Amsterdam

THE ROUGH GUIDE

There are more than seventy Rough Guide titles covering
destinations from Amsterdam to Zimbabwe

Forthcoming titles include
Britain • China • Hawaii • Mallorca & Menorca
Rhodes • Vietnam

Rough Guide Reference Series
Classical Music • The Internet • Jazz • World Music

Rough Guide Phrasebooks
Czech • French • German • Greek • Italian • Mexican Spanish
Portuguese • Spanish • Thai • Turkish

Rough Guide Credits

Text Editor:	Jack Holland
Series Editor:	Mark Ellingham
Editorial:	Martin Dunford, John Fisher, Jonathan Buckley, Greg Ward, Jules Brown, Graham Parker, Jo Mead, Samantha Cook
Production:	Susanne Hillen, Andy Hilliard, Gail Jammy, Vivien Antwi, Melissa Flack, Alan Spicer
Publicity:	Richard Trillo
Finance:	Celia Crowley, Simon Carloss

Acknowledgements

Thanks to Gareth Nash for proofreading; to Gail Jammy for typesetting; to Jane Holly and Kate Berens for emergency typing; and Matt Welton for map revisions.

We'd also like to thank all those who wrote in with **comments and updates** on the previous edition: Mattilda Gomez, Ian Watt, Georges van den Eshof, Dave Gorman and Eva Lartey, Richard Hovey, Doug Hall, Dave Jarratt, Glenn McDonald and Georgia Wood, Laura Miller, Harriet Gutjeurtz, Emma Louch, Sally Abbott, P. McManus, Erika Guttmann, N. Walton, Daniel Mack and Lorraine Ellis, Kathy Smith, Paul Zandbergen, Colin Costello, G. Light, John Humphries, Elaine Hughes. Apologies if we've spelt anyone's name wrong or have missed anyone out. And please keep writing!

Typography and **original design** by Jonathan Dear and The Crowd Roars.
Illustrations throughout by Ed Briant.

The publishers and authors have done their best to ensure the accuracy and currency of all information in *The Rough Guide to Amsterdam*; however, they can accept no responsibility for any loss, injury, or inconvenience sustained by any traveller as a result of information or advice contained in the guide.

This edition was published in 1994 by Rough Guides Ltd, 1 Mercer Street, London WC2H 9QJ. Reprinted October 1994, April 1995 & April 1996.

Distributed by the Penguin Group:

Penguin Books Ltd, 27 Wrights Lane, London W8 5TZ
Penguin Books USA Inc., 375 Hudson Street, New York 10014, USA
Penguin Books Australia Ltd, 487 Maroondah Highway, PO Box 257, Ringwood, Victoria 3134, Australia
Penguin Books Canada Ltd, 10 Alcorn Avenue, Toronto, Ontario, Canada M4V 1E4
Penguin Books (NZ) Ltd, 182–190 Wairau Road, Auckland 10, New Zealand

Previous editions published in the UK by Harrap Columbus.
Previous editions published in the United States and Canada as *The Real Guide Amsterdam*.

Printed in the United Kingdom by Cox & Wyman Ltd (Reading).

British Library Cataloguing in Publication Data
A catalogue record for this book is available from the British Library

ISBN 1-85828-086-9

Amsterdam

THE ROUGH GUIDE

Written and researched by
Martin Dunford and Jack Holland

With additional contributions by
Emile Bruls and Anna van Kemenade

THE ROUGH GUIDES

The Contents

A MAP OF AMSTERDAM

AMSTERDAM NORTH

DE RUYTERKADE

HET IJ

PR. HENDRIK-KADE

NIEUW-MARKT

WATERLOOPLEIN

Artis Zoo

PL. MIDDENLAAN

WEESPERSTR.

Amstel

SARPHATISTRAAT

MAURITSKADE

Muiderpoort Station

LINNEUSSTR.

Oosterpark

AMSTELDIJK

WIBAUTSTR.

VAN WOUSTR.

SOUTH

MIDDENWEG

PRINS BERNHARD PLEIN

Amstel Station

GOOISEWEG

VELTLAAN

PRES. KENNEDYLAAN

1 km

AMSTERDAM

Help us update
We've gone to a lot of effort to ensure that this edition of *The Rough Guide to Amsterdam* is accurate and up-to-date. However, things do change – places get "discovered", opening hours vary, restaurants close and hotels raise prices or lower standards. Any suggestions, comments or corrections would be much appreciated.

We'll credit all contributions, and send a copy of the next edition (or any other Rough Guide if you prefer) for the best letters. Send them to:

Rough Guides, 1 Mercer Street, London WC2H 9QJ

or Rough Guides, 375 Hudson Street, 3rd Floor, New York NY 10014.

Introduction

Amsterdam is a compact, instantly likeable capital. It's appealing to look at, pleasant to walk around, an enticing mix of the provincial and the cosmopolitan; it also has a welcoming attitude towards visitors, and a uniquely youthful orientation, shaped by the liberal counter-culture of the last two decades. It's hard not to feel drawn in by the buzz of open-air summer events, by the intimacy of the clubs and bars, or by the Dutch facility with languages; English, for example, is spoken by almost everyone.

The city's layout is determined by a web of canals radiating out from a medieval core, which, along with planned seventeenth-century extensions further out, provide elegant backdrops for living or wandering. The conventional sights are for the most part low-key – the **Anne Frank House** being a notable exception – but Amsterdam has developed a world-class group of museums and galleries. The **Van Gogh Museum** is, for many, reason enough to visit the city; add to it the **Rijksmuseum**, with its collections of medieval and seventeenth-century Dutch paintings, the contemporary and experimental **Stedelijk**, plus hundreds of smaller galleries, and the international quality of the art is evident.

However, it's Amsterdam's **population and politics** that constitute its most enduring characteristics. Notorious during the 1960s and 1970s as the heart of radical, "liberated" Europe, the city mellowed only marginally during the Eighties, and despite the inevitable late-Eighties yuppification retains a resilient laid-back feel, the keynote one of tolerance, and, as the Dutch say, *gezelligheid*, a hard-to-translate term, roughly meaning "cosiness", that perhaps best sums up the casual intimacy of the city. The authorities are trying to play down the counter-culture label, and boost Amsterdam's economy by cultivating a businesslike image for the city and a more conventional reputation for the arts, and it's true that battles over urban development and squatting rights have receded of late – although the divide between the long-established Social Democrat city council and the voters is growing. Perhaps in part to confront this problem, the council introduced a series of referenda on the way the city is managed, the first of which, a

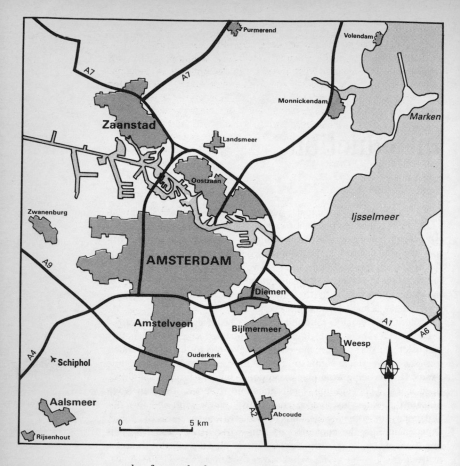

couple of years back, was on traffic and city centre congestion. The response to this was in fact resoundingly apathetic, although it did result in a narrow vote for a completely car-free centre – something that can only make the city more visitor-friendly in future.

Amsterdam has responded to its youth culture with a social and sensible attitude to soft drugs. Entertainment has a similarly innovative edge, exemplified by **multi-media complexes** like the *Melkweg*, whose offerings are at the forefront of contemporary film, dance, drama and music. There are some great **coffee shops**, serving cannabis products and soft drinks instead of alchohol, and more conventional **bars**, ranging from traditional, bare-floored brown cafés to new-wave designer haunts. The **club** scene is by contrast relatively subdued, even modest by the standards of other capital cities, and the emphasis is more on dancing than on posing. **Gay** men and women, though, will discover that Amsterdam has Europe's most active and convivial nightlife network.

Costs

Amsterdam is by no means a cheap city. But careful **spending** – picnicking or eating in the cheaper restaurants, camping, or sleeping in hostels – can make a visit possible on the tightest of budgets. Individual accommodation costs vary from around £8 ($12) a night for the cheapest dormitory bed, to around £15 ($22.50) per person sharing a double room in a bottom-line hotel. Main courses in most restaurants will cost somewhere between £6 and £10 ($9 and $15), while drinking a small glass of beer in a bar will set you back around £1 ($1.50). Obviously, costs for both food and drink drop considerably if you visit a supermarket. Overall, at the lowest level of spending, reckon on getting by on £20 ($30) a day as an absolute minimum; if you actually want to enjoy yourself, and sleep in an ordinary hotel, £35 ($50) a day would be a more realistic figure; £60 ($90) a day would mean you were living in some style.

When to go

Just about any time of year is a good time to visit Amsterdam, although it's advisable to avoid the mid-winter months – January and February – when the wind blowing off the canals can be bitterly cold. High summer can be unpleasant as well, since the city gets crowded and sticky and hotel rooms are at a premium. Spring is perhaps the best time to visit: the weather is comfortable for sightseeing and the canals are at their most alluring.

Getting out

Finally, don't fall into the trap of thinking that there's nothing to The Netherlands **beyond Amsterdam**. If you're here in spring or early summer the bulbfields are in full bloom, and the Randstad cities to the south of Amsterdam – Haarlem, Leiden and Utrecht – are worth a visit at any time of the year, not to mention the harbourside towns of Hoorn and Enkhuizen to the north of the city. Just about everywhere can be reached quickly and painlessly by train; for full details see Part Four, "Out of the City".

Average Maximum Temperatures												
	Jan	Feb	Mar	April	May	June	July	Aug	Sept	Oct	Nov	Dec
Min °C	-0.2	-0.5	1.5	3.8	7.5	10.5	12.5	12.5	10.5	7.3	3.8	1.1
Min °F	32	31	35	39	46	51	55	55	51	45	39	34
Max °C	4.3	4.9	8.1	11.6	16.0	19.1	20.5	20.5	18.3	14.0	8.8	5.7
Max °F	40	41	47	53	61	66	69	69	65	57	48	42

Part 1

The Basics

Getting There from Britain and Ireland

There is a wide range of ways to reach Amsterdam, which basically means deciding between a low-cost but time-comsuming ferry crossing and a swift but more expensive flight. Whichever alternative you opt for, you'll find a variety of competitive fares.

By Plane

Flights to Amsterdam Schiphol – 45 minutes' flying time from London – represent a considerable saving in time compared to the ferry connections. The large number of flights to Schiphol has led to a mass of cheap tickets, and it's reasonably easy to find a return fare from London for £80–120. To find the best bargains, study the ads in the Sunday travel sections of the quality newspapers, or, if you live in London, the back pages of the listings magazine *Time Out* or the *Evening Standard*. Alternatively, go to a **discount flight agent** such as *STA Travel, Campus Travel* or *Council Travel* (addresses below), who specialize in youth flights, and, if you're under 26 or a student, can offer savings on the price of a flight; they also sell ordinary discounted tickets.

Approaching the airlines direct, the **smaller operators**, such as *British Midland, Air UK* and *Transavia*, sometimes work out cheaper. But it's also worth trying the **national airlines** – *British Airways* and *KLM* – since their fares can be competitive with the cheaper operators. The best deal you'll get with a scheduled airline is with an APEX or Super Pex return ticket: these cost around £120 (a little more if you travel at the weekend) and normally must be booked fourteen days in advance; you have to spend one Saturday night abroad, and have no option to change your flight. To gain more flexibility you'll need to buy a standard return – which is likely to prove more expensive.

If you don't live in London, there are plenty of flights from various **UK regional airports** that can be good-value alternatives, particularly if you use the smaller operators. As a broad guide, APEX fares work out at £120–175, depending on where you travel from. It's also worth considering a **package deal** if you want to have your accommodation arrangements organized beforehand; these can be surprisingly good value (see pp.6–7 for more details).

By Plane from Ireland

There are no direct **ferry links** from Ireland to the Dutch coast, but there are direct **flights** to Amsterdam from Dublin, Cork, Shannon, Galway and Waterford. Ordinary scheduled APEX fares work out at about IR£180 from Dublin. If you are a student or under 26, *USIT* (see overleaf) can shave pounds off these prices. Several airlines also fly direct from Belfast at a cost of about £175 for an APEX fare, though *Belfast Student Travel* (again see overleaf) offer flights to Amsterdam for a little over £100 for students/under-26s, around £150 otherwise.

By Train

British Rail operates combined **boat-train services** from London to Amsterdam's Centraal Station. There are two daily departures from London Liverpool Street via Harwich to the Hook of Holland, one during the day, the other overnight; fares are £83 for an ordinary return, valid for two months, £63 for a five-day excursion and £49 for a single. Journey times are around

AIRLINE ADDRESSES AND ROUTES

Airline Addresses And Routes

Aer Lingus
223 Regent St,
London W1   ☎ 081/899 4747
Dublin to Schiphol.

Air UK
Stansted Airport   ☎ 0345/666 777
London (Stansted), Aberdeen,
Edinburgh, Glasgow, Humberside,
Leeds/Bradford, Newcastle, Norwich and
Teeside to Schiphol.

Birmingham European Airways
Birmingham Airport   ☎ 021/782 0711
Birmingham and Belfast
to Schiphol.

British Airways
156 Regent St,
London W1   ☎ 081/897 4000
London (Heathrow), Aberdeen, Belfast,
Birmingham, Edinburgh, Glasgow,
Manchester and Newcastle to Schiphol.

British Midland
Donnington Hall,
Castle Donnington,
Derby DE7 2SB   ☎ 0332/810552
London (Heathrow) and East Midlands to
Schiphol.

KLM
8 Hanover St,
London W1   ☎ 081/750 9000
London (Heathrow), Birmingham, Bristol,
Cardiff, Manchester, Newcastle and Belfast to
Schiphol.

Netherlines
8 Hanover St,
London W1   ☎ 081/750 9000
Birmingham, Luton, Southampton, Bristol,
Manchester and Teeside to Schiphol.

Suckling Airways
Cambridge Airport   ☎ 02205/3393
Cambridge to Schiphol.

Transavia   ☎ 0293/538181
London (Gatwick) to Schiphol.

Discount Flight Agents

Campus Travel
52 Grosvenor Gardens,
London SW1   ☎ 071/730 3402

Council Travel
28a Poland St,
London W1   ☎ 071/287 3337

STA Travel
86 Old Brompton Rd,
London SW7;

117 Euston Rd,
London N1   ☎ 071/937 9921

Travel Cuts
295 Regent St,
London W1   ☎ 071/255 1944

Addresses in Ireland

Belfast Student Travel
13b College St,
Belfast BT1 6ET   ☎ 0232/324073

KLM
42 Grafton St,
Dublin 2   ☎ 01/370011

USIT
Aston Quay,
O'Connell Bridge,
Dublin 2   ☎ 01/778117
and other branches countrywide.

eleven hours. There are also four daily departures from London Victoria via Dover and Ostend in Belgium: two by the faster jetfoil, which take about nine hours, two by ferry, which take around thirteen hours. Singles cost £53.50, five-day excursions £73, and ordinary two-month returns £99. Travelling at night on either route, you should add on the price of (obligatory) accommodation on the ferry – a minimum of £8 for a reclining seat, £10 upwards for a berth in a cabin. Tickets for all services can be bought from any *British Rail* ticket office, many high street travel agents, or *Eurotrain* (see below).

Fares can be cut drastically for those **under 26**, by way of *BIJ* youth tickets, which cost £62

return to Amsterdam; tickets are valid for two months and you can stop off en route as many times as you wish. For a little more money – £68 – *Eurotrain* will sell you a round-trip "explorer" ticket that takes in Brussels and Bruges as well. Another cash-saving possibility for those under 26 (and resident in Europe for six months) is the **InterRail pass**, currently costing £249 from any major UK railway station or student/youth travel agents, which is valid for one month's travel on all European (and Moroccan) railways, and gives around a third off rail travel within Britain and fifty percent off certain cross-Channel and North Sea ferries. This could cut costs significantly if Amsterdam is just part of your European travels.

4   BASICS

Train information

British Rail
European information line   ☎ 071/834 2345

Eurotrain
52 Grosvenor Gardens,
London SW1   ☎ 071/730 3402

Wasteels
121 Wilton Rd,
London SW1   ☎ 071/834 7066

Bus information

Hoverspeed City Sprint   ☎ 0304/240241

National Express/Eurolines
13 Regent St,
London SW1   ☎ 071/730 8235
and on other regional telephone numbers.

An alternative to this, worth considering if you intend only travelling within a limited area of Europe – say, Holland, Belgium, Luxembourg and France – is the **InterRail zonal pass**. Passes for a single zone, valid for fifteen days, cost £179; monthly passes for two and three zones cost £209 and £229 respectively. Contact larger BR stations or student travel offices for details.

By Bus

Travelling by long-distance **bus** is a good budget option if you're over 26, since fares are roughly the same as for under-26 rail travel. The choice is between coach and hovercraft (via Dover–Calais) and the slower coach and ferry. *Eurolines*, operated by *National Express*, offer two daily departures from London's Victoria coach station to Amsterdam beween May and the end of September (one in the morning, the other an overnight service); between October and April services run at least once daily, with two services daily on Wednesday and Sunday and – in April and October only – on Friday too. Prices are £30 single, £49 return, the journey time about thirteen hours. *Eurolines* also act as agents for *Hoverspeed*, who offer similar services, but with faster hovercraft crossings. Their Amsterdam service runs once daily and costs the same as *Eurolines* – journey time around twelve hours. Tickets for all services are bookable through most travel agents, *British Rail* travel centres, or from the companies direct, and there's an eight percent reduction for under-26s and students.

By Car: the Ferries

Until the Channel Tunnel opens, you can only take your car or caravan to The Netherlands by ferry. The most direct ferry crossings into Holland are via Harwich to the Hook of Holland, and from Sheerness to Vlissingen. It takes approximately one hour to drive from the Hook to Amsterdam; from Vlissingen it takes roughly two and a half hours. If you want to spend less time crossing the water, consider instead sailing either from Dover to Ostend, or from Felixstowe to Zeebrugge. A further option from the north of England are the Hull to Zeebrugge and Hull to Rotterdam services, the latter leaving you just an hour or so's drive from Amsterdam.

High street travel agents have numerous brochures offering various fares; it's worth shopping around for the most competitive deals. Booking ahead is strongly recommended for motorists; indeed it's essential in high season. Foot passengers and cyclists can normally just turn up and board, at any time of year. Prices vary with the month, day and even hour that you're travelling, how long you're staying, the size of your car – and the different ferry companies are always offering special fares to outdo their competitors. Since the price structures tend to be geared around one-way rather than return travel, you don't necesarily have to cross over and back using the same port. Bear in mind, though, that some sort of cabin or berth accommodation is obligatory on all night sailings, and should be added on to the price of an ordinary ticket. If

Ferry company addresses

North Sea Ferries
King George Dock,
Hedon Rd,
Hull HU9 5QA   ☎ 0482/77177

Olau Line
Olau Line Terminal,
Sheerness,
Kent ME12 1SN   ☎ 0795/666666

P&O European Ferries
Channel House,
Channel View Rd,
Dover,
Kent CT17 9TJ   ☎ 0304/203388

Stena Sealink
Charter House,
Park St,
Ashford,
Kent TN24 8EX   ☎ 0233/647047

Ferry Routes and Prices

	Operator	Frequency	Duration	Single fare	Foot Passenger
Dover–Ostend	*P&O*	8 daily	4hr	£110–150	£24
Felixstowe–Zeebrugge	*P&O*	2 daily	5hr 45min	£112–152	£24
Harwich–Hook of Holland	*Stena Sealink*	2 daily	6–9hr	£114–174	£30
Hull–Rotterdam	*North Sea*	1 daily	14hr	£151–179	£47–55
Hull–Zeebrugge	*North Sea*	1 daily	14hr 30min	£151–179	£47–55
Sheerness–Vlissingen	*Olau*	2 daily	6–8hr	£94–114	£27.50

* Fares and frequencies are for travel during the peak June–August period, and calculated for two people plus a small car.

Taking Your Bike

Most people who take their bikes to the Low Countries go by **train**. In order to do this, you must take your bike with you to the station at least an hour before departure and register it with *British Rail*. It's then loaded onto the train for you and delivered to the station of your destination. There's no guarantee it will turn up when you do. In practice, bikes can arrive anything up to 48 hours later – and you should plan accordingly. Taking your bike on the **ferry** presents few problems. Bicycles travel free on *Stena Sealink*, and for £2–7 on *P&O* and *Olau Lines*, depending on the time of sailing and the season. Simply turn up with your bike and secure it in the designated area. Travelling by **plane** with your bike is equally straightforward, provided you let the airline know at least a week in advance. Contact them directly to make a cargo booking for your bike, then take your machine with you when you travel. At the airport you'll need to detach the wheels and fold down the handlebars. The bike will be included in your luggage allowance (usually 20kg); if the total exceeds that, you'll need to pay for the difference. For more on cycling, see p.19.

you're just going for a weekend break, check out the short-period excursion fares offered by all the companies – usually 53-hour or five-day returns – which can cost much the same as a single. If you have kids, *Stena Sealink* have the best deals: on day crossings children under fourteen travel free, and at night go for fifty percent discount; other operators tend to give a fifty percent discount across the board. All also carry children under four free. Note that for students or those under 26, *Eurotrain* can knock a few pounds off ferry tickets.

Hitching

It's relatively easy to get lifts once in Holland or Belgium, so **hitching** can be a good way of cutting costs. Bear in mind, though, that since drivers have been made to account for unauthorized passengers, it's no longer possible to travel over on the ferry for free in a truck driver's cab. To make sure of a lift on arrival, talk to as many people as you can on the ferry and do your best to cajole them into picking you up on the other side of customs.

Inclusive holidays

Don't be put off by the idea of going on a **package holiday**: most consist of no more than travel and accommodation and can work out an easy way of cutting costs and hassle – especially if you live some distance from London, since many operators offer a good-value range of regional

Car Rental Companies

Avis	☎ 081/848 8733
Budget	☎ 0800/181181
Eurodollar	☎ 0895/233300
Europcar	☎ 081/950 5050
Hertz	☎ 081/679 1799
Holiday Autos	☎ 071/491 1111

25 Savile Row, London W1X 1AA
Reliable car rental specialist.

Tour Operators

Amsterdam Travel Service
Bridge House,
Ware,
Herts SG12 9DF   ☎ 0920/467444

Anglo Dutch Sports
30a Foxgrove Rd,
Beckenham,
Kent BR3 2BD   ☎ 081/650 2347

Cresta
1 Tabley Court,
Victoria St,
Altrincham,
Cheshire WA14 1EZ   ☎ 061/929 0000

Kirker
3 New Concordia Wharf,
Mill St,
London SE1 2BB   ☎ 071/231 3333

Olau Short Breaks
Olau Line Ferries,
Sheerness,
Kent ME12 1SN   ☎ 0795/662233

Thomson
Greater London House,
Hampstead Rd,
London NW1 7SD   ☎ 071/387 6510

Time Off
Chester Close,
Chester St,
London SW1X 7BQ   ☎ 071/235 8070

Travelscene
11–15 St Anne's Rd,
Harrow, HA1 1AS   ☎ 081/427 4445

flight departures. Depending on the type of hotel you opt for (anything from budget to five-star hotels are available with most companies), short breaks in Amsterdam start at around £85 per person for return bus or train and ferry or hovercraft travel and two nights' accommodation in a one-star hotel with breakfast, or from a little over £100 if you fly. A travel agent can advise further on the best deals available, or you can contact one of the operators listed above.

Getting There from Australasia

The cheapest option is to fly to London – for which there are plenty of good deals – and pick up a connection from there. Reckon on paying around AUS$1750 return from Sydney, NZ$2040 from Auckland. *STA*, 1a Lee St, Railway Square, Sydney 2000 (☎ 02/212 1255), and in New Zealand, *STS*, 64 High St, Auckland (☎ 09/309 0458), tend to have the best prices; see the phone book for branches in other cities.

Getting There from the USA and Canada

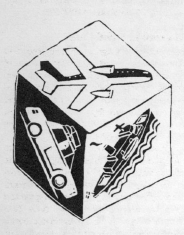

Amsterdam is among the most popular and least expensive gateways to Europe from North America, and getting a convenient and good-value flight is rarely a problem. Virtually every region of the United States and Canada is well served by the major airlines, though only two scheduled carriers offer nonstop flights – KLM (the Dutch national airline) and Delta. The rest go via London and other European centres. The cheapest fares are those sold by seat consolidators, who buy up unsold seats on major airlines and sell them to travellers for less than half the normal price; these are real bargains but impossible to change once you've booked. The best deal if you're travelling scheduled is to get an APEX fare; look out too for the deals offered by the Dutch charter company Martinair, who offer mid-priced seats on nonstop flights from a number of cities in the US and Canada. Prices quoted below include all applicable taxes, currently $22 in the US and CDN$40 in Canada.

Flights from the USA

KLM offers the widest range of **flights** to Amsterdam, with nonstop services from nine US cities and connecting services to dozens more on Northwest Airlines, with whom they've recently joined forces. Their APEX fares are usually identical to those offered by other carriers, so for convenience at least, KLM is the best bet. If you're travelling in late spring or summer, and are able to plan your trip well in advance, it's worth looking into the deals offered by Martinair, who operate three flights a week out of Newark and various Florida cities on the East Coast, as well as Los Angeles, Oakland and Seattle on the West Coast. One-way fares are rarely good value, but if you're set on one the best source is the seat consolidators advertising in the back pages of the travel sections of the major Sunday newspapers.

East Coast

KLM's round-trip **APEX fares** on nonstop flights out of New York (JFK) start at around $600 in low season, rising to around $750 in May and peaking under $900 in July and August; these fares are for midweek travel with a maximum stay of thirty days, and tickets must be bought fourteen days in advance. Nonstop fares out of Baltimore, Washington DC, Orlando, Atlanta, Detroit, Chicago and Minneapolis cost $50–100 more; connecting flights from other major cities are usually thrown in for free. Delta has similar fares on nonstops out of New York (JFK) and Atlanta, and most other carriers – United, American, British Airways – match these on their flights via London Heathrow. Especially during winter, many airlines have special offers which can lower fares to well under $500 round-trip.

Seat consolidators can generally find you a seat for about $200 one-way, $350 round-trip in winter; $250 one-way, $500 round-trip in summer. **Agents** like STA Travel can usually come close to these prices, and are almost always more flexible and easier to deal with. Martinair charter flights out of Newark cost $540 round-trip in May, $700 in July and August, and are available through most travel agents.

West Coast

KLM's round-trip **APEX fares** on nonstop flights out of Los Angeles, and one-stop flights from San Francisco, start at around $650 in low season, rising to $900 in May and peaking at around $1100 in July and August; again, these fares are for midweek travel with a maximum stay of thirty days, and tickets must be bought at least fourteen days in advance. Fares from other western cities usually cost from $50 to $100 more, and most international carriers will match these prices. Special offers sometimes lower the fares to under $500, though these are usually only available during winter. **Agents** like *STA* will find you the best available fare for the dates you want to travel. If price is your main concern, **seat consolidators**, who advertise in the travel sections of the Sunday *LA Times*, the *San Francisco Examiner* and *Chronicle* and other West Coast papers, offer round-trip fares from around $500 in winter and $650 in summer.

Balancing good value with convenience and reliability, *Martinair* is an especially good option for West Coast travellers. Their round-trip, nonstop fares out of Los Angeles, Oakland and Seattle start at about $650 in April and October, and rise to $900 during the summer peak season. You can make reservations through most travel agents and through *Rebel Tours* – see overleaf.

Flights from Canada

Again, *KLM* has the best range of routes, with nonstop flights from all major Canadian airports, and fares are approximately the same as they are from the US. Round-trip tickets out of Toronto start at under CDN$600 in the low season, stepping up to CDN$675 in May and reaching around CDN$900 in summer. Fares from Vancouver and Calgary range from a low of CDN$800 to a summer peak of CDN$1500. Neither *Air Canada* nor *Canadian Airlines* serves Amsterdam, though *Martinair* has nonstops out of Toronto for around CDN$100 less than *KLM's* fares, and *Sabena* flies from Montréal to Brussels – with connections to Amsterdam – on Wednesday, Friday and Sunday for a high season APEX fare of around CDN$1000.

Via Europe – and Eurail

Even though many flights from North America to Amsterdam are routed via London, because of the various special fares it often winds up being cheaper to stay on the plane all the way to Amsterdam. In general, you can't stop over and continue on a later flight – US and Canadian airlines are not allowed to offer services between European cities.

However, if you want to combine a trip to Amsterdam with visits to other European capitals, **London** makes the best – certainly the most inexpensive, flightwise – starting point. Besides speaking the same language and having the best range of inexpensive transatlantic flights (New York to London is the busiest and cheapest route), London also has excellent connections on to Amsterdam. **Paris** is also becoming an attractive route. *United* and *American Airlines*, as well as *British Airways* and the excellent-value smaller British carrier *Virgin Atlantic*, all have regular flights to London from various parts of the US; *Air France*, *United* and *American* have daily flights to Paris. See "Getting There from Britain", p.3, for details on travel from Britain to Amsterdam.

Eurail passes

If you intended Amsterdam to form just part of your European travels, or envisage utilizing the European rail network extensively, you should consider investing in a **Eurail pass**, valid for unlimited first-class travel throughout seventeen countries, including The Netherlands. It's available for periods of fifteen days ($498), 21 days ($648), one month ($798), two months ($1098) and three months ($1398). For Americans under 26, the **Eurail Youthpass** offers one or two months' unlimited second-class rail travel for $578 and $768 respectively. There's also a **Eurail Flexipass**, which entitles travellers to a range of options: five days of unlimited first-class travel over a fifteen-day period ($255); a one-month pass giving ten days of travel ($402); and

Discount Flight Agencies, Travel Clubs, Consolidators

Access International
101 W 31st St, Suite 104,
New York, NY 10001 ☎ 800/TAKE-OFF
Consolidator with good East Coast and central US deals.

Airkit
1125 W 6th St,
Los Angeles, CA 90017 ☎ 213/957-9364
West Coast consolidator with seats from San Francisco and LA.

Council Travel
205 E 42nd St,
New York, NY 10017 ☎ 212/661-1450
Head office of the nationwide US student travel organization. Branches in San Francisco, LA, Washington, New Orleans, Chicago, Seattle, Portland, Minneapolis, Boston, Atlanta and Dallas, to name only the larger ones.

Discount Club of America
61-33 Woodhaven Blvd,
Rego Park, NY 11374 ☎ 718/335-9612
East Coast discount travel club.

Discount Travel International
Ives Bldg,
114 Forrest Ave, Suite 205, ☎ 215/668-2182
Narbeth, PA 19072 or ☎ 800/221-8139
Good deals from the East Coast.

Encore Short Notice
4501 Forbes Blvd, ☎ 301/459-8020
Lanham, MD 20706 or ☎ 800/638-0830
East Coast travel club.

Interworld
3400 Coral Way,
Miami, FL 33145 ☎ 305/443-4929
Southeastern US consolidator.

Last-Minute Travel Club
132 Brookline Ave, ☎ 617/267-9800
Boston, MA 02215 or ☎ 800/LAST-MIN

Moment's Notice
425 Madison Ave,
New York, NY 10017 ☎ 212/486-0503
Travel club that's good for last-minute deals.

Nouvelles Frontières
12 E 33rd St,
New York, NY 10016 ☎ 212/779-0600

800 blvd de Maisonneuve Est,
Montréal, PQ H2L 4L8 ☎ 514/288-9942
Main US and Canadian branches of the French discount travel outfit. Other branches in LA, San Francisco and Quebec City.

Rebel Tours
25050 Avenue Kearny, ☎ 805/294-0900
Valencia, CA or ☎ 800/227-3235
Good source of deals with Martinair.

STA Travel
17 E 45th St, Suite 805,
New York, NY 10017 ☎ 212/986-9470

166 Geary St, Suite 702,
San Francisco, CA 94108 ☎ 415/391-8407
Main US branches of the originally Australian and now worldwide specialist in independent and student travel. Other offices in LA, Boston and Honolulu.

Stand Buys
311 W Superior St,
Chicago, IL 60610 ☎ 800/331-0257
Good Midwestern travel club.

TFI Tours
34 W 32nd Street, ☎ 212/736-1140
New York, NY 10001 or ☎ 800/825-3834
The very best East Coast deals, especially worth looking into if you only want to fly one-way.

Travac
1177 N Warson Rd,
St Louis, MO 63132 ☎ 800/872-8800
Good central US consolidator.

Travel Brokers
50 Broad St,
New York, NY 10004 ☎ 800/999-8748
New York travel club.

Travel Cuts
187 College St,
Toronto, ON M5T 1P7 ☎ 416/979-2406
Main office of the Canadian student travel organization. Many other offices nationwide.

Travelers Advantage
49 Music Square,
Nashville, TN 37203 ☎ 800/548-1116
Reliable travel club.

Travel Avenue
180 N Jefferson St, ☎ 312/876-1116
Chicago, IL 60606 or ☎ 800/333-3335
Discount travel agent.

Unitravel
1177 N Warson Rd,
St Louis, MO 63132 ☎ 800/325-2222
Reliable consolidator.

Worldwide Discount Travel Club
1674 Meridian Ave,
Miami Beach, FL 33139 ☎ 305/534-2082

a two-month pass which gives fifteen days of travel ($540). All of these passes must be bought from an authorized travel agent before you leave for Europe.

Inclusive tours

If you're short on time and want to avoid the hassle of finding a room and arranging transport, it may make sense to take some kind of package tour. Dozens of companies offer these, in various forms, although *KLM* offer the widest range, to suit all sorts of budgets and itineraries. Starting at around $1000 per person, their basic price includes round-trip flights from New York, four nights' accommodation, airport transfers and some meals. They also arrange tours which take in several different European cities, at little extra cost. Either contact your local travel agent or call the *KLM Vacation Centre* on ☎800/777-1668 for a brochure.

Red Tape and Visas

Citizens of Britain, Eire, Australia, Canada or the USA need only a valid passport to stay for three months in The Netherlands. The temporary British Visitor's Passport, obtainable from post offices, is valid for the same length of stay. On arrival, be sure to have enough money to convince officials you can stay alive. Poorer-looking visitors are often checked out, and if you can't flash a few travellers' cheques or notes you may not be allowed in.

If you want to stay longer, officially you need a *verblijfsvergunning* or residence permit. These are obtainable in advance from Dutch embassies, or, for EC citizens who have found a job in The Netherlands, from the *Vreemdelingendienst*, Aliens' Police, at Waterlooplein 9 (open to visitors Mon–Fri 8am–noon, during which time you can make an appointment – get there early as the queues build up fast). In reality restrictions are fairly loose for European Community passports –

they're not always date-stamped when entering the country – though if you are definitely planning to stay and work it's best to get a stamp anyway (see "Long-term Stays", p.42). Non-EC nationals, however, should always have their documents in order; their passports will always be stamped on arrival, and they should be aware that it's not possible to apply for a residence permit while in The Netherlands, even if they already have a job. Whether obtained before you leave home or from the Dutch Aliens' Police, residence permits are issued for a maximum term of one year. Work permits are even harder to get; your prospective employer must apply in The Netherlands while you simultaneously apply at home; both parties must await its issuance (by no means automatic) before proceeding. Applying from abroad, you need to show proof of income from sources other than employment in The Netherlands, or, if you're going there to study, proof of registration with a Dutch educational institution.

EC citizens do not need to apply for work permits in advance; indeed they can work for up to three months without one. After that period, work permits are issued on presentation of your *werkgeversverklaring,* a proof of employment. Non-EC citizens can only apply for work permits from their home country, in conjunction with their prospective employer, and cannot enter the country until all formalities have been completed.

Customs

For residents of EC countries the **duty-free allow-ance** is 300 cigarettes if bought tax-paid in the

---

Dutch Consulates

Australia
120 Empire Circuit,
Yarralumla,
Canberra ACT 2600 ☎ 062/273 3611

Canada
3rd Floor, 275 Slater St,
Ottowa, ON K1P 5H9 ☎ 613/237 5030

Great Britain
38 Hyde Park Gate,
London SW7 ☎ 071/585 5040

New Zealand
10th Floor, Investment House,
Balance and Featherstone St,
Wellington ☎ 04/738 652

USA
4200 Linnean Ave NW,
Washington, DC 20008 ☎ 202/244-5300

11th Floor, 1 Rockefeller Plaza,
New York NY 10020 ☎ 212/246-1429

Foreign Consulates in The Netherlands

Australia
Carnegielaan 12
The Hague
2517 KH ☎ 070/310 82 00

Canada
Sophialaan 7
The Hague
2514 JP ☎ 070/361 41 11

Great Britain
Koningslaan 44
Amsterdam
1075 AE ☎ 676 43 43

Ireland
Dr Kuyperstraat 9
The Hague
2514 BA ☎ 070/363 09 93

New Zealand
Mauritskade 25
The Hague
2514 HD ☎ 070/346 93 24

USA
Museumplein 19
Amsterdam
1071 DJ ☎ 664 56 61

EC, 200 if bought duty-free or outside the EC. These allowances are doubled for those who live outside the EC. Wherever you've come from you're allowed one litre of duty-free spirits (don't bother utilizing your five-litre wine allowance – it's cheaper to buy it in Amsterdam). Allowances are the same when returning to Britain and in all cases apply only to those over the age of 17.

British **customs officials** tend to assume that anyone youthful-looking and coming directly from The Netherlands is a potential dope fiend or pornographer – strip searches and other unpleasantness can be frequent. If it happens, unfailing politeness is the best tactic: those attempting to bring back drugs, pornography or flick knives can expect a hard time and most likely arrest.

Health and Insurance

As fellow members of the European Community, both Britain and Eire have reciprocal health agreements with The Netherlands. In theory, these provide for free medical advice and treatment on presentation of certificate E111. In practice many doctors and pharmacists charge, and it's up to you to arrange reimbursement from the DHS once you're home. To get an E111, fill in a form at any post office and you'll be issued with a certificate immediately. Without an E111 you won't be turned away from a doctor or hospital, but you will almost certainly have to contribute towards treatment.

Minor ailments can be remedied at a **chemist** (*drogist*), which supplies toiletries, non-prescription drugs, tampons, condoms and the like. A **pharmacy** or *apotheek* (open Mon–Fri 9.30am–5.30 or 6pm) is where you go to get a prescription filled. No pharmacy is open 24 hours, but the **Central Medical Service** (*Centrale Doktersdienst*; ☎664 21 11) will give the addresses of the nearest shop open outside normal business hours, and one that's open 24 hours. To get a prescription or **consult a doctor**, again phone the Central Medical Service – something the VVV tourist office will do for you if you need help (address on p.24). **Minor accidents** can be treated at the out-patients department of most **hospitals**; the most central one is the *Onze Lieve Vrouwe Gasthuis*, 1e Oosterparkstraat 179 (☎599 91 11) – tram #9 – or the VVV can advise on out-patient clinics. In **emergencies** dial ☎0611 to call an ambulance.

For urgent **dental treatment**, ring the *ADC Dentist Practice*, Wilhelmina Gasthuisplein 167 (Mon–Fri 8am–midnight, Sat 8am–9pm, Sun 1–5pm; ☎616 12 34), who will sort out an appointment for you, though without insurance the cost can be high. For advice and information on **sexually transmitted diseases**, there's a 24-hour phone line on ☎623 22 52; there's also a weekend clinic for gay men at 1e Helmerstraat 17 (☎685 33 31). For details of how to get contraceptive or "morning-after" pills, see p.40.

Insurance

It's a good idea to have some kind of **travel insurance**, since with this you're covered for loss of possessions and money, as well as the cost of all medical and dental treatment. Among British insurers, *Endsleigh* are about the cheapest, offering a month's cover for around £20. Their policies are available from most youth/student travel specialists or direct from their offices at 97–107 Southampton Row, London WC1 (☎071/580 4311). You must make sure you keep all medical bills, and, if you have anything stolen, get a copy of the police report – otherwise you won't be able to claim.

In the **US and Canada** you should check carefully the insurance policies you already have before taking out a new one. You may discover that you're covered already for medical and other losses while abroad. Canadians especially are usually covered by their provincial health plans, and holders of ISIC cards are entitled to be reimbursed (outside the USA) for $3000-worth of accident coverage and sixty days of in-patient benefits up to $100 a day for the period the card is valid. Students may also find their health coverage extends to vacations, and many bank and charge accounts include some form of travel cover; insurance is also sometimes included if you pay for your trip with a credit card. If you do want a specific travel insurance policy, there are numerous kinds to choose from: short-term combination policies, covering everything from baggage loss to broken legs, are the best bet and cost around $25 for ten days, plus $1 a day for trips of 75 days or more. One thing to bear in mind is that none of the currently available policies covers theft; they only cover loss while in the custody of an identifiable person – though even then you must make a report to the police and get their written statement. Two companies you might try are *Travel Guard*, 110 Centrepoint Drive, Steven Point, WI 54480 (☎715/345-0505 or 800/826-1300), or *Access America International*, 600 Third Ave, New York, NY 10163 (☎212/949-5960 or 800/284-8300).

Transport Connections

Points of arrival in Amsterdam are fairly central, with the exception of Schiphol Airport, which has, in any case, quickly and efficient connections with the city. The hub for most travel is Centraal Station, in the heart of the city and connected by tram, bus, and, to a lesser extent, the metro, with all parts of Amsterdam.

Schiphol Airport

Amsterdam has only one international airport, **Schiphol**. This is connected by train with Amsterdam's Centraal Station, a fast service leaving every fifteen minutes during the day, and every hour at night from 1am onwards; the journey takes twenty minutes and costs f5.25 oneway. There are also trains to Amsterdam RAI, Amsterdam Duivendrecht and Amsterdam Zuid – useful if you know you'll be staying nearby. As for Schiphol itself, its claim to be the businessperson's favourite airport is well founded: it's compact enough to keep walking to a minimum, directional signs are clear and plentiful, and the duty-free shop is the cheapest in Europe. There are **bureaux de change** in the arrivals hall, as well as a *GWK* **money exchange office** in Schiphol's train station (open daily 24hr), and a **post office** in the departures lounge (daily 6am until the last departure, usually somewhere between 9 and 11pm). **Left-luggage** is open from 7am to 11.45pm and costs f5 per item per day. If you need to freshen up after a long journey, there are **showers** too (daily 6am–11pm), which cost f2.50 per person.

Travel information		Airline offices	
Schiphol Airport Flight enquiries and arrivals information ☎ 601 09 66 .		**Aer Lingus** Heiligweg 14	☎ 623 86 20
Train Information ☎ 620 22 66 or 601 05 41 for international travel; ☎ 06/9292 for travel within The Netherlands (the latter is charged at 50c a minute).		**Air France** Strawinskylaan 813	☎ 675 48 81
		Air UK Building 22, Room 162, Schiphol Airport	☎ 601 06 33
Travel agents		**British Airways** Stadhouderskade 4	☎ 685 22 11
NBBS			
Leidsestraat 53	☎ 620 50 71	**British Midland** Strawinskylaan 1535	☎ 06/022 24 26
Rokin 38	☎ 624 09 89		
Ceinturbaan 294	☎ 679 93 37	**KLM**	
Haarlemmerstraat 115	☎ 626 25 57	G. Metsustraat 2–6	☎ 649 36 33
Kimberstraat 96	☎ 683 62 49	**Northwest Airlines**	
The nationwide student/youth travel organization, and the best source of discount train tickets, flights, etc.		Weteringschans 85c	☎ 622 00 22
Budget Air		**Sabena**	
Rokin 34	☎ 627 12 51	Weteringschans 26	☎ 626 29 66
Budget Bus		**Transavia**	
Rokin 10	☎ 627 51 51	PO Box 7777, Schiphol Airport	☎ 604 65 18
Nouvelles Frontières			
Van Baerlestraat 3	☎ 664 41 31		

Train and Bus Terminals

Amsterdam has a number of suburban **train stations**, but all major internal and international traffic is handled by **Amsterdam Centraal**.

Arriving here you are at the hub of all bus and tram routes and just five minutes' walk from Dam Square. The station's facilities include a *GWK* **bank and money-changing office** (open 24hr), **lockers** (daily 5am–11pm; small ƒ3.50, large ƒ5.50, for 72hr), as well as the usual array of shops, newsstands and restaurants (including a top-class French restaurant – see *Restaurants* for details).

Almost all long-distance **buses** arrive at **Centraal Station** too, except for Hoverspeed's *City*

Sprint service, which calls at **Stadionplein** before terminating at **Leidseplein**, which is linked to Centraal Station by trams #1, #2 and #5.

Road Connections

Coming in on either highway **A4** or **A2** from the south, you should experience few traffic problems, and, as soon as you approach Amsterdam's southern reaches, signs clearly direct you to the city centre. For the western portions of the city follow the A10 and watch the signs for the best exit to your destination; for other parts of the city follow the Ringweg-Zuid (A10) and get off at either the Olympic Stadium or the RAI exhibition centre exits.

City Transport

By European capital standards Amsterdam is small, its public transport is excellent, and most of the things you might conceivably want to see can be found in the city's compact centre. Getting around couldn't be easier.

Walking

The best way to get around is to **walk**: you'll see more (remember, this is a city built around canals) and virtually everything of interest is within walking distance. As a broad reference, it takes at most three-quarters of an hour to stroll from Centraal Station to the Rijksmuseum, which is about the longest walk you'd ever need to take. Bear in mind, however, that it takes a while to get used to the traffic, whose combination of cars, trams, buses and bicycles can make crossing the road a harzardous business.

Buses, trams and the metro

Apart from walking, **trams** – and, to a lesser extent, **buses** – offer the easiest transport alternative: the system is comprehensive and inexpensive. Your first stop should be the **GVB** public transport office in front of Centraal Station, next door to the VVV (Mon–Fri 7am–10.30pm, Sat & Sun 8am–10.30pm), where you'll find a free route map and an English guide to the **ticketing** system. Failing that, for details on all city public transport, phone ☎06/9292 (Mon–Fri 7am–11pm, Sat & Sun 8am–11pm; 50c per minute).

The most commonly used ticket is the **strippenkaart**. These are valid nationwide and work on a zonal basis whereby you cancel two strips

for one zone, three strips for two and so on, when you board the tram or bus (the driver will do it for you on a bus; on trams you're trusted to do it yourself). The most economical *strippenkaart* has fifteen strips (currently f10.75) and can be purchased at any *GVB* office (the others are in the Scheepvaarthuis at the corner of Prins Hendrikkade and Binnenkant, in the Amstel Station, and there is sometimes a portacabin parked outside the Stadsschouwburg on Leidseplein), post offices, selected tobacconists, or at train station ticket counters. There's also a 45-strip card available for f31 – useful if you intend to stay a little longer, or travel further afield. Otherwise two-, three- and eight-strip tickets are available from the driver – though they work out considerably more expensive. You'll rarely need to travel outside the central zone, so most of the time cancelling two strips is sufficient. Additional people can travel on the same *strippenkaart* by cancelling the requisite number of strips. Also, don't forget that the stamp made on the *strippenkaart* is timed and valid for an hour: you don't need to cancel it again if you change trams or buses within that time.

If you don't want to be bothered with cancelling a *strippenkaart*, the easiest thing to do is buy a **dagkaart** or day ticket – valid for as many days as you need, up to nine days: prices start at f11.50 for one day, going up to f24.45 for four days, plus f3.60 for each additional day. Those planning to stay for some time might consider investing in a *sterabonnement* or **season ticket**, valid weekly, monthly or yearly and available from the same outlets as a *strippenkaart*. A one-star weekly pass, valid for one zone only, currently costs f14.25, and you need a photograph and your passport to buy one.

The system is wide open to abuse. But lately the city has been eager to crack down on those who don't pay (known as *zwartrijders* – "black riders"), and wherever you're travelling, and whatever time of day, there's a good chance you'll have your ticket checked. If caught, you're liable for a f60 fine (plus the price of the ticket you should have bought), due on the spot, so it pays to be honest.

The *stippenkaart* system also works on the city's **metro**, which starts at Centraal Station and connects with the building complexes of Bijlmermeer to the east, and the new sneltrain running down to Amstekveen. Both lines are clean, modern and punctual, although it can be a bit frightening at night, and apart from a couple of stops in the eastern reaches of the centre, most of the stations are in the suburbs and used mainly by commuters.

All of the above services stop running at midnight, when a wide network of **night buses** rolls into action, about once an hour until 4am from Centraal Station to most parts of the city; the *GVB* has a leaflet detailing all the routes.

Bikes

Another possibility, and a practical one, is to go native and opt for a **bicycle**: the city's well-defined network of bicycle lanes (*fietspaden*) means that this can be a remarkably safe way of getting around. If you haven't brought your own, it's possible to **rent a bike** from the cycle store at Centraal Station (Mon–Sat 7am–10pm, Sun 9am–10pm; f7.50 a day, f30 a week, plus f200 deposit and either driving licence or passport), or from a number of similarly priced bike-rental firms scattered around town (see box on p.22), most of which ask for smaller deposits or accept a passport alone; some also do tandems for about f25 a day; see below for details. Also, if you're camping, it's usually possible to rent bikes from the campsite.

As for the **rules of the road**, remember that you are legally obliged to have reflector bands on both wheels. Bike lanes are denoted by a white bicycle on a blue background, or a small black oblong sign saying "Fietspad". Also, a **word of warning**: lock up your bike at *all times* (see "Police and Trouble", p.34). Bike theft is rife in Amsterdam, and it's not unusual to see the dismembered parts of bicycles still chained to railings, victims of sharp-eyed gangs armed with bolt cutters who roam the streets hawking their prizes at suspiciously low prices. Ironically, this is often the cheapest way to pick up a bike – and you can always sell it (often at a profit) when the time comes to go home. Should you prefer to buy a bike legally, however, see "*Shops and Markets*" for a list of bike shops.

Canal bikes and canoes

More for fun than for serious transport are the **canal bikes**, pedalboats that during the summer can be picked up (and dropped off) between 9.30am and 7pm every day (until 11pm in July and Aug) at one of four central locations – Leidseplein by the American Hotel, on the Singelgracht opposite the Rijksmuseum, Prinsengracht at the Westerkerk, and Keizersgracht near Leidsestraat. Between November and March only the Rijksmuseum pick-up point is in use. You're given a map to plan a route, and rental costs f19.50 an hour for a two-seater, f29.50 for four, plus f50 deposit. For further information phone ☎626 55 74. In addition, *Roell Watersport* on Mauritskade, (☎692 91 24), behind the Amstel Hotel, rents out machines for f18 per hour for two people, f26 for four. They also rent out one-person **canoes**, at a rate of f15 for ninety minutes on the water, plus f75 deposit and your passport. Their jetty is in front of the Amstel Hotel (daily 8.30am–10pm).

Taxis

Taxis are plentiful in Amsterdam. They can be found in ranks on the main city squares (Stationsplein, Dam Square, Leidseplein, etc) or by phoning ☎677 77 77 – you can't hail them. Most drivers know their way around fairly well, though rates are pricey by any standards – f2.50 a kilometre, with approximately ten percent premium after midnight.

Useful Cycling Terms	
Tyre	*Band*
Puncture	*Lek*
Break	*Rern*
Chain	*Keting*
Wheel	*Wiel*
Pedal	*Trapper*
Pump	*Pomp*
Handlebars	*Stuur*
Broken	*Kapot*

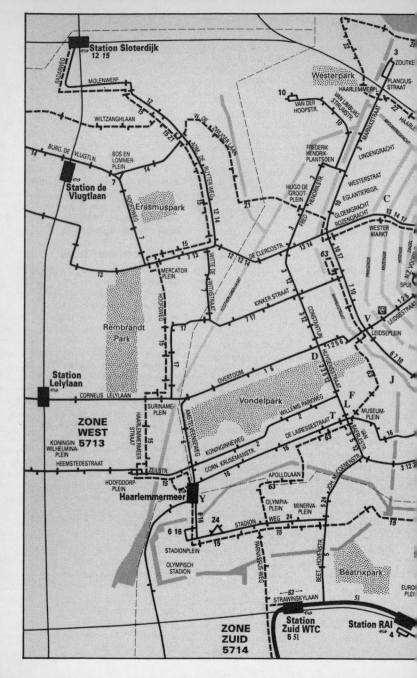

TRAMS, BUSES AND THE METRO

- - - 12 - - - Bus route
——— 10 ——— Tram route
——— 51 ——— Metro route
- - - - - - Zone boundary
———————— Railway line
(for reference only)

*GVB Offices
Opposite Central Station
(Mon-Fri 7 am–10.30 pm,
Sat & Sun 8 am–10.30 pm)

Prins Hendrikkade 108-114
(Mon-Fri 8.30 am–4.30 pm)

Amstel Station
(Mon-Fri 7 am–8.30 pm,
Sat & Sun 10.15 am–5 pm)

A. Allard Pierson Museum
B. Amsterdam Historical Museum
C. Anne Frank House
D. Dutch Film Museum
E. Museum Fodor
F. Vincent van Gogh Museum
G. Jewish Historical Museum
H. Technical Museum NINT
I. Rembrandt House
J. National Museum
K. Maritime Museum
L. Municipal Museum
M. Tropical Museum
N. Madamme Tussaud's
O. Begijnhof
P. Royal Palace
Q. Nieuwe Kerk
R. Oude Kerk
S. Carré Theatre
T. Concerthall
U. Musiektheater
V. Municipal theatre
W. Flower Market
X. Artis Zoo
Y. Trammuseum
Z. Hortus Botanicus

Cars

Taxis aside, it's generally unwise to travel **by car**: parking is either difficult or expensive (in general it costs around f3 an hour, or f19 per day in official car parks, but you need to buy a parking card from the *Dienst Parkenbekeer*, Prins Hendrikkade 108, Leidsegracht 101–105 or Bakkerstraat 13, to get these rates), and even if you have brought your own car it won't make any difference to the zealous traffic police, who will clamp or tow away your car whatever the registration plate says. Reclaiming a car from the pound costs at least f320; a clamp or parking ticket is cheaper, but still costs at least f120 plus the excess meter time; if your car is clamped, you have to present yourself personally at the nearest clamp office to get it removed. If you get caught and don't know what to do, call ☎626 69 11; the car pound is at Cruquiusweg 25 (☎555 98 00).

Even when you're mobile, the abundance of trams and bikes makes driving hazardous, to say the least. If you do **bring your own car**, an ordinary driver's licence is acceptable, and the Dutch automobile organization, *ANWB*, offers reciprocal repair/breakdown services to members of most foreign motoring organizations, as long as they hold a Letter of International Assistance – available from your home motoring organization. Their office in Amsterdam is at Museumplein 5 (Mon–Fri 8.45am–4.45pm, Sat 8.45am–noon; ☎673 08 44). Their repair service – *de Wegenwacht* – can be called nationwide on ☎06 08 88. If you're not a member of your home motoring organization, you can either pay for this service or, for a small fee, become a temporary member.

For getting out of town, it's better to **rent a vehicle** by the day or week. All the major agencies are represented in Amsterdam, although you will probably find the best deals with the local operators, whose prices start at around f45 a day plus a 35c charge per kilometre over 100km, or, even cheaper, by booking up in advance through a specialist agent like *Holiday Autos* (see p.6 for their address), whose rates normally substantially undercut all the competition. Briefly, the **rules of the road** include a maximum speed limit within the city of 50kph (31mph), and seatbelts must be worn by all drivers and front-seat passengers.

Car parks

De Bijenkorf
Beursplein, off Damrak

Europarking
Marnixstraat 250

Parking Byzantium
Tessekschadestraat 1

Parking Prinsengracht
Prinsengracht 540–542

*There are also **underground car parks**: at the Victoria Building, Prins Hendrikkade 20 (near Centraal Station), and under the Muziektheater and Museumplein.*

Car rental firms

Avis
Nassaukade 380   ☎683 60 61

Bakker
Hoordeweg 133   ☎612 40 47

Budget
Overtoom 121   ☎612 60 66

Diks
van Ostadestraat 278–280   ☎662 33 66

Eurodollar
Overtoom 196   ☎616 24 66

Europcar
Overtoom 51–53   ☎683 21 23

Hertz
Overtoom 333   ☎612 24 41

Kaspers en Lotte
van Ostadestraat 232–234   ☎662 66 14

Bike rental firms

Bulldog Rent-a-Bike
The Bulldog
Oude Zijds Voorburgwal 126   ☎624 82 48

Damstraat Rent-a-Bike
Pieter Jacobsdwarsstraat 11
off Damstraat   ☎625 50 29
Stationsplein 33   ☎625 38 45
Damrak 62   ☎622 32 07

Koenders
Utrechtsedwarsstraat 105   ☎623 46 57

Macbike
Nieuwe Uilenburgerstraat 116   ☎620 09 85
Marnixstraat 220   ☎626 69 64

Sint Nicolaas Rent-a-Bike
Sint Nicolaasstraat 14   ☎623 97 15

Zijwind
Ferdinand Bolstraat 168   ☎673 70 26

Organized tours: by boat, bus, tram and bike

One way of getting oriented is to take a **canal trip** on one of the glass-topped boats that jam the major canals during the summer season. While not exactly riveting, these trips are the best way to see the canal houses, and have a soporific charm if you're feeling lazy. There are many to choose from, dotted all over the city centre (*P. Kooij* is one of the better ones, with a refreshingly uncanned commentary); prices are around f10 per person, f6 for kids. However, the tours are so popular you may find you need to queue for a place in summer.

As far as regular **city tours** go, the *GVB* offers a ninety-minute tour by **tourist tram** each Sunday, departing hourly between noon and 4pm from Centraal Station and taking in the main sights of the immediate city centre for just f9 (children f5); and operators like *Lindbergh* (the cheapest), Damrak 26 (☎625 30 35), *Keytours*, Dam 19 (☎624 73 10), and *Holland International*, Damrak 6 (☎622 25 50), offer three-hour tours with stop-offs, and, again, live commentary for f35. The same organizations also run a range of **excursions** into the outlying regions of Holland – pick up a leaflet for details and prices. Finally, if you fancy a **cycle tour**, *Yellow Bike*, Nieuwezijds Voorburgwal 66 (☎620 69 40), organize 20km-long bike tours around the city, starting from Centraal Station. They cost f29, the bike is supplied, and tours leave daily at 9.30am and 1pm.

Other water transport services

If you want to combine a canal tour with real transportation, there is a **canal bus** service, which runs from Weteringschans opposite the Rijksmuseum to Centraal Station and back, with stops at Leidseplein, Leidsestraat/Keizersgracht and the Westerkerk. The whole journey takes

Canal trips

Amstel
Stadhouderskade, opposite Heinek
Brewery; ☎626 56 36. April–Sept da
5pm every 30min; Oct–March daily 1(
noon & 2–4pm.

Holland International
Stationsplein; ☎622 77 88. April–Oct daily 9am–6pm every 15min, 6–10pm every 45min; Nov–March daily 9am–4pm every 45min.

P Kooij
Opposite Rokin 125; ☎623 38 10. April–Oct daily 9.30am–6pm every 15min, 6–10pm every 30min; Nov–March daily 10am–5pm every 30min.

Lovers
Opposite Prins Hendrikkade 25; ☎622 21 81. April–Oct daily 9am–6pm every 15min; Nov–March daily 10am–5pm every 30min.

Meyers
Damrak, Jetties 4 & 5; ☎623 42 08. April–Sept daily 8am–6pm every 15min; Oct–March daily 9am–4pm every 30min.

about an hour, and boats leave the Rijksmuseum every twenty minutes – pick them up at any stop. A day ticket costs f15; more details on ☎623 98 86.

Another combination of a canal trip and real transportation is the latest addition to the boats jamming the canals, the so-called **Museumboat**. This runs a regular service, once every half-hour, between seven jetties located at the city's twenty major museums. A day ticket will cost you f19; a ticket including entrance to three museums of your choice costs f35. For more details call ☎622 21 81.

For the seriously moneyed, there are also **canal taxi** services. *Water Taxi*, outside Centraal Station (☎622 21 81), charges f120 per hour (f2 a minute) inside Amsterdam, with a maximum of eight people on board.

Before you leave it's worth contacting the Netherlands Board of Tourism, who put out a variety of glossy, informative (and free) booklets. Most of these cover Holland in its entirety, but some are specifically devoted to Amsterdam, with useful, if sketchy, introductory maps of the city and brief details of hotels, principal tourist attractions, annual events, etc.

Once in Amsterdam, the place to head for is the VVV, the nationwide tourist organization. They have a main branch at Stationsplein 10, immediately outside Centraal Station (May–Sept daily 9am–11pm; Oct–April daily 9am–5pm; ☎06/340 340 66 or 626 64 44), another at Leidseplein 1 (May–Sept daily 9am–9pm; Oct–April Mon–Sat 9am–5pm), and one at Stadionplein (daily 8am–8pm). This last is useful if you're arriving at Stadionplein via the *Hoverspeed* link bus. Each office can sell you a map, book accommodation for a ƒ3.50 fee (plus a ƒ4 "deposit" which you reclaim from the hotel), book theatre and concert tickets and provide informed answers to most other enquiries. In spring and summer months the Centraal Station office in particular gets very **crowded**, and you may have to queue for some time before being seen. Keep an eye on your belongings, and ignore the offers of the accommodation touts who hang around outside.

Our **maps** are adequate for most purposes, but if you need one on a larger scale, or with a street index, look for the "This is Amsterdam" map by *Falk* (ƒ3), available from the VVV and many bookshops. The traditional foldout *Falkplan* (ƒ7.50) is more detailed still, though *Falk's* ring-bound city atlas (ƒ10) is more convenient.

Netherlands Board of Tourism Offices	
Australia	
5 Elizabeth St, Suite 302, Sydney, NSW 2000	☎02/247 6921
Great Britain	
25–28 Buckingham Gate, London SW1E 6LD	☎0891/200277
Canada	
25 Adelaide St East, Suite 710, Toronto, ON M5C 1Y2	☎416/363 1577
USA	
355 Lexington Ave, 21st floor, New York, NY 10017	☎212/370-7360
225 N Michigan Ave, Suite 326, Chicago, IL 60601	☎312/819-0300
90 New Montgomery St, Suite 305, San Francisco, CA 94105	☎415/543-6772

The Media: Newspapers, Magazines, TV and Radio

There's no difficulty in finding **British newpapers** – they are on sale just about everywhere the same day they come out (the Centraal Station shop has a good selection). For those wanting to practise their Dutch, *NRC Handelsblad* is a right-of-centre paper that has perhaps the best news coverage and a liberal stance on the arts; it is the one favoured by the city's intellectuals. *De Volkskrant* is a progressive, leftish daily; *De Telegraaf* is a right-wing popular paper, although its financial pages are well respected; *Algemeen Dagblad* is a right-wing broadsheet, while the middle-of-the-road *Het Parool* ('The Password'), and the news magazine *Vrij Nederland*, are the successors of underground newspaper printing during the Nazi occupation. The Protestant *Trouw* ('Trust'), also an ex-underground paper, is also centre-left in orientation, but focuses on religion.

For information about **what's on**, the best source is *Time Out* (f4), a monthly English-language arts and entertainment guide owned by and similar to the London listings magazine. While sometimes adopting a rather pompous xenophobia, and often omitting Dutch-language events, it's a useful place to look for critical listings on clubs, live music, cinema and exhibitions, as well as local news articles. The VVV also issues a weekly listings guide, *What's On In Amsterdam*, which you can either pick up directly from their offices for f2.75, or obtain free from selected hotels, hostels and restaurants. Though more detailed than *Time Out*, its listings for

museums, the arts, shopping and restaurants are bland and uncritical. Of the many Dutch-language monthly freebies to be found in bars and restaurants, the best is *Agenda*, whose listings have a more youthful slant and whose addresses, phone numbers and numerous advertisements for various services could prove invaluable. *Uitkrant*, too, covers just about everything that is happening, albeit fairly uncritically.

TV and Radio

Dutch **TV** isn't up to much, although the quantity of English-language programmes, without subtitles, is high. If you're staying somewhere with cable TV (most places do have it in Holland), it's also possible to tune in to many non-Dutch TV channels, mostly for English-speakers, for example BBC1 and BBC2, but also various Belgian, German, French, and even Italian, Turkish and Arab-language stations. Most hotels also pick up a host of European-wide cable and satellite stations: *Superchannel* (which offers pop videos, reruns of British sitcoms, dramas and documentaries); *BSkyB*, which is fairly similar; the Euro version of *MTV* (24-hour pop videos); and the American-based all-news channel, *CNN*. Other Dutch TV channels, cable and non-cable, regularly run American and British movies with Dutch subtitles. As for **radio**, it's possible to pick up BBC Radio 4 on 1500m long wave, and the BBC World Service on 463m medium wave and at short wave frequencies between 75m and 49m at intervals throughout the day and night.

Money and Banks

The Dutch currency is the guilder, indicated by "f", "ff" and occasionally "Hfl", "Dfl" or "NLG". Each guilder is divided into 100 cents. You'll find 5c ("stuiver"), 10c ("dubbeltje"), 25c ("kwartje"), f1, f2.50 ("rijksdaalder") and f5 coins, along with f5, f10, f25, f50 and f100 notes, and, rarely, f250 and f1000 notes. Although prices are still given using individual cents, 1c coins are no longer available.

Guilders are available in advance from any high street bank: current exchange rates are around f2.7 to £1, f1.86 to US$1, and there are no restrictions on bringing currency into the country. The best way of carrying the bulk of your money is in **travellers' cheques**, available from most high street banks (whether or not you have an account) for the usual fee of one percent of the amount ordered. An alternative is the **Eurocheque** book and card, issued on request by most British banks to account holders, which can be used to get cash in the majority of Dutch (and European) banks and bureaux de change. This works out slightly more expensive than travellers' cheques but can be more convenient. Bear in mind that you always need your passport as well as the Eurocheque card to obtain cash at Dutch banks.

Changing money

Amsterdam **banks** usually offer the best deal for changing money. Hours are Monday to Friday 9am to 4pm, with a few banks also open Thursday 7–9pm or Saturday morning; all are closed on public holidays (see p.35). At other times you'll need to go to one of the many **bureaux de change** scattered around town. The best of these are – as in the rest of the country – the *GWK* (main branches at Centraal Station and Schiphol Airport, open 24hr), which tend to give the best rates, others include *Change Express* and *Thomas Cook*. You should, however, beware of places that offer seemingly good rates but then charge high commissions (see box above). You can also change money at post offices, major department stores like *Vroom & Dreesman* and *De Bijenkorf*, VVV counters or other bureaux de change, though again the deals they offer aren't so good. Hotels, hostels and campsites usually give poor rates of exchange.

Plastic money

Visa, Access/Mastercard/Eurocard, Diners Club and *American Express* cards can be used in most Dutch banks and bureaux de change – if you're prepared to withdraw a minimum of f300. *American Express* card holders can also take out cash or replace lost travellers' cheques by using the machine and office at Damrak 66. Credit cards are less popular than would be expected, although most mainstream shops, hotels and restaurants will take at least one brand. Check before you commit yourself to spending. Eurocheques are the most commonly used form of payment after cash.

Useful Addresses

City centre banks

These are only the most usefully placed: for full listings, look in the Yellow Pages.

ABN/AMRO, Vijzelstraat 68; Dam 2; Damrak 33; Leideseplein 2; Leidsestraat 1; Rozengracht 88; Rokin 80.

Rabobank, Dam 16; Nieuwmarkt 20.

NMB Bank, Damrak 80; Herngracht 580; Rozengracht 8.

Change Express

Damrak 86 (daily 8am–11.45pm; ☎ 624 66 81)
Leidsestraat 106 (daily 8am–midnight; ☎ 622 14 25)
Kalverstraat 150 (daily 8am–8pm; ☎ 627 80 87)

GWK

Centraal Station (open 24hr; ☎ 627 27 31)
Schiphol Station (open 24hr; ☎ 601 05 07)

Amstel Station (Mon–Sat 8am–8pm; ☎ 693 45 45)
Sloterdijk Station (daily 8am–8pm; ☎ 688 12 13)

Thomas Cook

Dam 23 (daily 9am–6pm; ☎ 625 09 22)
Damrak 1–5 (daily 9am–6pm; ☎ 620 32 36)
Leidseplein 31 (daily 9am–6pm; ☎ 626 70 00)
Muntplein 12 (daily 9am–6pm; ☎ 620 40 16)

American Express

Damrak 66 (Mon–Fri 9am–5pm, Sat 9am–noon; ☎ 520 77 77)

Lost credit cards

Access/Mastercard/Eurocard ☎ 10/207 07 89
American Express ☎ 642 44 88
Diners Club ☎ 557 84 07 (6.30pm–8am; ☎ 627 93 10)
Visa ☎ 660 0611
Lost Travellers' Cheques ☎ 06/022 01 00

Post and Phones

Amsterdam's main **post office** is at Singel 250–
256, and is open Monday to Friday from 9am
until 6pm (staying open until 8pm on Thurs) and
Saturday from 9am to 3pm (☎556 33 11).
Queues for stamps can be long (make sure you're
in the right one, labelled "postzegels") and it's
often easier, especially if you're sending post-
cards, to buy stamps from tobacconists. For the
record, **postal charges** right now are: within
Europe 70c for a postcard, 90c for a letter, and
outside Europe 90c for a postcard and ƒ1.60 for
air-mail letters up to 10g; aerogrammes cost
ƒ1.20. **Post boxes** are everywhere, but be sure to
use the correct slot – labelled *Overige* for destinations other than Amsterdam. To use the **poste**

restante, letters should be addressed to "Poste
Restante, Central Post Office, Amsterdam" and will
arrive at the main office. To collect a letter you'll
need your passport.

Telephones

The green-trim **telephone boxes** are similar to the
modern British kiosks and most others in Europe,
with a digital display of the amount of credit
remaining after depositing your money. The slots
take 25c, ƒ1 and ƒ2.50 coins; only wholly unused
coins are returned. More and more call boxes
taking only **phonecards** are appearing, and
buying a card is a good way to avoid queueing.
They're available from post offices and Centraal
Station – ƒ5 for the equivalent of twenty local
calls. Though you may have less idea of how
much you're spending while the call is in
progress, it's easier to make international calls
from the **Telehouse**, Raadhuisstraat 48–50 (open
24hr); a discount rate on international calls is in
effect between 8pm and 8am. Most hotels will
allow you to make international calls, but check
prices first as the charge is considerably higher
than from a booth or the Telehouse. Taking
advantage of recent privatization, there are also
commercial **phone centres**, like the *Tele Talk
Center*, Leidsestraat 101 (daily 10am–midnight),
and the *Telefoon Center* (directly opposite but
with an entrance in Lange Leidsedwarsstraat),
which offers phones, faxes, photocopying facilities
and suchlike, albeit a little more expensively. For

City centre post offices

Singel 250–256

Oosterdokskade 3, near Centraal Station
(open until 9pm)

St Antoniebreestraat 16

Keizersgracht 757

Kerkstraat 167

De Bijenkorf, Damrak 90a

Stadhuis, Waterlooplein 2

Plantage Middenlaan 167

Haarlemmerdijk 99

Bloemgracht 300

*For further locations, and information on
the postal service, call* ☎ *06 04 17 (free).*

International Dialling Codes

Great Britain	☎ 00 44
Northern Ireland	☎ 00 44
Eire	☎ 00 353
Australia	☎ 00 61
New Zealand	☎ 00 64
USA and Canada	☎ 00 1

Useful Numbers

Operator calls	☎ 06 04 10
National directory enquiries	☎ 06 80 08

open 8am–10pm; outside these times dial ☎ 06 899 11 33 (both 60c per call).

International directory enquiries (free) ☎ 06 04 18

Police	☎ 559 91 11
Fire	☎ 621 21 21
Ambulance	☎ 555 55 55
Fire, Police and Ambulance (nationwide alarm number)	☎ 06 11

Collect calls

Either ☎ 06 04 10, or for calls to the UK ☎ 06 022 99 44; to the USA and Canada ☎ 06 022 91 11; to Australia ☎ 06 022 00 61. *These numbers connect directly to the national operators and generally provide a quicker and cheaper service.*

See also the "Directory" section for help and information lines.

further assistance, the **Amsterdam Yellow Pages** (*Gouden Gids*) can be found in most bars and cafés and has useful information, including a 'Tourist Page" in English. To obtain your own copy, the customer service section can be contacted on ☎ 567 67 67.

All Amsterdam **phone numbers** are made up of seven figures, and either begin with "four", "five" or "six". The city's **area code**, which you use when dialling Amsterdam from anywhere outside its formal boundaries, is ☎ 020; calling from outside The Netherlands, omit the first zero. Where applicable, codes for other cities are stated in the text. It's useful to know, too, that any number that is prefixed by the code "06" is either toll-free – or (confusingly) less or more expensive than usual; legally, the rate should be stated near the number.

Eating and Drinking

Amsterdam is better known for **drinking** than eating, and with good reason: its selection of bars is one of the real pleasures of the city. As for **eating**, this may not be Europe's culinary capital, but there's a good supply of ethnic restaurants, especially Indonesian and Chinese, and the prices (by big-city standards) are hard to beat. And there are any number of *eetcafés* and bars which serve increasingly adventurous food, quite cheaply, in a relaxed and unpretentious setting.

In the *Restaurants* and *Bars and Coffee Shops* chapters you will find full lists of Amsterdam's bars, coffee shops and restaurants. They are also **cross-referenced** at the end of each area section in the "City" chapters.

Food

In all but the very cheapest hostels or most expensive hotels, **breakfast** (*ontbijt*) will be included in the price of the room. Though usually nothing fancy, it's always very filling: rolls, cheese, ham, hard-boiled eggs, jam and honey or peanut butter are the principal ingredients. If you're not eating in your hotel, many bars and cafés serve breakfast, and those that don't invariably offer at least rolls and sandwiches.

Fast food and snacks

For the rest of the day, eating cheaply and well, particularly on your feet, is no real problem, although those on the tightest of budgets may find themselves dependent on the dubious delights of **Dutch fast food**. This has its own peculiarities. Chips − *patat* in Amsterdam, *frites* in the south of the country − are the most common standby (*Vlaamse* or "Flemish" are the best), either sprinkled with salt or smothered with huge gobs of mayonnaise (sometimes known as *frite-saus*); some alternative toppings are curry, goulash, peanut or tomato sauce. Often, chips are complemented with *kroketten* − spiced minced meat covered with breadcrumbs and deep-fried − or *fricandel*, a franfurter-like sausage. All these are available over the counter at evil-smelling fast-food places (*Febo* is the most common chain), or, for a guilder or so, from heated glass compartments outside. As an alternative there are also a number of **Indonesian fast-food** places, serving saté and noodle dishes in a McDonald's type atmosphere.

Tastier, and good both as a snack and a full lunch, are the **fish specialities** sold from street kiosks: salted raw herrings, smoked eel, mackerel in a roll, mussels, and various kinds of deep-fried fish; tip your head back and dangle the fish into your mouth, Dutch-style. Other street foods include **pancakes** (*pannekoeken*), sweet or spicy, also widely available at sit-down restaurants; **waffles** (*stroopwafels*), doused with maple syrup; and *poffertjes*, shell-shaped dough balls served with masses of melted butter and icing sugar − an extremely filling snack. Try also *oliebollen*, greasy doughnuts traditionally served at New Year. Dutch **cakes and biscuits** are always good, and filling, best eaten in a *banketbakkerij* with a small serving area; or buy a bag and eat them on the go. Apart from the ubiquitous *appelgebak* − wedges of apple and cinnamon tart − things to try include *spekulaas*, a cinammon biscuit with a gingerbread texture; *stroopwafels*, butter wafers sandwiched together with runny syrup; and *amandelkoek*, cakes with a biscuity outside and melt-in-the-mouth almond paste inside.

As for the kind of food you can expect to encounter in bars, there are **sandwiches and rolls** (*boterhammen* and *broodjes*) − often open, and varying from a slice of tired cheese on old bread to something so embellished it's almost a complete meal − as well as more substantial fare. In the winter, *erwtensoep* (aka *snert*) is available in most bars, and at about *f*5.50 a shot it makes a great buy for lunch: thick pea soup with smoked sausage, and served with a portion of smoked bacon on *pumpernickel*. Or there's *uitsmijter* (literally, "bouncer"): one, two or three fried eggs on buttered bread, topped with a choice of ham, cheese or roast beef – at about *f*8, another good budget lunch.

Dutch cheese

Holland's **cheeses** have an unjustified reputation abroad for being bland and rubbery, possibly because they only export the nastier products and keep the best for themselves. In fact, Dutch cheese can be delicious, although there isn't the variety you get in, say, France or Britain. Most are based on the same soft, creamy *Goudas*, and differences in taste come with the varying stages of maturity – *jong*, *belegen* or *oud*. *Jong* cheese has a mild flavour, *belegen* is much tastier, while *oud* can be pungent and strong, with a flaky texture not unlike Italian parmesan. Generally, the older they get, the saltier they are. Among the other cheeses you'll find are the best-known round, red *Edam*, made principally for export and (quite sensibly) not eaten much by the Dutch; *Leidse*, simply *Gouda* with cumin seeds; *Maasdammer* and *Leerdammer*, strong, creamy and full of holes; and Dutch-made *Emmentals* and *Gruyères*. The best way to eat cheese here is the way the Dutch do it, in thin slices (cut with a special cheese knife or *kaasschaaf*) rather than large hunks.

Restaurant food

Dutch food tends to be higher in protein content than on imagination: steak, chicken and fish, along with filling soups and stews, are staple fare. Where possible stick to *dagschotels* (dish of the day), a meat and two vegetable combination for which you pay around *f*15, bottom-line, for what tend to be enormous portions. The fish is generally high-quality but not especially cheap (*f*20 and up, on average), while the three-course *tourist menu*, which the authorities push at several of the city's more mainstream restaurants, is, at *f*21.50, no great bargain, and usually extremely dull.

A wide selection of **vegetarian** restaurants offer full-course set meals for around *f*10–12. Bear in mind that they often close early. Another cheap standby is **Italian** food: pizzas and pasta

dishes start at a fairly uniform *f*10–11 in all but the ritziest places. **Chinese** restaurants are also common, as are (increasingly) **Spanish**, and there are a handful of **Tex-Mex** eateries, all of which serve well-priced, filling food. But Amsterdam's real speciality is its **Indonesian** restaurants, a consequence of the country's imperial adventures and well worth checking out. You can eat à la carte – *Nasi Goreng* and *Bami Goreng* (rice or noodles with meat) are ubiquitous dishes, and chicken or beef in peanut sauce (*saté*) is available everywhere too. Alternatively, order a *rijsttafel*: boiled rice and/or noodles served with a number of spicy side dishes and hot *sambal* sauce on the side. Eaten with the spoon in the right hand, fork in the left, and with dry white or rosé wine or beer, this doesn't come cheap, but it's delicious and is normally more than enough for two. (See p.137 for restaurant listings.)

Drink

Dutch **coffee** is black and strong, and often served with *koffiemelk* (evaporated milk); ordinary milk is offered only occasionally. If you want white coffee, ask for a *koffie verkeerd*. Most bars also serve cappuccino, although bear in mind that many stop serving coffee altogether around 11pm. **Tea** generally comes with lemon, if anything; if you want milk you have to ask for it. **Hot chocolate** is also popular, served hot or cold: for a real treat drink it hot with a layer of fresh whipped cream on top.

Beer, spirits, liqueurs

The beverage drunk most often in Amsterdam bars is **beer**. This is usually served in small (around half-pint) measures (ask for "een pils"), much of which will be a frothing head – requests to have it poured English-style meet with various responses, but it's worth trying. **Jenever**, or Dutch gin, is not unlike British gin, but is a bit weaker and a little oilier; it's made from molasses and flavoured with juniper berries. It's served in small glasses and is traditionally drunk straight, often knocked back in one gulp with much hearty back-slapping. There are a number of varieties: *Oud* (old) is smooth and mellow, *Jong* (young) packs more of a punch – though neither is terribly alcoholic. Ask for a *borreltje* (straight jenever), a *bitterje* (with angostura bitters), or, if you've a sweeter tooth, try a *bessenjenever* – blackcurrant-flavoured gin; for a

Glossary of Dutch Food And Drink Terms

Although most menus in Amsterdam include full English translations, the list below will help you to make specific requests.

Basics

Boter	Butter
Boterham/Broodje	Sandwich/roll
Brood	Bread
Dranken	Drinks
Eieren	Eggs
Gerst	Barley
Groenten	Vegetables
Honing	Honey
Hoofdgerechten	Main courses
Kaas	Cheese
Koud	Cold
Nagerechten	Desserts
Peper	Pepper
Pindakaas	Peanut butter
Sla/salade	Salad
Smeerkaas	Cheese spread
Stokbrood	French bread
Suiker	Sugar
Vis	Fish
Vlees	Meat
Voorgerechten	Starters/ hors d'oeuvres
Vruchten	Fruit
Warm	Hot
Zout	Salt

Starters and Snacks

Erwtensoep/snert	Thick pea soup with bacon or sausage
Huzarensalade	Egg salad
Koffietafel	A light midday meal of cold meats, cheese, bread, and perhaps soup
Patates/Frites	Chips
Soep	Soup
Uitsmijter	Ham or cheese with eggs on bread

Meat and Poultry

Biefstuk (duitse)	Steak
Biefstuk (hollandse)	Hamburger
Eend	Duck
Fricandeau	Roast pork
Fricandel	A frankfurter-like sausage
Gehakt	Minced meat
Ham	Ham
Kalfsvlees	Veal
Kalkoen	Turkey
Karbonade	Chop
Kip	Chicken
Kroket	Spiced minced meat in breadcrumbs
Lamsvlees	Lamb

Lever	Liver
Rookvlees	Smoked beef
Spek	Bacon
Worst	Sausages

Fish

Forel	Trout
Garnalen	Prawns
Haring	Herring
Haringsalade	Herring salad
Kabeljauw	Cod
Makreel	Mackerel
Mosselen	Mussels
Paling	Eel
Schelvis	Haddock
Schol	Plaice
Tong	Sole
Zalm	Salmon

Terms

Belegen	Filled or topped, as in Belegen broodje – a small roll topped with cheese, etc
Doorbakken	Well-done
Gebakken	Fried/baked
Gebraden	Roast
Gegrild	Grilled
Gekookt	Boiled
Geraspt	Grated
Gerookt	Smoked
Gestoofd	Stewed
Half doorbakken	Medium
Hollandse saus	Hollandaise (a milk and egg sauce)
Rood	Rare

Vegetables

Aardappelen	Potatoes
Boerenkool	Mashed potato and cabbage
Bloemkool	Cauliflower
Bonen	Beans
Champignons	Mushrooms
Erwten	Peas
Hutspot	Mashed potatoes and carrots
Knoflook	Garlic
Komkommer	Cucumber
Prei	Leek
Rijst	Rice
Sla	Salad, lettuce
Uien	Onions
Wortelen	Carrots
Zuurkool	Sauerkraut

Indonesian Dishes and Terms

Ajam	Chicken
Bami	Noodles with meat/chicken and vegetables
Daging	Beef
Gado gado	Vegetables in peanut sauce
Goreng	Fried
Ikan	Fish
Katjang	Peanut
Kroepoek	Prawn crackers
Loempia	Spring rolls
Nasi	Rice
Nasi Goreng	Fried rice with meat/chicken and vegetables
Nasi Rames	Rijsttafel on a single plate
Pedis	Hot and spicy
Pisang	Banana
Rijsttafel	Collection of different spicy dishes served with plain rice
Sambal	Hot, chilli-based sauce
Satesaus	Peanut sauce to accompany meat grilled on skewers
Seroendeng	Spicy fried, shredded coconut
Tauge	Bean sprouts

Sweets and Desserts

Appelgebak	Apple tart or cake
Drop	Dutch liquorice, available in zoet (sweet) or zout (salted) varieties – the latter being an acquired taste
Gebak	Pastry
IJs	Ice cream
Koekjes	Biscuits
Oliebollen	Doughnuts
Pannekoeken	Pancakes
Pepernoten	Dutch ginger nuts
Poffertjes	Small pancakes, fritters
(Slag) room	(Whipped) cream
Speculaas	Spice & honey-flavoured biscuit
Stroopwafels	Waffles
Taai-taai	Dutch honey cake
Vla	Custard

Fruits and Nuts

Aardbei	Strawberry
Amandel	Almond
Appel	Apple
Appelmoes	Apple purée
Citroen	Lemon
Druiven	Grape
Framboos	Raspberry
Hazelnoot	Hazelnut
Kers	Cherry
Kokosnoot	Coconut
Peer	Pear
Perzik	Peach
Pinda	Peanut
Pruim	Plum/prune

Drinks

Bessenjenever	Blackcurrant gin
Citroenjenever	Lemon gin
Droog	Dry
Frisdranken	Soft drinks
Jenever	Dutch gin
Karnemelk	Buttermilk
Koffie	Coffee
Kopstoot	Beer with a jenever chaser
Melk	Milk
Met ijs	With ice
Pils	Dutch beer
Proost!	Cheers!
Thee	Tea
Vruchtensap	Fruit juice
Wijn	Wine
(wit/rood/rosé)	(white/red/rosé)
Vieux	Dutch brandy
Zoet	Sweet
Anijsmelk	Aniseed-flavoured warm milk
Appelsap	Apple juice
Chocomel	Chocolate milk
Koffie verkeerd	Coffee with warm milk
Met slagroom	With whipped cream
Sinaasappelsap	Orange juice
Tomatensap	Tomato juice

glass of beer with a jenever chaser, ask for a kopstoot. Other drinks you'll see include numerous Dutch **liqueurs**, notably advocaat or eggnog and the sweet blue curacao; and an assortment of lurid-coloured **fruit brandies**, which are best left for experimentation at the end of an evening. There's also the Dutch-produced brandy, Vieux, which tastes as if it's made from prunes but is in fact grape-based.

Beer and jenever are both dirt cheap if bought by the bottle from a shop or supermarket: the commonest beers, Amstel, Grolsch and Heineken, all cost a little over f1 for a half-litre (about a pint), and a bottle of jenever sells for around f14. Imported spirits are considerably more expensive. **Wine**, too, is very reasonable – expect to pay around f6 or so for a bottle of fairly decent French white or red.

Police, Trouble and Drugs

You're unlikely to come into much contact with Amsterdam's police force (Politie), a laid-back bunch in dodgem-sized patrol cars. Few operate on the beat, and in any case Amsterdam is one of the safest cities in Europe: bar-room brawls are highly unusual, muggings uncommon, and street crime much less conspicuous than in many other capitals.

Nonetheless, it's always worth taking precautions against **petty crime**: secure your things in a locker when staying in a dorm; never leave any valuables in a tent; and if you've brought a car, remove everything that you might miss, especially the radio, and park in a well-lit public place if you can't find a car park. As far as **personal safety** goes, it's possible to walk anywhere in the city centre at any time of the day or night – though women might get tired of being hassled if they walk through the red-light areas alone; see p.40 for more on women and sexual harassment.

If you're unlucky enough to have something stolen, you'll need to report it to a police station immediately and get them to write a statement for your insurance company; see "Health and Insurance", above.

City centre police stations	
Elandsgracht 117	☎559 91 11
Kloveniersburgwal T/O 26	☎559 32 60
Lijnbaansgracht 219	☎559 23 10
N.Z. Voorburgwal 118	☎559 32 80
Prinsengracht 1109	☎559 34 50
Singel 455	☎559 32 95
Warmoesstraat 44	☎559 22 10
Amsterdam's police emergency number	☎06 11

Drugs

Some residents claim that the liberal municipal attitude to the sale of **drugs** has attracted all sorts of undesirables to the city. This is partly true, but the "cleaning up" of the Zeedijk, once Amsterdam's heroin-dealing quarter, though not wholly a success, seems to have made open trafficking less frequent and the city a safer place.

Amsterdam has sanctioned the sale of **cannabis** at the *Melkweg* and *Paradiso* nightspots, and at many coffee shops, since the 1960s. Buy it elsewhere, however, especially on the streets, and it's highly likely you'll be ripped off. The law is a little confusing. Though busts are rare, legally you're allowed to possess only 30 grams for personal use. However, even if you have less, the police are technically entitled to (and do) confiscate it. It's acceptable to smoke in some bars, but since many are strongly against it, don't make any automatic assumptions. If in doubt, ask the barperson.

The law is the same throughout the rest of the country, as is the liberal attitude, at least in the cities of the Randstad, although the legal niceties are perhaps more strictly interpreted. The one thing you shouldn't do is attempt to take cannabis products out of the country – this would be foolhardy in the extreme. Bear in mind, also, that while there's a lively and growing trade in **cocaine** and **heroin**, possession of either could mean a stay in one of The Netherlands' lively and growing gaols. For drug-related **problems**, the *Drug Advice Centre*, Keizersgracht 812 (open to walk-in visitors Mon–Fri 1–3pm; ☎570 23 35), offers help and advice. You could also try *Stichting Drugshulpverlening*, De Regenboog, Droogbak 1 (☎625 37 37), or *MDHG*, Binnenkant 46 (☎624 47 75).

Opening Hours

The Dutch weekend fades painlessly into the working week with many shops staying closed on Monday morning, even in central Amsterdam. **Opening hours** are usually from 9am to 5.30pm or 6pm, with many shops open later, especially on Thursday evenings – *Koopavond* or "shopping night" in Amsterdam – when many places stay open until 9pm. Some shops close on Wednesday afternoon. Things shut down a little earlier on Saturday, and only specific licensed shopkeepers open up on Sunday. For a list of **late-night shops** – "Avondwinkels" – see *Shops and Markets*.

Museums, especially those that are state-run, tend to follow a pattern: closed on Monday, open from 10am to 5pm Tuesday to Saturday and from 1 to 5pm on Sunday and public holidays. Though closed on Christmas, New Year's and Boxing Days, all state-run museums adopt Sunday hours on the remaining **public** **holidays**, when most shops and banks are closed. (For a full list of museums and galleries, and details of their opening hours, see *Museums and Galleries*).

Public Holidays
New Year's Day
Good Friday (many shops open)
Easter Sunday and Monday
April 30, Queen's Birthday (many shops open)
May 5, Liberation Day
May 28, Ascension Day
Whit Sunday and Monday
Dec 5, St Nicholas' birthday (early closing for shops)
Christmas Day
December 26

Festivals and Annual Events

Most of Amsterdam's **festivals** aren't so much street happenings as music and arts events, in addition to which there are a sprinkling of religious celebrations. Most, as you'd expect, take place in the summer; the Queen's Birthday celebration at the end of April is rapidly becoming the city's most touted and most exciting annual event, with half the city given over to an impromptu flea market. On a more cultural level, the Holland Festival, throughout June, attracts a handful of big names. Check with the VVV for further details, and remember that many other interesting happenings, such as the Easter performance of Bach's *St Matthew Passion* in Naarden or the *North Sea Jazz Festival* in The Hague, are only a short train ride away.

Diary Of Events

February
• Last week: *Commemoration of the February Strike* around the *Docker Statue* on J. D. Meijerplein, Feb 25 (see p.90).
• February is also normally *Carnaval* month – basically six weeks before Easter – though the three-day celebrations are confined to the south of The Netherlands, centring on Breda, Hertogenbosch and Maastricht. There is, however, also a parade through Amsterdam itself.

March
• March–Oct: *Arts and Crafts Markets* every Sun, on Thorbeckeplein and on Spui.
• Second week: *Stille Omgang* procession through the streets to the Sint Nicolaaskerk on the Sunday closest to March 15.
• Third week: *Blues Festival* at the Meervaart Theatre.
• Last week: *Head of the River* rowing competition on the Amstel river.

April
• April–Aug: *Vondelpark Open Air Theatre* – free theatre, dance and music throughout the summer.
• April–Aug: *Arts and Crafts Market* every Sun 10am–6pm on Spui.

• April–Aug: *Stadsilluminatie* – not really a festival, but in April the canal bridges are lit up at night until October – a lovely sight.
• Second or third week: *Paasopenstelling* – the Royal Palace open day.
• Last week: *Nationaal Museumweekend* – free entrance to all the museums in The Netherlands.
• April 30: *Koninginnedag* (Queen's birthday), celebrated by a fair on Dam Square, street markets, and fireworks in the evening. A street event par excellence, which seems to grow annually and is almost worth planning a visit around, though some people claim it has become too commercialized over recent years.

May
• May–Sept: *Nieuwmarkt Antique Market* every Sun.
• Throughout May: *World Press Photo Exhibition* in the Nieuwe Kerk.

June
• Throughout June: *Holland Festival*, the largest music, dance and drama festival in the Low Countries; see *Nightlife* for details.

July
• Last week: *Zomerfestijn*, an informal international festival of modern theatre, music, dance, and mime.

August

• First or second week: *Amsterdam 700* weekend-long football tournament with Ajax Amsterdam and top European clubs.

• *Uitmarkt*, a weekend where every cultural organization in the city advertises itself, with music, theatre, dancing, etc; either on Museumplein or by the Amstel.

• Last week: *Prinsengrachtconcert*, an evening of classical music on Prinsengracht outside the *Pulitzer Hotel*.

September

• Through Sept: *Open Monumentendag* – most of the state-owned monuments have an open day.

• First week: *Bloemencorso*, the Aalsmeer–Amsterdam flower pageant in the city centre. Vijzelstraat is the best place to see things, but it's not really worth a special trip.

• Second week: *Hiswa te Water*, state-of-the-art boat show at the Oosterdok. Illuminated canoe-row at night.

• Second or third week: *Jordaan Festival*, street festival in a friendly neighbourhood. There's a commercial fair on Palmgracht, talent contests on Elandsgracht and a few street parties.

• Last week: *Amsterdam City Marathon*.

November

• Second or third week: *Parade of Sint Nicolaas*, with the traditional arrival of *Sinterklaas* near the Sint Nicolaaskerk, on a Sat.

December

• Dec 5: Though it tends to be a private affair, December 5, or *Pakjesavond*, rather than Christmas Day, is when Dutch kids receive their Christmas presents. If you're here on that day and have Dutch friends, it's worth knowing that it's traditional to give a present together with an amusing poem you have written caricaturing the recipient.

• Dec 31: *New Year's Eve* is a big thing in Amsterdam, with fireworks everywhere, especially outside Chinese restaurants. Some bars and discos are open all night.

Gay Amsterdam

In keeping with the Dutch reputation for tolerance, no other city in Europe accepts **gay men** as readily as Amsterdam. Here, more than anywhere, it's possible to be openly gay and accepted by the straight community. Gays are prominent in business and the arts, the age of consent is sixteen, and, with the Dutch willingness to speak English, French and just about any other language, Amsterdam has become a magnet for the international gay scene – a city with a dense sprinkling of advice centres, bars, clubs and cinemas.

It says much for the strength of the community that the arrival of **AIDS** was not accompanied by the homophobia seen elsewhere. Rather than close down clubs and saunas, the city council has funded education programmes, encouraged the use of condoms, and generally conducted an open policy on the disease. If anything AIDS has created an even greater solidarity among Amsterdam's gays, a feeling tangibly manifested in the *Homomonument*, unveiled in 1987 as a memorial to gays and lesbians murdered in the Nazi concentration camps (see p.81).

The city has four recognized **gay areas**: the most famous and most lively centres on **Kerkstraat** and **Reguliersdwarsstraat**, a neighbourhood as popular with locals as it is with tourists; the riverside bars along the **Amstel** are popular too, as is the cruisy and mainly leathergeared **Warmoesstraat**. There's also a gay-oriented enclave near the **Station**, up **Nieuwe Zijds Voorburgwal** and along **Spuistraat**, though this is harder territory, more associated with drugs and prostitution than anything else.

You'll find descriptions of all **bars and nightclubs** in *Bars and Coffee Shops*, *Restaurants* and *Nightlife*, and recommended **gay hotels** on p.123. If you want more **information**, get hold of a copy of the **map** of gay Amsterdam produced by *Holland Boys International*, which has information, addresses and locations and is available

from most gay hotels; or call them for a copy on ☎692 26 83. You could also invest in a copy of the *Best Guide to Amsterdam* (f13.95), a comprehensive gay **guide** (in English), available from any of the shops listed below and most other gay bookshops around the world, or by post from *Best Guide*, Nieuwe Zijds Voorburgwal 66, 1012 SC Amsterdam. For up-to-the-minute listings, the fortnightly **newspaper** *De Gay Krant* (f4.95) has all the details you could conceivably need, though it is in Dutch only.

Contacts and resources

COC, Rozenstraat 14; ☎623 11 92; information on ☎623 40 79; women ☎626 83 00. A national gay and lesbian body with help, advice, social activities, coffeeshop and contacts. Mon–Fri 9am–5pm. *COC* also broadcasts gay and lesbian information (occasionally in English) at 102.4 FM.

Documentatiecentrum Homostudies, Oude Zijds Achterburgwal 185; ☎525 26 01. A gay studies information centre, now in new and enlarged premises. Fri 2–5pm.

Gay and Lesbian Switchboard ☎623 65 65. An English-speaking service providing information on the gay and lesbian scenes in general. Also a good source of help and advice. Daily 10am–10pm.

Gay Radio. If your Dutch is up to it, *MVS Radio* is a gay and lesbian radio station broadcasting on 104.9, 106.8 and, via cable, 103.8 FM. The English-language programme *Alien*, on Sundays from 6 to 8pm, is especially for gay foreign visitors to the city.

Gay Jewish Group (*Sjalhomo*), Postbus 2536, 1000 CM Amsterdam; ☎673 06 29. Monthly discussion groups for gay and lesbian Jews.

Op Je Flikker Gehad !?, Postbus 55556, 1007 NB Amsterdam; ☎24 63 21. Support and help group for victims of assault, rape and blackmail.

Tijgertje Stichting Homoverdediging, Postbus 10521; ☎664 94 24. Self-defence for homosexuals.

The legal **age of consent** for gay men in The Netherlands is 16

Health

AIDS Infoline ☎06/022 22 20. Mon–Fri 2–10pm.

Body Positive Helpline ☎624 50 05. Offers a sympathetic ear and legal advice to HIV-positive men. Wed & Sun 9–11.30pm.

Jhr Mr. J. A. Schorerstichting, P.C. Hooftstraat 5; ☎662 42 06. Gay and lesbian counselling centre offering professional and politically conscious help and advice on identity, sexuality and lifestyle. Mon 6–7pm, Thurs 9–10am.

Mandate, Prinsengracht /15; ☎623 49 36. Sports school for gays, teaching self-defence along with oriental fighting techniques.

NVSH, Blauwburgwal 7–9; ☎623 93 59 or 622 66 90. The Amsterdam branch of the *Netherlands Society for Sexual Reform*, with booklets on safe sex and supplies of *Gay Safe*, a condom specially designed for anal sex. Mon–Fri 11am–6pm, Sat 11am–4pm.

Polikliniek voor Geslachtsziekten en Aids, 1e Helmerstraat 17; ☎685 33 31. Gay-run clinic specializing in counselling for those suffering from sexually transmitted diseases, including AIDS. Thurs 10am–noon, Fri & Sat 7–9pm, Sun 2–3pm.

STD Clinic, Groenburgwal 44; ☎622 37 77. Major state-run clinic offering free medical examinations and a testing service for sexually transmitted diseases. Not specifically gay. Daily 9am–5pm.

Bookshops

Bronx, Kerkstraat 55; ☎623 15 48. Books, magazines, videos. Strictly a porno place.

Intermale, Spuistraat 249–251; ☎625 00 09. Amsterdam's largest serious gay bookshop, with a good stock of English-language books, as well as cards, newspapers and magazines.

Vrolijk, Paleisstraat 135; ☎623 51 42. Gay and lesbian bookshop in new premises near Dam Square. English-language books, magazines and posters.

Other shops

Expectations, Warmoesstraat 32; ☎624 55 73. Rubber, leather and latex wear – made on the premises.

Manstore, Hobbemastraat 1–11; ☎671 07 34. Designer underwear, swimwear and nighclothes.

RoB gallery, Weteringschans 253; ☎625 46 86. Top quality made-to-measure leatherwear.

Ronin and Rik, Runstraat 30; ☎627 89 24. Leather clothes and belts.

Services

Thermos Day Sauna, Raamstraat 33; ☎623 91 58. Sauna, steam room, whirlpool, cinema and coffee bar. Mon–Fri noon–11pm, Sat noon–6pm. Admission f21.

Thermos Night Sauna, Kerkstraat 58–60; ☎623 49 36. Saunas, whirlpool, video room and cabins. If nothing else, a cheap place to spend the night. Daily 11pm–7am. Admission f22.50.

Toff's Tours, Ruysdaelkade 167; ☎664 94 79. Informal tours of the gay scene in Amsterdam – or anywhere else that takes your fancy. Useful for first-time visitors with plenty of cash.

Women's Amsterdam

Just over a century ago the only women out at night in Amsterdam were prostitutes, and a respectable woman's place was firmly in the home. Today the city has an impressive **feminist infrastructure**: support groups, health centres and businesses run by and for women, and there's a good range of bars and discos, a few exclusively for women.

Unless you're here for an extended stay, however, much of this can remain invisible. Both the Dutch lesbian scene and Amsterdam feminist circles are generally indifferent to travellers; most of the contacts you'll make will be with other visitors to the city. Outside the capital you'll frequently be reminded of just how parochial The Netherlands is: attitudes and behaviour acceptable in Amsterdam will be frowned on elsewhere, especially in the Catholic south.

Amsterdam, though, maintains equality of the sexes in high profile; the atmosphere is refreshing. The city streets are relatively safe for women travellers, although the brashness of its main **Red Light district** around Oude Zijds Achterburgwal can be initially intimidating. Walking with a friend is a good idea here, if only to ward off unwelcome leers. When it comes to exploring by yourself, remember to project a confident attitude – if you feel that the night is yours as well as his, problems shouldn't arise. However, the smaller backstreet red-light areas, such as those around the northern end of Spuistraat, are best avoided.

What follows are information/health/services listings; for **women's bars**, see p.133.

Health, support and crisis centres

AIDS Infoline ☎06/022 22 20. Mon–Fri 2–10pm.

Aletta Jacobshuis, Overtoom 323; ☎616 62 22. Named after the country's first female doctor, the Jacobshuis offers sympathetic information and help on sexual problems and birth control. It's possible to get prescriptions for contraceptive pills here, as well as morning-after pills and condoms. Mon–Thurs 9am–noon & 7.15–9pm.

Drugs Vrouwen Crisis Centrum, Stadhouderskade 125; ☎675 07 41. Drug crisis centre for addicted women.

De Maan, Roemer Visscherstraat 8; ☎616 38 91. Women's therapy centre with competent, concerned staff.

Meidentelefoon ☎623 14 01. Hotline for all matters of interest to women. Mon–Fri 6–9pm.

MR '70, Sarphatistraat 620–626; ☎624 54 26. Independent abortion clinic.

De Rode Draad, Kloveniersburgwal 47; ☎624 33 66. Prostitutes' support group. Mon & Thurs 1–4.30pm.

Rechtenvrouw, Singel 373; ☎624 94 33. A group of lawyers who provide feminist legal advice.

Rechtshulp voor Vrouwen, Wilemsstraat 24; ☎624 03 23. Legal help for women, especially in cases involving women's rights.

Tegen Haar Wil ☎612 75 76. Hotline for victims of rape and sexual harassment. Daily 10.30am–11.30pm.

Vrouwengezondheidscentrum, Obiplein 4; ☎693 43 58. Women's health project, offering self-help groups for eating disorders, pregnancy and menopausal problems, along with a referral service to help find non-sexist, non-homophobic doctors, therapists and clinics. Tues 9am–noon, Thurs 7–10pm, Fri 1–4pm.

Vrouwen Opvanghuis voor Vrouwen ☎626 80 80. Battered women's shelter.

Vrouwen bellen Vrouwen ☎625 01 50. Women's support and information hotline. Tues & Thurs 9am–noon & 8–11pm.

Vrouwen Tegen Verkrachting, Herengracht 65; ☎624 76 44. Rape helpline. Mon 7.30–10.30pm, Thurs & Fri 2–4pm.

Centres and groups

Avalon, Roerstraat 79; ☎664 65 30. Feminist spirituality centre offering a wide range of workshops and weekend courses.

For **babysitting services** see *Kids' Amsterdam*; for names of recommended **nurseries and daycare centres**, phone ☎085/33 66 41.

Gay Jewish Group (*Sjalhomo*), Postbus 2536, 1000 CM Amsterdam; ☎673 06 29. Monthly discussion groups for gay and lesbian Jews. If no answer, phone the Lesbian and Gay Switchboard.

De Hippe Heks, Confuciusplein 10; ☎611 22 68. Women's meeting place.

Kenau, Overtoom 270; ☎616 29 13. Self-defence centre with summer weekend courses on oriental defence techniques for women.

Vrouwen in de Beeldende Kunst, Entrepot Dok 66; ☎626 65 89. A foundation for women artists.

Vrouwenhuis, Nieuwe Herengracht 95; ☎625 20 66. Organizing centre for women's activities and cultural events. Bar, self-defence classes, chess club and other activities. Worth dropping in to check out what's happening. Mon–Thurs 7–11pm.

Bookshops and galleries

Amazone, Singel 72; ☎627 90 00. Women's art gallery and exhibition centre for cultural and social topics affecting women. Tues–Fri 10am–4pm, Sat 1–4pm.

Lorelei, Prinsengracht 495; ☎623 43 08. Secondhand booksellers with a lesbian-feminist stock and clientele. Tues–Fri noon–6pm, Sat noon–5pm.

Villa Baranka, Prins Hendrikkade 140; ☎627 64 80. Cross-cultural art studio with performance art, literature and poetry readings by and for women. See *Nightlife* and *Uitkrant* for more details.

Vrolijk, Paleisstraat 135; ☎623 51 42. Bookshop with an international range of lesbian magazines and secondhand books. Mon–Fri 10am–6pm, Thurs until 9pm, Sat 11am–5pm.

Vrouwenindruk, Westermarkt 5; ☎624 50 03. Feminist secondhand bookshop.

Xantippe, Prinsengracht 290; ☎623 58 54. Amsterdam's foremost women's bookshop with a wide selection of feminist titles in English.

Archives

International Information Centre and Archives for the Women's Movement (IAV), Keizersgracht 10; ☎624 42 68. Up-to-date clippings service from important international feminist magazines, and a major archive for the women's movement

containing an elaborate historical collection from international soureces. Also has a referral service for women's studies. Mon–Fri 10am–4pm, Tues until 8.45pm.

Feminist businesses

Freewheel, Akoleienstraat 7; ☎627 72 52. Bike repairs and sales.

Knalpot, Postbus 3910; ☎665 32 18. Garage where women teach you how to fix your car. Mon & Tues only.

Vrouwenfietsenmakkerij, 2e Ceramstraat 23–25; ☎665 32 18. Bicycle repair shop run by the same women. Mon, Wed & Fri 9am–5.30pm, Thurs noon–5.30pm, Sat 9am–5pm.

Zijwind, Ferdinand Bolstraat 168; ☎673 70 26. Bicycle repair shop run by women; they also rent bikes. Tues–Fri 9am–6pm, Sat 9am–5pm.

Lesbian Amsterdam

The city's native **lesbian scene** is smaller and more subdued than the gay one. Many of Amsterdam's politically active lesbians move within tight circles, and it takes time to find out what's happening. Good places to begin are the *Saarein*, the oldest and best established of Amsterdam's *vrouwencafés*, or any of the women's bars listed in *Bars and Coffee Shops*.

Help and information

COC, Rozenstraat 14; ☎623 40 79. Help, advice, non-commercial social activities, coffee shop and noticeboard for men and women, and a gay and lesbian disco. Open noon to midnight. COC also broadcasts lesbian information (occasionally in English) at 102.4 FM.

Gay and Lesbian Switchboard ☎623 65 65. English-speaking information service on health, communtly services and the gay and lesbian scene. Daily 10am–10pm.

Lesbian Radio. For the frequencies of Amsterdam's gay and lesbian radio station, see "Gay Amsterdam" above.

Lesbian Archives, 1e Helmerstraat 17; ☎618 58 79. Mainly Dutch reference centre for contemporary lesbian culture and history. Tues & Fri 2–4.30pm.

Jhr Mr. J. A. Schorerstichting, PC Hooftstraat 5; ☎662 42 06. Lesbian and gay counselling centre.

Long-term Stays: Finding Work And Accommodation

Many people come to Amsterdam for a visit and decide to stay. This isn't necessarily advised, and in any case only EC citizens are eligible to work in The Netherlands. However, if you are keen to stay in the city for a prolonged period of time, the following should provide you with a few basic pointers to how to go about it.

Finding work

EC nationals do not need a work permit in order to work legally in The Netherlands, although if you want to stay on after the official three-month period you have to have a job. If you are planning on staying, try to get your passport stamped on entry – just ask firmly at passport control. This is useful because the only proof of long-standing residence the police will accept is a stamped passport. Within eight days of your decision to stay on in The Netherlands, you should report to the Aliens' Police (address on p.45), and upon proof of employment – a *werkgeversverklaring*, a written statement from your employer – you'll be granted a residence permit – a *verblijfsvergunning* – for the duration of your job, with a maximum term of one year.

Non-EC nationals, on the other hand, need an official work permit – a *werkvergunning* – which must be applied for in advance. You're only granted one of these (and the resulting

preliminary residence permit) once you have a job (with the exception of some highly specialized and trained labourers), which means basically that you have to have a job *before* you arrive. One exception to this rule are US citizens, who have the same rights as EC nationals, although even they should check the current regulations with their nearest Dutch consulate before leaving home. Once in The Netherlands, all EC nationals should report to the Aliens' Police in order to convert their preliminary residence permit into a full one.

Whether you're an EC national or not, obtaining a residence permit means tangling with Dutch **bureaucracy**, which can be extremely labyrinthine; be prepared before beginning, or you'll end up in a terrible mess. Above all, make sure you bring all possible documentation – birth or marriage certificates, letters of employment, contracts, etc – with you, and put on business-like clothes when attending any official interviews. For help and advice, the **Information Centre** and **Municipal Service Center**, in the Stadhuis on Waterlooplein (Mon–Fri 9am–5pm, Thurs until 7pm; ☎624 11 11), provides information on all municipal policies and answers general questions about Amsterdam. You can also pick up various helpful brochures and leaflets, including the extremely useful "Amsterdam Information", which has details on the job market, social security, housing, health care, education and the like. If still in doubt, the **Sociaal Raadslieden** (Citizens' Advisors), at the Municipal Service Centre (Mon–Fri except Wed 9am–noon), offer free personal – and confidential – advice on a wide range of questions. If you can't or don't want to go into the office they can also be contacted by writing to PO Box 202, 1000 AE Amsterdam.

Actually **finding a job** isn't easy, though lately the (previously terrible) employment situation seems to have stabilized. **Temp agencies** (*uitzendburos*) provide the main source of casual, quasi-legal work, particularly during the summer.

If you're prepared to tramp around to such offices twice a day and are willing to take any job, you'll normally find something, especially if you're under 23 (employers have to pay substantially more to older individuals). The sort of jobs you'll find in this way vary enormously, but in the summer there's some demand in the hotel and catering industry – though you may have better results applying directly to tourist establishments. It's often possible for people with typing/secretarial skills to pick up temporary jobs as English-speaking typists, particularly in the holiday season. Summer jobs in the glass-houses and bulbfields can also occasionally be found; the best way of doing so is to head down to Aalsmeer and the bulb areas around Haarlem, although, as with all these kind of jobs, bear in mind that they will be low-paid and exploitative. You could also try scanning the newspapers, though this normally isn't much use save for irregular adverts from *uitzendburos* and cleaning agencies. For a more stable – and wholly legal – job you'd do better to head straight for the *arbeidsburo* (labour exchange) at Singel 202 (Mon–Thurs 8.15am–4pm, Fri 8.15am–nooon), which has a complete file of registered job openings and has been known to find work for non-Dutch speakers, mainly as skilled manual workers – although this seems to have dried up considerably.

Finding rented accommodation

Reasonably priced **rented accommodation** in Amsterdam is in short supply, and flat-hunting requires a determined effort. With the exception of tiny apartments, and places in Amsterdam Zuid-Oost, most of the housing with a monthly rent of under f525 is controlled by the **council**, and can only be rented with a *woonruimteverklaring*, a housing permit, in most cases in combination with an *urgentiebewijs*, a certificate of urgency. These documents are issued by the **Gemeentelijke Dienst Herhuisvesting**, the municipal department for the reallocation of housing (Mon–Thurs 8.30am–3pm, Fri 8.30am–noon; ☎680 68 06), where you'll find all kinds of information on housing in Amsterdam, including the addresses of non-commercial letting agencies. However, you will only be issued a housing permit or *urgentiebewijs* if you have been registered as living in Amsterdam for two years. Anyone planning to stay a while should therefore register at the **Bevolkingsregister**,

Amstel 1 (the Stadhuis; Mon–Fri 8.30am–3.30pm, Thurs also 5–7pm; ☎551 99 11) as quickly as possible after arriving, since it's this date that counts as the official beginning of your stay in Amsterdam. Bear in mind, however, that you should do this only once you've registered with the Aliens' Police, and that you should keep both places informed of any change of address during the two-year period – otherwise things can get confused.

In the meantime, though, you're forced to seek accommodation in other ways, which can prove expensive. One way of cutting costs is to look for a place in **Amsterdam Zuid-Oost**, an unpopular and somewhat notorious concrete extension to the city that is a great deal cheaper than any other neighbourhood – for obvious reasons, once you're there. That said, the apart-ments are spacious and generally in good condi-tion, with rents of f400–500 a month; also, although you're a long way out of the centre, there's a fast metro link. The *Herhuisvesting* can give you details of letting agencies down here, or try the **Nieuw Amsterdam** agency direct (☎567 51 00), which handles accommodation exclusively in Bijlmermeer, a particularly unpopu-lar high-rise corner of Amsterdam Zuid-Oost.

Otherwise, in the **private sector**, there's little chance of finding anything for much under f600 a month. Some of the old warehouse buildings around the central harbour area have been converted into small studios and rooming houses, which are comparatively cheap, if a little tacky; ask in *'t Anker* bar, behind Centraal Station at De Ruyterkade 100 (☎622 95 60), for more information. Otherwise, the **newspapers** *De Telegraaf* and *De Volkskrant* are a must, with large "To Let" (*Te Huur*) sections, particularly on Friday and Saturday – though it's well worth buying them every morning (at the crack of dawn for any sort of chance; look out in bars for roving sellers of the Saturday edition on Friday night). The free weekly papers, notably *De Echo*, should also be closely scrutinized. Apartment-finding **agencies** advertise regularly in the news-papers and are another useful source if you can afford the fee – normally one or two months' rent for finding a place – but beware of agencies that ask for money before they hand out an address, since fly-by-night operators are common. Bear in mind, too, that whether you rent through an agency or not, an *overname* – key-money paid to the previous tenant to cover fixtures and fittings – is often charged. This varies tremendously and can be exorbitant, but it's usually unavoidable and can only be recovered by charging it to the next tenant when you move out. Landlords also sometimes ask for a *borgsom* – a refundable security deposit.

When all's said and done, though, a lot of housing is found by **word of mouth**. A remarkable grapevine springs up in the summer among the travelling community; people are constantly coming and going, looking for apartment-sharers or temporary house-sitters. Just let everyone you meet know you're homeless. It's also worth keeping an eye on **noticeboards** everywhere: the main public library at Prinsengracht 587 has a good one, as do bars and student eating places such as the *mensas* and *Egg Cream* (addresses in *Restaurants*). **Student dorms** have noticeboards which often advertise temporary accommodation in students' rooms – not a bad short-term option since rooms are very cheap. You might also try the boards in **supermarkets** and **tobacconists' windows**, as the Dutch tend to take long summer holidays and often need house-sitters to take care of the cats and plants while they're away.

Squatting

The other way to solve your housing problem is to find a **squat** or *kraak*, though it's important to remember that the foreign squatter faces special problems – principally police harassment and deportation. If the police want you out, your rights as an EC citizen don't count for much, and being deported is an unpleasant and expensive experience. To avoid this it's essential to gain the support, and listen to the advice of, the local squatting group, although they aren't always terribly helpful to foreigners. Since Dutch squatters regard their own activities as community-oriented and politically motivated, they don't always welcome people whom they suspect are looking for a short rent-frree stay in Holland. Become involved with a local group, get to know the people and keep looking for an empty place yourself – don't expect it all to be done for you.

A **short-term** squat of an empty flat in blocks due for demolition within about six months is probably the best solution for the temporary visitor. For a variety of reasons, these are likely to dry up in the future but, for the moment at least, they do exist. You have to be quick and get in

before the wreckers, though, who are sent in by the council to make places uninhabitable. Lately this has become more important than ever, since in response to the city's heroin problem and the resultant colonies of junkies, the council is amazingly efficient about trashing the premises first. You really need to be tipped off or actually see people moving out and get in that evening; local squatters may be able to provide information. Once you're in, chances are there won't be any trouble, but again, your local squatting group or the *Bureau voor Rechtshulp*, a free legal advice centre, will be able to help. Having established a claim on the property, your next problem is lack of furniture, gas and electrical appliances, etc. These are surprisingly easy to pick up – often off the street on rubbish-collection night – and a place can be made habitable in a couple of weeks with next to no cash outlay.

Long-term squats are much more complicated: they have to be observed for some time and thoroughly investigated before being attempted; the help of a squatters' group is imperative. The main aim of this type of squatting is to get a licence from the local council, and the best chance of success is in a place that is already in an unrentable condition.

The big **community squats** are much more than just a way of alleviating the housing problem. They are overtly political in nature and present a challenge to the establishment by opposing the activities of property developers in a very practical way. Most of the larger premises used for squatting were abandoned factories, hotels or warehouses – destined to be demolished and replaced by luxury apartments or office complexes, or simply left until land prices rose, enabling resale at a profit. Large groups of squatters moved in and set about creating a complete environment from nothing, building living spaces, workshops, studios and often even shops, cheap cafés, day care centres, etc. These communities house many people and try to provide services which are lacking in inner-city areas. Though it seems as if their popularity is waning, and that the days of the big community squats are over, many still exist. Living in one entails quite a commitment – you have to be prepared to participate fully in the community and spend a lot of time and energy on the squat – so they shouldn't be seen as a solution to the short-term housing problem of someone just passing through.

Useful addresses

Aliens' Police (Vreemdelingendienst)
Bijmerdreef 90; ☎ 691 91 00. Open Mon–Fri
8.30am–noon – you can make an appointment.

Arbeidsburo
Singel 202; ☎ 520 09 11. Mon–Thurs 8.15am–
4pm, Fri 8.15am–noon.

Bevolkingsregister
Amstel 1 (the Stadhuis, Waterlooplein); ☎ 551
99 11. Mon–Fri 8.30am–3.30pm, also Thurs 5–
7pm.

Bureau voor Rechtshulp
Spuistraat 10; ☎ 626 44 77. Free legal advice
centre.

Gemeentelijke Dienst Herhuisvesting
Weesperplein 4; ☎ 680 68 06. Mon–Thurs
8.30am–3pm, Fri 8.30am–noon..

Information Centre
Stadhuis, Waterlooplein; ☎ 624 11 11. Mon–Fri
9am–5pm, Thurs until 7pm.

Job Centre
Singel 202–208; ☎ 520 08 88. Mon–Fri 8.30am–
5pm.

Nieuw Amsterdam
Letting office for Bijlmermeer; ☎ 567 51 00.
Mon–Fri 8.30am–noon & 1.30–5pm..

Openbare Bibliotheek
Prinsengracht 587; ☎ 523 09 00.

Sociaal Raadslieden
Municipal Service Centre, Stadhuis. Mon–Fri
9am–noon, closed Wed.

Student Housing Office
Weesoerstraat 51; ☎ 683 58 19. Individual
student halls are listed under "Studentenhuis"
in the telephone directory.

Uitzendburo Randstad
Head Office: Amstelveenseweg 182; ☎ 676 66 61.
Also Muntplein 2 (☎ 523 91 00) and Leidseplein
1–3 (☎ 551 05 51).

Volksuniversiteit
Herenmarkt 93; ☎ 626 16 26. They run cheap
and basic courses in Dutch – good for getting a
toehold on the language early on.

Directory

BABIES When booking rooms, remember that some hotels don't accommodate babies, or will only do so during the low season, so be sure to first verify the situation with the hotel. For baby-sitting services and recommended nurseries, see *Kids' Amsterdam*.

BRING . . . Toiletries, film and English-language books, all of which are expensive in Amsterdam.

CHURCHES Services in English at the *English Reformed Church*, Begijnhof 48 (☎624 96 65), Sun at 10.30am; the *Anglican Church*, Groenburgwal 42 (☎624 88 77), Sun at 10.30am and 7.30pm; English Catholic Mass at the church of *St John and Ursula*, Begijnhof (☎622 19 18), Sun at 12.15pm. For details of other religious services, consult the VVV.

CONTRACEPTIVES Condoms are available from *drogists* or the *Condomerie* (see *Shops and Markets*), but to get the pill you need a doctor's prescription – see "Health and Insurance".

DIAMONDS The industry was founded here in the late sixteenth century by refugee diamond workers from Antwerp, but since World War II it has depended on tourists for a livelihood. Currently around twenty diamond firms operate in Amsterdam. All are working factories, but many open their doors to the public for viewing the cutting, polishing and sorting practices, and (most importantly) for buying. City tours often include diamond factories (see p.23), but a few

can be visited individually. Among them are *Coster*, Paulus Potterstraat 2–6 (☎676 22 22), *Van Moppes*, Albert Cuypstraat 2–6 (☎676 12 42), and the *Amsterdam Diamond Centre*, Rokin 1 (☎624 57 87). Admission is free.

DISABLED VISITORS Though Amsterdam's public transportation system has no facilities for disabled passengers, most of the city's major museums, concert halls, theatres, churches and public buildings are accessible to visitors in wheelchairs. *Netherlands Railways* offer a comprehensive service for disabled travellers, including a timetable in Braille, free escort service and assistance at all stations. Get more details by calling ☎030/33 12 53 (Mon–Fri 8.30am–4pm), or from The Netherlands Board of Tourism leaflet, *Holland for the Handicapped*, which also describes hotel and camping facilities throughout the country. There is also a desk in the Schiphol Arrivals Hall, North section (daily 6am–11pm), to help disabled people through the airport. Last but not least, paper currency has dots in the corner to indicate its value to the visually impaired.

DOG SHIT Step carefully when walking the streets as Amsterdam's dog-owners have yet to train their animals to use the gutters – something the council seems unwilling (or unable) to do anything about.

ELECTRIC CURRENT 220v AC – effectively the same as British; American apparatus requires a transformer; both will need new plugs or an adaptor.

ISIC CARDS Student ID won't help gain reduced admission to anything in the city – for this you need a museumcard or CJP (see *Museums*).

LAUNDERETTES *The Clean Brothers* is the best, at Jakob Van Lennepkade 179, Kerkstraat 56 and Rozengracht 59 (daily until 9pm). Other launderettes are at: Warmoesstraat 30, Oude Doelenstraat 12, Haarlemmerdijk 102 and Herenstraat 24. Otherwise look under *Wassalons* in the Yellow Pages.

LIBRARIES No one will stop you from using any of the public libraries or *Openbare Bibliotheken* for reference purposes, but to borrow books you'll need to show proof of residence and pay around f25 for a card. The main branch at Prinsengracht 587 (Mon 1–9pm, Tues–Thurs 10am–9pm, Fri & Sat 10am–5pm) has English newspapers and magazines, photocopiers and a cheap snack bar.

LOST PROPERTY For items lost on the trams, buses or metro, contact *GVB* Head Office, Prins Hendrikkade 108–114 (☎551 49 11). For property lost on a train go to the *Gevonden Voorwerpen* office at the nearest station. Amsterdam's is at the Centraal Station (☎557 85 44); after ten days, all unclaimed property goes to 2e Daalsedijk 4, Utrecht (☎030/35 39 23). If you lose something in the street or a park, try the police lost property at Waterlooplein 11 (walk-in visitors Mon–Fri 11am–3.30pm; phone enquiries noon–4pm; ☎559 80 05).

MOSQUITOES These thrive in Holland's watery environment, and bite their worst at the campsites. An antihistamine cream such as *Phenergan* is a good antidote, available all over Amsterdam, as is the popular Autan stick, which can keep mosquitoes away for eight hours at a time.

NOTICEBOARDS Most "brown cafés" have noticeboards with details of concerts, events and the like, occasionally displaying personal notices too. Both *Egg Cream* (see p.139) and the main library (see above) have noticeboards useful for apartment- and job-hunting, sharing lifts, etc. Try also the supermarkets, most of which have noticeboards.

PHOTO BOOTHS Scattered around town, but most reliably on the first floor of *Vroom & Dreesmann* on Kalverstraat, or at Centraal Station. You'll pay around f5 for four pictures.

TAMPONS On sale at all *drogists* (chemists) and supermarkets. There are rarely machines in women's loos in bars, restaurants, etc.

TELEPHONE HELPLINES AND SERVICES In English: *Legal Hotline* (☎548 26 11); *Mental and Social problems* (☎555 52 09); *Tram, Bus and Metro Information* (☎06/92 92); *Wake-up Service* (☎06/96 55). In Dutch: *Road Conditions* (☎06/910 910 910); *Time* (☎06/80 02); *Weather* (☎06/ 80 03); *House Party info line* (☎06/350 320 15).

TIME One hour ahead of Britain, six hours ahead of Eastern Standard Time.

TIPPING Don't bother, since restaurants, hotels, taxis, etc, must include a fifteen percent service charge by law. Only if you're somewhere really upmarket is it considered proper to round up the bill to the nearest five guilders.

WINDMILLS The most central windmill in Amsterdam is *De Gooyer* in the Eastern Islands district. But the best place to see windmills is Kinderdijk near Rotterdam; they're also very much part of the landscape in the polderlands north of Amsterdam. Some have been moved and reassembled in the open-air museums at Zaanse Schans, near Zaandam, and just outside Arnhem.

The City

Chapter 1

Introducing the city

Amsterdam is an easy city to find your way around. Centraal Station, where you're likely to arrive, lies on the northern edge of the city centre, on the banks of the river IJ: on the far side lies Amsterdam North, an area almost entirely outside your range of interest unless you're camping; in the other direction, the city fans south in a cobweb of canals surrounded by expanding suburbs.

The city is small enough not to have any really distinct neighbourhoods: it's easier just to distinguish between the central core and its artery, Damrak, and the main canals that encircle it. The neighbourhoods outside this broad half-circle are residential for the most part, although they do hold a number of attractions, not least the city's major

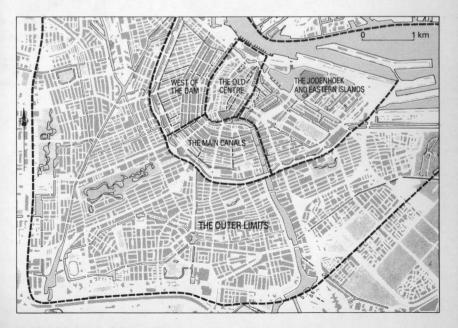

52   THE CITY: CHAPTER 1

AMSTERDAM CITY CENTRE

Het Ij

Dijksgracht

Oosterdok

thuis

ontelbaanstoren

PRINS HENDRIKKADE

KATTENBURGERSTRAAT

Maritime Museum

KATTENBURGERGRACHT

Nieuwe

WITTENBURGERGRACHT

Vaart

OOSTENBURGERGRACHT

gracht

Kerk

Herengracht

MUIDERSTRAAT

HOOGTEKADIJK

ENTREPOTDOK

Kromhout Museum

PLANTAGE DOKLAAN

Artis Zoo

PLANTAGE MIDDENLAAN

eizersgracht

NIEUWE KERK STRAAT

PLANTAGE MUIDERGRACHT

Prinsengracht

Singelgracht

Muiderpoort

WEESPERPLEIN

Nieuwe

Achtgracht

SARPHATISTRAAT

Tropenmuseum

MAURITSKADE

Oosterpark

WIBAUTSTRAAT

0   500 m

museums and its largest central open space, the Vondelpark, and as such are often near the top of most people's travel agendas.

We've divided Amsterdam into the headings which follow for convenience; because of the nature of the city they don't always refer to uniform areas and are certainly not itineraries to be followed slavishly. Amsterdam is a city of low-key attractions and charms, and wandering its streets and canals is as good a way as any to explore it.

The centre of the city – along with the main canals, the area in which you'll spend most of your time – is the old **medieval core**, which fans south from Centraal Station, taking in the main artery of Damrak, Dam Square and Rokin. This area is Amsterdam's commercial heart, and boasts the best of its bustling street life: it is home to shops, many bars and restaurants and, not least, the infamous **Red Light district**. The area is bordered by the Singel, first of the **big canals**, on the far side of which curl Herengracht, Keizersgracht and Prinsengracht. These canals are part of a major seventeenth-century urban extension and, with the radial streets of Leidsestraat, Vijzelstraat and Utrechtsestraat, create Amsterdam's distinctive cobweb shape. This is the Amsterdam you see in the brochures: still, dreamy canals, crisp reflections of seventeenth-century townhouses, railings with chained bicycles – an image which even today is not far from authentic.

Further out, the **Jordaan** grew up as a slum and immigrant quarter and remains the traditional heart of working-class Amsterdam, though these days there is a yuppie edge to the area. On the other side of town, the **Jodenhoek** was, as its name suggests, once home to the city's Jewish community. Since the construction of the Muziektheater and metro here it's probably Amsterdam's most visibly changed district since World War II.

Across the Singelgracht, which marks the outer limit of today's centre, lie the largely residential districts of **Amsterdam South**, **West** and **East**, in themselves not of great interest, though with attractions (principally the main museums) that could tempt you out that way. Amsterdam **North**, on the other hand, remains a quite distinct, though nondescript, entity, which most people visit for its campsite – though it is good cycling country. The VVV has details of routes, best of which are those along the Buiten IJ.

Chapter 2

The Old Centre

A msterdam's **central core** pokes south into the elegant girdle of the major canals, the city's busiest and most vigorous district by far, lacking the gracious uniformity of much of the rest of the city centre, but making up for it in excitement. Given the dominance of Centraal Station on most transport routes, the old centre is where you'll almost certainly arrive. It's a small but varied area, ranging from the vigour of Stationsplein, the city's major traffic junction and home of the VVV tourist office, to the strategic tourist trap of Damrak and the studied sleaze of the Red Light District, not surprisingly one of Amsterdam's biggest attractions, though also home to a couple of its most beautiful canals.

Historically, the old centre divides into a new and an old side. The "New Side" was the western half of the medieval city, bordered by Nieuwe Zijds Voorburgwal ("New Side Town Wall") and Damrak. On the other side of Damrak, the "Old Side" is the oldest part of Amsterdam, much of it dating back to the fifteenth century and focusing on the city's oldest street, Warmoesstraat, which connected the Dam with the river. It was bordered by two canals. One of these, Oude Zijds Voorburgwal, ran in front ("voor") of the city wall; the other, Oude Zijds Achterburgwal, ran behind ("achter").

Stationsplein and around

The neo-Renaissance **Centraal Station** is an imposing prelude to the city. When built on an artificial island late in the last century, this was a controversial structure, as it obscured the views of the port that brought Amsterdam its wealth. Since then, however, shipping has moved out to more spacious dock areas to the west and east, and the station, embellished with all manner of Victorian ornament by its architect P.J.H. Cuypers (also designer of the not dissimilar Rijksmuseum) is now one of Amsterdam's most resonant landmarks, and a natural focal point for urban life. Stand here and all of Amsterdam, with its faintly oriental skyline of spires and cupolas, lies before you.

AMSTERDAM

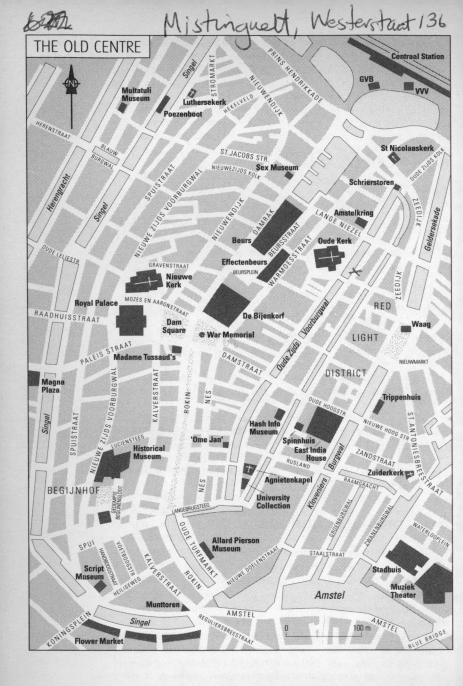

Mistinguett, Westerstraat 136

THE OLD CENTRE

Multatuli Museum

Luthersekerk

Poezenboot

St.JACOBS STR.

NIEUWEZIJDS KOLK

Sex Museum

St Nicolaaskerk

Schrierstoren

Amstelkring

Beurs

Effectenbeurs

BEURSPLEIN

Oude Kerk

Nieuwe Kerk

GRAVENSTRAAT

Royal Palace

MOZES EN AARONSTRAAT

Dam Square

War Memorial

De Bijenkorf

RAADHUISSTRAAT

Waag

RED

LIGHT

NIEUWMARKT

DISTRICT

PALEIS STRAAT

Madame Tussaud's

Magna Plaza

Trippenhuis

OUDE HOOGSTR

Hash Info Museum

'Ome Jan'

Spinnhuis

East India House

RUSLAND

ZANDSTRAAT

Zuiderkerk

Historical Museum

BEGIJNHOF

Agnietenkapel

University Collection

RAAMGRACHT

LANGEBRUGSTEEG

Allard Pierson Museum

STAALSTRAAT

WATERLOOPLEIN

Script Museum

NIEUWE DOELENSTRAAT

Stadhuis

Muziek Theater

Munttoren

Amstel

KONINGSPLEIN

Singel

AMSTEL

REGULIERSBREESTRAAT

0   100 m

AMSTEL

BLUE BRIDGE

Flower Market

Centraal Station

GVB

VVV

PRINS HENDRIKKADE

Beaurs

Blauw aan de Wal 020 3

Stationsplein, immediately outside, is a messy open s
mented by ovals of water and dotted with barrel organs, c
and "M" signs indicating the city's spanking new but rapi
metro. Come summer, there's no livelier part of the city,
performers compete for attention with the careening tr
converge dangerously from all sides. It's without a doubt a p
place to arrive, and with that in mind the municipal author
cleaning up the area's image, notably in the southeastern
where there's a spanking new luxury hotel and development
encouraged along the once-notorious Zeedijk.

Close by here, the dome of the **St. Nicolaaskerk** catches the eye.
Despite a dilapidated exterior, it's the city's foremost Catholic church,
having replaced the clandestine Amstelkring (see below) in 1887. Even
if you manage to coordinate your visit with the limited opening hours
(April–Sept Tues–Sat 11am–4pm, Sun 10am–3pm; Oct Sat 11am–4pm,
Sun 10am–3pm), you'll find that there's not much of note inside –
except, on the high altar, the crown of Austro-Hungarian Emperor
Maximilian, very much a symbol of the city and one you'll see again and
again (on top of the Westerkerk and on much of the city's official literature). Amsterdam had close ties with Maximilian: in the late fifteenth
century he came here as a pilgrim and stayed on to recover from an
illness. The burghers funded many of his military expeditions; in return
he let the city use his crown in its coat of arms, which gave the upstart
port immediate prestige in the eyes of the rest of the world.

Along Damrak

Above all, though, Stationsplein acts as a filter for Amsterdam's
newcomers, and from here **Damrak**, an unenticing avenue lined by
tacky restaurants, bureaux de change, and the bobbing canal boats of
Amsterdam's considerable tourist industry, storms south into the heart
of the city. Just past the boats is the Stock Exchange, or **Beurs** –
known as the "Beurs van Berlage" – designed at the turn of the century
by the leading light of the Dutch modern movement, H. P. Berlage,
and, with its various styles from Romanesque to Neo-Renaissance
interwoven with a minimum of ornamentation, is something of a semi-
nal work. These days it's no longer used as an exchange, and, not
surprisingly, often hosts visiting theatre groups and exhibitions. If you
get the chance, look into the main hall, where exposed ironwork and
shallow-arched arcades combine to give a real sense of space. The
much duller **Effectenbeurs**, flanking the eastern side of Beursplein, is
the home of such trading as remains these days (Mon–Fri 10.30am–
4.30pm) – phone for an appointment (☎523 4567) to view the
proceedings from the visitors' gallery.

On the other side of the street at Damrak 18, the **Sex Museum**
(daily 10am–11pm; ƒ3.95), is frankly more of a commercial enterprise
than a museum, although it does display – should such things be of
interest – erotic pictures, statues, cartoons and examples of early

rnographic films. Further up on the same side, one of Amsterdam's best bookshops, **Allert de Lange**, is the contemporary outlet of a pioneering Jewish publisher, who in the 1930s made available much of the work of refugee authors from Nazi Germany, such as Bertholt Brecht and Max Brod. Crossing over the street again, the **De Bijenkorf** (literally "beehive") department store building, facing the Beurs and extending as far as Dam Square, was another successful Jewish concern – so much so that during the occupation the authorities, fearing altercations with the Jewish staff, forbade German soldiers to shop on the ground floor. Today *De Bijenkorf* is a nationwide chain.

more on shopping, see Shops and Markets.

The Red Light District

Left off Damrak before the Beurs is the **Red Light District**, known locally as the "Walletjes", bordered by the oldest street in the city, Warmoesstraat, and stretching across the two canals which marked the edge of medieval Amsterdam, **Oude Zijds Voorburgwal** and **Oude Zijds Achterburgwal**. The prostitution here is sadly, but perhaps inevitably, one of the real sights of the city, and one of its most distinctive draws, and the two main canals and narrow connecting passages are on most evenings of the year thronged with people here to discover just how shocking it all is. The atmosphere is a festive one, with entertainment for all, as entire families titter and blush at the invitations to various kinds of illicit thrills. Men line the streets hawking the peep shows and "live sex" within, while the women sit bored behind glass, in shop windows that take their place among more conventional businesses on the same street. There's a nasty edge to the district too, oddly enough sharper during the daytime, when the pimps hang out in shifty gangs and drug addicts wait anxiously, assessing the chances of scoring their next hit.

Warmoesstraat

Soliciting hasn't always gone on here, and the rich facades of Oude Zijds Voorburgwal – known in the sixteenth century as the "Velvet Canal", because it was home to so many wealthy people – point to a more venerable past. As the city prospered, and the then-nearby docks grew busier, the area grew sleazier as more and more prostitutes were required to service the growing population of itinerant seamen. Today narrow **Warmoesstraat** is seedy and uninviting, but it was once one of the city's most fashionable streets, and home of Holland's foremost poet, **Joost van der Vondel**, who ran his seventeenth-century hosiery business from number 110 in between writing and hobnobbing with the Amsterdam elite. Vondel is a kind of Dutch Shakespeare: his *Gijsbrecht van Amstel*, a celebration of Amsterdam during its Golden Age, is one of the classics of Dutch literature, and he wrote regular, if ponderous, official verses, including well over a thousand lines on the inauguration of the new town hall. His house no longer stands, but a little way down on the right, by the wall of the city's stock exchange, a statue of the poet marks its site. After his son had frittered away the modest family fortune, Vondel lived out his last few years as doorkeeper of the pawn shop on Oude Zijds Voorburgwal (see below), dying at the age of 92 of hypothermia brought on by his advanced years. Unassuming to the end, his own suggested epitaph ran:

> *Here lies Vondel, still and old*
> *Who died – because he was cold.*

Also on Warmoesstraat, at number 67, the **Geels & Co. Museum** (Fri & Sat noon–5pm; free) displays mills, machinery and assorted paraphernalia related to the consumption of coffee and tea above its venerable old shop.

The Oude Kerk

Just off Warmoesstraat, the precincts of the **Oude Kerk** (April–Oct Mon–Sat 11am–5pm, Sun 1.30–5pm; Nov–March Mon–Sat 1–3pm, Sun 1–3pm; ƒ3; tower June–Sept Wed–Sat 2–5pm; ƒ3.50) offer a reverential peace after the excesses of the Red Light district – though even here some of the houses have the familiar *Kamer te huur* ("Room to Let") sign and window seat. There's been a church on this site since the late-thirteenth century, even before the Dam was built, but most of the present building dates from the fourteenth century. In the Middle Ages, many pilgrims flocked to Amsterdam – and specifically to this church – thanks to a mid-fourteenth-century miracle in which a dying man regurgitated the Host he had received at Communion, which was thrown on a fire yet did not burn. It was placed in a chest (now in the Amsterdam Historical Museum), and a chapel was erected somewhere between Nieuwe Zijds Voorburgwal and Kalverstraat, close to where the miracle happened. When this burnt down and the Host still didn't burn, a plaque was put up in the Oude Kerk to commemorate the event. In the manner of such tales, the Host began to turn up in different spots all over town, attracting pilgrims in droves. The faithful still come to take part in the annual commemorative *Stille Omgang*, a silent nocturnal procession terminating at the Oude Kerk on the Sunday closest to March 15 that is normally joined by some ten thousand people.

Having been stripped bare during the Reformation and recently very thoroughly restored, the Oude Kerk is nowadays a survivor rather than any sort of architectural masterpiece. Its handful of interesting features include – apart from a few faded vault paintings – some beautifully carved misericords in the choir, the tomb of one of seventeenth-century Holland's naval heroes, Admiral J. van Heemskerk, and the memorial tablet of Rembrandt's wife, Saskia van Uylenburg, who is also buried here. Her tomb was apparently sold by the bankrupt Rembrandt to pay for the burial of his second wife.

The Amstelkring

Further down Oude Zijds Voorburgwal, the clandestine **Amstelkring**
(Mon–Sat 10am–5pm, Sun 1–5pm; ƒ4.50) at the Zeedijk end is also of
interest, once the principal Catholic place of worship in the city and
now one of the city's best and least demanding small museums, and a
tranquil and still relatively undiscovered escape from the surrounding
sleaze. Seventeenth-century Holland was, by the standards of its
contemporaries, a remarkably tolerant society: in Amsterdam many
religions were accepted if not exactly encouraged, and most freedoms
could be bought, either with hard cash or a proven popularity.
Catholics, however, had to confine their worship to the privacy of their
own homes – an arrangement which led to the growth of so-called
clandestine Catholic churches throughout the city. Known as "Ons
Lieve Heer Op Solder" – or "Our Dear Lord in the Attic" – this is the
only one left; it occupies the loft of a wealthy merchant's house,
together with those of two smaller houses behind it. The **church** itself
is delightful, three balconied storeys high and reaching from the
massive organ (which must have been heard all over the
neighbourhood) to a mock marble altar decorated with a chubby
Baptism of Christ by Jacob de Wit – one of three painted for the
purpose. In addition, the **house** itself has been left beautifully
untouched, its original furnishings reminiscent of interiors by Vermeer
or de Hooch.

The Hash Info Museum and the Spinhuis

There's little else along this part of Oude Zijds to stop for, although the
Hash Info Museum at Oude Zijds Achterburgwal 148, the next canal
across (daily 11am–10pm; ƒ6), is still going strong between intermit-
tent battles with the police, with displays of various types of dope and
numerous ways to smoke it. Pipes, books, videos and plenty of souvenirs are also on display, though these days there are lots of empty
spaces where the police have removed the exhibits.

While you're on Oude Zijds Achterburgwal, stop off at the
Spinhuis, at no.28. This used to be a house of correction for "fallen
women", who would work at looms and spinning wheels to atone for
their wayward ways – ironic given its position in the centre of the Red

The Cul De Sac
*bar, down an
alleyway at
Achterburgwal 99,
is a good place for
a drink.*

Light District now. Oddly enough, places like this used to figure on
tourist itineraries: for a small fee the public were allowed to watch the
women at work, and at carnival times admission was free and large
crowds came to jeer and mock. Shame was supposed to be part of the
reforming process, although it's undoubtedly true that the city fathers
also made a nice return on their unfortunate inmates. You can't go in
now – the building is given over to muncipal offices – but the facade
remains pretty much intact, with an inscription by the seventeenth-
century Dutch poet Pieter Cornelisz Hooft: "Cry not, for I exact no
vengeance for wrong but to force you to be good. My hand is stern but
my heart is kind".

Zeedijk

Just past here, **Zeedijk** itself is much cleaned up now but was a pretty
lurid spot in the mid-Eighties, when you had to run the gauntlet of
Surinamese heroin dealers trying to fast-talk you into a quick sale
while idle groups of policemen looked on. The police claim to have the
area under control now – part of the Eighties city-wide push to polish
up Amsterdam's tarnished reputation as a tourist centre – and
certainly this narrow street is less intimidating than it once was, a
process hastened by the completion of the luxury *Barbizon Plaza
Hotel* nearby. But there's still some way to go: Zeedijk remains dilapidated, and the heroin dealers – albeit much depleted in number – are
creeping back to shoot up in doorways and hustle passers-by for small
change; really, though it's only the area towards Nieuwmarkt that has
any vicious overtones.

East of the Red Light District

Zeedijk opens out on to **Nieuwmarkt** and the top end of
Geldersekade, which together form the hub of Amsterdam's tiny
Chinese quarter, consisting of a handful of oriental supermarkets and
a couple of bookshops. As its name suggests, Nieuwmarkt was once
one of Amsterdam's most important markets, first for fish, later for the
cloth traders from the adjacent Jewish quarter, and nowadays for
antiques on Sunday and a few stalls selling fish, fruit and vegetables
during the week. During the last war it was surrounded by barbed wire
behind which Jews were penned while awaiting deportation.

  The main focus of the square, the turreted **Waag** or old **Sint
Antoniespoort**, has played a variety of roles over the years. Originally
part of the fortifications that encircled Amsterdam before the seventeenth-century expansion, it later became the civic weighing house,
and for a time was used by a number of the city's guilds, including the
Surgeons' – the young Rembrandt's *Anatomy Lesson of Dr. Tulp* was
based on the activities here. After a spell as the Amsterdam Jewish
Museum, the Waag is now waiting for a new role, possibly either as a
home for a piggy-bank museum and children's book centre, or a
museum of advertising.

Kloveniersburgwal

Kloveniersburgwal, which leads south from Nieuwmarkt, was the
outer of the three eastern canals of sixteenth-century Amsterdam.
Although it is not a particularly attractive waterway, it does boast, on
the left, one of the city's most impressive canal houses. Built for the
Trip family in 1662, and large enough to house the Rijksmuseum
collection for most of the nineteenth century, the **Trippenhuis** is a
huge overblown mansion, its Corinthian pilasters and grand frieze
providing a suitable reflection of the owners' importance among the

*The
Engelbewaarder at
Kloveniersburg-
wal 59 is an
attractive brown
café, and has live
jazz on Sundays.*

Amsterdam *Magnificat* – the name given to the clique of families (Six, Trip, Hooft, Pauw) who shared power during the Golden Age. The Trips, incidentally, made their fortune from arms dealing; today their house contains the Dutch Academy of Sciences.

Directly opposite, on the right bank of the canal, there's another, quite different, house which gives an idea of the sort of resentment such ostentatious displays of wealth engendered. Mr Trip's coachman was so taken aback by the size of the new family residence that he exclaimed he would be happy with a home no wider than the Trips' front door. Which is exactly what he got, and 26 Kloveniersburgwal is known as the **House of Mr Trip's Coachman** – not surprisingly, at a yard or so across, it is the narrowest house in town.

Further up the canal, on the corner of Oude Hoogstraat, the redbrick former headquarters of the **Dutch East India Company** is a monumental building, built in 1606 shortly after the founding of the company. It was from here that the Dutch organized and regulated the trading interests in the Far East which made the country so profitable in the seventeenth century. Under the greedy auspices of the East India Company, The Netherlands (especially its most prosperous provinces, Holland and Zeeland) exploited the natural resources of the group of islands now known as Indonesia for several centuries, satisfying the whims of Amsterdam's burghers with shiploads of spices, textiles and exotic woods. For all that, the building itself is of little interest, being occupied these days by offices and the university: enter by the small gate in Oode Hoogstraat for a quick look.

Around the University

It's better to continue on towards the southern end of Kloveniersburgwal, to where the **Oudemanhuispoort** passage leads through to Oude Zijds Achterburgwal. This was once part of an almshouse for elderly men, but is now filled with secondhand bookstalls and a group of buildings serving Amsterdam University. On Oude Zijds Achterburgwal you look across to the pretty **Huis op de Drie Grachten**, the "House on the Three Canals", on the corner of Grimburgwal, which runs alongside more university buildings. A little way down Oude Zijds Voorburgwal on the right, through an ornate gateway, is the fifteenth-century **Agnietenkapel** (Mon–Fri 9am–5pm; f2.50), also owned by the university and containing its so-called **Historical Collection**, made up of collections of books, prints, letters and suchlike, related to the history of the city's university – real specialist stuff on the whole. Roughly opposite, the building at Oude Zijds Voorburgwal 300 has for years been known as **"ome Jan"** ("Uncle John's") for its function as central Amsterdam's pawn shop, established 350 years ago in a typically enlightened attempt to put a stop to the crippling activities of moneylenders who were making a killing among the city's poor. The poet Vondel ended his days working here, and a short verse above the entrance extols the virtues of the pawn shop and the evils of usury.

't Gasthuys, Grimburgwal 7, is a bar popular with students and has outside seating in summer.

At the corner a passage cuts through to **Nes**, a long, narrow street, once home to the philosopher Spinoza; or you can make your way back up Oude Zijds past the **Galerie Mokum** at number 334, named after the old Jewish moniker for the city, now in general use. From here it's just a few yards to Rokin, and, beyond, Kalverstraat.

Dam Square

At the far end of Damrak, **Dam Square** gives the city its name: in the thirteenth century the river Amstel was dammed here, and the small fishing village that grew around it became known as "Amstelredam". Boats could sail right into the square and unload their imported grain in the middle of the rapidly growing town, and the later building of Amsterdam's principal church, the Nieuwe Kerk, along with the Royal Palace, formally marked Dam Square as Amsterdam's centre.

Though robbed a little of its dignity by the trams that scuttle across it, the square is still the hub of the city, with all the main streets zeroing in on the maelstrom of buskers, artists and dope dealers who find an instant and captive clientele in the passers-by. At the centre there's a **War Memorial**, an unsightly stone tusk designed by J.J.P. Oud that's filled with soil from each of The Netherlands' eleven provinces and Indonesia, and which also serves as a gathering place for the square's milling tourists and dubious looking characters selling dope to gullible teenagers. The Square's single commercial tourist pull is the newly enlarged and improved Amsterdam branch of **Madame Tussaud's** at Dam 20.

The Royal Palace

Across the square, the **Royal Palace** (daily 12.30–5pm; ƒ5, no museumcards) seems neither Dutch nor palatial – understandably so since it was originally built from imported stone as the city's town hall. The authorities of Europe's mercantile capital wanted a grandiose declaration of civic power, a building that would push even the Nieuwe Kerk into second place, and Jacob van Campen's then startlingly progressive design, a Dutch rendering of the classical principles revived in Renaissance Italy, did exactly that. At the time of its construction in the mid-seventeenth century, it was the largest town hall in Europe, supported by 13,659 wooden piles driven into the Dam's sandy soil; the poet Constantyn Huygens called it "the world's Eighth Wonder/with so much stone raised high and so much timber under". It's the magisterial interior that really deserves this praise, though; the Citizen's Hall proclaims the pride and confidence of the golden age, with the enthroned figure of Amsterdam looking down on the world and heavens laid out at her feet, the whole sumptuously inlaid in brass and marble. A good-natured and witty symbolism pervades the building: cocks fight above the entrance to the Court of Petty Affairs, while Apollo, god of the sun and the arts, brings harmony to the disputes; and a plaque above the door of the Bankruptcy Chamber aptly shows the Fall of Icarus, who flew too close to the sun, surrounded by marble carvings depicting an empty chest and unpaid bills, around which scurry hungry rats. On a more sober note, death sentences were pronounced at the High Court of Justice at the front of the building, and the condemned were executed on a scaffold outside.

Otherwise, the Palace's interior is dull, darkened with the grand but uninspired paintings of the period. Rembrandt, whose career was waning, had his sketches for the walls rejected by the city fathers; today's city council must bemoan their predecessors' lack of judgement, since there's a good chance they'd now be sitting on one of Europe's major art treasures. The building received its royal designation in 1808 when Napoleon's brother Louis commandeered it as the one building fit for a king. Lonely and isolated, Louis briefly ruled from here, until he was forced to acquiesce to Napoleon's autocratic demands. On his abdication in 1810 he left behind a sizeable amount of Empire furniture, most of which is exhibited in the rooms he converted.

The Nieuwe Kerk

Vying for importance with the Palace is the **Nieuwe Kerk** (daily 11am–5pm; ƒ6) – which, despite its name, is a fifteenth-century structure rebuilt several times after fires. Though impressive from the outside, the Nieuwe Kerk has long since lost out in rivalries with the Oude Kerk and the Royal Palace (it was forbidden a tower in case it outshone the new town hall), and is now used only for exhibitions, organ concerts and state occasions: Queen Beatrix was crowned here in 1980. The interior is neat and orderly, its sheer Gothic lines only slightly weighed down by seventeenth-century fixtures such as the massive pulpit and organ. Of the catalogue of household names from Dutch history, Admiral de Ruyter, seventeenth-century Holland's most valiant naval hero, lies in an opulent tomb in the choir, erected in 1681 on what was formerly the high altar; and the poet Vondel is commemorated by a small urn near the entrance.

South of Dam Square

South from Dam Square, the broad sweep of **Rokin** follows the old course of the Amstel River, lined with grandiose nineteenth-century mansions – Amsterdam's *Sotheby's* is here, and, further down, the elaborate *fin-de-siècle* interior of the *Maison de Bonneterie* clothes store. Rokin gives trams running to and from Dam Square their single chance to accelerate in the city, so cross with care. Running parallel with Rokin, **Kalverstraat** has been a commercial centre since it hosted a cattle market in medieval times; now it has declined into a standard European shopping mall, an uninspired strip of monotonous clothes shops differentiated only by the varying strains of disco music they pump out.

The Allard Pierson Museum

On the left-hand side of Rokin, across the short stretch of water at Oude Turfmarkt 127, the **Allard Pierson Museum** (Tues–Fri 10am–5pm, Sat & Sun 1–5pm; f5) is the city's archaeological display, a small and excellent museum, which manages to overcome the fatigue normally induced by archaeological collections by arranging its high-quality exhibits in intimate galleries that encourage you to explore. Also simple background information personalizes what might otherwise be meaningless objects. The museum's highlights include a remarkably well-preserved collection of Coptic clothes and artefacts from the sixth century, good Greek pottery and jewellery, and fine gold and precious stones from all periods.

The Amsterdam Historical Museum

A short walk from the Allard Pierson, a lopsided and frivolous gateway on Kalverstraat forms an unexpected entrance to the **Amsterdam Historical Museum**, Kalverstraat 92 (Mon–Fri 10am–5pm, Sat & Sun 11am–5pm; f6.50; phone ahead on ☎523 18 22 to book places on the guided tours, which run on Weds at 2pm & 3pm). Housed in the restored seventeenth-century buildings of the Civic Orphanage, this attempts to survey the city's development with artefacts, paintings and documents from the thirteenth century onwards. Much is centred on the "golden age" of the seventeenth century: a large group of paintings portrays the city in its heyday and the art collection shows how the wealthy bourgeoisie decorated their homes. Sadly, though, most of the rest of the museum is poorly documented and lacks continuity. Still, it's worth seeing for the nineteenth-century paintings and photos and, more notably, the play-it-yourself carillon and the Regents' Chamber, unchanged since the Regents dispensed civic charity there three hundred years ago. Directly outside the museum, the glassed-in **Civic Guard Gallery** draws passers-by with free glimpses of the large company portraits – there's a selection ranging from the earliest of the 1540s to the lighter affairs of the seventeenth century.

Muntplein and the Flower Market

Kalverstraat comes to an ignoble end in a stretch of ice-cream parlours and fast-food outlets before reaching **Muntplein**. Originally a mint and part of the old city walls, the **Munttoren** was topped with a spire by Hendrik de Keyser in 1620 and is possibly the most famous of the towers dotting the city, a landmark perfectly designed for postcards when framed by the flowers of the nearby floating **Bloemenmarkt** (flower market). From here, Reguliersbreestraat turns left toward the gay bars and loud restaurants of Rembrandtsplein, while Vijzelstraat heads straight out to the edge of the Amsterdam crescent.

See Shops and Markets *for full details of all Amsterdam's markets.*

Along Nieuwe Zijds Voorburgwal

Even before Amsterdam's seventeenth-century expansion, the town could be divided into old and new sectors; the outer boundaries were lined by a defensive wall, and it's this that gives **Nieuwe Zijds Voorburgwal** ("New Sides Town Wall") its name. The wall itself disappeared as the city grew, and in the nineteenth century the canal that ran through the middle of the street was filled in, leaving the unusually wide swathe that runs from just below Prins Hendrikkade to Spui. Nieuwe Zijds used to be the home of most of the capital's newspaper offices. Sadly, rising costs have forced most of these out but you can still see the names of the papers on some of the buildings, and the old journo's watering hole, *Scheltema*, at no. 242, is still a good place for a drink.

The northern end of Nieuwe Zijds

Nieuwe Zijds begins with a bottleneck of trams swinging down from the Centraal Station, and one of the first buildings you see is the **Holiday Inn**, built on the site of an old tenement building called "Wyers". The 1985 clearance of squatters from Wyers ranks among the most infamous of the decade's anti-squatting campaigns, having involved much protest and some violence throughout the city. The squatters had occupied the building in an attempt to prevent another slice of the city from being handed over to a profit-hungry multinational and converted from residential use. Although widely supported by the people of Amsterdam, they were no match for the economic muscle of the American company, and it wasn't long before the riot police were sent in; construction of the hotel soon followed.

The Flying Dutchman, close to the Holiday Inn at Martelaarsgracht 13, is Amsterdam's best-known English bar.

The fate of the **Luthersekerk**, directly west from here on Kattengat, hasn't been much better. With its copper-green dome, which gives this area the label of **Koepelkwartier** or "Dome Neighbourhood", it was deconsecrated and acquired as a conference centre for the luxury Sonesta Hotel nearby, before being destroyed by fire in 1993. Currently, it's undergoing reconstruction. Across the water, the redbrick building at **Singel 140–2** was once home of Captain Banning Cocq, the central character of Rembrandt's *Night Watch*. But more noticeable (and audible) is the quaintly named **Poezenboot** ("cat boat"), a refuge for the city's stray and unwanted cats, moored a little further along the Singel. It's open for visits daily between 1pm and 3pm. Directly east, **Spuistraat** begins at a fork in Nieuwe Zijds Voorburgwal, with a small red light area edging around the St. Dominicus Kerk. These are the red lights the tourists miss, and the business here has the seamy feel of the real thing.

West of Spuistraat, between the Singel and Herengracht, the **Multatuli Museum** at Korsjespoortsteeg 20 (Tues 10am–5pm, other times phone ☎638 19 38 for an appointment; free) – just one large room basically – was the birthplace of Multatuli, the pen name of **Eduard Douwes Dekker**, Holland's most celebrated nineteenth-century writer and a champion of freethinking. Disgusted with the behaviour of his fellow Dutch in their East Indies colonies, he returned home to enrage the establishment with his elegantly written satirical novel, *Max Havelaar*, now something of a Dutch literary classic. The museum is filled with letters, first editions, and a small selection of his furnishings, including the chaise longue on which he breathed his last. There's no information in English, but the attendant will keep you informed.

South to Spui

The trees that fringe Nieuwe Zijds conceal some impressive canal houses, and the specialized shops and private galleries try hard to preserve the refinement the street must have had before canal traffic gave way to trams. You need only compare it to the parallel **Nieuwendijk** to see how Nieuwe Zijds has retained some character. Nieuwendijk is a shabby, uninviting stretch of cheap shops and not-so-cheap restaurants, and the dark side streets have a frightening atmosphere of illicit dealings that hurries you back to the main roads. Things only improve as you approach the Nieuwe Kerk: there's a medieval eccentricity to the streets here, and all seediness vanishes as designer clothes shops appear in the old workshops clustered around the church. Walk down the wonderfully named Zwarte Handsteeg ("Black Hand Alley") and you're back on Nieuwe Zijds. Just across the road, the old **Post Office** manages to hold its own against the Nieuwe Kerk and Royal Palace. Built in 1899, its whimsical embellishments continue the town's tradition of sticking towers on things – here, as everywhere, purely for the hell of it. The city's main post office has since moved around the corner from here, to a building on Singel, and the old office has been converted into a stylish American-style **shopping mall** called Magna Plaza, complete with *Virgin Megastore* and other chain names.

Spui and around

Nieuwe Zijds broadens south of the post office, the streets running west, to Spuistraat and beyond, mostly filled with antique and stamp shops, and some of Amsterdam's oldest and most expensive restaurants. On Wednesdays and Saturdays (11am–4pm) there's a stamp and coin market along Nieuwe Zijds' southern end. Both Spuistraat and Nieuwe Zijds culminate in **Spui**, a chic corner of town with a mixture of bookshops, fashionable restaurants and packed bars and cafés centring on a small, rather cloying statue of a young boy – known as 't **Lieverdje** ("Little Darling") – which was a gift to the city from a large cigarette company. Twenty years ago this was the scene of a series of demonstrations organized by the Provos, an anarchist group that grew out of the original squatters' movement. With the alternative culture then at its most militant, the Provos labelled 't Lieverdje a monument to tomorrow's addiction to capitalism and turned up in force every Saturday

One of the best of the many bars in the area is Hoppe, the ex-local of Freddie Heineken.

evening to preach to the Spui's assembled drinkers. When the police arrived to break up these small "happenings", they did little to endear themselves to the public – and much to gain sympathy for the Provos.

Around the corner in the university library at Singel 425, the **Script Museum** (Mon–Fri 9.30am–1pm & 2–4.30pm; free) is an offbeat collection of different alphabets from around the world, in which – thankfully – the medium is often more interesting than the message; stones, snakeskins, and tree bark providing note pads for some weird hieroglyphs. Further along the canal, **Heiligeweg** or "Holy Way", which connects Singel with Kalverstraat, is so named for its position on the route pilgrims took to Amsterdam (see p.59, the Oude Kerk, for details). On the right, close by the corner with Kalverstraat at Heiligeweg 19, is the gateway of the old **Rasphuis** or "house of correction", topped with a sculpture of a woman punishing two delinquents chained at her sides. Underneath is the single word "Castigatio" or "punishment", beneath which is a carving by Hendrik de Keyser showing wolves and lions cringing before the whip, and an inscription that reads, "It is a virtue to subdue those before whom all go in dread".

The Begijnhof

The main attraction around Spui is however, less obvious. Perhaps those who run the **Begijnhof** want it this way: enclosed on three sides, this small court of buildings is an enclave of tranquillity which is typically Dutch and totally removed from the surrounding streets. Most of the houses are seventeenth-century, but one, no. 34, dates from 1475 – the oldest house in Amsterdam, and built before the city forbade the construction of houses in wood, an essential precaution against fire. *Hofjes* (little courtyards) are found all over the Low Countries. Built by rich individuals or city councils for the poor and elderly, the houses usually turn inwards around a small court, their backs to the outside world. This sense of retreat suited the women who, without taking full vows, led a religious life in the *hofjes*, which often had their own chapel. Here the order was known as *Begijnen*, and such was its standing in the city community that it was allowed to quietly continue its tradition of worship even after Catholicism was suppressed in 1587. Mass was inconspicuously celebrated in the concealed **Catholic Church**, a dark Italianate building with a breath-holding silence that seems odd after the natural peace outside. There's none of this sense of mystery about the **English Reformed Church** which takes up one side of the Begijnhof. Plain and unadorned, it was handed over to Amsterdam's English community when the Begijns were deprived of their main place of worship and, like the *hofje* itself, it's almost too charming, a model of prim simplicity. Inside are several old English memorial plaques, and pulpit panels designed by the young Piet Mondrian.

See West of the Dam *for details of some of the city's other hofjes.*

The Main Canals:
Raadhuisstraat to Amstel

T he central part of Amsterdam was originally encircled by the
Singel, which was part of Amsterdam's original protective moat
but is now just the first of the five **canals** that reach right
around the city centre. These were dug in the seventeenth century as
part of a comprehensive plan to extend the boundaries of a city no
longer able to accommodate its burgeoning population. The idea was
that the council would buy up the land around the city, dig the canals,
and lease plots back to developers on strict conditions. The plan was
passed in 1607, and work began six years later, against a backdrop of
corruption (Amsterdammers in the know bought up the land they
thought the city would subsequently have to purchase).

Increasing the area of the city from 450 to 1800 acres was a
monumental task, and the conditions imposed by the burghers were
tough. The three main waterways, Herengracht, Keizersgracht and
Prinsengracht, were set aside for the residences and offices of the
richer and more influential Amsterdam merchants, while the radial
canals were left for more modest artisans' homes. Even the richest
burgher had to conform to a set of stylistic rules when building his
house, and taxes were levied according to the width of the properties.
This produced the loose conformity you can see today: tall, narrow
residences, with individualism restricted to heavy decorative gables
and sometimes a gablestone to denote name and occupation. Even the
colour of the front doors was regulated, with choice restricted to a
shade that has since become known as "Amsterdam Green" – even
now, difficult to find outside Holland. It was almost the end of the
century before the scheme was finished – a time when, ironically, the
demise of great Amsterdam had already begun – but it remains to the
burghers' credit that it was executed with such success.

Of the three main canals or *grachten*, **Herengracht** ("Gentlemen's
Canal") was the first to be dug, and so attracted the wealthiest
merchants and the biggest, most ostentatious houses. The other two,
Keizersgracht ("Emperor's Canal") and especially **Prinsengracht**

("Prince's Canal"), ended up with noticeably smaller houses – though both still hold some of the most sought-after properties in the city. Today, Herengracht remains the city's grandest stretch of water, especially between Leidsestraat and Vijzelstraat (see below), but you may find the older and less pretentious houses and warehouses of Prinsengracht more appealing. It's hard to pick out any particular points to head for along the three main canals. A lot of the houses have been turned into offices or hotels, and there's little of specific interest apart from museums. Rather, the appeal lies in wandering along selected stretches and admiring the gables while taking in the tree-lined canals' calm, so unusual in the centre of a modern European capital. For shops, bars, restaurants and the like, you're better off exploring the streets that connect the canals.

> The main canals extend north beyond Radhuisstraat, enclosing the western edge of the city centre, beyond which lies the Joordaan. As it is a somewhat distinct area from the main central stretch of the canal, this area is covered in the following chapter *West of the Dam*.

Herengracht: Raadhuisstraat to Vijzelstraat

The most touted but perhaps least memorable stretch of Herengracht is known as the "**Golden Bend**", between Leidsestraat and Vijzelstraat, where the double-fronted merchant residences of the sixteenth and seventeenth centuries – principally numbers 441–513 and 426–480 – try to outdo each other in size if not in beauty. Most of the houses here date from the eighteenth century, with double stairways (the door underneath was the servants' entrance) and the slightly ornamented cornices that were fashionable at the time. The two-columned portal at 502 Herengracht indicates that this is the Mayor's official residence; and there are a couple of neat facades across Vijzelstraat, at number 539 and numbers 504–510, the second of which carries carved figures of dolphins on its crest. But otherwise the houses in this part of town are mainly corporate offices, and markedly less fascinating than the tourist authorities claim. One exception, for its contents at least, is the **Kattenkabinet** ("Cats' cabinet) at Herengracht 468 (Tues–Sat 11am–5pm, Sun noon–5pm; f7.50). This is an enormous collection of art and artefacts relating to cats, housed in a seventeenth century canal house with some original decor and paintings by Jacob de Wit; moggiephiles will be delighted.

There are more imposing facades across Leidsestraat, notably that of **Herengracht 380**, an exact copy of a Loire château – stone again, with a main gable embellished with reclining figures, and a bay window with cherubs, mythical characters, and an abundance of acanthus leaves. Further along, just beyond Leidsegracht on the left,

THE CITY: CHAPTER 3

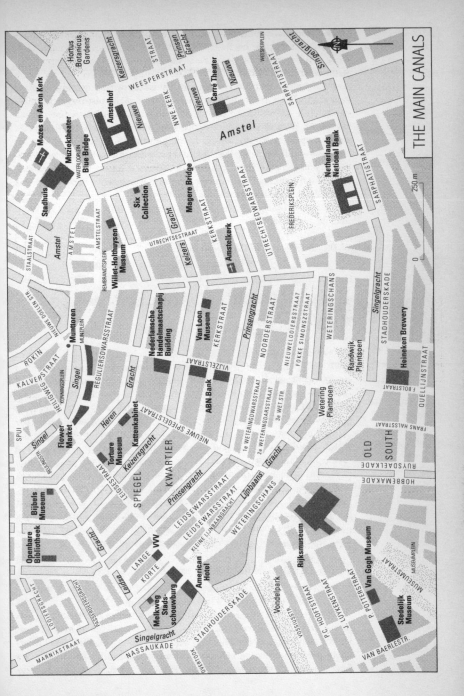

THE MAIN CANALS

there's also the **Bijbels Museum**, which occupies a four-gabled, seventeenth-century stone house frilled with tendrils, carved fruit and scroll-work, at Herengracht 366 (Tues–Sat 10am–5pm, Sun 1–5pm; ƒ3). Inside there's an elaborate eighteenth-century painted ceiling by Jacob de Wit, and a small but imaginative museum with engaging displays relating to Jewish daily life, religious ritual and the history of the Bible in Dutch – refreshingly ecumenical, making connections across all faiths. At Herengracht 255 is the **Ferdinand Domela Nieuwenhuis museum** (Mon–Fri 10am–4pm, appointment only; free), which contains exhibits from the life of Ferdinand Domela, a turn-of-the-century anarchist. The **Netherlands Theatre Institute**, ten minutes' walk away across Raadhuisstraat at Herengracht 168 (Tues–Sun 11am–5pm; ƒ5), is also worth a look, both for the house it is installed in – a fine old place with eighteenth-century murals by Jacob de Wit – and its bold exhibition space, with lively, provocative recreations of contemporary stage sets alongside models that trace the earlier days of the theatre in The Netherlands. It's also a resource centre, with a library, bookshop and historical collections (including video).

*Two good places to
drink – and eat –
on Keizersgracht
are next door to
each other:*
Morlang,
*Keizersgracht 451
and* Land van
Walem,
Keizersgracht 449.

Keizersgracht: Raadhuisstraat to Vijzelstraat

On the next canal, **Keizersgracht**, the one mansion you'll notice in your wanderings is the **Felix Meritis** building at Keizersgracht 324, a heavy neoclassical monolith built in the late eighteenth century to house the artistic and scientific activities of the society of the same name. For most of the nineteenth century this was very much the cultural focus of the city, at least for the very wealthy, and it aped the refined manners of the rest of "cultured" Europe in a way only the Dutch could: badly. It's said that when Napoleon visited the city the entire building was redecorated for his reception only to have him stalk out in disgust, claiming that the place stank of tobacco; and in spite of its use as a model for the later Concertgebouw, the concert hall was well known among musicians for its appalling acoustics. It used to be the headquarters of the Dutch Communist Party; but they sold it to the council who now lease it to the *Felix Meritis Foundation*, a centre for experimental and avant-garde arts.

The Van Loon Museum

A little further along, on the opposite side of the canal, the **Van Loon Museum** at Keizersgracht 672 (Mon 10am–5pm, Sun 1–5pm; ƒ5) is perhaps the finest accessible canal house interior in Amsterdam, a less grand and more likeable alternative to its rival, the nearby Willet-Holthuysen Museum (see below), with a pleasantly down-at-heel interior of peeling stucco and shabby paintwork. Built in 1672, the house's first tenant was the artist Ferdinand Bol; fortunately he didn't suffer the fate of many subsequent owners who seem to have been cursed with a series of bankruptcies and scandals for over two hundred years. The van Loon family bought the house in 1884. The last family member to occupy the whole house, one Thora van Lojon-Egidius, was "dame du paleis" to Queen Wilhelmina, the highest ranking female position in the land. Of German extraction, she was proud of her roots and apparently used to entertain high-ranking Nazi officials here during the occupation – which meant she was later shunned by the royal family. The current van Loons still live upstairs, in the attic rooms, but the rest of the house is filled with homely bits and pieces that stretch from 1580 to 1949; there are lots of family portraits, and various upstairs rooms are sumptuously decorated with eighteenth-century wall paintings. Look, too, at the ornate copper balustrade on the staircase, into which are worked the names "Trip" and "Van Hagen" – former owners of the house; the van Loons later filled the spaces between the letters with fresh iron curlicues to prevent their children falling through.

Leidsestraat, Leidseplein, the Spiegelkwartier, Vijzelstraat

On the corner of Keizersgracht and Leidsestraat, the designer department store, **Metz & Co**, with its corner dome by Gerrit Rietveld, has a top-floor restaurant and tea room with one of the best views of the city. **Leidsestraat** itself is a long, slender passage across the main canals chocked with airline and tourist offices, and with trams that crash along the narrow thoroughfare, dangerously scattering passers-by. At Leidestraat 27, the **Museum of Torture** (daily 10am–7pm; ƒ7.50) is made up of a macabre and comprehensive collection of medieval punishment equipment, including a nasty-looking rack, a guillotine, a (used) garotte and that favourite of the Inquisition, the chair of nails. There is good English information which is well documented with contemporary posters. There's a grill for roasting heretics, a wheel for spinning them on, a contraption for crunching their skulls and even a so-called "flute of shame", which was used on bad musicians, though perhaps the most horrific item is the one that simply manacles the victim into a crouched position until they go mad with muscle cramps – a device apparently used on Guy Fawkes. It's not just a frivolous display, either, as an Amnesty International note reminds you: torture is not just a thing of the past.

A little way north of Leidsestraat, at Prinsengracht 653, Het Molenpad is a cosy and popular place to drink and eat.

Leidseplein and around

At its southern end, Leidestraat broadens into **Leidseplein**, the hub of Amsterdam's nightlife but by day a rather unattractive open space littered with sandwich boards touting the surrounding American burger joints. There's probably a greater concentration of bars, restau-

*One long-standing
and great-value
restaurant in the
Leidesplein area
is the Indonesian
Bojo – see p.141.*

*For full details on
how to go about
joining the lounge
lizards in the
Holland Casino,
see* Sports and
Outdoor Activities.

rants and clubs here than anywhere else in the city, and the streets extend off the square in a bright jumble of jutting signs and neon lights; around the corner, in a converted dairy, lurks the famous **Melkweg** (see *Nightlife*). As for the square itself, on summer nights especially, it can ignite with an almost carnival-like vibrancy, drinkers spilling out of cafés to see sword-swallowers and fire-eaters do their tricks, while the restaurants join in enthusiastically, placing their tables outside so you can eat without missing the fun. On a good night Leidseplein is Amsterdam at its carefree, exuberant best.

On the far corner, the **Stadsschouwburg** is the city's prime performance space after the Muziektheater, while behind, and architecturally much more impressive, is the fairy-castle **American Hotel** – the traditional meeting place of Amsterdam media folk, although these days the renowned turn-of-the-century terrace room is mainly popular with tourists. Even if you're not thirsty it's worth a peek inside, the leaded stained glass, shallow brick arches, chandeliers and carefully coordinated furnishings as fine an example of the complete stylistic vision of Art Nouveau as you'll find.

A few steps southeast of Leidseplein, just past the Paradiso, **Max Euwe Plein** is part of Amsterdam's recent attempt to spruce itself up, a glitzy new complex of retail outlets, riverlike fountains and the new **Holland Casino**, housed in a former jail – Amsterdam's only venue for roulette, blackjack and other such decadent pursuits. Max Euwe was Holland's most famous chess player and only world champion to date, and the **Max Euwe Centre** (Mon–Fri 10.30am–4pm; free) here contains an interesting exhibition on the history and development of competitive chess, and a review of Max Euwe's career. Chess sets are available if you feel so inspired, both the real thing and the computer variety. Whether you intend to play (or gamble) or not, it's worth wandering around Max Euwe Plein for a brief look, taking in the general atmosphere and many contemporary sculptures. One of these, an "invisible" pyrex cube, used to house a floating ƒ100 note. Predictably, however, this was broken into and snatched within weeks of the centre's opening.

The Spiegelkwartier, Kerkstraat, Vijzelstraat, Weteringplantsoen

Walking east from here, **Weteringschans**, and, running parallel, **Lijnbaansgracht**, ring the modern city centre. On the right the **Rijksmuseum** looms large across the canal; left, Spiegelgracht and, further on, Nieuwe Spiegelstraat lead into the **Spiegelkwartier**, the focus of the Amsterdam antique trade. It's a small area, but has around fifty dealers here – none, as you might expect, particularly inexpensive.

Kerkstraat, a narrow street featuring an odd mixture of gay bookshops and art galleries, leads east from here to connect with **Vijzelstraat** at the **ABN Building**, through which the street runs. The ABN, bland and plastic-looking on the whole, doesn't merit a second glance today – but its construction in the 1950s was the subject of one of Amsterdam's biggest property controversies. During that decade many canals had been filled in and large parts of the city torn down to make way for increased traffic. The tension between the conservationists and developers had been mounting for some time, and when the collapse of a building between Keizersgracht and Prinsengracht left this plot vacant, the scene was set for confrontation. There was immediate protest when it turned out that the *Algemene Bank Nederland* was to buy up the land for office use, and diverse groups of Amsterdammers joined together to keep the bank out. The architect had already defaced part of the city with the overbearing State Bank building on Fredericksplein, and many people felt he shouldn't be given the opportunity again – particularly not on the banks of one of the city's most beautiful canals. That the bank's offices stand now is proof enough that the conservationists lost, but it was an important early skirmish in the city's continuing struggles to keep property barons at bay.

Looking towards Muntplein, the oversized **Nederlandsche Handelsmaatschapij Building** (now also owned by *ABN*) is another bank building totally unsympathetic to its surroundings. Though a much worthier work architecturally than the later bank, it would look more at home in downtown Manhattan than on the banks of a Dutch canal. In the other direction, Vijzelstraat becomes the filled-in **Vijzelgracht**, which culminates in a roundabout at **Weteringplantsoen**, and, on its southern side, one of Amsterdam's saddest spots: it was here, on April 3, 1945, that twenty people were shot by the Nazis – an example, in the last few weeks of their power, to anyone who might consider opposing them. On the wall is an excerpt from a poem by H.M. van Randwijk, recalling the incident with carefully levelled restraint:

The Heineken brewery, celebrated for its tours, overlooks Weteringplantsoen. For details, see p.108.

> *When to the will of tyrants,*
> *A nation's head is bowed,*
> *It loses more than life and goods –*
> *Its very light goes out.*

Rembrandtsplein and around

Towards the Amstel, the area cornered by Herengracht's eastern reaches is dominated by **Rembrandtsplein**, a dishevelled bit of greenery fringed with cafés and their terraces. This claims to be one of the centres of city nightlife, though the square's crowded restaurants are today firmly tourist-targeted; expect to pay inflated prices. Rembrandt's pigeon-spattered statue stands in the middle, his back wisely turned against the square's worst excesses, which include live (but deadly) outdoor music. Of the cafés, only the bar of the **Schiller Hotel** at number 26 stands out, with an original Art Deco interior reminiscent of a great ocean liner.

Rembrandts-plein and around

The streets leading north from Rembrandtsplein to the Amstel river are more exciting, containing many of the city's mainstream gay bars – accessible to all, and less costly than their upstart neighbours. **Amstelstraat** is the main thoroughfare east, crossing the river at the **Blauwbrug** ("Blue Bridge"), and affording wonderful views across the new **Muziektheater** and **Town Hall** complex (see below). Heading west, **Reguliersbreestraat** links Rembrandtsplein to Muntplein, and, tucked in among slot-machine arcades and sex shops, houses the **Tuschinski**, the city's most famous cinema, with an interior that's a wonderful example of the Art Deco excesses of the 1920s. Opened in 1921, there are Expressionist paintings, coloured marbles, and a supremely colourful carpet handwoven in Marrakesh in 1984 by sixty women to an original design. Obviously you can see all this if you're here to watch a film (the Tuschinski shows all the most popular general releases); if you're not, guided tours are laid on during July and August on Sunday and Monday mornings at 10.30am (ƒ5 per person).

The block of streets behind the Tuschinski was once known as **Duivelshoek** ("Devil's Corner"), and, although it's been tidied up and sanitized, enough of the backstreet seediness remains to make it a spot most people avoid at night. To the south of Rembrandtsplein, **Thorbeckeplein** scores points for having a thinner concentration of clog and card shops, but is hardly a fitting memorial for Rudolf Thorbecke, a politician whose liberal reforms of the late nineteenth century furthered the city tradition of open-minded tolerance, and whose statue stands a short way from the topless bars and sex shows. An occasional art market brightens the square on Sundays. **Reguliersgracht** flows south from here, a broad canal of distinctive steep bridges that was to have been filled in at the beginning of the century, but was saved when public outcry rose against the destruction of one of the city's more alluring stretches of water.

The Willet-Holthuysen Museum

The three great *grachten* nearby don't contain houses quite as grand as those to the west, but a couple of buildings can be visited, notably the **Willet-Holthuysen House** at Herengracht 605 (Mon–Fri 10am–5pm, Sat & Sun 11am–5pm; ƒ5). Splendidly decorated in Rococo style, the house was opened to the public as a museum in 1895, after the last owner, Sandra Willet-Holthuysen, died childless. In those days it was a lot less remarkable as a patrician period piece than it is now, and was so little visited that people used to joke that it was the best place for a man to meet his mistress without being noticed. Nowadays it is more a museum than a home, and very much look-don't-touch territory, with displays of Abraham Willet's large collection of glass and ceramics, a well-equipped replica of a seventeenth-century kitchen in the basement, and, out the back, an immaculate eighteenth-century garden – worth the price of the admission alone.

The Six Collection

Another good example of a seventeenth-century patrician canal house,
the **Six Collection**, close by at Amstel 218 (guided tours on Mon, Wed
& Fri at 10am & 11am; free), has an easily absorbed group of paintings
in a remarkably unspoiled mansion – though the current Baron Six, who
still lives there, has a policy of actively discouraging visitors (you must
apply first, with your passport, at the Rijksmuseum information desk
for a ticket). Rembrandt was a friend of the burgomaster and his
Portrait of Jan Six is the collection's greatest treasure. Painted in
1654, it's a brilliant work, the impressionistic treatment of the hands
subtly focusing attention on the subject's face. Also here are
Rembrandt's *Portrait of Anna Wijmer*, Six's mother, and Hals's
portrait of another figure prominent in Rembrandt's oeuvre, *Dr Tulp*, a
great patron of the arts whose daughter married Jan Six. Other connections between the Six family and their collection are well explained by
the staff, and the whole group of paintings is a must if you have any
interest in seventeenth-century painting – or indeed in the period at all.

South of Rembrandtsplein and across the Amstel

As the canals approach the Amstel, their houses become increasingly
residential. Even **Kerkstraat** is tamed of its bars and clubs, turning east
of Reguliersgracht into a pleasant if unremarkable neighbourhood that
lies beside the **Amstelveld**, a small square-cum-football pitch that few
visitors happen upon. The **Amstelkerk**, a seventeenth-century graffiti-
covered wooden church with a nineteenth-century Gothic interior
marks the corner, and a Monday **flower market** here adds a splash of
colour. **Utrechtsestraat**, the other artery that flows to and from
Rembrandtsplein, is probably Amsterdam's most up-and-coming strip
and contains most of the area's commercial activity, much of it in the
shape of mid- to upper-bracket restaurants. It ends in the concrete
wasteland of **Frederiksplein** – more a glorified tram stop than a square,
presided over by the massive glass box of the **Nederlandse Bank**.
Leading off Frederiksplein, **Sarphatistraat** crosses the wide and windy
reaches of the **Amstel River**, whose eastern side is stacked with chunky
buildings such as the **Carré Theatre**, built as a circus in the early
1900s, but now more often a space for music and drama. Just beyond,
the **Magere Brug**, ("Skinny Bridge") is (inexplicably) the focus of much
attention in the tourist brochures, and hence the most famous of the
city's swinging bridges. More worthy of a serious look is the **Amstel
Hof**, a large and forbidding former *hofje* that was one of a number of
charitable institutions built east of the Amstel after a seventeenth-
century decision to extend the major canals eastward towards the new
harbour and shipbuilding quarter. Takers for the new land were few,
and the city had no option but to offer it to charities at discount prices.

*Sluizer,
Utrechtsestraat
45, is one of the
better of many
restaurants along
this street.*

Across the Amstel

Move east from this part of the Amstel and you're heading toward the edges of the old Jewish area, though, as in the Jodenhoek proper, there are scant traces of the community that thrived here before World War II. The development of Weesperplein as a major traffic route (and the building of the metro beneath it) removed most of what little remained, but one painful reminder of the war years still stands at **Nieuwe Keizersgracht 58**. From 1940, this house was the headquarters of the *Judenrat* or Jewish Council, an organization used by the Nazis to cover up the fact that Jews were being deported from the city to their deaths. The council helped implement the day-to-day running of the deportations, thereby furthering the belief among Jews that they were being taken to new employment in Germany. Just how much the council leaders knew isn't clear, but a good many workers within the organization complied with Nazi orders, believing their own skins would be saved. After the war the surviving leaders of the Jewish Council successfully defended themselves against charges of collaboration, stating that they effectively prevented far stricter deportation schemes. But the presence of the council office had already given this stretch of Keizersgracht a new name – "Nieuwe Martelaarsgracht", the canal of the New Martyrs.

Not far away at Nieuwe Prinsengracht 130, there's another museum, the **Geological Museum** (Mon–Fri 9am–5pm; free), made up of the geological collection of Amsterdam University: boring boulders, monotonous minerals and other assorted rubble; strictly for rock fans only.

Chapter 4

West of the Dam

U nlike the Jodenhoek to the east, the area west of Amsterdam's immediate centre is one of the city's most untouched neighbourhoods – and one of its loveliest. The **Prinsengracht** here has a gentle beauty quite unlike its grander rivals, and holds the Anne Frank House as a specific draw; and the **Jordaan**, just beyond, with its narrow waterways spotted with tiny shops and bars, is as good (and as pretty) a place for idle strolling as you'll find. The areas around what used to be the quays and warehouses of Amsterdam's **western docks** are gradually becoming gentrified, and integrated with the city's mainstream.

Raadhuisstraat and the Westerkerk

From behind the Royal Palace, **Raadhuisstraat** runs west past the elegant curve of the nineteenth-century Art Nouveau **Utrecht Building** towards **Westermarkt**, a glorified tram stop with a couple of fish stalls between Keizersgracht and Prinsengracht. The seventeenth-century French philosopher René Descartes lived at Westermarkt 6 for a short time, happy that the business-oriented character of the city left him able to work and think without being disturbed. As he wrote at the time, "Everybody except me is in business and so absorbed by profit-making I could spend my entire life here without being noticed by a soul".

The Westerkerk

However, it's the **Westerkerk** (Tues–Sat 10am–4pm; tower April–Sept Mon–Sat 10am–5pm; ƒ3.50) that dominates the square, its tower – without question Amsterdam's finest – soaring graciously above the gables of Prinsengracht. On its top perches the crown of Kaiser Maximilian, a constantly recurring symbol of the city and an appropriate finishing touch to what was only its second place of worship built expressly for Protestants. The church was designed by Hendrik de Keyser (architect also of the Zuiderkerk and Noorderkerk) as part of the general seventeenth-century enlargement of the city, and completed in 1631. But while this is probably Amsterdam's most

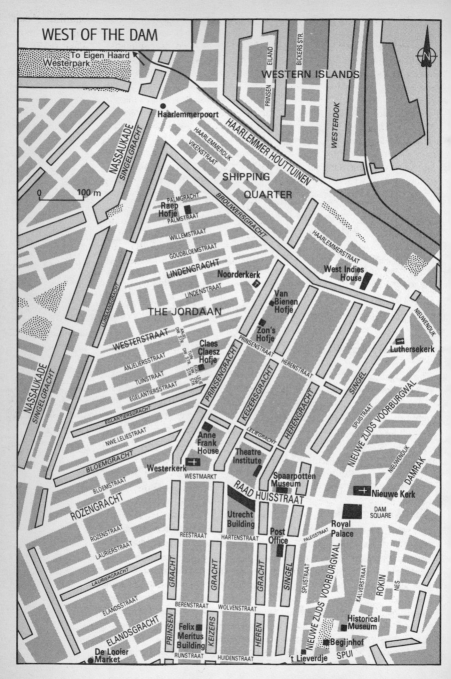

WEST OF THE DAM

To Eigen Haard
Westerpark

WESTERN ISLANDS

PRINSEN EILAND

BICKERS STR.

WESTERDOK

Haarlemmerpoort

NASSAUKADE

SINGELGRACHT

HAARLEMMERDIJK

VIKENSTRAAT

HAARLEMMER HOUTTUINEN

SHIPPING

QUARTER

0   100 m

PALMGRACHT

Raep
Hofje

PALMSTRAAT

BROUWERSGRACHT

HAARLEMMERSTRAAT

WILLEMSTRAAT

GOUDBLOEMSTRAAT

West Indies
House

LINDENGRACHT

Noorderkerk

LINDENSTRAAT

Van
Bienen
Hofje

NIEUWENDIJK

THE JORDAAN

WESTERSTRAAT

Zon's
Hofje

Luthersekerk

Claes
Claesz
Hofje

ANJELIERSSTRAAT

PRINSENSTRAAT

HERENSTRAAT

TUINSTRAAT

EGELANTIERSSTRAAT

SINGEL

NIEUWENDIJK

NASSAUKADE

SINGELGRACHT

EGELANTIERSGRACHT

PRINSENGRACHT

KEIZERSGRACHT

HERENGRACHT

SPUISTRAAT

NIEUWE ZIJDS VOORBURGWAL

NWE LELIESTRAAT

LELIEGRACHT

BLOEMGRACHT

Anne
Frank
House

Theatre
Institute

DAMRAK

Westerkerk

WESTMARKT

Spaarpotten
Museum

Nieuwe Kerk

BLOEMSTRAAT

RAAD HUISSTRAAT

ROZENGRACHT

Utrecht
Building

DAM
SQUARE

ROZENSTRAAT

REESTRAAT

HARTENSTRAAT

Post
Office

Royal
Palace

PALEISTRAAT

LAURIERSTRAAT

NIEUWE ZIJDS VOORBURGWAL

LAURIERGRACHT

GRACHT

GRACHT

GRACHT

SINGEL

SPUISTRAAT

KALVERSTRAAT

ROKIN

NES

ELANDSSTRAAT

BERENSTRAAT

WOLVENSTRAAT

ELANDSGRACHT

PRINSEN

KEIZERS

HEREN

Historical
Museum

Felix
Meritus
Building

De Looier
Market

RUNSTRAAT

HUIDENSTRAAT

Begijnhof

't Lieverdje

SPUI

visually appealing church from the outside, there's little within of special note.

Rembrandt, who was living nearby when he died, is commemorated by a small memorial in the north aisle. His pauper's grave can no longer be located; indeed, there's a possibility that he's not here at all, since many of the bodies were moved to a cemetery when underground heating was installed. The memorial is, however, close to where Rembrandt's son Titus is buried. Rembrandt worshipped his son – as is evidenced by numerous portraits – and the boy's death dealt a final crushing blow to the ageing and embittered artist, leading to his own death just over a year later. During recent excavations, bones have been unearthed which could be those of Titus and even Rembrandt – which has made the church authorities very excited about the resultant tourist possibilities. The only thing that can prove it one way or the other is the analysis currently taking place of the lead content of the bones, which in the case of an artist such as Rembrandt should be unusually high, since lead was a major ingredient of paint.

Behind the church, on the corner of Keizersgracht and Westermarkt, are the pink granite triangles of the **Homo-Monument**. Designed by Karin Daan, these commemorate not only those homosexuals who died in concentration camps – during the occupation all homosexuals were forced to wear pink cloth triangles on their jackets – but also known homosexuals who fought with the Allies and whose names were omitted from other remembrance monuments. The inscription, by the gay Dutch writer Jacob Israel de Haan, reads – "Such an infinite desire for friendship".

Along Prinsengracht

Directly outside the Westerkerk stands a small, simple statue of **Anne Frank** by the Dutch sculptor Mari Andriessen – a careful and evocative site, since it was just a few steps from here, at Prinsengracht 263, that the young diarist used to listen to the Westertoren bells until they were taken away to be melted down for the Nazi war effort. The story of Anne Frank, her family and friends is well known. Anne's father, Otto, was a well-to-do Jewish businessman who ran a successful spice-trading business and lived in the southern part of the city. By 1942 the Nazi occupation was taking its toll: all Jews had been forced to wear a yellow star, and were not allowed to use public transport, go to the theatre or cinema or stray into certain areas of the city; roundups, too, were becoming increasingly common. As conditions became more difficult, and it looked as if the Franks themselves might be taken away, Otto Frank decided – on the advice of two Dutch friends and colleagues, Mr Koophuis and Mr Kraler – to move into their warehouse on the Prinsengracht, the back half of which was unused at the time. The Franks went into hiding in July 1942, along with a Jewish business partner and his family, the Van Daans, separated from the eyes of the outside world by a bookcase that doubled as a door. As far as everyone else was concerned, they had fled to Switzerland.

So began the two-year occupation of the *achterhuis*, or back annexe. The two families were joined in November of 1942 by a Mr Dussel, a dentist friend, and supplies and news of the outside world – which, for the Jews, was becoming daily more perilous – were brought regularly by Koophuis or Kraler, who continued working in the front office. In her diary Anne Frank describes the day-to-day lives of the inhabitants of the annexe: the quarrels, frequent in such a claustrophobic environment; celebrations of birthdays, or of a piece of good news from the Allied Front; and her own, slightly unreal, growing up (much of which, it's been claimed, was deleted by her father).

Two years later, the atmosphere was optimistic: the Allies were clearly winning the war, and it was thought that it wouldn't be long before the fugitives could emerge. It wasn't to be. One day in the summer of 1944 the Franks were betrayed by a Dutch collaborator; the Gestapo arrived and forced Mr Kraler to open up the bookcase, whereupon the occupants of the annexe were all arrested and quickly sent to Westerbork – the northern Netherlands German labour camp where all Dutch Jews were processed before being moved to Belsen or Auschwitz. Of the eight from the annexe, only Otto Frank survived; Anne and her sister died of typhus within a short time of each other in Belsen, just one week before the German surrender.

De Prins, Prinsengracht 124, is a good place to stop off for a drink and a bite to eat.

The Anne Frank House

Anne Frank's diary was among the few things left behind in the annexe. It was retrieved by one of the people who had helped the Franks and handed to Anne's father on his return from Auschwitz; he later decided to publish it. Since its appearance in 1947, it has been constantly in print, translated into 54 languages and has sold thirteen million copies worldwide. In 1957 the Anne Frank Foundation set up the **Anne Frank House** (Mon–Sat 9am–5pm, Sun 10am–5pm; closed Yom Kippur – Oct 9; ƒ7, no museumcards; ☎626 45 33), now one of the most deservedly popular tourist attractions in town; bearing this in mind, the best time to visit is early morning before the crowds arrive.

The rooms the Franks lived in for two years are left much the same as they were during the war, even down to Anne's movie star pin-ups in her bedroom and the marks on the wall recording the children's heights. A number of other rooms offer background detail on the war and occupation, one offering a video biography of Anne, from her frustrated hopes in hiding in the annexe up to her death in 1945, another detailing the gruesome atrocities of Nazism, as well as giving some up-to-date examples of fascism and anti-Semitism in Europe which draw pertinent parallels with the war years. Anne Frank was only one of 100,000 Dutch Jews who died during that time, but this, her final home, provides one of the most enduring testaments to the horrors of Nazism.

The Jordaan

Across Prinsengracht, between Brouwersgracht on the north and Leidsegracht on the south, **The Jordaan** is a likeable and easily explored area of narrow canals, narrower streets and simple, architecturally varied houses. The name is said to come from the French *jardin*, and many of the streets are named after flowers. Falling outside the seventeenth-century concentric-canal plan, the area was not subject to municipal controls, which led to its becoming a centre of property speculation, developing as a series of canals and streets that followed the original polder ditches and rough paths. In contrast to the splendour of the three main *grachten*, the Jordaan became Amsterdam's slum quarter, home of artisans, tradespeople, and Jewish or Huguenot refugees who had fled here to escape religious persecution at home. Though tolerated, the immigrants remained distinct minorities and were treated as such, living in what were often cramped and unsanitary quarters. Later, after much rebuilding, the Jordaan became the inner-city enclave of Amsterdam's growing industrial working class – which, in spite of increasing gentrification, to some extent remains.

Of the many bars in the Jordaan, among the best are De Reiger, Nieuwe Leliestraat 34; De Tuin, *2e Tuindwarsstraat 13; and the old-fashioned* Nol *at Westerstraat 109.*

The last couple of decades have seen the Jordaan gain a reputation as the home of young "alternative" Amsterdam. However, partly thanks to a decree issued by the Amsterdam city authorities in 1972 that any development would have to enhance the historic character of the area and therefore be primarily residential, there's a core population of residents who retain long-standing roots in the district. Today, working-class, family-oriented Jordaaners live shoulder-to-shoulder with educated, mostly single newcomers.

The Jordaan's hofjes

Other than a handful of bars and restaurants, some posh clothes shops and the odd outdoor market, there's nothing very specific to see (though it's a wonderful neighbourhood for a wander) apart from its **hofjes** – seventeenth-century almshouses for the city's elderly population. There were – and are – *hofjes* all over the city (most famously the Begijnhof – see "The Old Centre"), but there's a concentration in the Jordaan, and if you're passing through, it is worth looking in on a courtyard or two; many of them have real charm. Bear in mind, though, that most are still lived in, and be discreet.

Of those that warrant a specific visit, the **Van Bienen Hofje**, opposite the Noordermarkt at Prinsengracht 89–133, is the grandest, built in 1804, according to the entrance tablet, "for the relief and shelter of those in need". A little way down the canal at Prinsengracht 157–171, **Zon's Hofje** has a leafier, more gentle beauty; and, back in the main grid of the Jordaan, the **Claes Claesz Hofje** on 1e Egelantierdwarsstraat, a much earlier almshouse (built in 1616 for poor widows), is now noisily occupied by students of the Amsterdam Conservatory of Music. A little further north, look also at the buildings of **Raep Hofje**, Palmgracht 26–38, funded by the Raep family and sporting a carved *raep* (turnip) above the entrance. For more on *hofjes* – and an account of one of the country's most famous, the Frans Hals Museum in Haarlem – see "Out from the City".

Rozengracht to Lindengracht

More general wanderings start on **Rozengracht**, the filled-in canal where, at number 184, Rembrandt once lived – though the house itself has long since disappeared and only a plaque marks the spot. Though not the Jordaan proper, the area south of this street is a likeable one, centring on the pretty Lauriergracht and including, at Elandsgracht 109, the **De Looier** (pronounced "lawyer") indoor antique market, where a leisurely browse may unearth a bargain (see *Shops and Markets*). North of Rozengracht the Jordaan's streets and canals run off diagonally, bordering Prinsengracht. The main street of the district is **Westerstraat** (where there's a general Monday market of clothes and textiles), which runs down to join Prinsengracht at **Noordermarkt** and Hendrik de Keyser's **Noorderkerk** (occasionally open on Saturdays). This church, finished in 1623, is probably the architect's least successful creation in Amsterdam; nor is the square particularly attractive being part car park, part children's playground. Outside the church, the **statue** of three figures clinging to each other commemorates the Riots of 1934, which prevented a proposed reduction in government benefit payments during the Depression. The inscription reads: "The strongest chains are those of unity". Nowadays the square is the site of a Monday antiques market and the regular Saturday **Boerenmarkt** ("farmers' market") – a lively affair full of avuncular characters selling organic produce, handicrafts, homemade goods and wine. Cross an unmarked border and you'll find a different set of people selling, rather cruelly, a selection of exotic birds in very small cages – perhaps a leftover from the Boerenmarkt's origins as a cattle market: look at the gables of Noordermarkt 17, 18 and 19 and you'll see a cow, a chicken and a sheep, a reminder of the old days..

The next street over, **Lindengracht**, is home to another, general Saturday market. If you're interested in shopping, also check out **Tweede Anjelierdwarsstraat** and **Tweede Tuindwarsstraat** – two streets which hold the bulk of the Jordaan's ever-increasing trendy stores and clothing shops, and some of its liveliest bars and cafés for restorative sipping.

Try the Indonesian food at Speciaal, Nieuwe Leliestraat 142.

The Shipping Quarter and Western Islands

Brouwersgracht, just beyond, is one of Amsterdam's most picturesque and most photographed canals, marking what is in effect the northern boundary of the Jordaan and the beginning of a district loosely known as the **Scheepvaartsbuurt** or "Shipping Quarter", which centres on the long arteries of **Haarlemmerstraat** and **Haarlemmerdijk**. In the seventeenth century this district was at the cutting edge of Amsterdam's trade: *Brouwersgracht* means "brewers' canal", and there were once many breweries along here, brewing ale for export via the harbour: in the days of polluted water, beer was one of the more reilable drinks available. The warehouses along Brouwersgracht provided storage space for the spoils brought back from the high seas, and the building on Haarlemmerstraat at Herenmarkt, the **West Indies House**, was the home of the Dutch West Indies Company, who administered much of the business. Today it's a good area for cheap restaurants and offbeat shops: the warehouses have been largely taken over and converted into spacious apartments, and the West Indies Company Building has a courtyard containing an overstated statue of Peter Stuyvesant, governor of New Amsterdam (later named New York), and a swanky restaurant named after the seventeenth-century Dutch naval hero Piet Heijn.

't Smackzeyl, Brouwersgracht 101, is a decent local bar, with food.

The Western Islands

At the far end of Haarlemmerdijk, the **Haarlemmerpoort** is an oversized and atypical former gateway to the city, built for the arrival in the city of William II in 1840. Beyond this you can either walk on to the **Westerpark**, one of the city's smaller and more enticing parks, or duck under the railway lines to the **Western Islands** district, made up of the artificial islands of **Bickerseiland**, **Prinseneiland**, and, just to the north, **Realeneiland**. Ships were once loaded and unloaded here, and there are more rows of gaunt warehouses. It's an atmospheric area, in part still largely deserted, though becoming increasingly sought after. The painter G. H. Breitner had his studio here – in the modern house beside the **Sloterdijkbrug** – and the area is still a favourite with artists, some of whom have moved in to exploit the space offered by the old warehouses.

Across the Westerkanaal on Spaarndammerplantsoen and Zaanstraat, the **Eigen Haard** housing project is probably the most central example you'll see of the Amsterdam School of architecture. Designed by Michael de Klerk, this was one of a number of new schemes that went up in Amsterdam in the early part of this century, a result of legislation passed to alleviate the previously appalling housing conditions of the city's poor. Modern municipal architects – Dutch ones included – could learn a lot from the style, which is typical of the Amsterdam School. Rounded corners, turrets, and bulging windows and balconies lend individuality to what would otherwise be very plain brick residences.

For more on the Amsterdam School see H.P. Berlage's "New South" and Piet Kramer's De Dageraad estate, also in the South.

Chapter 5

The Jodenhoek and the Eastern Islands

T hough hardly any visible evidence remains, from the sixteenth century onward Amsterdam was the home of Jews escaping persecution throughout Europe. Under the terms of the Union of Utrecht, Jews enjoyed a tolerance and freedom unknown elsewhere, and they arrived in the city to practise diamond processing, sugar refining and tobacco production – effectively the only trades open to them since the city's guilds excluded Jews from following traditional crafts. This largely impoverished Jewish community lived in one of the city's least desirable stretches, the old dock areas around Jodenbreestraat, which became known as the **Jodenhoek**. The docks moved east to Kattenburg, Wittenburg and Oostenburg – the **Eastern Islands**.

The Jodenhoek

By the early years of this century Jewish life was commercially and culturally an integral part of the city, the growing demand for diamonds making Jewish expertise invaluable and bringing wealth to the community, concentrated in the **Jodenhoek**, for the first time. In the 1930s the community's numbers swelled with Jews who had fled persecution in Germany. But in May 1940 the Nazis invaded, sealing off the area to create a ghetto. Jews were not allowed to use public transport or own a telephone, and were placed under a curfew. Roundups and deportations continued until the last days of the war: out of a total of 80,000 Jews in the city, 75,000 were murdered in concentration camps.

After the war the Jodenhoek lay deserted: those who had lived here were dead or deported, and their few possessions were quickly looted. As the need for wood and raw materials grew during postwar shortages, many houses were slowly dismantled and finally destroyed in the 1970s with the completion of the metro that links the city centre to the outer suburbs. Today few people refer to the Jodenhoek by that name, and many Amsterdammers are unaware of its history.

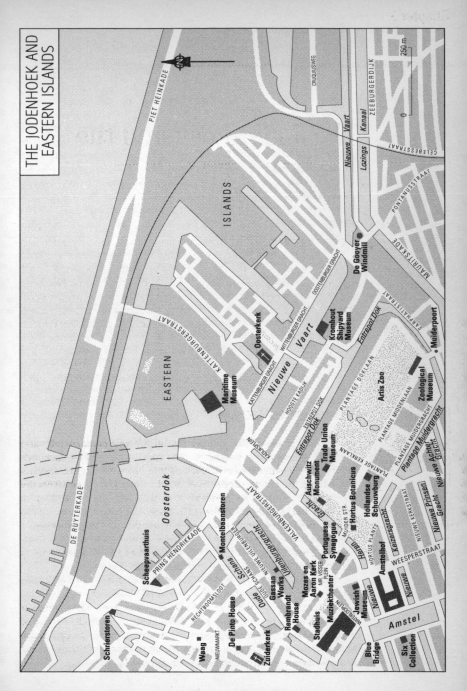

THE JODENHOEK AND
EASTERN ISLANDS

Along Jodenbreestraat

Nieuwmarkt signals the beginning of what was the Jodenhoek, and St Antoniesbreestraat leads to its heart, an uncomfortably modernized street whose original old houses were demolished to widen the road for the heavy traffic that the Nieuwmarkt redevelopment (see below) would bring. Only the **De Pinto House** at no. 69 survives, easily spotted by its creamy Italianate facade. Isaac De Pinto, a Jew who had fled Portugal to escape the Inquisition, was a founder of the East Indies Company and used some of the wealth he had accrued to decorate his house; today it's a branch of the public library, and worth dropping into for a glimpse of the elaborately painted ceiling. Nearby, on Zandstraat, the decorative landmark of Hendrik de Keyser's **Zuiderkerk** (Mon–Wed & Fri noon–5pm, Thurs noon–8pm) is similarly surrounded by new development. Inside there's an exhibition on city planning, though the church's best feature, its tower, is currently closed undergoing restoration.

St Antoniesbreestraat runs into **Jodenbreestraat**, at one time the Jodenhoek's principal market and centre of Jewish activity. After the shipbuilding industry moved further east, this area, made up of the small islands of Uilenburg and Marken, became the site of the worst living conditions in the city: cramped, dirty streets which housed the very poorest Jews, those who weren't able to find employment in the diamond factories such as the **Gassan Works** (daily 9am–5pm; free), whose buildings still stand on the southwest corner of Uilenburgergracht. It wasn't until 1911 that the area was declared a health hazard and redevelopment was started. Jodenbreestraat itself was modernized and widened in the 1970s and it lost much of its character as a result; only when you reach the **Rembrandt House** at number 6 (Mon–Sat 10am–5pm, Sun 1–5pm; ƒ5) do you find any continuity with the past.

Rembrandt bought the house at the height of his fame and popularity, living here for over twenty years and spending a fortune on furnishings – an expense that helped lead to his bankruptcy. An inventory made at the time details a huge collection of paintings, sculptures and art treasures he'd amassed, almost all of which went in the bankruptcy hearings, and in 1660 he was forced to move to a more modest house on Rozengracht in the Jordaan. The house itself is disappointing – mostly a reconstruction and with no artefacts from Rembrandt's life on exhibit – but you can view a great variety of the artist's engravings here. The biblical illustrations attract the most attention, though the studies of tramps and vagabonds are more accessible; an informative accompanying exhibit explains Rembrandt's engraving techniques.

Dantzig, Zwanenburgwal 15, is a popular place to eat and drink.

Waterlooplein

Jodenbreestraat runs parallel to its sibling development, the **Muziektheater** and **Town Hall** – the so-called "Stopera" complex – on **Waterlooplein**, whose building occasioned the biggest public dispute the city had seen since the Nieuwmarkt was dug up in the 1970s to make way for the metro. The Waterlooplein, a marshy, insanitary area that rapidly became known as the poorest patch of the city, was the first neighbourhood to be settled by the Jews. By the latter part of the nineteenth century things had become so bad that the canals that crossed the area were completely filled in and the shanty houses in the area were razed; the street markets were then shifted here from their previous sites in St. Antoniesbreestraat and Jodenbreestraat. The Waterlooplein quickly became the largest and liveliest market in the city, and a link between the Jewish community and the predominantly Gentile one across the Amstel. During the war it became infamous again, this time as a site for Nazi roundups; in the 1950s it regained some of its vibrancy with the establishment of the city's flea market here.

Later, when the council announced the building of a massive new opera complex that would all but fill the square, opposition was widespread. People believed it should be turned into a residential area at best, a popular performance space at the least – anything but an elitist opera house. Attempts to prevent the building failed, but since opening in 1986 the Muziektheater has successfully established itself with visitors and performers alike, and the **flea market** has come back after being moved for a few years to nearby Valkenburgstraat. If you'd like to explore backstage and get an idea of the workings of the Muziektheater, guided tours run throughout the year, except in July (Wed & Sat 4pm; *f*8.50; phone for information ☎551 8054). To find out what the city is up to today in terms of planning and building, drop into the **Architecture Centre Amsterdam** (*ARCAM:* Tues–Sat 1–5pm; free) at Waterlooplein 213, which has changing exhibitions on the city's architecture.

You'll find full details of the flea market in Shops and Markets.

In the public **passageway** between the theatre and town hall a series of glass columns give a salutary lesson on the fragility of The Netherlands, one containing water indicating the sea levels in the Dutch towns of Vlissingen and IJmuiden, and another recording the (much higher) levels experienced during the 1953 flood disaster. Downstairs a plaque shows what is known as "Normal Amsterdam Level" (NAP), originally calculated in 1684 as the average water level in the river IJ and still the basis for measuring altitude above sea level across Europe (Mon–Fri 8.30am–4pm except Thurs 8.30am–7pm, occasionally Sat & Sun also). Three water columns show the tides at IJmuiden and Vlissingen, a few feet high, and the level reached during the 1953 floods, which is far above your head. Downstairs – and so below sea level – is a bronze knob which represents the zero point from which altitude is measured.

Outside the Muziektheater, the outline of a house has been marked on the ground, in remembrance of a Jewish boys' orphanage that once stood here. During the Nazi era, its occupants were all sent to the Sobibor concentration camp, from which none returned.

Mr Visserplein and around

Just behind the Muziektheater, on the corner of Mr Visserplein, is the **Mozes en Aaron Kerk**, originally a small (clandestine) Catholic church that was rebuilt in rather glum, neoclassical style in the mid-nineteenth century. The philospher Spinoza was born in a house on this site, and as a Jew, quickly came into conflict with the elders of the Jewish community over his radical views. When he was 23 the religious authorities excommunicated him, and he was forced to move to the Hague and take up work as a lens polisher.

The area around Mr Visserplein, today a busy and dangerous junction for traffic speeding towards the IJ tunnel, contains the most tangible mementoes of the Jewish community. The brown and bulky **Portuguese Synagogue** (May–Oct daily except Sat 10am–5pm, Nov–April Mon–Fri 10am–4pm; free) was completed in 1675 by Sephardic Jews who had moved to Amsterdam from Spain and Portugal to escape the Inquisition, and who prospered here in the seventeenth and eighteenth centuries. During the war Amsterdammers kept the building under constant surveillance to ensure no harm came to it. A glance inside gives you an idea of just how wealthy the community was, the high barrel vault emphasizing the synagogue's size, the oak and jacaranda wood its riches. When it was completed the Portuguese Synagogue was the largest in the world; today the Sephardic community has dwindled to thirty or forty.

Across from the Portuguese Synagogue, the **Jewish Historical Museum** (daily 10am–4pm; closed Yom Kippur; ƒ5) is cleverly housed in a complex of High German synagogues dating from the late seventeenth century. For years after the war the buildings lay in ruins, and it's only recently that the museum was installed. In addition to photos and mementoes from the holocaust, the museum gives an introduction to Jewish beliefs and life and is one of the most modern and impressive in western Europe; it won the 1988 European Museum of the Year award. The Nieuwe Synagogue of 1752 is the starting point of the exhibition, which includes memorabilia from the long – and, until the Nazi occupation, largely unoppressed – history of Jews in The Netherlands. Inevitably, the most poignant part of the exhibition is from the war years, but the main focus of the display is the religious traditions of the Dutch community rather than the holocaust. As a lesson in how to combine ancient and modern, spiritual and historical, it's hard to beat.

Between the museum and the Portuguese Synagogue is **J.D. Meijerplein**, where a small statue marks the spot on which, in February 1941, around four hundred young Jewish men were rounded up, arrested, loaded on trucks, and taken to their eventual execution at Mauthausen in reprisal for the killing of a Nazi sympathizer in a street fight between members of the Jewish resistance and the Dutch Nazi party. The arrests sparked off the "February Strike", a general strike led by transport workers and dockers and organized by the outlawed Communist party in protest against the deportations and treatment of

the Jews. Although broken by mass arrests and some violence after only
two days, it was a demonstration of solidarity with the Jews that was
unique in occupied Europe and unusual in The Netherlands, where the
majority of people had done little to prevent or protest against the
actions of the SS. Mari Andriesson's statue of **The Dockworker** on J.D.
Meijerplein commemorates the event, but a better memorial, tinged
with Amsterdam humour, is the legendary slogan – "Keep your filthy
hands off our filthy Jews". The strike is still commemorated annually by
a wreath-laying ceremony on February 25.

Along Plantage Middenlaan

Leaving Mr Visserplein via Muiderstraat, to the right is the prim **Hortus
Botanicus** (April–Oct Mon–Fri 9am–5pm, Sat & Sun 11am–5pm; Nov–
March Mon–Fri 9am–4pm, Sat & Sun 11am–4pm; ƒ6. Guided tours
each Sunday at 2pm; call first on ☎625 8411), a pocket-sized botanical
garden whose six thousand plant species make a wonderfully relaxed
break from the rest of central Amsterdam. It's worth wandering into for
the sticky pleasures of the hot houses, its terrapins, and for the world's
oldest (and probably largest) potted plant. Stop off for coffee and cakes
in the orangery.

   Across Muiderstraat from the Hortus is Wertheimplantsoen, a small
park containing the **Auchwitz monument,** moved here from the Nieuwe
Oosterbegraafplaats in the east of the city. Designed by the Dutch
writer Jan Wolkers, it's a simple affair with symbolically broken mirrors
and a cracked urn containing the ashes of some of the Jews who died in
Buchenwald: the inscription reads *Nooit meer Auschwitz*, "Auschwitz –
Never Again". There was some consternation at the monument's unveil-
ing, when it was found to have been badly damaged. At first it was
assumed that this was the work of Fascists, and for a week or so the
papers were full of sententious editorials about the rise of right-wing
extremism in Holland; later it was discovered that the damage was done
by a disgruntled employee of the company that made the glass. The
monument is still awaiting full repair.

   Further along Plantage Middenlaan, you reach another sad relic of
the war at number 24, the **Hollandse Schouwburg**, a predominantly
Jewish theatre that after 1940 became the main assembly point for
Dutch Jews prior to their deportation to Germany. Inside, there was no
daylight and families were packed in for days in conditions that fore-
shadowed the camps. The house across the street, now a teacher training college, was used as a day nursery. Some, possibly hundreds,
managed to escape through here and a plaque outside extols the
memory of those "who saved the children". Inside, on the second floor
of the adjacent building, there's an **exhibition** (summer daily 11am–
4pm; free) on World War II and Germany's destruction of the Jews,
aimed specifically at children. There's also a history of the Hollandse
Schouwburg as a theatre: this area was once full of theatres, and the
centre of the city's theatre world.

The Hollandse Schouwburg is today little more than a shell. Its facade is still intact, but the roof has gone and what used to be the auditorium is now a quiet, grassy courtyard. A memorial – a column of basalt on a base in the form of a Star of David – stands where the stage once was. It seems understated, a failure to grasp the enormity of the crime. Off the beaten track and with few visitors, it is a temptation to the local kids, whose shouts bring an attendant from his office; a battered vending machine offers a leaflet and photographs. It's almost impossible now to imagine the scenes that went on here, but the sense of emptiness and loss is strong. If sometimes there seems to be a hollow ring to fun-loving Amsterdam, this place is why.

In the street behind, at Henri Polacklan 9, the **Trade Union Museum** (Tues–Fri 11am–5pm, Sun 1–5pm; *f*5) is a small exhibition of documents, cuttings and photos relating to the Dutch labour movement that is inevitably of fairly esoteric interest. The building. however, is worth a look. Built by Berlage in 1900 for the mainly Jewish Diamond Workers' Union, it soon became known as the "Rode Burgt" ("Red Stronghold") and includes Berlage's trademark arches, and clever use of light and space. Inside, take a look at the main hall and committee room, and the murals by the Dutch impressionist painter, R.N. Roland Holst.

For full details, see Kids' Amsterdam.

Further along Plantage Middenlaan, on the left-hand side, is the **Artis Zoo** (daily 9am–5pm; *f*18.50, children *f*11) and **Zoological Museum** where you could pass a (pricey) couple of hours.

Prins Hendrikkade and the Eastern Islands

The broad boulevard that fronts the grey waters of the Oosterdok is **Prins Hendrikkade**, a continuation of the road that leads to Stationsplein in the west and goes on deep into the docks of eastern Amsterdam. Since the city emerged as a maritime power in the sixteenth century, this strip, along with its twin to the west, served as a harbour front to the ships which carried its riches: merchant vessels brought grain from the Baltic and took diamonds, fabric and wines to the north, vastly increasing the city's importance as a market and bringing about the prosperity of the Golden Age. Today Prins Hendrikkade is a major artery for cars flowing north via the IJ tunnel, and the only ships docked here belong to the police or navy. But the road is lined with buildings that point to a more interesting nautical past.

The first of these, the squat **Schreierstoren**, was traditionally the place where, in the Middle Ages, tearful women saw their husbands off to sea (the name could be translated as "weepers' tower"), though this is probably more romantic invention than fact. A sixteenth-century inlaid stone records the emotional leave-takings, while another much more recent tablet recalls the departure of Henry Hudson from here in

1609 – the voyage on which he inadvertently discovered Manhattan. A little further along, the **Scheepvaarthuis** at Prins Hendrikkade 108 is covered inside and out with bas-reliefs and other decoration relating to the city's maritime history; it's also embellished with slender turrets and expressionistic masonry characteristic of the Amsterdam School of architecture that flourished early in this century.

Several of the houses along Prins Hendrikkade and the streets nearby have similarly impressive facades: **Kromme Waal**, opposite the Scheepvaarthuis, has a fussy collection of gables, and the building at Prins Hendrikkade 131 was once the home of Amsterdam's greatest naval hero, Admiral de Ruyter; he's depicted in a stern frieze above the door. A little further along, the wide **Oude Schans** was the main entrance to the old shipbuilding quarter, and the **Montelbaanstoren** tower that stands about halfway down was built in 1512 to protect the merchant fleet. A century later, when the city felt more secure and could afford such luxuries, it was topped with a decorative spire by Hendrik de Keyser, the architect who did much to create Amsterdam's prickly skyline.

For a drink, try the friendly De Druif, Rapenburgerplein 83.

The chief pillar of the city's wealth in the sixteenth century was the **Dutch East India Company**. Its expeditions established links with India, Sri Lanka, the Indonesian islands, and later China and Japan, using the Dutch Republic's large fleet of vessels to rob the Portuguese and Spanish of their trade and the undefended islanders of their wood and spices. Dutch expansionism wasn't purely mercantile: not only had the East India Company been given a trading monopoly in all the lands east of the Cape of Good Hope, but also unlimited military, judicial and political powers in the countries which it administered. Behind the satisfied smiles of the comfortable burghers of the golden age was a nightmare of slavery and exploitation.

The Maritime Museum

The twin warehouses where the East India Company began its operations still stand at Prins Hendrikkade 176, but a better picture of the might of Dutch naval power can be found in the **Maritime Museum** on Kattenburgerplein (Tues–Sat 10am–5pm, Sun noon–5pm; ƒ10), a well-presented display of the country's maritime past housed in a fortress-like former arsenal of the seventeenth century. Much of it seems to be an endless collection of maps, navigational equipment and weapons, though the large and intricate models of sailing ships and men-of-war that date from the same period as the original ships are impressive. A detailed English guidebook is available (necessary as all the labelling is in Dutch), and if ships and sailing are your passion you'll doubtless find the place fascinating; for the non-nautical it can be a little tedious. Best go for the highspots: a cutaway outrigger of 1840, the glitteringly ostentatious Royal Barge, and the museum's periscope for a seagull's-eye view of the city. Be sure, also, to check out the eighteenth-century East India trading ship moored outside.

Prins
Hendrikkade
and the
Eastern
Islands

The Eastern Islands

As the wealth from the colonies poured in, the old dock area to the southeast around Uilenburg was no longer able to cope, and the East India Company financed a major reclamation of, and expansion into, the marshland to the east of the existing waterfront, forming the three **Eastern Islands – Kattenburg**, **Wittenburg**, and **Oostenburg**. A ship-building industry developed, and in time the Eastern Islands became the home of a large community working in the shipfitting and dock-yard industries. The nineteenth century brought the construction of iron ships, and at a wharf at Hoogte Kadijk 147 an old shipyard is now the **Kromhout Museum** (Mon–Fri 10am–4pm; ƒ3.50, no museum-cards), a working museum which patches up ancient boats and offers a slide show that's a useful introduction to the area's history. The Kromhout was one of the few survivors of the decline in shipbuilding during the nineteenth century. It struggled along producing engines and iron ships until it closed in 1969 and was saved from demolition by being turned into this combination of industrial monument, operat-ing shipyard, and museum. Money is still tight, which means that little shipbuilding or restoring is going oŋ at the moment, but the enthusias-tic staff and good explanatory background material make this an up-and-coming place, and a useful adjunct to the nearby Maritime Museum.

Entredok,
Entrepot Dok 64,
is one of the best of
the growing
number of bars in
the
neighbourhood.

See p.166 for
details of the zoo.

In time, the shipyards of the Eastern Islands declined, the working-class neighbourhood shrank, and today there's not much to see of a once-lively community. The **Oosterkerk**, across the water from the Kromhout, was, like the East India Company building and the Maritime Museum, designed by Daniel Stalpaert; now it functions as a social and exhibition centre, part of an attempt to give back this area some of its former identity; you'll see a local newspaper on sale, and the people here still refer to themselves as "Islanders". South of the Kromhout it's worth wandering through to the **Entrepot Dok**, a line of old ware-houses, each bearing the name of a destination above its door. Recreated as hi-tech offices and apartments, and with weird animal sounds coming from the **Artis Zoo** across the way, it seems an odd sort of end for the Eastern Islands' rich maritime tradition.

See p.130

Keep going down Oostenburgergracht and you'll reach "**De Gooyer**", a windmill that dates from 1814. Once, mills were all over Amsterdam, pumping water and grinding grain; today this old corn mill is one of the few that remains, now converted into a brewery called 't IJ , though its sails still turn on the first Saturday of the month – wind permitting.

Chapter 6

The Outer Limits: South, East and West

A msterdam is a small city, and most of its residential **outer neigh-bourhoods** can be easily reached from the city centre. Of these, the **South** holds most interest, with all the major museums, the Vondelpark (a must on summer Sundays), the raucous "De Pijp" quarter and the 1930s architecture of the New South more than justifying the tram ride. As for the other districts, you'll find a good deal less reason for making the effort. The **West** is nothing special, aside from the occasional park and one lively immigrant quarter; nor is the **East**, although this does have one conceivable target in the Tropenmuseum.

The Old South: the major museums

During the nineteenth century, unable to hold its mushrooming population within the limits of its canals, Amsterdam began to expand, spreading into the neighbourhoods beyond the Singelgracht which now make up the district known as the **Old South** – a large and disparate area that includes the leafy residential quarters immediately south of Leidseplein as well as the working-class enclaves further east. Most people visit this part of Amsterdam for its role as home to some of the city's best museums, a number of which – the **Rijksmuseum**, **Van Gogh** and **Stedelijk** – are imposingly grouped around the grassy wedge of **Museumplein**, which extends south from Stadhouderskade to Van Baerlestraat. It's a bare and rather windswept open space, but in summer hosts a variety of outdoor activities, and can be a lively place for a stroll; it's also one of the city's favoured spots for demonstrations.

About halfway down, you'll see a group of slim steel blocks which commemorate the women of the wartime concentration camps, particularly Ravensbruck, where some 92,000 died through starvation, disease, or extermination. A "Vrouwen van Ravensbruck" committee organizes annual antifascist events, and the text on the right reads: "For those women who until the bitter end refused to accept fascism".

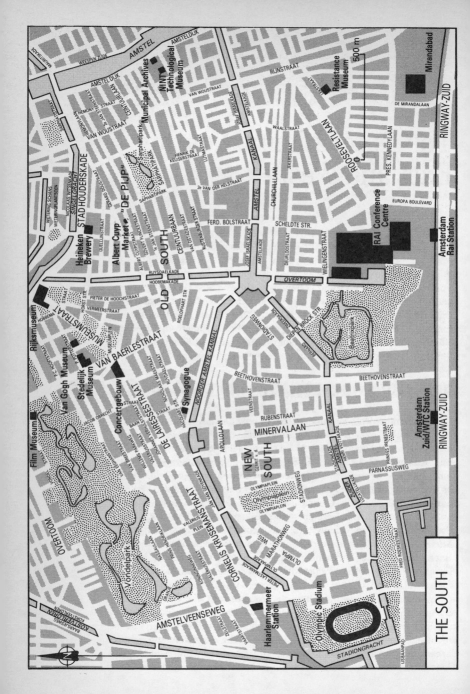

THE SOUTH

Plans for Museumplein

Plans are afoot for a rearrangement of Musemplein, and the area around
Museumstraat. The whole area will be pedestrianized, and a huge underground car park excavated, capable of containing 600 cars and 25 coaches.
Above ground, it's proposed that a large shallow pond be dug, designed to
provide a public skating rink in winter. At the moment all these ideas are still
just paperwork, but if the go-ahead is given Museumplein might be trans-
formed into an interesting city space.

The Rijksmuseum

At the head of Museumplein, facing onto Stadhouderskade and the
Singelgracht, the **Rijksmuseum** (Tues–Sat 10am–5pm, Sun 1–5pm;
f10), housed in a whimsical neo-Gothic structure built by P. J. H.
Cuijpers – the architect of Centraal Station – in 1885, is the one
museum you shouldn't leave Amsterdam without visiting, if only
briefly. Its seventeenth-century Dutch paintings constitute far and
away the best collection to be found anywhere, with twenty or so
Rembrandts alone, as well as copious arrays of works by Steen, Hals,
Vermeer and many other Dutch artists of the era – all engagingly
displayed with the layperson in mind. There are, too, representative
displays of all other pre-twentieth-century periods of Dutch and
Flemish painting, along with treasures in the medieval art and Asiatic
sections that are not to be missed. To do justice to the place demands
repeated visits; if time is limited, it's best to be content with the core
paintings and a few selective forays into other sections.

Paintings of the fifteenth and sixteenth century

Starting from the first floor shop, the eastern wing runs chronologically through the Rijksmuseum's collection of Low Countries painting.
First off are works from the early **Netherlandish Period**, when divi-
sions between present-day Holland and the Flemish south weren't as
sharp as they are today. The canvases here are stylized, commissioned
either by the church or by rich patrons who wanted to ensure a good
deal come the Day of Judgement, and thus tended to illustrate religious themes. This means they're usually full of symbols and allusions,
and set against a suitably ecclesiastical backdrop – as with the
Madonna Surrounded by Female Saints, painted by an unknown
artist referred to (after this picture) as the **Master of the Virgin
Among Virgins**. Of the artists here, though, the work of **Geertgen tot
Sint Jans** is the most striking: his *Holy Kindred*, painted around
1485, is a skilfully structured portrait of the family of Anna, Mary's
mother, that illustrates the symbolism of the period. The Romanesque
nave represents the Old Testament, the Gothic choir the New; Mary
and Joseph in the foreground parallel the figures of Adam and Eve in
the altarpiece; lit candles on the choir screen bring illumination, and
Joseph holds a lily, emblem of purity, over Mary's head. Alongside are
Geertgen's *Adoration of the Magi*, full of humility and with an

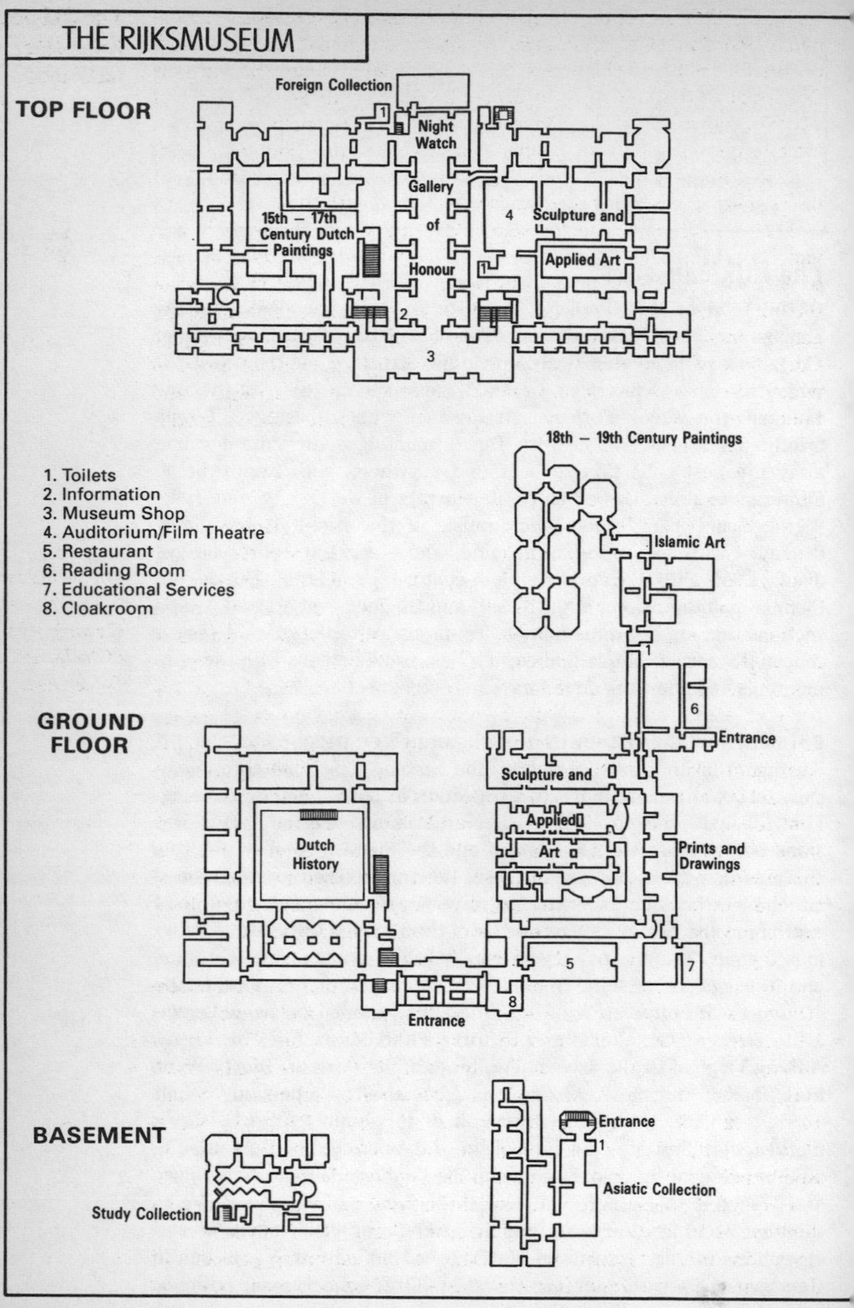

THE RIJKSMUSEUM

TOP FLOOR

Foreign Collection

1

Night
Watch

Gallery

of

15th — 17th
Century Dutch
Paintings

4   Sculpture and

Honour

Applied Art

1

2

3

1. Toilets
2. Information
3. Museum Shop
4. Auditorium/Film Theatre
5. Restaurant
6. Reading Room
7. Educational Services
8. Cloakroom

18th — 19th Century Paintings

Islamic Art

6

Entrance

GROUND FLOOR

Dutch
History

Sculpture and

Applied

Art

Prints and
Drawings

5

7

8

Entrance

BASEMENT

Entrance

1

Study Collection

Asiatic Collection

engaging fifteenth-century backdrop of processions, castles and mountains, and Jan Mostaert's *Tree of Jesse*, crammed with tumbling, dreamlike medieval characters. An even clearer picture of the Low Countries in the Middle Ages comes across in *The Seven Works of Charity*, attributed to the **Master of Alkmaar**. Originally hung in St. Laurenskerk in Alkmaar, each panel shows the charitable acts expected of those with sufficient piety (and cash): alms are doled out to the poor against a toytown landscape of medieval Alkmaar.

The rooms move into the sixteenth century with the work of **Jan van Scorel**, represented here by a voluptuous *Mary Magdalen*, next to which is his pupil **Maerten van Heemskerck's** portrait of Master of the Mint *Pieter Bicker*, shiftily counting out the cash. Further on, the gallery opens out to reveal soft, delicate compositions, most notably **Cornelis Cornelisz van Haarlem's** *Bathsheba* and *Fall of Man*, in which the artist (typically) is more concerned with the elegant and faintly erotic arrangement of his nudes than with the biblical stories that inspired them.

Paintings of the Dutch Golden Age

After this begin the classic paintings of the **Dutch Golden Age**: portraits by Hals and Rembrandt, landscapes by Jan van Goyen and Jacob van Ruisdael, the riotous scenes of Jan Steen and the peaceful interiors of Vermeer and Pieter de Hooch. First, though, are some early seventeenth-century works, including **Frans Hals'** expansive *Isaac Massa and His Wife* and more sensational paintings such as **Dirck van Baburen's** *Prometheus in Chains* – a work from the Utrecht School, which used the paintings of Caravaggio as its model. Through a small circular gallery devoted to the miniatures of Hendrik Avercamp (skating scenes mostly) and Adriaen van Ostade (grotesque peasants) are a number of thoroughly Dutch works, among them the soft, tonal river scenes of **Salomon van Ruisdael** and the cool church interiors of **Pieter Saenredam**. Search out especially Saenredam's *Old Town Hall of Amsterdam*, in which the tumbledown predecessor of the current building (now the Royal Palace) is surrounded by black-hatted townsmen in a set piece of seventeenth-century daily life.

See Contexts *for a full rundown on the major artists of the Dutch Golden Age.*

Beyond this is a mixed selection of canvases from the hands of **Jacob van Ruisdael** – Salomon's nephew but, though also a landscapist, quite different in style – and of **Rembrandt** and some of his better-known pupils. Perhaps the most striking is the *Portrait of Maria Trip*, but look, too, at Ferdinand Bol's *Portrait of Elizabeth Bas*, Govert Flinck's *Rembrandt as a Shepherd* – interesting if only for its subject – and the *Portrait of Abraham Potter* by **Carel Fabritius**, this last a restrained, skilful work painted by one of Rembrandt's most talented (and shortest-lived) students.

The next rooms take you into the latter half of the seventeenth century, and include works ranging from **Gerrit Berckheyde's** crisp depictions of Amsterdam and Haarlem, to the carousing peasants of **Jan Steen**. Steen's *Morning Toilet* is full of associations, referring either to pleasures just had or about to be taken, while his *Feast of St. Nicholas*, with its squabbling children, makes the festival a celebration of pure greed – much like the drunken gluttony of the *Merry Family* nearby. The out-of-control ugliness of *After the Drinking Bout* leaves no room for doubt about what Steen thought of all this ribaldry.

It's in the last few rooms, though, that the Dutch interior really comes into its own, with a gentle moralizing that grows ever more subtle. **Vermeer's** *The Letter* reveals a tension between servant and mistress – the lute on the woman's lap was a well-known sexual symbol of the time – and the symbolism in the use of a map behind the *Young Woman Reading a Letter* hints at the far-flung places her loved one is writing from. **Gerard ter Borch**, too, depicts apparently innocent scenes, both in subject and title, but his *Lady with a Mirror* glances in a meaningfully anxious manner at her servants, who look on with delicate irony from behind dutiful exteriors, and the innocently named *Interior Scene* is clearly taking place in a brothel. The paintings of **Pieter de Hooch** are less symbolic, more exercises in lighting, but they're as good a visual guide to the everyday life and habits of the seventeenth-century Dutch bourgeoisie as you'll find. So, too, with **Nicholas Maes**, whose *Woman Saying Grace* is not so much a moral tableau as a simple celebration of experience.

Mingling with these interior scenes are more paintings by **Hals** and **Rembrandt** – later works, for the most part, from the painters' mature periods. Hals weighs in with a handful of portraits, including the boisterous *Merry Toper*, while Rembrandt – at his most private and expressive best here – is represented by a portrait of his first wife *Saskia*, a couple of his mother, and a touching depiction of his cowled son, *Titus*. All are in marked contrast to studio mate **Jan Lievens'** stiff though perceptive *Constantin Huygens* on the opposite wall, a commissioned work if ever there was one. There was some criticism of this painting among Huygens' high-ranking friends, though Huygens himself seemed pleased enough with it, claiming that the thoughtful expression accurately "reflected the cares of my heart".

The Gallery of Honour

A small room off to the side of the last one offers an introduction to the **Gallery Of Honour** and one of the Rijksmuseum's great treasures: **Rembrandt's** *The Night Watch*, the most famous and most valuable of all the artist's pictures, recently restored after being slashed by a vandal in 1975. The painting is a so-called Civil Guard portrait, named after the bands of militia that got together in the sixteenth century to defend the home front during the wars with the Spanish. They later grew into social clubs for local dignitaries – most of whom would commission a group portrait as a mark of prestige. This painting, of the Guards of the Kloveniersdoelen in Amsterdam, was erroneously tagged *The Night Watch* in the nineteenth century – a result both of the romanticism of the age and the fact that for years the painting was covered in soot. There are other misconceptions about the painting, most notably that it was this work that led to the downward shift in Rembrandt's standing with the Amsterdam elite. In fact, there's no evidence that the militia group weren't pleased with the picture, or that Rembrandt's commissions flowed in any more slowly after he had completed it. Though not as subtle as much of the artist's later work, it's an adept piece, full of movement and carefully arranged – these paintings were collections of individual portraits as much as group pictures, and part of the problem in creating one was to include each individual face while simultaneously producing a coherent group scene. The sponsors paid for a prominent position in the painting, and the artist also had to reflect this.

The surrounding paintings also depict various companies of the Kloveniersdoelen, and they make for interesting comparison. Two are by **Bartholomeus van der Helst**: that on the left of the *Night Watch* is probably the best of the lot; it's lively and colourful, but like the other three its arrangement and lighting are static. Van der Helst's painting to the right also includes (as was usual) a self-portrait, here on the far left of the picture – as does that by **Govert Flinck**, on the top far right of his picture, and in both of his other portraits. It seems Rembrandt didn't bother with his, though art historians have been speculating for centuries about whether the pudgy face peering out from the back of the *Night Watch*, between the soldier and the gesticulating militiaman, could be the artist making a rare Hitchcockian appearance.

Elsewhere, the Gallery of Honour houses the large-scale works from the museum's collection of Dutch paintings. Some of these are notable only for their size – the selection of naval battles particularly – but a number do stand out, and would in any museum. Two of Rembrandt's better-known pupils crop up here: **Nicholas Maes**, with one of his typically intimate scenes in *Dreaming*, and **Ferdinand Bol**, both in his *Regents of the Nieuwe Zijds Workhouse* and the elegantly composed *Venus and Adonis*. The dashing *Self-portrait* is his too, a rich and successful character leaning on a sleeping cupid. By way of contrast, **Rembrandt** himself follows with a late *Self-portrait*, caught in mid-shrug as the Apostle Paul, a self-aware and defeated old man. Opposite, *The Staalmeesters* is an example of one of his later commissions and, as do so many of Rembrandt's later works, it demonstrates his ability to capture a staggering range of subtle expressions. Nearby is *The Jewish Bride*, one of his very last pictures,

---

Rembrandt's Dirty Pictures

Fans of Rembrandt will be pleased to hear that seven of his works owned by the Rijksmuseum have returned to display after a thorough restoration and cleaning that has revealed new details in some of the works. The paintings are *Portrait of Titus as a Monk*, *Self-portrait as the Apostle Paul*, *Still Life with two Red Peacocks*, *The Staalmeesters*, *The Denial of Peter*, *The Jewish Bride* and the recently purchased *Portrait of Johannes Uyttenbogaerts*.

---

finished in 1665. No one knows who the people are, nor whether they are actually married (the title came later), but the painting is one of Rembrandt's most telling, the paint dashed on freely and the hands joined lovingly in, as Kenneth Clark wrote, a "marvellous amalgam of richness, tenderness and trust".

The Foreign Collection

Tucked away in a small gallery behind the *Night Watch*, the Rijksmuseum's collection of **Foreign Paintings** is undoubtedly overshadowed by the quality of the surrounding homegrown works. Aside from a scattering of **Belgian** artists – the lusty scenes of Jordaens and the bloated pink subjects of Rubens and van Dyck – **Italian** works are the collection's mainstay. These include a beautiful embossed *Mary Magdalen* by Crivelli, a dignified *Portrait of a Nobleman* by Paolo Veronese and a couple of *Portraits* by Pietro di Cosimo. A tiny collection, and one, not surprisingly, often overlooked.

This section of the museum is closed until 1995; however, the paintings mentioned below can be found scattered throughout the other galleries.

Later Dutch Painting

To pick up chronologically where the Gallery of Honour left off, it's necessary to move down to the ground floor, where the **eighteenth- and nineteenth-century Dutch Paintings** collection begins with the work of **Cornelis Troost**, whose eighteenth-century comic scenes earned him the dubiously deserved title of the "Dutch Hogarth". More enduring are the later pictures, notably the pastels of Pierre-Paul Prud'hon & Jan Ekels' *The Writer* – small and simple, the lighting and attention to detail imitative of Vermeer.

After this, rooms follow each other in haphazard fashion, with sundry landscapes and portraiture from the lesser nineteenth-century artists. **Jongkind** is the best of the bunch, his murky *River Landscape in France* typical of the Impressionism that was developing in the nineteenth century. The chief proponents of Dutch Impressionism originated from or worked in The Hague, and the handy label of the **Hague School** covers a variety of styles and painters who shared a clarity and sensitivity in their depiction of the Dutch landscape. Of the major Hague School painters, the Rijksmuseum is strongest on the work of **Jan Weissenbruch**, whose land- and seascapes, such as *View near the Geestbrug*, hark back to the compositional techniques of van Ruisdael and the **Maris Brothers**. Jacob Maris' sultry landscapes are the most representative of the School, while the younger Willem Maris' work is more direct and approachable – his *Ducks* being a good example. **Anton Mauve** is similar, filling such pictures as *Morning Ride on the Beach* with shimmering gradations of tone that belie the initial simplicity of the scene.

While members of the Hague School were creating gentle landscapes, a younger generation of Impressionist painters working in Amsterdam – the **Amsterdam School** – was using a darker palette to capture city scenes. By far the most important picture from this turn-of-the-century group is **G. H. Breitner's** *Singelbrug near*

Paleisstraat in Amsterdam, a random moment in the street recorded and framed with photographic dispassion. Breitner worked best when turning his attention to rough, shadowy pictures of the city as in *Rokin* and *Damrak*. Isaac Israëls' work is lighter in tone and mood, with canvases likr *Donkey Rides on the Beach* showing how close he was to the French Impressionists of the period.

Dutch History

The Dutch history section starts promisingly with exhibitions depicting aspects of life in the Golden Age, and not surprisingly focuses on the naval might that brought Holland its wealth. Fearsome model ships impress, but more revealing of everyday life are the maritime odds and ends from the *Witte Leeuw*, an East Indian vessel that sank in 1613 laden with a cargo of pepper and Chinese porcelain. The galleries off this room, however, are for the most part uninspired, filled with relics of Holland's naval and colonial past. The prize for the most conspicuous exhibit goes to Willem Pieneman for his painting of the *Battle of Waterloo*, a vast canvas that took six years to complete. All the big names of the battle are there (the artist spent two years on the portrait studies alone) but nevertheless it's a laboured and rather arid piece.

Sculpture and Applied Art

The Rijksmuseum has a huge amount of applied art, so unless your tastes are eclectic it's wise to restrict yourself to a single period: easily the most impressive is the first-floor collection of Medieval and Renaissance applied art. Beginning with a handful of Byzantine trinkets and Limoges enamels, the collection leads off the main hall with the magnificent *Ten Mourners*, sensitive fifteenth-century figures taken from the tomb of Isabelle de Brabant in Antwerp. Contemporaneous with these is the fifteenth-century carving, especially the work of Adriaen van Wesel of Utrecht, whose scenes (for example, the *Meeting of the Magi*) are packed with vigour and expression. Look out, too, for the *Anna te Drieën*, carvings of the infant Jesus with Mary and her mother Anna – a popular grouping in the Low Countries at this time.

Other galleries here are stuffed from floor to ceiling with delftware, the blue-and-white ceramics to which Delft gave its name in the seventeenth century. The original designs were stylized copies of Chinese ceramics imported by the Dutch East Indies Company, but the patterns quickly fell into the domestic traditions of landscapes, animals and comic figures. By the early years of the eighteenth century, Delft's craftspeople had become confident enough to create vases, jars and even musical intruments, in polychrome as well as the traditional blue and white. Examples of each and every period are here, but you'll need an inexhaustable interest to cope with so large a collection.

Of the rest, much of the ground floor is a warehouse of furniture, ceramics and textiles from the sixteenth century on: it's dull beyond belief, with only the dolls' houses providing diversion.

The Old South:
the major
museums

*This section of the
museum is closed
until 1995;
however, the
works mentioned
below can be
found scattered
throughout the
other galleries.*

The Asiatic Collection

Holland's colonial connection with the East means that Asian art can
be found in most of the museums' collections, but the Asian collection
proper holds its most prized treasures. Of the different cultures, China
and Japan are best represented: the striking twelfth-century *Statue of
Avalokiteshvara* and graceful *Paintings* by Kao Ch'i-p'ei, drawn with
his fingernails, are highlights of the Chinese collection, while the
seventeenth-century ceramics and lacquerwork are the best of the
Japanese. If you're interested, you'll find much more, from twelfth-
century Indonesian gold jewellery to Cambodian carving. An excellent
collection, and one to linger over.

The Rijksmuseum Vincent Van Gogh

Vincent van Gogh is arguably the most popular, most reproduced and
most talked about of all modern artists, so it's not surprising that the
Rijksmuseum Vincent Van Gogh (Tues–Sat 10am–5pm, Sun 1–5pm;
f 10), opened in 1973 and comprising the extensive collection of the
artist's art-dealer brother Theo, is Amsterdam's top tourist attraction.
Housed in an angular building designed by the aged Gerritt Rietveld,
it's a gentle and unassuming introduction to the man and his art – and
one which, due both to the quality of the collection and the building,
succeeds superbly well.

The museum starts with a group of works by van Gogh's better-
known friends and contemporaries, many of whom influenced his work
– Gauguin, Emile Bernard, Adolph Monticelli and others. It moves on
to the works of the man himself, for the most part chronologically. The
first go back to the artist's early years in Nuenen, southern Holland,
where he was born: dark, sombre works for the most part, ranging
from an assortment of drab grey and brown *Still Lifes* to the gnarled
faces and haunting, flickering light of *The Potato Eaters* – one of van
Gogh's best-known paintings, and the culmination of hundreds of studies of the local peasantry.

Across the hall, the sobriety of these early works is easily trans-
posed on to the Parisian urban landscape, particularly in his *View of
Paris*, where the city's domes and rooftops hover below Montmartre
under a glowering, blustery sky. But before long, under the sway of
fellow painters and, after the bleak countryside of North Brabant and
the sheer colour of the city itself, his approach began to change. This
is most noticeable in the views of Montmartre windmills, a couple of
self-portraits, and the pictures from Asnières just outside Paris, where
the artist used to travel regularly to paint. Look also at *A Pair of
Shoes*, a painting that used to hang in the house van Gogh shared with
Gauguin in Arles, at *Woman in the Café Tambourin* (actually a
portrait of the owner, with whom the artist was friendly), and at the
dazzling movement of *Edge of a Wheatfield*.

In February 1888, van Gogh moved to Arles, inviting Gauguin to
join him a little later. With the change of scenery came a heightened

interest in colour, and the predominance of yellow as a recurring motif: it's represented best in such paintings as *Van Gogh's Bedroom* and the *Harvest at La Crau*, and most vividly in *The Yellow House*. A canvas from the artist's *Sunflowers* series is justly one of his most lauded works, intensely, almost obsessively, rendered in the deepest oranges, golds and ochres he could find. Gauguin told of van Gogh painting these flowers in a near trance, and there were usually sunflowers in jars all over their house.

At the asylum in **St. Remy**, where van Gogh committed himself after snipping off part of his ear and offering it to a local prostitute, nature took a more abstract form in his work: trees bent into cruel, sinister shapes, skies coloured purple and yellow, as in the *Garden of St Paul's Hospital*. Van Gogh is at his most expressionistic here, the paint applied thickly – often with a palette knife, especially in the final, tortured paintings done at **Auvers**, including *Undergrowth*, *The Reaper*, or *Wheatfield with Crows*, in which the fields swirl and writhe under black, moving skies. It was a few weeks after completing this last painting that van Gogh shot and fatally wounded himself.

On the second floor, the museum shows a revolving selection from its vast stock of van Gogh's **drawings**, notebooks and letters, and also affords space to relevant temporary exhibitions. The top floor is used as a **temporary exhibition space** year round, usually showing works loaned from other galleries that illustrate the artistic influences on van Gogh, or his own influence on other artists. As well as the usual post-cards, the museum **shop** sells large prints of the more famous paintings for around *f*7; ask for a strong triangular box (*f*2) to protect your purchase.

The Stedelijk Museum

Despite its reputation as Amsterdam's number one venue for modern art, the **Stedelijk Museum** (daily 11am–5pm; *f*7.50) can be a bit of a disappointment. True, its temporary exhibitions are often of world renown, and worth catching if you happen to be in town, but the museum is primarily devoted to displays of contemporary art on loan. Should you want to see something of its extensive permanent collection (impressively complete from the nineteenth century onwards) you'll need to be here in the summer, when the museum's holdings are shown through much of July and August. However, with a new director now in charge, this policy may change.

This said, the Stedelijk *is* the city's most important contemporary art exhibition space. The **ground floor** is usually given over to at least a couple of temporary exhibits, often by living European artists (some, though not all, from the museum's own stock), as is the bright two-storey **extension** at the back. Justifiably, current Dutch art often gets a thorough showing (as it does at the nearby *Museum Overland*), so keep an eye out for the work of such painters as Jan Dibbets, Rob Scholte, and Marlene Dumas.

The Old South: the major museums

Of the museum's **permanent collection**, there's always a good (rotating) smattering hanging on the **first floor**. Briefly, and broadly, this starts off with drawings by Picasso, Matisse and their contemporaries, and moves on to paintings by major Impressionists – Manet, Monet, Bonnard – and Post-Impressionists: Ensor, van Gogh, and Cezanne. Farther on, Mondrian holds sway, from the early, muddy-coloured abstractions to the cool, boldly coloured rectangular blocks for which he's most famous. Similarly, Kasimir Malevich is well represented, his dense attempts at Cubism leading to the dynamism and bold, primary tones of his "Suprematist" paintings – slices, blocks and bolts of colour that shift around as if about to resolve themselves into some complex computer graphic. You may find a good stock of Marc Chagall's paintings (the museum owns a wide selection of his work), and a number of pictures by American Abstract Expressionists Mark Rothko, Ellsworth Kelly, and Barnett Newman. Jean Dubuffet, too, with his swipes at the art establishment, may well have a profile, and you might catch Matisse's large cutout, *The Parakeet and the Mermaid*.

Two additional large-scale attractions are on the ground floor – Karel Appel's *Bar* in the foyer, installed for the opening of the Stedelijk in the 1950s, and the same artist's wild daubings in the museum's restaurant. But perhaps the single most interesting permanent exhibit is Ed Kienholz's *Beanery* (1965) in the basement of the museum: modelled on his local bar in Los Angeles, in this tableau the clock-faced figures, the hum of conversation, and the music create a nervous, claustrophobic background to the horror of the newspaper headline in the vending machine – "Children Kill Children in Vietnam Riots". For Kienholz, this is *real* time, and that inside the bar is "surrealist time . . . where people waste time, lose time, escape time, ignore time".

The Old South: the Vondelpark, De Pijp and the Heineken Brewery

Five minutes' walk west of Museumplein, the **Vondelpark** is the city's most enticing park. Named after the seventeenth-century poet Joost van der Vondel, and funded by local residents, it was landscaped in the latter part of the last century in the English style, with a bandstand and an emphasis on nature rather than on formal gardens. Today it's a regular forum for drama and other performance arts in the summer, and at weekends young Amsterdam flocks here in force to meet friends, laze by the lake, buy trinkets from the flea markets that spring up in the area or listen to music – in June, July and August bands give free concerts here every Sunday at 2pm.

At the park's bottom right-hand corner there's a fine neo-Gothic church by Cuijpers, as well as the **Netherlands Film Museum** (Mon–Fri 3–9.30pm, Sat–Sun 4–9.30pm; free. Library & documentation centre Tues–Sat 11am–5pm; ƒ2.50. Film shows daily 4–9.30pm; specific times vary; ƒ8.50), housed in a pavilion near the Vondelstraat entrance.

Essentially, this is a showcase for obscure films on a variety of subjects – not always Dutch and usually organized by theme. The library has a well-catalogued collection of books, magazines and journals, some in English, but the museum is really worth visiting only if the movies being shown seem appealing. Check the usual listings sources for details, and look out for the Sunday market outside the museum – a dozen or so stalls selling books and posters about films past and present.

The area around the Vondelpark is one of Amsterdam's better-heeled residential districts, with designer shops and delicatessens along chic **P. C. Hooftstraat** and **Van Baerlestraat**, and some of the city's fancier hotels (and plenty of its cheaper ones, too) on their connecting streets. On Van Baerlestraat, at the bottom end of Museumplein, is the **Concertgebouw**, completed in 1883 and renowned for its marvellous acoustics and its famed – and much recorded – resident orchestra. The building was given a major £12 million facelift a few years ago following the discovery that the wooden piles on which it rested were rotting, causing subsidence. The foyer has been moved around to the side, housed in a new, largely glass wing which contrasts nicely with the redbrick and stone of the rest of the building.

De Pijp and around

The Old South isn't all culture, however; nor is it all wealthy. Walking east from Museumplein, across Hobbemakade, you enter the busy heart of the Old South, known as **"De Pijp"** ("The Pipe") after its long, sombre canyons of brick tenements that went up in the nineteenth century as the city grew out of its canal-girded centre. The population here is densely packed, much of it made up of immigrants, and De Pijp has always been one of the city's closest-knit communities – and one of its liveliest. A few years ago it was forced to absorb some of the worst residue of Amsterdam's heroin-dealing trouble spots (those which were "cleaned up" in the tourist-conscious city centre by the police), and despite several big roundups and raids, and a higher than usual police presence, the selling of stolen goods and heroin dealing still goes on in many coffee shops. But it's still a cheerful area, its hub the long slim thoroughfare of **Albert Cuypstraat**, whose daily general **market** – which stretches for about a mile between Ferdinand Bolstraat and Van Woustraat – is the largest in the city, with a huge array of stalls selling meat, fish, cheeses, buckets of olives, cheap clothes, and anything else you're prepared to seek out. Watch out, too, for the bargain-basement and ethnic shops which flank it on each side, and check out the Indian and Surinamese restaurants – they're often cheaper than their equivalents in the city centre.

A few blocks south of the Albert Cuyp market, there's the small but pretty **Sarphatipark**, while beyond, the **Municipal Archives**, by the river at Amsteldijk 67 (Mon–Fri 8.45am–4.45pm, Sat 9am–12.15pm; free) holds regular exhibitions on subjects related to the city's history – although extensive research facilities are its chief concern. Starting

Keyser, van Baerlestraat 96, is a long-established and elegant place for a quick drink or a full meal.

For details on how to get Concertgebou tickets, see Nightlife.

Saray Lokantasi, G. Doustraat 33, is a great local Turkish eatery.

The Old South: the Vondelpark, De Pijp and the Heineken Brewery

with Count Floris V's grant of toll privileges to the city in 1275 (the oldest document to mention Amsterdam by name), the Archives have a mass of material on the city; perhaps the most interesting is the photo collection, documenting changes to each of Amsterdam's streets from the nineteenth century on. All births, marriages and deaths on record from the early sixteenth century are here, and there's an extensive array of newspapers, posters, and Amsterdam-related ephemera.

Perhaps more interesting, especially if you have kids in tow, is the **NINT Technological Museum**, Tolstraat 129; for full details, see "Museums" in *Kids' Amsterdam*.

The Heineken Brewery

On the northern edge of De Pijp, on the corner of Stadhouderskade and Ferdinand Bolstraat, the **Heineken Brewery** (Mon–Fri 9.30am, 11am, 1pm, 2.30pm and in summer only 4.30pm; ƒ2) remains one of the city's best-known sights. Although the brewery recently stopped production, and has mostly been demolished, it's still interesting to explore the old plant, viewing aspects of the beer-making process. Afterwards, you are given snacks and free beer, and the atmosphere is convivial – as you'd imagine when there are 200 people downing as much free beer as they can drink. Whether you have just one, or drink yourself into a stupor, it's a diverting way to get a lunchtime aperitif.

The New South

There's little else to detain you in the Old South, and you'd be better off either walking or catching a tram down into the New South – a real contrast to its neighbour and the first properly planned extension to the city since the concentric canals of the seventeenth century. The Dutch architect H. P. Berlage was responsible for the overall plan, but he died before it could be started and the design was largely carried out in the 1930s by two prominent architects of the Amsterdam School, Michael de Klerk and Piet Kramer. De Klerk and Kramer were already well known for their housing estates in west and southeast Amsterdam, and Kramer had also been responsible for the distinctive lettering design on the city's bridges. Cutbacks in the city's subsidy led them to tone down the more imaginative aspects of the scheme, and most of the buildings are markedly more sober than previous Amsterdam School works (such as the Scheepvaarthuis on Prins Hendrikade). But otherwise they followed Berlage faithfully, sticking to the architect's plan of wide boulevards and crooked sidestreets (a deliberate attempt to achieve the same combination of monumental grandeur and picturesque scale as the great seventeenth-century canals), and adding the odd splash of individuality to corners, windows and balconies.

Nowadays the New South is one of Amsterdam's most sought-after addresses. **Apollolaan**, **Stadionweg** and, a little way east, **Churchillaan**, especially, are home to luxury hotels and some of the city's most sumptuous properties, huge idiosyncratic mansions set back from the street behind trees and generous gardens. **Beethovenstraat**, the main street of the New South, is a fashionable shopping boulevard, with high-priced, slightly staid stores catering for the district's wealthy residents.

The New South achieved a brief period of notoriety in 1969, too, when John Lennon and Yoko Ono staged their famous week-long "Bed-In" for peace in the **Amsterdam Hilton** at Apollolaan 138. The press came from all over; fans crowded outside, hanging on the couple's antiwar proclamations, and the episode was seen as the beginning of John and Yoko's subsequent campaign for worldwide peace. Rather exploitatively, the suite they stayed in has recently been decorated with Beatles memorabilia, and rents out for around £500 a night.

Umeno, Agamamnou-straat 27, is a reasonably priced Japanese restaurant just off Stadionweg

The New South and World War II

It's hard to believe that once there were few takers for the apartments down here, and that soon after it was finished the area had become a second ghetto for Jews fleeing the terror in Nazi Germany. The Frank family, for example, lived in the South, on Merwedeplein, and there's a whimsical brick **synagogue** on Jacob Obrechtplein, built in the Expressionist style of the 1930s.

If you can read Dutch, the Jewish novel *Tramhalte Beethovenstraat* by Grete Weil will give you a candid picture of the years of occupation in this part of the city. Otherwise, the New South still has plenty of reminders of the war period, when it was the scene of some of the Nazis' worst excesses. The bedraggled **trio** at the intersection of Apollolaan and Beethovenstraat was sculpted to commemorate the reprisal shooting of 29 people on this spot in 1944. The **school** on Gerrit van der Veenstraat, itself named after an Amsterdam resistance fighter who was shot for organizing false identity papers for Jews and attacking Nazi strongholds in the city, was once headquarters of the Gestapo – and where the Frank family were brought after their capture. The former synagogue at Lekstraat 63 houses the excellent **Resistance Museum** (*Versetmuseum*; Tues–Fri 10am–5pm, Sat & Sun 1–5pm; ƒ4.50), charting the rise of the resistance from the German invasion of The Netherlands in May 1940 to the country's liberation in 1945. The fascinating collection includes photos, illegal newsletters, anti-Jewish propaganda and deportation orders, and also generates interest by being interactive: slide shows and radio broadcasts start at the touch of a button, while mock-up hiding places and prison cells complete with piped-in prison sounds recreate some of the horrors faced by Dutch resistance fighters. The museum is primarily designed for those too young to have first-hand knowledge of the period, and though purists may balk at the gimmickry, its aim of revealing the brutality and thoroughness with which the Wehrmacht forces routed resistance members is forcefully achieved. The English exhibition guide, available for ƒ1.50, is essential.

The Southern Reaches

At the opposite end of Beethovenstraat, the dense trees and shrubs of the **Beatrixpark** flank the antiseptic surroundings of the adjacent **RAI exhibition centre**: a complex of trade and conference centres which was built as part of the city's plan to attract more business people to Amsterdam – along with their considerable expense accounts. It's of little general appeal (though one hall very sporadically hosts concerts), but if you're at a loose end you may find one of its many exhibitions interesting. The **Olympic Stadium**, built for the 1928 games, though currently under threat of demolition, is a useful landmark; just north of it is the **Haarlemmermeer Station**, terminus of a summer museum tram – the Museum Tramline – which runs several times a day to the Amsterdamse Bos further south, technically outside the city limits in Amstelveen (one way ticket ƒ2.50, return ƒ4). See *Kids' Amsterdam* for details.

New San Kong, Amstelveenseweg 338–344, is an excellent Chinese restaurant, with good dim sum.

The Amsterdamse Bos

The **Amsterdamse Bos** is the city's largest open space, a 2000-acre woodland park planted during the 1930s in a mammoth project to utilize the energies of the city's unemployed. Once a bleak area of flat, marshy fields, it combines a rural feel with that of a well-tended city park. The Bosbaan, a 1km-long canal in the north of the park, is used for boating and swimming; there are children's playgrounds and spaces for various sports, including ice skating; there's a reserve in the south containing bison and buffalo; or you can simply jog your way around a choice of fourteen planned trails. If it's out of season or you're not into old trams, take one of the buses (#170, #171, #172) which run directly from Stationsplein. Once there, the best way to get around is to hire a bicycle (March–Oct) from the main entrance on Van Nijenrodeeweg and follow the 27 miles of path. It's also possible to hire canoes, canal bikes and motorboats. The **Bosmuseum** on Koenenkade (daily 10am–5pm; free), a few kilometres along the Bosbaan from the main entrance, has maps and basic information on the park's facilities, as well as an exhibition on its history and its contemporary role.

The East

A cupolated box splattered with graffiti and topped with a crudely carved pediment, the sturdy **Muiderpoort** marks the boundary between the centre of Amsterdam and the beginning of Amsterdam **East**.

The Tropenmuseum

Across the canal the gabled and turreted **Royal Tropen Institute** – a more respectable label for what was once home of the Royal Colonial Institute – has a marble and stucco entrance hall which you can peek into, though the only part open to visitors is the excellent

Tropenmuseum, just around the corner at Linnaeusstraat 2 (Mon–Fri 10am–5pm, Sat–Sun noon–5pm; ƒ7.50). As part of the Institute, this used to display only artefacts from the Dutch colonies. Since the 1950s, however, when Indonesia was granted independence, it has collected applied arts from all over and its holdings now cover the world. Most of the collection is on permanent exhibit and is imaginatively displayed through a variety of media – slides, videos and tapes. All of this makes for an impressively unstuffy exposition of contemporary Third World life and problems – both urban, covering the ever-expanding slum dwellings of cities such as Bombay, and rural, examining such issues as the dangerous wholesale destruction of the world's tropical rainforests. The best sections are those devoted to Africa, India and (not surprisingly) Indonesia, but it's really all worth seeing, even if you have little interest in ethnography. Also, have a look in on the **bookshop**, which has a good selection of books on Third World subjects, the popular **restaurant** which features dishes from many countries at reasonable prices (book a table on ☎568 8200), and the **Soeterijn Theatre** downstairs, which specializes in cinema, music and dance from a non-Western or political angle (see *Nightlife*). Kids might be interested in the **TM Junior Museum** – see *Kids' Amsterdam*.

The Oosterpark and east

Behind the Tropen Institute, the **Oosterpark** is a peaceful oblong of green, and a gentle introduction to the area, which extends south and east – a solidly working-class district for the most part, particularly on the far side of Linnaeustraat. There's a high immigrant presence here, and the street names – Molukkenstraat, Madurastraat, Javaplein – are

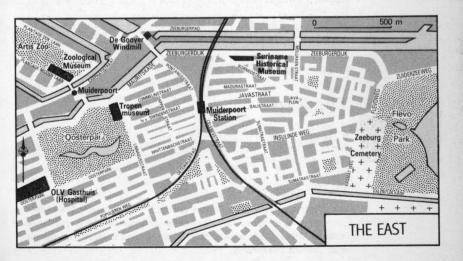

THE EAST

reminiscent of Holland's colonial past, an era which, after the war, ended in defeat and humiliation as the Dutch struggled to hang on to territories they were in no position to defend.

Today the housing is still relatively poor, though there's ambitious urban renewal going on, and many of the ageing terraced houses have been torn down to make way for new and better-equipped public housing. As in the Old South, there's an underlying drug problem in this area, but while you're unlikely to need (or want) to come out here, it's by no means a forbidding district. Two things which may make you decide to visit (apart from the Zeeburg campsite) are the **Dapperstraat market** – a kind of Eastern equivalent to the Albert Cuyp – and, at the end of tram routes #3 and #10, the **Flevopark**, dull in itself but giving access to the IJsselmeer and patches of Dutch countryside right out of Ruisdael. Just in front, the drab **Zeeburg Jewish cemetery** was once the city's major burial place for impoverished Jews, but few graves remain today.

A couple of museums in this part of town you might look in on: first is the **Netherlands Press Museum**, housed in the International Institute for Social History at Cruquiusweg 31 (Mon–Fri 9.30am–5pm, Sat 9.30am–1pm; free), although its displays on the history of the Dutch press since 1903, as revealed in newspapers, leaflets, posters and political cartoons, are of pretty specialized interest. The collection of the Institute itself will be of interest to students of the working class movement and international socialism, with original letters and writings of Marx, Lenin, Bakhunin and other left-wing (and anarchist) luminaries. Secondly the **Suriname Historical Museum** (Mon–Sat 10am–5pm, Sun noon–5pm; ƒ5) at Zeeburgerdijk 21 gives an impression of the old and new Surinam, which in 1975 became the last major colony to be relinquished by the Dutch. Surinamers form a high proportion of the Netherlands' ex-colonial immigrants, and the high incidence of unemployment among them, along with the fact that some turn to drug dealing, has made them the target of racist attacks. The common vernacular tag of "Suris" has the same underlying racist slur as the English "Pakis".

The West

Of all Amsterdam's outer central districts, Amsterdam West is probably the least interesting for the visitor, primarily a residential area with only a couple of nondescript parks as possible attractions. There's the **Old West**, whose busy Turkish and North African immigrant-based streetlife can be worth checking out if you find yourself in the vicinity: **Kinkerstraat** is a good place to bargain-hunt if you're not after anything fancy, and there's also the vigorous **ten Katestraat market**, about halfway down Kinkerstraat on the right. Outside of this zone, in the districts of Bos en Lommer and Overtoomse Veld, there's little other than the large but on the whole mediocre **Rembrandtpark** to draw you out this far.

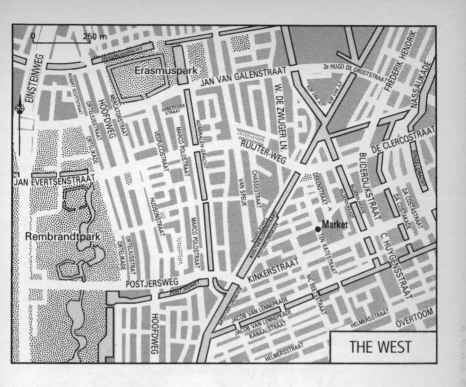

Amsterdam: Listings

Chapter 7

Accommodation

Unless you're camping, **accommodation** in Amsterdam is a major expense: even hostels are pricy for what you get, and hotels are among the most expensive in Europe. The city's size means that you'll inevitably end up somewhere central, but you'll still need to search hard to find a bargain. At peak periods throughout the year – July and August, Easter, Christmas – it's advisable to book ahead of time; rooms can be swallowed up remarkably quickly, especially during the summer. You can reserve rooms in advance from abroad at no extra charge by contacting the *National Booking Centre*, PO Box 404, 2260 AK Liedschendam, The Netherlands (☎070/320 25 00; fax ☎070/320 26 11). Once in The Netherlands, VVV's all over the country will make advance hotel reservations for a ƒ3.50 fee, as will the VVV in Amsterdam (see "Information and Maps" in *Basics*, for

Amsterdam locations and opening times); they will also book accommodation on the spot for the same fee, or simply sell you a booklet on hotels in Amsterdam for ƒ2.50. Note that all tram line directions given below are from Centraal Station.

Hostels

The bottom line for most travellers is taking a dormitory bed in a **hostel**, and there are plenty to choose from official IYHF places, unofficial private hostels, even Christian youth hostels; in fact you'll probably be accosted outside the train station with numerous offers of beds. Most hostels expect you to provide your own sleeping bag (bed linen is often available for a small fee), and many, for security reasons, lock guests out of the dormitories for a short period each day and set some kind of nightly curfew– though it's usually late enough not to be a problem. The cheapest deal you'll find is around ƒ18 per person a night (at the *Sleep-In*); prices rise sharply at better-furnished and more central hostels to an average somewhere between ƒ20 and ƒ30. If you want a little extra privacy, many of these also offer triples, doubles and singles for much less than you'd pay in a regular hotel, though their rates rarely include breakfast, which hotel rates generally do.

Official youth hostels

Stadsdoelen, Kloveniersburgwal 97; ☎624 68 32. The closest of the two official hostels to the station (on the edge of the Red Light district), and with slightly more

Accommodation

inviting dorms than its rival, although there are no double rooms. Beds go for ƒ26.50 a head (rising to ƒ29 in July and August), including breakfast; there's a ƒ5 discount on these prices for IYHF members. The bar serves good-value, if basic food, and there's a 2am curfew. Open March–Dec and for a week around New Year. Tram #4, #9, #14, #16, #24, #25, or the metro to Nieuwmarkt.

Vondel Park, Zandpad 5; ☎683 17 44. For facilities, the better of the two official hostels, with a bar, restaurant, TV lounge and kitchen; it's also well located for the summer events in the park and has the advantage of being bookable in advance from other city youth hostels. The only disadvantage is that in July and August only IYHF members are allowed in. Rates are also ƒ30.50 per person, including breakfast, with a ƒ5 discount for IYHF members; use of secure lockers costs 25c. Double rooms cost ƒ90 and upwards. Curfew 2am. Tram #1, #2, #5.

Christian youth hostels

Eben Haezer, Bloemstraat 179; ☎624 47 17. Don't be put off: though you may be given a booklet on Jesus, and the slogans on the walls may not be the ones you'd put up on yours, Amsterdam's two Christian youth hostels aren't evangelical, but simply provide neat, clean dormitories for rock-bottom prices – ƒ15 per person including bed linen and a hearty breakfast; there's also a refundable deposit of ƒ10 for a locker. Curfew 1am on weekends; age limit 35, though this is negotiable. Tram #13, #14, #17.

The Shelter, Barndesteeg 21; ☎625 32 30. Smack in the middle of the Red Light district, this is the less appealing of the two, though it's within walking distance of Centraal Station. Rates (breakfast included), curfew, and age limit are the same as *Eben Haezer*. Metro stop Nieuwmarkt.

Other hostels

Adam and Eva, Sarphatistraat 105; ☎624 62 06. Outside the centre but virtually opposite Weesperplein metro and tram stops #6 or #10. Dorm beds ƒ21.50, not including breakfast.

Arrive, Haarlemmerstraat 65; ☎622 14 39. A recently spruced-up hostel which has dorm beds for ƒ40, single rooms for ƒ75 and doubles for ƒ100 – essentially real hotel prices. Bed linen and breakfast included. Ten minutes walk from Centraal Station.

Boatel Amstel, Pier 5, De Ruyterkade; ☎626 42 47. The only survivor of a number of barge hotels which used to be moored behind Centraal Station, most are now closed due to fire risks. This was always the largest and best known, and still makes for a cheap and central place to stay. Prices range from ƒ68 for a double room with private shower and toilet. All private rooms have a phone and TV; all prices include breakfast.

Bob's Youth Hostel, Nieuwe Zijds Voorburgwal 92; ☎623 00 63. An old favourite of backpackers, this has small, clean dorms for ƒ20 per person including breakfast in the coffee shop on the ground floor; the curfew is 3.30am. A short, 5–10 min walk from Centraal Station.

Euphemia, Fokke Simonszstraat 1; ☎622 9045. Well situated – a short walk from Leidseplein and the Riksmuseum/Van Gogh museums – Euphemia has a likeable laid-back atmosphere: rooms are big and basic, with free showers and TVs, and prices are very reasonable, which means it's usually full. Doubles ƒ85, three-bedded rooms ƒ40 per person, four-bedded ƒ30 per person. Tram #16, #24, #25.

Hans Brinker, Kerkstraat 137; ☎622 06 87. Another well-established Amsterdam hostel, though more upmarket than most of the others, with dorm beds going for ƒ38.50, singles for ƒ73 and doubles for ƒ103 – breakfast included. The facilities are good, but at these prices you may as well go for an ordinary hotel. Tram #1, #2, #5.

Kabul, Warmoesstraat 38–42; ☎623 71 58. Reasonable dorm rates (ƒ23), with singles at ƒ67 and doubles at ƒ79; triples and four-bedded rooms are available too. Also on the plus side, there's no lockout or curfew, it's an easy walk from the station, and there's a late-opening bar next door. Breakfast ƒ6 extra.

Keizersgracht, Keizersgracht 15; ☎625 13 64. Terrific location close to the station, with singles for ƒ60, doubles for ƒ105 and upwards, and a good mixture of triples and four-bedded rooms from ƒ40 per person. Spotless rooms, although breakfast is extra.

Last Waterhole, Oude Zijds Armsteeg 12; ☎ 644 48 14. Long-established Amsterdam dosshouse with beds in large and fairly unprepossessing dorms for about ƒ25, breakfast not included. Handy for the station, though.

Meeting point, Warmoesstraat 14; ☎627 74 99. Central city hostel with space in ten-bed dorms going for ƒ25 per person, breakfast not included. Close to Centraal Station.

Sleep-In,'s -Gravesandestraat 51; ☎694 74 44. A little way out of the centre, but the city's cheapest accommodation with beds at ƒ17.50 per person, ƒ22.50 for less crowded dorms, doubles for ƒ80 plus ƒ40 deposit, though these prices don't include breakfast. Lockers are available for ƒ10 deposit, refunded on leaving. Dorms are enormous, and facilities include a bar, restaurant and information centre. Concerts on Wednesday, Thursday and Friday, films on Tuesday, and a weekly dance night on Friday and Saturday complete a full list of activities. Also, around 600 beds means you're unlikely to be turned away. Open year-round, but closed between noon and 4pm. Can also take wheelchairs. Weesperplein metro or tram #6.

Hotels

Apart from a couple of ultra-cheap places, most of Amsterdam's **hotels** start at around ƒ75 for a double, and although a filling Dutch breakfast is normally included at all but the most expensive places, some middle-range hotels can give the barest value for money. There are exceptions, but don't be afraid to ask to see the room first – and to refuse it if you don't like it.

The hotels here are divided by price and listed alphabetically; we've also included a list of gay hotels. Many hotels in Amsterdam are run by gays, and, although by no means are all exclusively gay, the ones in our list are those that have a predominantly gay clientele and/or are situated in the main gay

areas. Unless otherwise stated, the prices quoted are for the cheapest rooms in high season (without private bath), including breakfast; most places have cheaper off-season prices.

Inexpensive hotels (ƒ110 and under)

Abba, Overtoom 122; ☎618 30 58. Well-worn but clean rooms above a garage on the very busy Overtoom. Doubles ƒ105. Tram #2, #6.

De Admiraal, Herengracht 563; ☎626 21 50. Friendly hotel just off Rembrandtsplein. Doubles from ƒ95. Tram #4, #9.

Aspen, Raadhuisstraat 31; ☎626 67 14. One of a number of budget hotels on Raadhuisstraat, with doubles from ƒ85, not including breakfast. Tram #13, #14, #17.

Asterisk, Den Texstraat 16; ☎626 23 96. Good-value budget hotel on the edge of the city centre, just across the canal from the Heineken Brewery, with some doubles from ƒ90. Tram #6, #7, #10.

Bema, Concertgebouwplein 19b; ☎679 13 96. Small but friendly place, handy for concerts and museums. Doubles from ƒ85. Tram #3, #5, #12.

Beursstraat, Beursstraat 7; ☎626 37 01. Nestling behind Berlage's Stock Exchange, a basic but very cheap hotel with doubles from ƒ50, not including breakfast. A short walk from Centraal Station. Some complaints have reached us about surly management and room prices being raised after bookings had been confirmed.

De Bloeiende Ramenas, Haarlemmerdijk 61; ☎624 60 30. A cross between hostel and hotel, with comfortable rooms, friendly and welcoming management (and atmosphere), and sensible prices: ƒ85 for a double room, including breakfast. Only disadvantage is the location, to the north-west of the centre and away from any action. Bus #22.

Brian, Singel 69; ☎624 46 61. Cheap at ƒ80 for a double, including breakfast, and with equally inexpensive triple and quadruple rooms available too. But if you're looking for something peaceful, this isn't the place. Tram #1, #2, #5, #13, #17.

Accommodation

Accommodation

Casa Cara, Emmastraat 24; ☎662 31 35. Homely hotel five minutes from the Concertgebouw and major museums. Doubles from ƒ70. Tram #2, #16.

Clemens, Raadhuisstraat 39; ☎624 60 89. One of a number of inexpensive hotels situated in the Art Nouveau crescent of the Utrecht Building. Clean, neat and good value for money, with doubles at ƒ90. As this is one of the city's busiest streets, it makes sense to ask for a room at the back. Tram #13, #14, #17.

Galerij, Raadhuisstraat 43; ☎624 88 51. One of the Raadhuisstraat budget options. Doubles from ƒ80, not including breakfast. Tram #13, #14, #17.

De Harmonie, Prinsengracht 816; ☎622 80 21. Small rooms, but a nice central setting just down from the Amstel and within easy reach of Rembrandtsplein. Doubles from ƒ110. Tram #4.

Hegra, Herengracht 269; ☎623 78 77. Relatively cheap for the location at ƒ95 for a double including breakfast.

King, Leidsekade 85–86; ☎624 96 03. Nicely situated hotel with doubles from ƒ110. Tram #1, #2, #5, #7, #10.

Kitty, Plantage Middenlaan 40; ☎622 68 19. A little bit out from the centre, but decent-sized rooms for ƒ95 a double, including as much breakfast as you can eat. Good value. Tram #9 or #14, get off at the zoo.

De Lantaeme, Leidsegracht 111; ☎623 22 21. Well located, just shouting distance from the *Melkweg*, but rather seedy, despite the elegant building. It can get noisy too, and the management are none too friendly. Doubles for ƒ100. Tram #1, #2, #5, #6, #7, #10.

De Leydsche Hof, Leidsegracht 14; ☎623 21 48. Stately canal house on one of the smaller and quieter canals. Doubles for ƒ85, not including breakfast. Tram #1, #2, #5.

Museumzicht, Jan Luykenstraat 22; ☎671 52 24. Conveniently located for the main museums, with plain rooms from ƒ100. Tram #2, #3, #5, #12.

Van Onna, Bloemgracht 102 ☎626 58 01. A quiet, comfortable little family-run place in the Jordaan. ƒ110 for a double, including breakfast.

Van Ostade, Van Ostadestraat 123; ☎671 52 13. Friendly, youthful place near the Albert Cuyp market that bills itself as a "bicycle hotel", renting bikes (ƒ1.80 per day) and giving advice on routes, etc. Peacefully situated out in the Old South. Basic but clean rooms for ƒ90 a double. Also unusual in having garage facilities for cars. Tram #12, #25.

Pax, Raadhuisstraat 37; ☎624 97 35. Basic city centre cheapie with fair-sized doubles from ƒ65 – breakfast is extra. As with most of the hotels along here, ask for a room at the back. Tram #13, #14, #17.

Piet Hein, Vossiusstraat 53; ☎662 72 05. Calm, low-key and clean, tucked away behind the Concertgebouw. Doubles from ƒ95. Tram #2, #3, #12.

Prinsenhof, Prinsengracht 810; ☎623 77 72. One of the city's best budget options, this tastefully decorated hotel has doubles from ƒ95. Best rooms at the back. Tram #4.

Rokin, Rokin 73; ☎626 74 56. Something of a bargain considering the location, with doubles from ƒ98, including breakfast. Tram #4, #9, #14, #16, #24, #25.

Ronnie, Raadhuisstraat 41; ☎624 28 21. Owned by the American cousins of the *Clemens*' owners, and with equally good prices and facilities. Friendly and helpful, with doubles from ƒ100. Three-, four-, and five-person rooms, too. Tram #13, #14, #17.

Schroder, Haarlemmerdijk 48b; ☎626 62 72. Out on the western edge of the city centre, with doubles from ƒ80, breakfast not included. Bus #18.

Seven Bridges, Reguliersgracht 31; ☎623 13 29. One of the city's most beautiful and best-value hotels, with a lovely (and convenient) canalside location and beautifully decorated rooms. Doubles start at about ƒ110, including breakfast served in your room. Tram #4.

Utopia, Nieuwe Zijds Voorburgwal 132; ☎626 12 95. Doubles from ƒ80; triples and quadruples too. Also (for guests) an all-night coffee shop and bar. Tram #1, #2, #5, #13, #17.

Verdi, Wanningstraat 9; ☎676 00 73. Small and simple hotel near the Concertgebouw with double rooms starting at ƒ110. Tram #3, #5, #6, #12.

Vullings, P. C. Hooftstraat 78; ☎671 21 09. Small, elegantly located hotel with doubles from ƒ95. Tram #2, #3, #5, #12.

Moderate hotels (ƒ110–250)

Acacia, Lindengracht 251; ☎622 14 60. Amicable hotel run by a young married couple. Doubles from ƒ120. They let self-catering apartments too. Tram #3, bus #18.

Acca, Van de Veldestraat 3a; ☎662 52 62. Intimate hotel close to the major museums with double rooms for ƒ150. Beginning to look a little tatty. Tram # 2, #3, #5, #12.

Acro, Jan Luykenstraat 44; ☎662 05 26. Excellent, modern hotel which has been completely refurbished with stylish rooms, a plush bar and self-service restaurant. Doubles from ƒ140 (slightly more if you stay only one night) but well worth the money. Tram #2, #3, #5, #12.

Adolesce, Nieuwe Keizersgracht 26; ☎626 39 59. Nicely situated just off the Amstel, with a choice of doubles at ƒ120. Tram #4, #9, #14, bus #31, or Waterlooplein metro station.

Agora, Singel 462; ☎627 22 00. Nicely located, small, amicable hotel near the flower market, with doubles for upwards of ƒ125, three- and four-bedded rooms for proportionately less. Tram #1, #2, #5.

Armada, Keizersgracht 713–715; ☎623 29 80. Large if slightly tatty rooms that go for around ƒ165 a double. Sympathetic to gay and lesbian visitors.

Atlas, Van Eeghenstraat 64; ☎676 63 36. Situated just south of the Vondelpark, this Art Nouveau building is on the inside a personable modern hotel with every convenience and comfort. Small, tranquil and very welcoming. Dinner is served on request. Doubles from around ƒ195. Tram #2.

Canal House, Keizersgracht 148; ☎622 51 82. Magnificently restored seventeenth-century building, centrally located on one of the principal canals. American family-run with a friendly bar and cosy rooms from

around ƒ195 a double. Tram #13, #14, #17.

Cok, Koninginneweg 34; ☎664 61 11. Actually two hotels on one site: Tourist Class, with double rooms for ƒ210; and First Class, with doubles for ƒ320. Packed with facilities, but rather a soulless place to stay. The majority of its trade comes from package holidaymakers, which means it's packed out during summer months. Tram #2.

Continental, Damrak 40–41; ☎622 33 63. Though on the noisy tourist drag of Damrak, a clean and friendly hotel with doubles for ƒ125. The main advantage is the location, a short walk from Centraal Station.

Crown, Oude Zijds Voorburgwal 21; ☎626 96 64. Friendly budget hotel in the Red Light area. Doubles at ƒ110–120.

Estherea, Singel 305–307; ☎624 51 46. Pleasant middle-of-the-road hotel in a blandly converted canal house, with doubles from ƒ275. Tram #1, #2.

Eureka,'s-Gravelandseveer 3–4; ☎624 66 07. Considering you're only across the Amstel from Rembrandtsplein, this is a surprisingly quiet part of town. Rooms are small but clean and pleasant, the staff friendly, and you're perfectly positioned for nightlife. ƒ120, including breakfast.

Fantasia, Nieuwe Keizersgracht 16; ☎623 82 59. Large, popular and welcoming hotel, with neat if unspectacular rooms and a large dining room and bar. From ƒ115. Tram #1, #2, #5.

De Filosoof, Anna Vondelstraat 4–6; ☎683 30 13. Hospitable hotel on the northern edge of the Vondelpark that for some reason names each of its rooms after a different philosopher. Rates are from about ƒ175 a double. Tram #1, #6.

Fita, Jan Luykenstraat 37; ☎679 09 76. Mid-sized, friendly hotel in a quiet spot on the far side of the Vondelpark. Doubles from ƒ170. Tram #2, #5.

Gerstekorrel, Damstraat 22–34; ☎624 97 71. Small, simple hotel which is located about as centrally as it's possible to get. Doubles from ƒ120. Tram #4, #9, #16, #24, #25.

Accommodation

Accommodation

De Gouden Kettingh, Keizersgracht 268; ☎624 82 87. Rambling old canal house popular with British/business clientele. The fanciest and best rooms overlook the canal. Doubles start at ƒ150 and up. Tram #13, #14, #17.

Het Leidseplein, Korte Leidsedwarsstraat 79; ☎ 627 25 05. Smart, mid-sized hotel sandwiched between the calm of Leidsegracht and the frenetic Leidseplein. Doubles from ƒ195. Tram #1, #2, #5, #6, #7, #10.

Jan Luyken, Jan Luykenstraat 58; ☎573 07 30. Elegant hotel with doubles starting at ƒ290. Tram #2, #ƒ5.

Maas, Leidsekade 91; ☎623 38 68. Recently renovated hotel with clean and nicely decorated rooms starting at ƒ150 a double. Ask for the waterbed! Tram #1, #2, #5.

De Munck, Achtergracht 3; ☎620 66 47. Quiet, clean and convenient hotel not far from Frederiksplein with a friendly, laid-back proprietor. The breakfast room sports a period jukebox with a good collection of Sixties hits. Doubles for ƒ125. Tram #4, #6, #7, #10.

Museum, P.C. Hoofstraat 2; ☎662 14 02. Large and luxurious hotel next door to the Rijksmuseum. Doubles from ƒ245. Tram #6, #7, #10.

De La Poste, Reguliersgracht 3–5; ☎623 71 05. Slightly shabby rooms from ƒ160 for a double. Tram #4.

Prinsen, Vondelstraat 38; ☎616 23 23. Affable hotel on the edge of the Vondelpark. Doubles from around ƒ195. Tram #2, #3, #5, #12.

Smit, P.C. Hoofstraat 24–28; ☎671 47 85. Slightly variable doubles from ƒ135. Tram #2, #3, #5, #12.

Titus, Leidsekade 74; ☎626 57 58. Variable rooms from ƒ120. One of several similiarly priced hotels to be found in this area. Tram #1, #2, #5, #10, #17.

Toren, Keizersgracht 164; ☎622 60 33. Fine example of a seventeenth-century canal house and once the home of a Dutch prime minister. Somewhat worn out these days, though still OK. Doubles from ƒ165. Tram #13, #14, #17.

Toro, Koningslaan 64; ☎673 72 23. Lovely hotel in a peaceful location out by the Vondelpark. Doubles from about ƒ200. Tram #2.

Vondel, Vondelstraat 28–30; ☎612 01 20. Overpriced and unfriendly, with doubles at ƒ185 plus. Tram #2, #3, #12, #15.

Vondelhof, Vondelstraat 24; ☎612 22 21. Busy hotel with large comfortable doubles with private bath, TV, etc, for around ƒ195. Tram #2, #3, #12.

Zandbergen, Willemsparkweg 205; ☎676 93 21. Light, airy hotel near the Vondelpark that has clean and spacious doubles for around ƒ175. Tram #2.

Expensive hotels (ƒ250 and over)

Many pricier hotels discount their rates, especially out of season and at weekends – sometimes by 35 percent or more. If you can be flexible, it's worth phoning around to see what's on offer during your stay.

American, Leidsekade 97; ☎624 53 22. Art Deco, landmark hotel bang on Leidseplein with double rooms that start at about ƒ425. If you can't afford this, soak up some of the atmosphere over a drink at the period-piece café downstairs. See also p.30. Tram #1, #2, #5.

Amstel, Prof. Tulpplein 1; ☎ 622 60 60. Perhaps the best place in town to spend one night of ultimate class – an experience that will set you back ƒ600 or so (ƒ450 at weekends) for a double room. Tram #6, #7, #10.

Dikker & Thijs, Prinsengracht 444; ☎626 77 21. Stylish hotel attached to the restaurants and shop of the same name. Doubles go for ƒ315, not including breakfast, so it's not exactly a bargain, although the canal-facing rooms are nice.

De l'Europe, Nieuwe Doelenstraat 2–8; ☎623 48 36. True nineteenth-century elegance for around ƒ550, though it has been claimed that the hotel to some extent rests on its reputation. Tram #4, #9, #16, #24, #25.

Grand Hotel, Oude Zijds Voorburgwal 197; ☎555 31 11. The mòst recent of the city's upscale hotels, the Grand used to be the

City Hall before it was moved to the Stopera complex. It's wonderfully plush without being overstated, with all mod cons and good attention to detail. Doubles from ƒ625, and they don't even throw in the breakfast for that price. Tram #4, #9, #14, #16, #24, #25.

Hilton, Apollolaan 138–140; ☎678 07 80. Way outside the centre in the New South, and only really worth staying at if you want – and can afford – to soak up a bit of Sixties nostalgia in its refurbished Lennon and Ono suite, where the couple had their notorious "Bed-In" in 1969. Regular doubles go for around ƒ500. Tram #5, #24.

Krasnapolsky, Dam 9; ☎554 91 11. A great, if not terribly peaceful, location right on Dam Square, and, with doubles for around ƒ390, a little cheaper than its slightly more sumptuous rivals. Tram #4, #9, #16, #24, #25.

Pulitzer, Prinsengracht 315–331; ☎523 52 35. About twenty seventeenth-century canal houses converted into a determinedly luxurious hotel that charges around ƒ450 plus for its double rooms. Tram #13, #14, #17.

Schiller Karena, Rembrandtsplein 26–36; ☎623 16 60. Once something of an artists' hangout, and still home to one of the city's best-known and most atmospheric bars on its ground floor, double rooms go for around ƒ315 plus. The drawback is the location on tacky Rembrandtsplein. Tram #4, #19, #14.

Gay hotels

Aero, Kerkstraat 49, second floor; ☎622 77 28. In the middle of Amsterdam's main gay street, an almost exclusively gay hotel with sixteen rooms, many of which have shower and/or toilet. Prices range from ƒ110 for a double, ƒ159 for a triple. No singles. Tram #1, #2, #5.

Anco, Oude Zijds Voorburgwal 55; ☎624 11 26. Small and rather sleazy exclusively gay, male, leather hotel in the Red Light district. Doubles from ƒ110. A short walk from the station.

ITC (International Travel Club), Prinsengracht 1051; ☎623 17 11. Close to the major gay areas and perhaps the least

expensive gay hotel of this quality. Singles from ƒ75, doubles ƒ135, off-season seven nights for the price of six. Tram #4.

Monopole, Amstel 60; ☎624 62 71. Overlooking the Amstel, very close to the Muziektheater, and right next door to the Monopole Taveerne. Singles from ƒ75, doubles from ƒ95. Triples and quadruples too. Tram #4.

New York, Herengracht 13; ☎624 30 66. Exceptionally popular, exclusively gay hotel, noted for its high standards, consisting of three modernized seventeenth-century houses – a short walk from Centraal Station. singles from ƒ150, doubles ƒ175.

Orfeo, Leidsekruisstraat 14; ☎622 81 80. Very pleasant, gay hotel, with doubles without bath for around ƒ100, a small sauna for guests and decent breakfasts served until midday.

Quentin, Leidsekade 89; ☎626 21 87. Not a gay hotel, but gays (especially women) made welcome. Excellent value, and very friendly, with singles from ƒ60, doubles from ƒ85. Tram #1, #2, #5.

Stablemaster, Warmoesstraat 23; ☎624 55 73. Small hotel in the heart of the red light action. Doubles go for ƒ120 upwards. Tram #4, #9, #16, #24, #25.

Toff's Apartments, Ruysdaelkade 167; ☎673 85 29. Self-catering apartments scattered all over the city that sleep two for ƒ150 a night, ƒ2500 a month. Toff's also run personalised guided tours of Amsterdam's gay scene – see Basics.

Unique, Kerkstraat 37; ☎624 47 85. A convenient and exclusively gay hotel with singles at ƒ75, doubles around ƒ130. Tram #1, #2, #5.

Waterfront, Singel 458; ☎623 97 75. Recently opened smart hotel, handy for the gay bars, but on the pricey side, with singles for ƒ160, doubles at ƒ195. Tram #1, #2, #5.

West End, Kerkstraat 42; ☎624 80 74. Another conveniently located hotel for the Kerkstraat area, with the Cosmo Bar as its main attraction; singles go for ƒ70, doubles ƒ90, breakfast not included. Tram #1, #2, #5.

Accommodation

Accommodation

Campsites

There are several **campsites** in Amsterdam, most of which are easily accessible by public transport or by car. The VVV directs most visitors to the "youth campsites" of *Vliegenbos* and *Zeeberg*, open April to September, while grown-ups and those with caravans or campers are advised to use one of the other sites.

Youth Campsites

Vliegenbos, Meeuwenlaan 138; ☎ 636 88 55. A relaxed and friendly site, just a ten-minute bus ride from the station. Facilities include a general shop, bar and bike rental. Rates are *f*5.75 a night per person, *f*7 if you're over 30, plus *f*1 for a tent, *f*2.25 for a motorbike, *f*3.25 for a car. Hot showers *f*1.25.

Vliegenbos also has a few camping huts with bunk beds and basic cooking facilities, for *f*46 per night for four people; phone ahead to check availability. Open April–Sept only. Bus #32, from Centraal Station, night bus #77. It's also possible – and an enjoyable alternative – to catch the free ferry from round the back of Centraal Station to North Amsterdam, and walk or cycle from

there (about 20 minutes on foot) – ask at the camp office for exact directions.

Zeeberg, Zuiderldijk 44; ☎ 694 44 30. Slightly better equipped than the *Vliegenbos*, in that it has a bar, but more difficult to get to. Rates are *f*5 per person, plus *f*2.50 for a tent, *f*3 for a motorbike, *f*5 for a car. Hot showers *f*1.50. Tram #3 or #10 to Muiderpoort Station, then bus #37, then a ten-minute walk; also served by night bus #76.

Other Campsites

Amsterdamse Bos, Kleine Noorddijk 1, Aalsmeer; ☎ 641 68 68. Many facilities, but a long way out. Rates are *f*7.60 a head, hot showers included, plus *f*2.60 for a motorbike or car, camper or caravan. Open April–Oct. Yellow bus #171 or #172 and a short walk.

Gaasper Camping, Loosdrechtsedreef 7; ☎ 696 73 26. Amsterdam's newest campsite, just the other side of the Bijlmermeer housing complex. Rates are *f*5 per person, plus *f*4.25 per tent, *f*1.75 for a motorbike, *f*3.50 for a car. Hot showers *f*1.50. Open March–Nov. Metro to Gaasperplas station and a five minute walk; night bus #75.

Chapter 8

Bars and Coffee Shops

Bars

Amsterdam is better known for drinking than eating, and with good reason: its selection of **bars** is one of the real pleasures of the city. There are two kinds of Amsterdam bar. The traditional, old-style bar is the **brown café** – a *bruin café* or *bruine kroeg* – cosy places so named because of the dingy colour of their walls, stained by years of tobacco smoke. A more recent backlash are slick, self-conciously modern **designer bars**, many lately known as "grand cafés", which are normally as un-brown as possible and geared towards a largely young crowd. We've included details of the more established ones, although these places come and go – something like seventy percent apparently disappear within a year of opening. Most bars, of any kind, open until around 1am during the week, 2am at weekends (sometimes until 3am), though some don't open until lunchtime, or even about 4pm. Other drinking spots are the **tasting houses** (*proeflokalen*), originally the sampling rooms of small private distillers, now tiny places that sell only spirits and close around 8pm, though there are very few of these places left.

Prices are fairly standard everywhere, and the only time you'll pay through the nose is when there's music, or if you're foolish (or desparate) enough to step into the obvious tourist traps around Leidseplein and along Damrak. Reckon on paying roughly ƒ2.50 for a small beer (note that some bars serve larger, approximately pint-size measures, which work out proportion-ately cheaper). You can also use bars as a place for **budget eating**. Many – often designated *eetcafés* – offer a complete menu, and most will make you a sandwich or a bowl of soup; at the very least you can snack on hard-boiled eggs from the counter for a guilder or so each. Some of the more restaurant-like places are listed in the *Restaurants* chapter.

There are around 1400 bars and cafés in Amsterdam – roughly one for every 700 people – and what follows is inevitably very selective. It does, however, cover a very broad crosssection of places across the city, so wherever you are, and, what-ever your tastes, you should be able to find something nearby to suit you. The places we've listed are divided geographically, between those in inner central Amsterdam (on and within the area bordered by the Singel canal); those on and around the other major canals and in the Jordaan – the outer centre; and a handful of others outside the Singelgracht. The **map** on p.126–7 should make it possible to coordi-nate your eating or sightseeing with an evening's drinking.

For details of the mechanics of drinking in The Netherlands, see "Eating and Drinking", p.30

Inner Centre Bars

Belgique, Gravenstraat 2. Minute bar near the Nieuwe Kerk that specializes in brews from Belgium.

Bem, Nieuwmarkt 9. Casual and inexpen-sive brown café patronized by a predomi-nantly arty clientele. Run by a native of Switzerland, its speciality is, not surprisingly, fondue.

AMSTERDAM LISTINGS: CHAPTER 8

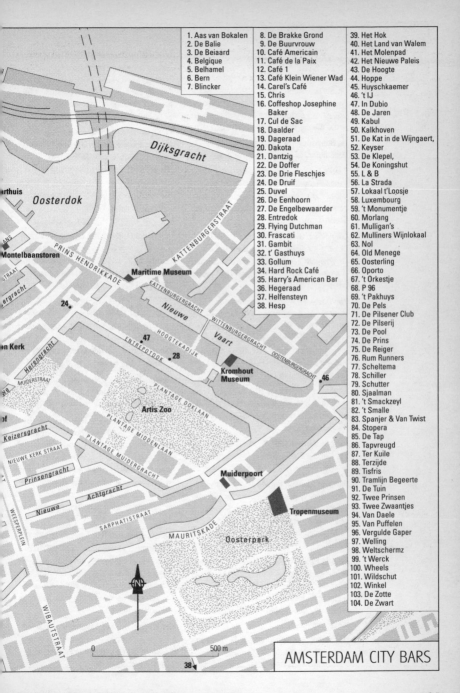

1. Aas van Bokalen
2. De Balie
3. De Beiaard
4. Belgique
5. Belhamel
6. Bern
7. Blincker
8. De Brakke Grond
9. De Buurvrouw
10. Café Americain
11. Café de la Paix
12. Café 1
13. Café Klein Wiener Wad
14. Carel's Café
15. Chris
16. Coffeeshop Josephine Baker
17. Cul de Sac
18. Daalder
19. Dageraad
20. Dakota
21. Dantzig
22. De Doffer
23. De Drie Fleschjes
24. De Druif
25. Duvel
26. De Eenhoorn
27. De Engelbewaarder
28. Entredok
29. Flying Dutchman
30. Frascati
31. Gambit
32. t' Gasthuys
33. Gollum
34. Hard Rock Café
35. Harry's American Bar
36. Hegeraad
37. Helfensteyn
38. Hesp
39. Het Hok
40. Het Land van Walem
41. Het Molenpad
42. Het Nieuwe Paleis
43. De Hoogte
44. Hoppe
45. Huyschkaemer
46. 't IJ
47. In Dubio
48. De Jaren
49. Kabul
50. Kalkhoven
51. De Kat in de Wijngaert,
52. Keyser
53. De Klepel,
54. De Koningshut
55. L & B
56. La Strada
57. Lokaal t'Loosje
58. Luxembourg
59. 't Monumentje
60. Morlang
61. Mulligan's
62. Mulliners Wijnlokaal
63. Nol
64. Old Menege
65. Oosterling
66. Oporto
67. 't Orkestje
68. P 96
69. 't Pakhuys
70. De Pels
71. De Pilsener Club
72. De Pilserij
73. De Pool
74. De Prins
75. De Reiger
76. Rum Runners
77. Scheltema
78. Schiller
79. Schutter
80. Sjaalman
81. 't Smackzeyl
82. 't Smalle
83. Spanjer & Van Twist
84. Stopera
85. De Tap
86. Tapvreugd
87. Ter Kuile
88. Terzijde
89. Tisfris
90. Tramlijn Begeerte
91. De Tuin
92. Twee Prinsen
93. Twee Zwaantjes
94. Van Daele
95. Van Puffelen
96. Vergulde Gaper
97. Welling
98. Weltschermz
99. 't Werck
100. Wheels
101. Wildschut
102. Winkel
103. De Zotte
104. De Zwart

AMSTERDAM CITY BARS

Bars and Coffee Shops

Blincker, St Barberenstraat 7–9. Squeezed between the top end of Nes and Oude Zijds Voorburgwal, this hi-tech theatre bar, all exposed steel and hanging plants, is more comfortable than it looks.

De Brakke Grond, Nes 43. Modern, high-ceilinged bar full of people trying not to discuss the performances they've just seen at the theatre of the same name.

De Buurvrouw, St Pieterspoortsteeg 29. Dark, noisy bar with a wildly eclectic crowd.

Carel's Café, Voetboogstraat 6. Large, youth-oriented bar serving slightly over-priced food – though the *dagschotels* are a good buy. Also at Frans Halsstraat 76 and Saenredamstraat 32.

Cul de Sac, Oude Zijds Achterburgwal 99. Down a long alley in what used to be a seventeenth-century spice warehouse, this is a handy retreat from the red Light district. Small, quiet and friendly.

Van Daele, Paleistraat 101. Worth mention-ing more for what it was than what it is, this used to be the city's most infamous punk bar, called *No Name*; later it became a squatters' bar, then a women's restaurant. Today it's a fairly ordinary bar in what used to be a large squat.

Dageraad, Paleisstraat 103–105. An *eetcafé* housed in a former squat near Dam Square, with food and occasional live music. Next door to *Van Daele*.

Dakota, Nieuwe Zijds Voorburgwal 256. Cosy, and a livelier choice than *Scheltema* nearby.

Dantzig, Zwanenburgwal 15. Recently opened, easy-going bar of the "grand café" variety, with comfortable chairs, friendly service and a low-key, chic atmosphere. Food served at lunchtime and in the evenings.

De Drie Fleschjes, Gravenstraat 16. Tasting house for spirits and liqueurs, which would originally have been made on the premises. No beer, and no seats either; its clients tend to be well heeled or well soused (often both).

De Eenhoorn, Warmoesstraat 16. Wine and cheese shop with raw brick walls, oak beams, paintings and classical music. A stark contrast to the surrounding Red Light district.

De Engelbewaarder, Kloveniersburgwal 59. Once the meeting place of Amsterdam's bookish types, this is still known as the "literary café". Relaxed and informal, it has live jazz on Sunday afternoons.

Flying Dutchman, Martelaarsgracht 13. Principal watering hole of Amsterdam's British expatriate community and not a word of Dutch is to be heard. Usually packed with stoned regulars crowding in to use the pool table or dartboards, or simply to cash in on the *Dutchman's* reasonably priced large-sized beers.

Frascati, Nes 59. Theatre bar, elegantly brown with mirrors and a pink marble bar, popular with a young, media-type crowd. Good, too, for both lunchtime and informal evening eating, with full meals for under ƒ20, snacks and soups for less. Recommended.

't Gasthuys, Grimburgwal 7. Convivial brown café packed during the school year with students from the university across the canal. Features include good food and summer seating outside by the water.

Gollum, Raamsteeg 4. Small, noisy bar with a huge array of different beers. A genial barman dispenses lists to help you choose.

Hard Rock Café, Oude Zijds Voorburgwal 246. Not the overblown burger joint found in London, but a small, crowded (smoking) bar serving 1970s-style videos to 1970s-style customers. Patronized mainly by those in Amsterdam for the weed. There's another, smaller branch, not a whole lot more appealing, at Korte Leidsedwarsstraat 28.

Harry's American Bar, Spuistraat 285. One of a number of would-be sophisticated hangouts at the top end of Spuistraat, *Harry's* is primarily a haunt for Amsterdam's more elderly *bon vivants*, with easy listen-ing jazz and an unhealthily wide selection of cocktails.

De Hoogte, Nieuwe Hoogstraat 2a. Small café on the edge of the Red Light district. Good music, engaging atmosphere, and beers a little cheaper.

Hoppe, Spui 18. One of Amsterdam's longest-established and best-known bars, and one of its most likeable, frequented by the city's dark-suited office crowd on their wayward way home. Summer is especially good, when the throngs spill out on to the street ten deep.

De Jaren, Nieuwe Doelenstraat 20–22. Large bar/restaurant overlooking the Amstel; three floors, two terraces and as much trendiness as you could wish for. Serves reasonably priced food too, and has a great salad bar, although the service can be poor.

Coffeeshop Josephine Baker, Oude Hoogstraat 27–29. Once known as the *Café de Dood* – "Café of the Dead", after the studiously wasted youth who patronize it – this is the loudest and most squalid hangout in the area.

Kabul, Warmoesstraat 38. Bar of the adjacent budget hotel, and consequently open late.

De Koningshut, Spuistraat 269. In the early evening, at least, it's standing room only in this small, spit-and-sawdust bar, popular with office people on their way home or to dinner. For middle-aged swingers only.

Ter Kuile, Torensteeg 8. A new-style brown café and a pleasant place to overlook this stretch of the Singel. Serves food at the usual *eetcafé* prices.

Lokaal 't Loosje, Nieuwmarkt 32–34. Quiet old-style brown café that's been here for 200 years and looks its age. Used by many of the locals living in the neighbourhood. Ignore the parrot.

Luxembourg, Spui 22–24. The latest watering hole of Amsterdam's advertising and media brigade. It's crowded too. If you can get in, it's actually an elegant bar with a good (though pricey) selection of snacks. Overlooks the Singel at the back.

Het Nieuwe Paleis, Paleisstraat 16. Bar currently in vogue with students from the adjoining university buildings. Laid-back and likeable.

Oporto, Zoutsteeg 1. Welcoming and surprisingly unchanged bar in the web of touristy streets just off Damrak. It serves beer by the pint if you want it, and has dartboard.

't Pakhuys, Voetboogstraat 10. One of a clutch of bars that line this tiny street, an inviting place serving food at ƒ15–120.

De Pilsener Club, Begijnensteeg 4. More like someone's front room than a bar – indeed, all drinks mysteriously appear from a back room. Photographs on the wall record generations of sociable drinking.

De Pilserij, Gravenstraat 10. Roomy bar behind the Nieuwe Kerk that has a comfortable back room and plays good jazz. Above all, though, you drink here for the bar's authentic nineteenth-century surroundings – little has changed, right down to the cash register.

De Pool, Oude Hoogstraat 8. Pleasant bar, somewhat quieter than most of the others along this stretch.

Scheltema, Nieuwe Zijds Voorburgwal 242. Journalists' bar, now only frequented by more senior newshounds and their occasionally famous interviewees, since all the newspapers that had their headquarters along here moved to the suburbs. Faded turn-of-the-century feel, with a reading table and meals for under ƒ25.

De Schutter, Voetboogstraat 13–15. Former folk music hangout, now simply a spacious upstairs bar, full of people munching on the cheap and basic food.

Spanjer & Van Twist, Nes 41. A gentle prelude to *De Buurvrouw*, just around the corner.

Stopera, Nieuwe Hoogstraat 41. Dubbed after the name of the campaign to prevent the building of the Stadthuis/Opera/Musiektheater a few years back, and sited right in the middle of the controversially developed jodenhoek quarter. Despite that, it's a fairly ordinary bar, pleasant enough but not really worth going out of your way for.

La Strada, Nieuwe Zijds Voorburgwal 93–95. Exceptionally trendy bar whose interior changes monthly as aspiring – but not always inspiring – local artists are given free reign with the decor. Occasional fully fledged exhibitions, poetry readings and live music on Saturdays. Good food too – pasta dishes start at ƒ16, main courses for around ƒ25.

Bars and Coffee Shops

Bars and Coffee Shops

Tapvreugd, Oude Hoogstraat 11. Far and away the most amicable of the loud, crowded music bars on this and surrounding streets. Like most of these places, though, its music and its regulars are strictly mid-1970s.

Tisfris, St Antoniesbreestraat 142. Split-level café and bar near the Rembrandt House. Youthful and popular.

Zwart, Dam Square. About as central as you can get. However, although recently modernized, not a place you'd want to spend the evening.

De Zwart, Spuistraat 334. Less businesslike neighbour of the more famous *Hoppe* across the alley, but similarly crowded.

Outer Centre Bars

Aas van Bokalen, Keizersgracht 335. Unpretentious local bar, with good food from ƒ17. Great collection of Motown tapes. Very small, so go either early or late.

Café Americain, American Hotel, Leidseplein 28–30. The terrace bar here has been a gathering place for Amsterdam media people for years, and it's worth coming here at least once for the decor: Art Nouveau frills coordinated down to the doorknobs. A place to be seen, with prices not surprisingly above average. Good fast lunches, too.

De Balie, Kleine Gartmanplantsoen 10. Big high-ceilinged haunt of the city's trendy lefties. Not especially inspiring, but, if you're stuck on Leidseplein on a Saturday night, it provides a welcome change of atmosphere.

De Beiaard, Herengracht 90. Light and airy Fifties-style bar for genuine beer aficionados. A wide selection of bottled and draught beers selected with true dedication by the owner, who delights in filling you in on the relative properties of each.

Belhamel, Brouwersgracht 60. Kitschy bar/restaurant with an Art Nouveau style interior and excellent, though costly, French food. The main attraction in summer is one of the most picturesque views in Amsterdam.

Chris, Bloemstraat 42. Very proud of itself for being the Jordaan's (and Amsterdam's) oldest bar, dating from 1624. Comfortable, homely atmosphere.

Daalder, Lindengracht 90. A relatively new Jordaan drinking place, normally filled with locals, that makes a good alternative to *De Tuin*.

Docksider, Entrepot Dok 7–10. Strange combination of bar, Japanese restaurant and snooker hall, out in the booming Eastern Islands district.

De Doffer, Runstraat 12. Small, affable bar with food and a billiards table.

De Druif, Rapenburgerplein 10. One of the city's most beguiling bars, and one that hardly anyone knows about. Its popularity with the locals lends it a village pub feel.

Entredok, Entrepot Dok 64. First and perhaps the best of a growing number of bars in this up-and-coming area. The clientele hail from the surrounding hi-tech offices, though increasingly from the residential blocks in between, too.

Gambit, Bloemgracht 20. Chess bar, with boards laid out all day until midnight.

De Geus, Korte Leidsedwarstraat 71. Cheerful place with a limited but tasty menu of Dutch food.

Hegeraad, Noordermarkt 34. Old-fashioned, lovingly maintained brown café with a fiercely loyal clientele.

Het Hok, Lange Leidsedwarstraat 134. Games bar, where you can play backgammon, chess or draughts, or just drink against a backdrop of clicking counters. Pleasingly unpretentious after the plastic restaurants of the rest of the street, though women may find the overwhelmingly male presence off-putting.

Huyschkaemer, Utrechtsestraat 137. Recently reopened in interior-designed glory, and already established as the favourite watering hole of arty students.

Café I, Nieuwe Spiegelstraat. New, very stylish bar, and surprisingly the only café in this area.

't IJ, in the De Gooyer windmill, Funenkade 7. Situated in the base of an early nineteenth-century windmill, where the beers (called *Natte*, *Zatte* and *Struis*) are brewed on the premises and are extremely strong. A fun place to drink yourself silly. Open Fri, Sat & Sun 3–8pm.

In Dubio, Entrepot Dok 36. One of the increasing number of bar/restaurants out in the Eastern Island quarter.

Kalkhoven, Prinsengracht 283. One of the city's most characteristic brown cafés. Nothing special, but warm and welcoming.

De Kat In de Wijngaert, Lindengracht 160. Hefty *bessenjenevers* and an enticing name.

Café Klein Wiener Wad, corner of Utrechtestraat and Utrechtsedwarstraat. Small self-conciously modern café; trendy and unavoidably intimate.

De Klepel, Prinsenstraat 22. Quiet bar whose speciality is chess playing. English newspapers.

L & B, Korte Leidsedwarsstraat 82. A cosy bar, rather misplaced among the touristy restaurants and clubs of this part of town. Has a selection of 200 different whiskies and bourbons from around the world. Open until 3am.

Het Land van Walem, Keizersgracht 449. Walem is one of Amsterdam's nouveau-chic cafés: cool, light, and vehemently un-brown. Clientele are stylish in taste and dress, while the foodis a kind of hybrid French-Dutch with full meals going for around ƒ22; there's also a wide selection of newspapers and magazines that includes some in English. Usually packed.

Het Molenpad, Prinsengracht 653. Thinking persons' bar and art gallery filled with academic types from the public library just along the canal.

't Monumentje, Westerstraat 120. Unspectacular Jordaan local haunt that plays good music. Likeable and cheap.

Morlang, Keizersgracht 451. Bar/restaurant of the new wave, yuppie variety (much like the *Walem* next door), serving good food for around ƒ18. Live music Tues.

Mulligan's, Amstel 100. Lively Irish bar usually full of expats. Serves food and hosts sporadic live music.

Mulliners Wijnlokaal, Lijnsbaansgracht 267. Upmarket wine bar (prices around ƒ5 a glass, ƒ25 a bottle) with food from ƒ15. Good atmosphere.

Nol, Westerstraat 109. Probably the epitome of the jolly Jordaan singing bar, a luridly lit dive, popular with Jordaan gangsters and ordinary Amsterdammers alike. Opens and closes late, especially on weekends, when the back-slapping joviality and drunken sing-alongs keep you here until closing time at least.

Oosterling, Utrechtsestraat 140. Stone-floored local bar-cum-off-licence that's been in the same family since the middle of the last century. Very quiet – home to some serious drinkers.

Café de la Paix, Wolvenstraat 22–24. More of a restaurant than a bar, really, but a friendly place whose drinks are much more reasonably priced than the unremarkable food. Modern music and a youthful crowd.

De Pels, Huidenstraat 25. Few surprises in this, one of Amsterdam's quieter but more pleasant bars.

De Prins, Prinsengracht 124. Boisterous student bar, with a wide range of drinks and a well-priced menu that includes fondues. A good place to drink in a great part of town.

P 96, Prinsengracht 96. A little way down the canal from *de Prins*, this bar is open late and, should you feel like a game, sports a dartboard.

Van Puffelen, Prinsengracht 377. More a restaurant than a café, and consequently only open from 4pm, but an appealing place to drink, with a huge choice of international beers and a reading room by day, restaurant by night. Food is French in style, and, although not cheap (ƒ25 and upwards), is usually well worth it.

De Reiger, Nieuwe Leliestraat 34. The Jordaan's main meeting place, an old-style café filled with modish Amsterdammers. Affordable food.

Rum Runners, Prinsengracht 277. Tropical-type bar/restaurant converted with neo-colonial chic from the old Westerkek hall. A broad range of cocktails, but the food – and the service – can be dire.

Schiller, Rembrandtsplein 26. Art Deco bar of the upstairs hotel, authentic in both feel

Bars and Coffee Shops

Bars and Coffee Shops

and decor, and although it's suffered something of a decline of late, offering a genteel escape from the tackiness of most of the rest of Rembrandtsplein. Main dishes in the restaurant next door go for around ƒ27.50.

Sjaalman, Prinsengracht 178. Small bar with a pool table and exotic food. Good in summer when the church tower is lit.

't Smackzeyl, Brouwersgracht 101. Boisterous drinking hole on the fringes of the Jordaan frequented by well-doused tourists in various stages of inebriation. Guiness on tap, and a light, inexpensive menu.

't Smalle, Egelantiersgracht 12. Candle-lit and comfortable, with a barge out front for relaxed summer afternoons.

De Tap, Prinsengracht 478. Roomy bar with a balcony and more individuality than you'd expect, two minutes from the Leidseplein.

Terzijde, Kerkstraat 59. Within a stones' throw of Leidsestraat, this is a peaceful, authentic brown café used by the locals.

De Tuin, 2e Tuindwarsstraat 13. The Jordaan has some marvellously unpretentious bars, and this is one of the best: agreeably unkempt and always filled with locals.

Twee Prinsen, Prinsenstraat 27. Cornerside people-watching bar that's a useful starting place for touring the area. Its heated terrace makes it possible to sit outside, even in winter.

De Twee Zwaantjes, Prinsengracht 114. Tiny Jordaan bar whose live accordian music and raucous singing you'll either love or hate. Fun, in an oompah-pah sort of way.

De Vergulde Gaper, Prinsenstraat 30. Opposite the *Twee Prinsen*, this offers much the same kind of low-key attraction – though it's somewhat larger and there's a wider choice of food. Has a heated terrace if you fancy sitting outside.

Weltschermz, Lindengracht 62. Modern new-waveish café, busy late in the evening, sometimes with impromptu concerts.

't Werck, Leliegracht 60. Small and brown café with good-value tasty food. Don't, however, come here if you're in a hurry.

Wheels, Wolvenstraat 2–4. Deceptively like any other brown café to look at, but actually the firmly British haunt of a number of expats. Expect to be served by a friendly north London soul boy.

Winkel, Noordermarkt 43. A popular, though not particularly brown, café, where the main language seems to be English and the food – well-priced and good – largely Italian-oriented.

De Zotte, Raamstraat 29. Belgian *eetcafé* on the edge of the Jordaan. Food from ƒ12.50, and hundreds of different types of beer.

Bars outside the Singelgracht

Duvel, 1e Van der Helstraat 59. An *eetcafé* on a pedestrianized street adjacent to the Albert Cuypstraat. Handy if you've come to shop in the market.

Helfensteyn, Overtoom 28. Popular and agreeable *eetcafé* about five minutes' walk from Leidseplein. Food is pricey, though, with a fixed-price menu at ƒ37.50, and main courses from ƒ20.

Hesp, Weesperzijde 130. Quite a way out, but with a real old-fashioned atmosphere, and not at all known to most tourists. Frequented by hacks from the nearby *de Volkskrant*, *Trouw*, and *Het Parool* newspapers.

Keyser, Van Baerlestraat 96. In operation since 1905, and right next door to the Concertgebouw, this café/restaurant exudes *fin-de-siècle* charm, with ferns, gliding bow-tied waiters, and a dark, wood-carved interior. Slightly higher prices, especially for the food, but a great place to idle away an hour over coffee. You'll need to make bookings for the restaurant, and dress accordingly.

Old Manege, Vondelstraat 140. Well-hidden and touristed café on the north side of the Vondelpark that is the chosen watering hole of horse enthusiasts from the adjacent riding school.

't Orkestje, Van Baerlestraat 51. Pleasant *eetcafé* with musical-theme decor – the Concertgebouw is just across the street. Not cheap.

Tramlijn Begeerte, van Limburg Stirumplein 4. Popular Staatsleidenbuurt neighbourhood bar (off Haarlemmerweg), especially crowded in summer, when everybody crowds onto the large terrace and pavement. Curiously enough, the Virgin Mary has appeared here over recent years on a number of occasions, a manifestation marked by a stone in the pavement outside.

Welling, J.W. Brouwerstraat 32. Supposedly the traditional haunt of the gloomy Amsterdam intellectual, *Welling* is usually packed solid with performers and visitors from the Concertgebouw next door.

Wildschut, Roelof Hartplein 1. Large and congenial bar whose Art Deco trimmings attract the New South's trendies. The best bet for this area.

Women-only bars

Many of Amsterdam's women-only bars have a strong lesbian following, though straight women are welcome everywhere.

Van den Berg, Lindengracht 95. Likeable local café with good food and a billiard table. Frequented mainly by lesbian women.

Coffeeshop Françoise, Kerkstraat 176. Lively and elegant atmosphere, with good breakfasts and lunches, and a small gallery. Men allowed. Mon–Sat 9am–6pm.

Groep 7152. A non-political group of lesbian and bisexual women that organizes open meetings (usually in the Creagebouw, but ask around) every third Sunday in the month.

Monica Bar, Lanfe Niezel 15. Hard-core lesbian bar.

Saarein, Elandstraat 119. Though some of the former glory of this café is gone, still a useful starting point for contacts and information, even for joining a women's football team. Mon 8pm–1am, Tues–Thurs 3pm–1am, Fri & Sat 3pm–2am, Sun 3pm–1am.

La Strada, Nieuwe Zijds Voorburgwal 93–95. Chic, stylish bar popular with lesbians: see "Inner Centre Bars" for listing.

Vive la Vie, Amstelstraat 7. Small, stylish but non-exclusive bar. Open noon–1am, except Fri & Sat when it's open until 2am.

Gay Men's Bars

Amstel Taveerne, Amstel 54. Well-established, traditional gay bar with regular sing-alongs. Always packed, and at its most vivacious in the summer when the crowds spill out onto the street.

Anco, Oude Zijds Voorburgwal 55. Late-night hotel and leather bar with a large back room.

April, Reguliersdwarsstraat 27. On the itinerary of almost every gay visitor to Amsterdam. Lively and cosmopolitan, with a good selection of foreign newspapers, cakes and coffee, as well as booze.

Argos Club, Warmoesstraat 95. Amsterdam's oldest leather bar, with two bars and a raunchy cellar. Not for the faint-hearted.

Backstage Coffeeshop, Utrechtsedwarsstraat 67. See "non-smoking" coffee shops. p.136

't Balkje Coffeeshop, Kerkstraat 46–48. Popular though not exclusively gay meeting place. Good-value meals and snacks.

Casa Maria, Warmoesstraat 60. Mixed gay bar in the heart of the Warmoesstraat scene.

Chez Manfred, Halvemaansteeg 10. Camp and often outrageous small bar. Can be packed at peak times, when everyone joins in the sing-along.

Clib Jaecques, Warmoesstraat 93. Bar for leather and denim types. A meeting place for locals, but appropriate visitors are made welcome.

Cockring (C-Ring), Warmoesstraat 96. Leather bar with a spacious dancefloor and a cruisy back room.

Company, Amstel 106. Western-style leather bar. Fills up later in the evening.

Cosmo Bar, Kerkstraat 42. Comfortable, quiet bar, part of the *West End Hotel* (see p.123). Opens at midnight: a good place for late night/early morning drinks.

Cuckoo's Nest, Nieuwe Zijds Kolk 6. A Warmoesstraat area leather bar with a long reputation, this is described as "the best place in town for chance encounters (dark room downstairs)".

Bars and Coffee Shops

Bars and Coffee Shops

Doll's Place, Vinkenstraat 57. A mixed bar, rather off the beaten track but popular with local gays and lesbians.

Coffeeshop Downtown, Reguliersdwarsstraat 31. A favourite with tourists. Relaxed and friendly, with inexpensive meals.

The Eagle, Warmoesstraat 86. Long-established leather bar popular with men of all ages. Gets very busy after 1am. Open until 5am.

The Eighties, Brouwersgracht 139. Tries for a hi-tech ambience, but suffers from an extremely small menu and out-of-place black plastic furnishings. Open until 8pm, 10pm in summer.

Favourite Tavern, Korte Reguliersdwarsstraat 10. Cosy, traditional brown café with a welcoming atmosphere.

Fellows, Amstel 50. Civilized and immaculately clean bar on the river. An ideal location in summer.

Gaiety, Amstel 14. Small gay bar with a warm welcome. One of the most popular gay haunts in Amsterdam.

G-Force, Oudezijds Amsteeg 7. All sexual preferences are catered for in this fairly recent bar.

Havana, Reguliersdwarsstraat 17. Stylish and would-be sophisticated hangout patronized by those who like to be seen out on the town.

Krokodil, Amstelstraat 34. Amiable, if noisy, bar in between the discos and clubs.

Mankind, Weteringstraat 60. Tucked-away bar with its own terrace and landing stage. Lovely in summer.

Meia Meia, Kerkstraat 63. Good if you like the combination of gay and Guinness, with good jazz music.

Monopole Taveerne, Amstel 60. Semi-leather bar, popular with both tourists and locals, especially on hot afternoons.

Montmartre de Paris, Halve Maansteeg 17. A convivial brown café, with the emphasis on music and entertainment.

The Otherside, Reguliersdwarsstraat 6. See "smoking" coffee shops, below.

Route 66, Kerkstraat 66. American-style bar popular with clones and middle-aged regulars.

Shako Bar, 's Gravelandseveer 2. Friendly bar across the Amstel with an interesting decor.

De Spijker, Kerkstraat 4. Leather and jeans bar that has made a name for itself with its twice-monthly, safe sex "jack off" parties, which raise funds for AIDS organizations.

Stablemaster, Warmoesstraat 23. A leather bar with English-speaking staff and a British following.

Taveerne De Pul, Kerkstraat 45. Pleasant mix of friendly regulars and foreign visitors. Worth a visit for the ceiling alone, which is covered with a collection of beer mugs from around the world.

The Web, St Jacobsstraat 6. Strict rubber, leather and denim bar with a dance floor, back rooms and a pool table.

The Web Club, Oude Zijds Voorburgwal 15–17. Leather bar with dancefloor and dark room. Open Wed–Sun from 11pm; women only Friday nights, when it becomes the *Clit Club* (see "Lesbian Clubs" in *Nightlife*).

Why Not, Nieuwe Zijds Voorburgwal 28. Long-running, intimate bar with a porno cinema above.

Coffee Shops

As with bars, there are two types of Amsterdam **coffee shops**: those whose principle business is the buying, selling and consuming of dope, and the more traditional places that sell neither dope nor alcohol but do serve sandwiches or a light menu for lower prices than you'd pay in a fully fledged restaurant; some also offer pastries or chocolates.

Smoking Coffee Shops

The so-called **"smoking" coffee shops** are easy to identify: pumping out varieties of acid house or hard rock, brightly lit, with starkly modern furniture and an accent on healthy food; they're about as far from the cosy Dutch *brown café* as it's possible to get. Indeed you'll rarely see Amsterdammers in these places – they're usually filled with tourists. Smoking dope is the primary pastime (all sell a range of hash and grass), and most also have video screens, (loud) music, and a selection of games from baccarat to pool; they're open roughly from late morning or midday until around midnight. There are a couple of chains and a number of established places – *The Bulldog, Fancy Free, Extase* – and new places seem to be opening up all the time. There are pressures, too, from all quarters to properly legalize cannabis in The Netherlands, so as to make it possible to control the quality of the stuff, and make the revenue it produces taxable.

Biba, Hazenstraat 15. In a street of coffee shops, this is one of the best.

The Bulldog, Leidseplein 15; Oude Zijds Voorburgwal 90; corner of Singel and Brouwersgracht. The biggest and most famous of the coffee shop chains, and a long way from its pokey Red Light district dive origins. The main Leidseplein branch (the "Palace"), housed in a former police station, has a large cocktail bar, coffee shop, juice bar and souvenir shop. It's big and brash, not at all the place for a quiet smoke, though the dope they sell (packaged up in neat little brand-labelled bags), is reliably good.

Dreadlock, Oude Zijds Voorburgwal, opposite Oude Kerk. Welcoming coffee shop that plays loud music and shows big screen cartoons. Very convivial, highly recommended.

Extase, Oude Hoogstraat 2. Part of a chain run by the initiator of the *Hash Info Museum*. Considerably less chi-chi than the better-known coffee shops.

Fairy Nuff, 2e Laurierdwarsstraat 1b. Small and quiet, with a low-key atmosphere.

Fancy Free, Martelaarsgracht 4; Haarlemmerstraat 64. Slick, pink, plush and commercial, very much in the *Bulldog* mould.

Free City, Marnixstraat 233. Crowded coffee shop that's favoured by Amsterdammers in the know. Good dope.

Goa, Kloveniersburgwal 42. A member of the Extase chain (see above).

Grasshopper, Nieuwe Zijds Voorburgwal 57; Utrechtsestraat 21. One of the city's more welcoming "smoking" coffee shops, though at times overwhelmed by tourists. The Utrechtsestraat branch is the quieter of the two.

Just a Puff, 2e Tuindwarsstraat 1. Instantly recognizable, friendly Jordaan smoking hole. Open irregularly, though.

De Lach, 1e Bloemdwarsstraat 6; Singel 237. Quite unlike a normal "smoking" coffee shop – and much the better for it.

Mellow Yellow, Vijzelgracht 33. Sparse but bright coffee shop with a small but good quality dope list. No alcohol but great, fresh orange juice; very friendly too.

The Otherside, Reguliersdwaarsstraat 6. Gay coffee shop, (in Dutch "being from the otherside" is a euphemism for being gay). Youthful venue facing stiff competition from its more established neighbours. good value snacks and meals.

Pie in the Sky, 2e Lauriersdwarsstraat 64. Beautiful canal-corner setting, great for outside summer lounging.

Prix d'Ami, Haringpakkersteeg 5. Long-established but characterless coffee shop.

La Rocka, Damrak 36. Centrally situated coffee shop that plays ear-splitting hard rock to a mixed clientele. Prices slightly above average. OK if you like that sort of thing.

Rusland, Rusland 16. One of the first Amsterdam coffee shops, a cramped but vibrant place that's a favourite with both dope fans and tea addicts (it has 43 different kinds). A little worse for a recent extension, but a still a cut above the rest.

Siberië, Brouwersgracht 11. Set up by the former staff of *Rusland* and notable for the way it has avoided the over-commercialization of the larger chains. Very relaxed, very friendly, and worth a visit whether you want to smoke or not.

So Fine, Prinsengracht 30. Long-established coffee shop, big on atmosphere at night with good food and music, a pool table, and a video room.

Bars and Coffee Shops

For real dope-heads there's also the Hash Info Museum *– see p.60. For more on dope, see p.34.*

Bars and Coffee Shops

Sturgis, Brouwersgracht 137. Very loud music.

De Tweede Kamer, Heisteeg 6. A busy coffee shop that's more "brown" than most of its rivals.

"Non-smoking" coffee shops

The growth of "smoking" coffee shops has made "straight" places increasingly defensive, and all of the coffee shops listed as "non-smoking" go to great lengths to emphasize that they don't sell dope, and that its consumption on the premises is strictly forbidden; some are even considering calling themselves "tea rooms" to avoid confusion. If you're not sure, ask. Basically the recommendations below are good places to take time out from shopping or sightseeing to have a cup of tea or coffee, or are good stopoffs for a light lunch or snack.

Arnold Cornelis, Elandsgracht 78. Confectioner with a snug tea room.

Backstage Coffee Shop, Utrechtsedwarsstraat 67. Run by the former cabaret stars, the Christmas Twins, this offbeat place also sells knitwear and African jewellery. Popular with gays.

Baton, Herengracht 82. Convivial coffee shop with a huge array of sandwiches. In a central location, handy for cheap lunches.

J. G. Beune, Haarlemmerdijk 156. Age-old chocolatier with a tea room attached.

Cocky's Coffeebar, Raadhuisstraat 8. Good no-nonsense coffee shop with a wide variety of sandwiches.

Dialoog, Prinsengracht 261a. A few doors down from the Anne Frank House, one long room filled with paintings, restrained classical music, and downstairs, a gallery of Latin American art. A good choice of sandwiches and salads, too.

Errol Trumpie, Leidsestraat 46. The place for pastries and chocolates, with a small tea room at the back. Try the *koffie complet de patisserie* – a pot of coffee and plate of heavy calorific pastries for around ƒ15.

Granny, 1e van der Helststraat 45. Just off the Albert Cuyp market, with terrific *appelgebak* and *koffie verkeerd*.

Greenwood's, Singel 103. Small, English-style coffee shop in the basement of a canal house. Pies and sandwiches, pots of tea – and a decent breakfast.

Karbeel, Warmoesstraat 58. Once run by the presnt owner of *De Eenhoorn* (see p.128), and similiar in style and setup.

Lindsay's Teashop, Kalverstraat 185. An attempt to recreate a little piece of England in the unlikely location of the basement of the American Discount Book Centre. The food, though, is fine: real English cream teas, with homemade pies and trifles. And it's a refreshing escape from the Kalverstraat shopping mafia.

Café Panini, Vijzelgracht 3–5. Coffee shop-cum-restaurant that features good sandwiches and, in the evening, pasta dishes.

Pompadour Patisserie, Huidenstraat 12. A great patisserie specializing in handmade chocolates.

Puccini, Staalstraat 21. Lovely cake, chocolate shop and café, with wonderful handmade cakes, pastries and good coffee.

Café de Stoep, Singel 415. Peaceful, rather ordinary café that is a good bet for a simple, light lunch.

Studio 2, Singel 504. Pleasantly situated, airy coffee shop with a delicious selection of rolls and sandwiches. Recommended.

Tatsun, Nieuwendijk 45. Turkish coffee shop with sticky pastries and suchlike.

Caffe Toto, 2e Anjeliersdwarsstraat 6. Small coffee shop that serves very tasty hot chocolate.

De Utrechtsepoort, Utrechtsestraat 113. Small, homely and serving delicious pancakes.

Café Vertigo, Netherlands Film Museum, Vondelpark 3. Basement museum café that's a nice place for a beer, coffee or snack. On Sundays a literary radio programme is broadcast from here.

Villa Zeezicht, Torensteeg. Small, centrally located place with excellent rolls and sandwiches.

Chapter 9

Restaurants

Amsterdam may not be Europe's culinary capital, but there's a good supply of ethnic **restaurants**, especially Indonesian and Chinese, and the prices – by big-city standards – are hard to beat. There are also a number of *eetcafés* and bars that serve increasingly adventurous food, quite cheaply, in a relaxed and unpretentious setting.

Apart from a short section on budget eating at the city's mensas, the following restaurants and *eetcafés* are grouped by cuisine and listed alphabetically: you'll find some indication of what each place is likely to cost within its listing, but as a broad guide, very few will cost more than *f*30 for a main course, and many charge much less than this; Dutch restaurants and *eetcafés* in particular serve plenty of smaller dishes for much less. Bars are also worth checking out: many serve food, and at lunchtime it's possible to fill up cheaply with a bowl of soup or a french bread sandwich.

The majority of bars are **open** all day; most restaurants open around 5pm. The Dutch eat out early – rarely later than 9pm – and in both restaurants and bars, kitchens are normally closed by 11pm at the latest; vegetarian restaurants tend to shut their doors even earlier.

Mensas

These are Amsterdam's student cafeterias, and as such are not frequented so much for the quality of the food as for the prices, which at *f*7.50–10 for a full meal can hardly be beaten. The food itself isn't bad, filling enough if not especially tasty.

Atrium, Oude Achterburgwal 237; ☎525 39 99. Mon–Fri noon–2pm and 5–7pm.

Agora, Roeterstraat 11; ☎525 26 99. Mon–Fri noon–2pm and 5–7pm.

Dutch

De Bak, Prinsengracht 193; ☎625 79 72. Good portions at moderate prices, though lately somewhat of a tourist hangout with a menu that seems to have shrunk down to spare ribs and not much else. See also *De Bak's* sister restaurant, *Sing Singel*, below.

De Bijenkorf, Dam 1; ☎621 80 80. Restaurant of the top-notch department store, and one of the best places for a full Dutch breakfast and good-value lunches for *f*10 upwards.

De Blauwe Hollander, Leidsekruisstraat 28; ☎623 30 14. Dutch food in generous quantities – something of a boon in an otherwise touristy, unappealing part of town. Most meals *f*20–30.

Claes Claesz, Egelantiersstraat 24–26; ☎625 53 06. Exceptionally friendly Jordaan restaurant that attracts a good mixed crowd and serves excellent Dutch food, though not at all cheaply. Reckon on paying *f*25 or more for a main course. Live music most nights. Often has (pricey) special menus to celebrate specific occasions – carnival, Easter, the Queen's Birthday, etc; best check first. Closed Mon–Wed.

Dikker & Thijs, Leidsestraat 80; ☎626 77 21. Self-conciously chic – and rather pretentious – brasserie run by the gourmet deli people, which has three-course menus

For some tips on Dutch food, reading the menu and other restaurant practices, see "Eating and Drinking" p.30.

Check the bar listings in the previous chapter for good-value eating.

Restaurants

from *f*45 and *dagschotels* for *f*30. The upstairs restaurant is more expensive.

De Eenhoom, 2e Egelantiersdwarsstraat 6; ☎ 623 83 52. A less attractive alternative to *De Eettuin* (see below) but handy if it's full.

De Eettuin, 2e Tuindwarsstraat 10; ☎ 623 77 06. Hefty portions of Dutch food, all with a salad from a serve-yourself bar for *f*17–24. Non-meat eaters can content themselves with the large, if dull, vegetarian plate, or the delicious fish casserole.

Haesje Claes, Spuistraat 275; ☎ 624 99 98. Dutch cuisine at its best. Extremely popular – go early to get a table.

Keuken van 1870, Spuistraat 4; ☎ 624 89 65. Basic, traditional Dutch cooking, a good deal if money's short, though the service can be pretty dreadful.

Koevoet, Lindenstraat 17; ☎ 624 08 46. Traditional Jordaan *eetcafé* that serves unpretentious food at good prices. The name means "cow's foot" or "crowbar".

Koffiehuis van de Volksbond, Kadijksplein 4; ☎ 622 12 09. Formerly a communist party café (and apparently the place where the local dockworkers used to receive their salaries at the end of each week), this is now a cheap Eastern Islands neighbourhood restaurant, with variable food for low prices – between *f*15 and *f*25 for three courses.

Leto, Haarlemerdijk 114; ☎ 626 56 95. Unexciting food but colourful management.

Moeder's Pot, Vinkenstraat 119; ☎ 623 76 43. Ultra-cheap Dutch food, usually of good quality, though recent reports have warned of under-cooking and watery flavours.

Sing Singel, Singel 101; ☎ 625 25 81. Sister restaurant to *De Bak*, above.

Zemmel, Prinsengracht 126; ☎ 620 65 25. A good place to eat in summer, with a nice position by the water. Simple food, not too expensive at around *f*30 for a main course. You can go just for a drink too.

't Zwaantje, Berenstraat 12; ☎ 623 23 73. Old-fashioned Dutch restaurant with a nice atmosphere and well-cooked, reasonably priced food.

Fish

Albatros, Westerstraat 264; ☎ 627 99 32. Family-run restaurant serving some mouth-wateringly imaginative fish dishes – though at around *f*40, for no mean cost. A place to splash out and linger over a meal.

Lucius, Spuistraat 247; ☎ 624 18 31. Pricey, but one of the best fish restaurants in town, though the service they give – particularly to credit card-paying customers – leaves something to be desired.

Noordzee, Kalverstraat 122; ☎ 623 73 37. The central Amsterdam branch of a chain that specializes in cheap fish lunches, sandwiches and take away fish and chips. Meals for around ƒ12, sandwiches ƒ5.

De Oesterbar, Leidseplein 10; ☎ 626 34 63. Pricey veteran overlooking the Leidseplein action, popular with a largely older crowd. Main courses ƒ25 or more, and not really worth it.

Sluizer, Utrechtsestraat 45; ☎ 626 35 57. Next door to its trendy meat-based partner, main courses here go for ƒ23–50 – which, for the quality of the food, service and decor, is fine value.

Pancakes

Bredero, Oude Zijds Voorburgwal 244; ☎ 622 94 61. On the edge of the Red Light district, one of the city's best pancake deals.

The Pancake Bakery, Prinsengracht 191; ☎ 625 13 33. Open all day; has a large selection of pancakes from ƒ10.

Vegetarian and Health Food

Bolhoed, Prinsengracht 60; ☎ 626 18 03. Health food place with set lunches for ƒ15, dinner for ƒ22.50. The food is healthy with a vengeance; try the natural beer to wash it down. Open until 10pm.

Egg Cream, St. Jacobstraat 19; ☎ 623 05 75. Amsterdam's most famous vegetarian restaurant, cheap and atmospheric, though the food isn't always exclusively veggie. Set lunches ƒ10, dinners ƒ15. Bear in mind the early closing time of 8pm.

Gimsez, Huidenstraat 19; ☎ 624 97 47. Pleasant and tasty food, though the ambience is a bit clinical and service can be slow. Good lunch specials.

Golden Temple, Utrechtsestraat 126; ☎ 626 85 60. Laid-back place with a little more soul than the average Amsterdam veggie joint. Gentle live music. Open until 9pm.

Klaver Koning, Koningstraat 29; ☎ 626 10 85. Excellent upmarket vegetarian restaurant, with decent wine and a refreshingly carefree atmosphere. But not cheap.

Het Noorden, Fredrik Hendrikstraat 115; ☎ 684 91 15. Housed in a former squat, this place is still full of idealism. From the fixed menu (changed daily), you can choose between fish (ƒ12) and vegetarian (ƒ9) meals.

Schizen, Kerkstraat 148; ☎ 622 86 27. Japanese macrobiotic restaurant, with dishes from ƒ17 upwards.

Sisters, Nes 102; ☎ 626 39 70. A busy vegetarian restaurant serving delicious *dagschotels* and other main courses for around ƒ16, as well as penty of snack-type items. Excellent value. Open (irregularly) for lunch until 4pm, dinner until 9pm.

De Vliegende Schotel, Nieuwe Leliestraat 162; ☎ 625 20 41. Very basic and very cheap, with a good noticeboard.

De Vrolijke Abrikoos, Weteringschans 76; ☎ 624 46 72. All ingredients, produce and processes are organic or environmentally friendly in this restaurant that serves fish and meat as well as vegetarian dishes.

Chinese, Japanese, Thai and Filipino

Dynasty, Reguliersdwarsstraat 30; ☎ 626 84 00. Festive choice of Indo-Chinese food, but not for the shoestring traveller. A rather middle-aged crowd.

De Klaas Compaen, Raamgracht 9; ☎ 623 87 08. Good Thai food at affordable prices.

Lana Thai, Warmoesstraat 10; ☎ 624 21 79. Among the best Thai restaurants in town, with seating overlooking the water of Damrak. Quality food, chic surroundings but high prices. Closed Tues.

Mango Bay, Westerstraat 91; ☎ 638 10 39. Slow service and high prices for the Filipino food, but the cocktails are deadly.

New San Kong, Amstelveenseweg 338–344; ☎ 662 93 70. Don't be put off by the ranch style of the decor; the Cantonese food is excellent and inexpensive (try the *dim sum*). Take tram #24 to the end of the line.

Oriental Palace, Oude Doelenstraat 1; ☎ 620 70 40. Chinese fast-food restaurant. Not the sort of place you'd want to linger.

Restaurants

Restaurants

Roeng Warie, Rokin 85; ☎626 79 13. Thai food, well priced and centrally located among the costlier reaches of Rokin.

Tom Yam, Staalstraat 22; ☎622 95 33. Expensive, but tasty (especially if you like chillis) Thai restaurant. Set menus from ƒ40.

Umeno, Agamemnonstraat 27; ☎676 60 89. Reaonably priced Japanese restaurants are hard to find, but this one, though down in the residential New South, has cooking and prices that are well worth the journey. Closed Mon. Tram #24.

Yoichi, Weteringschans 128; ☎ 622 68 29. High-class Japanese cuisine in an improbable dark-brown, old Dutch atmosphere. Closed Mon.

French and Belgian

Beddington's, Roelof Hartstraat 6–8; ☎676 52 01. Beddington's refined French cuisine blended with Japanese delicacy is always original, never disappointing. The subtlety of flavours is matched by Japanese inspired presentation (especially for the fish dishes), and a meal here can be memorable, if not cheap. ƒ65 and upwards.

Bistro de Vlier, Prinsengracht 422; ☎623 22 81. Fairly basic cooking in an affable atmosphere; main meals from ƒ25, three-course menus ƒ29. Open Sun, which is a boon.

Brasserie van Baerle, Van Baerlestraat 158; ☎662 20 90. Light and airy restaurant serving good food that's run by a couple of ex-*KLM* flight attendants. Very popular, especially on Sun; booking advised.

Café Cox, Marnixstraat 427; ☎620 72 22. Stylish but amicable bar and restaurant underneath the Stadtsschouwburg which serves a wide range of dishes, most for around ƒ25. *Dagschotels* from ƒ19.50.

't Fomuis, Utrechtsestraat 33; ☎626 91 39. A slightly cheaper alternative to *Orient Express* (see below), though it's usually very busy. Main courses ƒ26 or more.

Café Le Garage Restaurant, Ruysdaelstraat 54–56; ☎679 71 76. This elegant restaurant has quickly become popular with a media crowd and their hangers on, since it's run by a well-known Dutch TV cook. An eclectic French and Italian menu – ƒ60 for three courses – and sporadic fashion shows. A place to be seen.

Georges & Betsie, Herenstraat 3. A highly rated upmarket Belgian eatery. The set menu costs ƒ42.50, and is very meaty.

De Gouden Reael, Zandhoek 14; ☎623 38 83. Fine French food at reasonable prices. Closed Sun.

Grand Café Restaurant, Eerste Klas, Platform 2, Centraal Station; ☎625 01 31. Gourmet French cuisine with well-balanced menu in the train station's restored late-nineteenth-century restaurant. Good value, and it also has a wide array of snacks.

Hemelse Modder, Oude Waal 9; ☎624 32 03. Tasty meat, fish and vegetarian food in French-Italian style at reasonable prices in an informal atmosphere. Highly popular (especially among the gay community). Best phone ahead.

Intermezzo, Herenstraat 28; ☎626 01 67. Good French-Dutch cooking at above-average prices, but worth every penny.

Jardin Parisien, Utrechtsestraat 30a; ☎626 80 93. Cheap and straightforward, with around thirty different menus on offer, most of which seem to start with prawn cocktail. Two-course meals for ƒ22.50–30.

Café Jansen, Voetboogstraat 12; ☎638 64 70. Inexpensive nouvelle cuisine. Trendy but nice.

De Kikker, Egelantiersstraat 130; ☎627 91 98. Two-tier, top quality restaurant that has a downstairs *eetcafé* with three-course meals for around ƒ30. Upstairs is only really accessible for the well-dressed, wealthy and committed gourmet.

De Lieve, Herengracht 88; ☎ 624 96 35. Belgian restaurant with menus from ƒ40, and main courses for ƒ30. A pleasant atmosphere, although reports of the food are mixed.

Luden, Spuisstraat 304–308; ☎622 89 79. Excellent French restaurant that does fine value prix-fixe menus from ƒ45.

Orient Express, Utrechtsestraat 29; ☎ 620 51 29. Not cheap, but very good French food; you can also choose from a menu which changes every month, including French-flavoured items from each of the countries the Orient Express passes through.

Paris Brest, Prinsengracht 375; ☎ 627 05 07. Next door to *Van Puffelen* (see p.131) and owned by the same man, this is the designer alternative: all chrome and glass and black leather filofaxes. Excellent and clever main courses for around *f*28, and a very reasonable set menu at *f*41.

Robert & Abraham Kef, Marnixstraat 192; ☎ 626 22 10. Not a restaurant or bar but a cheese shop with a few tables for sampling the (mainly French) cheeses with a bottle of wine. Ideal for lunch or a snack. Open Tues–Sat until 6pm.

Sluizer, Utrechtsestraat 43; ☎ 622 63 76. French-oriented food, in one of Amsterdam's most atmospheric restaurants. There's a fish restaurant of the same name next door – see above.

De Smoeshaan, Leidsekade 90; ☎ 627 69 66. First-floor theatre restaurant, or downstairs bar, with inexpensive French cuisine.

Greek, Balkan, Turkish

Aphrodite, Lange Leidsedwarsstraat 91; ☎ 622 73 82. Refined Greek cooking in a street where you certainly wouldn't expect it. Fair prices too.

Filoxenia, Berenstraat 8; ☎ 624 42 92. Small, friendly, reasonably priced – and filling.

Kroation, Hobbemakade 64–65; ☎ 671 94 95. Good range of Yugoslav specialities, either à la carte or from a choice of set menus. However, it's a long way to trek unless you're a fan of the cuisine of the now defunct country.

To Ouzeri, De Clerqstraat 106; ☎ 618 14 12. Greek *eetcafé* where you can compose your own meal and make it as cheap – or as expensive – as you like.

Plaka, Egelantiersstraat 124; ☎ 627 93 38. Enormous plates of greasy Greek grub for *f*16–30; vegetarian dishes too. Popular (either book ahead or turn up early) and friendly.

Saray Lokantasi, Gerard Doustraat 33; ☎ 671 92 16. Excellent and cheap Turkish eatery down in the De Pijp neighbourhood. Popular with students.

Indian

Koh-I-Noor, Westermarkt 29 (☎ 623 31 33); Rokin 18 (☎ 627 21 18). One of the city's better Indian restaurants, with two central branches, and not overpriced. The Westermarkt branch is the more popular of the two.

Mogul, Rokin 107; ☎ 624 24 16. Above-average and centrally located restaurant serving Pakistani food.

New Delhi, Overtoom 350; ☎ 616 78 58. On the far side of the Vondelpark, but well worth the journey. Northern-style, very filling dishes for around *f*15.

Purna, Hartenstraat 29; ☎ 623 67 72. The speciality here is spicy tandoori; they also sell Indian silk paintings.

Rishi Roti Room, 1e Oosterparkstraat 91; ☎ 692 86 28. Cheap and cheerful restaurant.

Shiva, Reguliersdwarstraat 72; ☎ 624 87 13. Comes highly recommended as the city's outstanding Indian restaurant. Has a good selection for vegetarians, and isn't expensive – around *f*22 should get you three courses.

Tandoor, Leidseplein 19; ☎ 623 44 15. Doesn't live up to its excellent reputation, but pretty good nonetheless. The tandoori dishes are very tasty, and, if nothing like as cheap as the *New Delhi* (see above), still won't break the bank.

Indonesian

Asli, Waterlooplein 341; ☎ 638 65 03. Well-known Indonesian restaurant serving decent and authentic food at reasonable prices. Good saté.

Bojo, Lange Leidsedwarsstraat 51; ☎ 626 89 90. Possibly the best-value – if not the best – Indonesian place in town, and open until 6am. Expect to wait for a table, though – we weren't the first to discover it. Recommended, but the service can be slow.

Restaurants

Restaurants

Jaya, 1e Anjeliersdwarsstraat 18; ☎624 01 22. One of the smallest and finest of the city's Indonesian restaurants, with classical music as an accompaniment to your food. Bookings advised.

Sama Sebo, P.C. Hooftstraat 27; ☎662 81 46. Amsterdam's best-known Indonesian restaurant, especially for *rijstaffel* – though the prices may put you off. However, it's easy to eat quite reasonably by choosing your dishes à la carte, and the food is usually great. Bookings advised.

Sjaalman, Prinsengracht 178; ☎620 24 40. Indonesian *eetcafé* with huge and tasty vegetarian specials for around ƒ15.

Speciaal, Nieuwe Leliestraat 142; ☎624 97 06. Moderately priced and generally agreed to be one of the best in town.

Tempo Doeloe, Utrechsestraat 75; ☎625 67 18. Reliable place close to Rembrandtsplein. As with all Indonesian restaurants, be guided by the waiter when choosing a *rijstaffel* – some of the dishes are very hot indeed. Not cheap.

Italian

Burger's Patio, 2e Tuindwarsstraat 12; ☎623 68 54. Moderately priced, young and convivial Italian restaurant. Despite the name, not a burger in sight.

Capri, Lindengracht 63; ☎624 49 40. Inexpensive pizza place and coffee shop that's extremely tolerant towards children, and hence popular with parents shopping in the nearby markets.

Casa di David, Singel 426; ☎624 50 93. Solid-value Italian restaurant with a long-standing reputation. Pizzas from wood-fired ovens, freshly made pasta, and more substantial fare. Best seats are by the window. There's also a companion self-service place at Kalverstraat 180.

Mamma Mia, 2e Leliedwarsstraat 13; ☎ 625 82 38. Good selection of pizzas, from ƒ10, in a pleasant, family atmosphere.

Mascagni, Utrechtsestraat 65; ☎ 620 66 24. Authentic and homely Italian restaurant, family-run, and serving a very large choice of well-cooked dishes.

Miafiori, Hobbemastraat 2; ☎ 662 30 13. Upmarket Italian restaurant with a reputa-

tion as one of the town's best. Three courses for around ƒ40 means it's by no means unaffordable.

Orvieto, Nieuwendijk 9; ☎6266842. Centrally located and inexpensive.

Pizzeria Mimo, Lange Leidsedwarsstraat 37; ☎ 622 79 35. Perhaps the best of the dozens of Italian restaurants in this street.

Pizzeria Pastorale, Haarlemmerdijk 139; ☎625 99 28. Good-value pizzas.

Tartufo, Singel 449; ☎627 71 75. Two-tiered, two-menu place with a good choice of fair-priced pasta dishes downstairs.

Toscana di Romana, Haarlemmerdijk 176; (☎622 03 53); and Haarlemmerstraat 130. Fairly average food, but the pizzas and pasta dishes are all half-price Mon to Thurs. At other times, prices start at ƒ11. The Haarlemmerstraat branch is marginally the better of the two.

Toscanini Caffé, Lindengracht 75; ☎623 28 13. A step up in price from more average Italian places, but well worth the expense.

Vasso, Rosenboomsteeg 12–14; ☎626 01 58. Small expensive Italian restaurant with a good reputation.

North African

Artist, 2e jan Steenstraat 1; ☎671 42 64. A small Lebanese restaurant just off Alber Cuypstraat. Main dishes go for between ƒ15 and ƒ20.

Hamilcar, Overtoom 306; ☎683 79 81. Particularly good for its couscous, usually prepared by the chef and owner. Prices range from ƒ15 to ƒ35.

Marakech, Nieuwe Zijds Voorburgwal 134; ☎623 50 03. Inexpensive couscous place with veggie options.

Soulayma, Haarlemmerdijk 49; ☎625 75 79. Morrocan lunchroom that does rolls and sandwiches mostly, along with hot dishes like couscous for ƒ20 and less.

North, Latin and South American

Alfonso's, Korte Leidsedwarsstraat 69 (☎627 05 80); Utrechtsestraat 32 (☎ 625 94 26). Substantial helpings of relatively bland Mexican food for around *f*20 per person for the main course. Good value for Leidseplein, and not too touristy, but avoid the *margaritas*, which are watery and overpriced.

Café Pacifico, Warmoesstraat 31; ☎624 29 11. If you like Mexican food, or its Californian adaptation (or both), this is the place – only minutes from Centraal Station.

Cajun Louisiana Kitchen, Ceintuurbaan 256–260; ☎664 47 29. Not cheap, but it offers authentic Cajun flavours.

Canecao Rio, Reguliersdwarsstraat 8; ☎625 05 92. Brazilian food with live music.

Caramba, Lindengracht 342; ☎627 11 88. Steamy, busy Mexican restaurant in the heart of the Jordaan. The *margaritas* are almost on a par with Rose's (see below).

Curly's, Nieuwe Zijds Voorburgwal 22; ☎624 60 92. The food, plentifully supplied, is only average Tex-Mex fare. But relaxed atmosphere, music and service.

Lafitte Cajun, Westerstraat 20; ☎623 42 70. A more central Cajun alternative than the *Louisiana Kitchen*.

Mexico, Prinsengracht 188; ☎624 65 28. A cheaper and more amiable alternative to the glossier, more central eateries. Jolly owners, excellent food.

Mister Coco's, Thorbeckeplein 8–10. Bustling, determinedly youthful American restaurant that lives up to its own slogan of "lousy food and warm beer". Cheap, though (try the spare ribs), and very lively.

Rose's Cantina, Reguliersdwarsstraat 38; ☎625 97 97. In the heart of trendy Amsterdam, this qualifies as possibly the city's most crowded restaurant. No bookings, but you'll almost certanly have to wait, but it's no hardship to sit at the bar nursing a cocktail and watching the would-be cool bunch; the *margaritas* should carry a public health warning. The Tex-Mex food is good too, at around *f*25.

Sarita's Cantina, Lange Leidsedwarsstraat 29; ☎627 78 40. Nothing like as nice as Rose's (above), but serving good food at similiar prices.

Spanish and Portuguese

La Cacerola, Weteringstraat 41; ☎626 53 97. Small and secluded, with likeable if eccentric service – and erratic opening hours. Certainly closed Thurs & Sun.

Casa Tobio, Lindengracht 31; ☎624 89 87. Small Jordaan restaurant which doles out vast servings of Spanish food for around *f*25 a head, less if you risk annoying the management by sharing a paella for two between three – a good general rule for all Spanish places. Recent reports have been of unfriendliness though.

Centra, Lange Niezel 29; ☎622 30 50. A wonderful selection of Spanish food, masterfully cooked and genially served. In the running for Amsterdam's best Spanish food.

Eucalipto, Haarlemmerdijk 40; ☎623 07 94. Portuguese place, less crowded than *Girassol* (below) but still popular. Slightly more expensive, but with a pleasant and quieter atmosphere. Food varies in quality.

Girassol, Weesperzijde 135; ☎692 34 71. Close to Amstel Station, this place is a fair hike out from the centre, but easily merits the journey. A friendly, family-run Portuguese restaurant that food-loving Amsterdammers head out to. Best to book.

Iberia, Kadijksplein 16; ☎623 63 13. A little more expensive than some of the others listed here, but good service and great food.

Surinamese and Caribbean

Aurora, Rozengracht 5. Basic and typical Surinamese takeaway, with a few tables.

Riaz, Bilderdijkstraat 193; ☎683 64 53. Out in the Old West, an excellent, inexpensive Surinamese restaurant.

Rum Runners, Prinsengracht 277; ☎627 40 79. Caribbean-style bar/restaurant situated in the old Westerkek hall. Expensive cocktails but well-priced if not always devastatingly tasty food. Summer terrace and live South American music Wed–Sun evening.

Sin Doe, 1e van der Helstraat 62; ☎662 46 90. Very cheap Surinamese takeaway with a couple of bare tables.

Warung Swietie, 1e Sweelinckstraat 1; ☎671 58 33. Surinamese/Javanese *eetcafé*. Cheap and cheerful; closed Wed.

Restaurants

Chapter 10

Nightlife

Amsterdam is not a major cultural centre, by any standards. Its performance spaces are small for the most part, and the city is not a regular stop on the touring circuits of major companies. Rather, it's a gathering spot for fringe performances, and buzzes with places offering a wide – and often inventive – range of affordable entertainment.

As far as live music goes, Amsterdam is a regular stop for many bands, and a testing ground for current **rock** bands, especially British acts, although the city doesn't have a really major **rock music** venue, and the real superstars usually go to Rotterdam (the Ahoy sports hall or Feyenoord stadium) or Utrecht (the Music Centre Vredenburg). However, the city's many multi-media centres provide a constant and varied supply of music, as do *Paradiso* and a number of other smaller places. Look out, too, for the city's clubs and discos which sporadically host performances by live bands, and the many outlets for **jazz**, including **salsa** and **Latin American** music, which is well represented in a number of small bars and clubs.

For **classical music**, there's the perennial *Concertgebouw*, and the latest, biggest, and most prestigious outlet for **opera** is the *Muziektheater* by the Amstel on Waterlooplein – home of the national opera and ballet companies and part of a *f*306-million complex that includes the new town hall. It's not one of the city's more successful modern buildings, and caused considerable controversy when it went up. But it's now firmly part of the Amsterdam

skyline – and its cultural scene. As for **theatre**, a number of companies perform regularly in English, and **cinemas** rarely dub English-language films into Dutch.

The city's **multi-media centres**, at which you could find pretty much any of the above activities, are listed first along with the larger concert halls, and, along with other appropriate places, are **cross-referenced** at the end of each relevant section. Programmes everywhere can be varied and unpredictable, so always check listings sources carefully.

Information and Tickets

A good first stop is the **Uitburo**, in the Stadsschouwburg on the corner of Marnixstraat and Leidseplein (Mon–Sat 10am–6pm, Thurs until 9pm; ☎ 621 12 11), which offers advice on anything remotely cultural, sells tickets and is a source of the major **listings magazines**. Of these, there is the monthly *Uitkrant*, which is comprehensive and free, or the rather bland fortnightly *What's On In Amsterdam* (*f*3.50). Perhaps the best source for nightlife listings is the monthly *Time Out* (*f*4), aimed at the English speaking expat community. In Dutch, *Het Parool's* Wednesday entertainment supplement, *Uit en Thuis*, is the most up-to-date reference. Look too at the Uitburo's *Uitlijst* noticeboards, which include a weeekly update on pop music performances.

Tickets for most performances can be bought at the Uitburo and VVV offices (fees *f*2 and free respectively), or reserved by phone through *Uitlijn* (*f*5) or again, the VVV. Some major entertainment venues – the

Carre, Muziektheater, Stadsschouwburg and others – sell tickets for each other's productions at no extra cost through the *Kassadienst* plan. You can also book seats, again free of charge, through the *National Bookings Centre* (☎070/320 25 00), whereby you can make bookings at the really large venues (the Concertgebouw and *Muziektheater*, for example) from other European countries.

Festivals and Annual Events

Aside from the first two weeks of August, when many places are closed, summer sees a citywide expansion on the entertainment scene; walk the streets and you'll often be entertained whether you like it or not. There are free concerts and theatre performances in the **Vondelpark** from the beginning of June to the end-of-August up to five days a week. The end-of-August **Uitmarkt** is a three-day jamboree during which hundreds of cultural groups and organizations from all over Holland arrive with their new season's programmes, providing hours of free indoor and outdoor entertainment.

The largest of the festivals is the annual **Holland Festival**, a prestigious and international, if slightly highbrow, series of opera, music, theatre and dance performances held throughout the city (programmes, in English, from the Uitburo). Ther's also the annual gay **Festival van Verleiding** at the *Melkweg*, coinciding with Gay Pride Week at the end of June, which consists of exhibitions and performances of everything from erotic art to camp comedy. Watch out, too, for the **Amsterdam Roots Meeting** from mid-May to the first week of June, which – in a number of different theatres – concentrates on the culture of ethnic minorities; and during the first two weeks of November, the **Stagedoor Theatre Festival**, which is held at the Balie, Engelenbak and Soeterijn theatres. The **Over Het IJ Festival** features experimental theatre and performances (including the celebrated *DOG-troep*) at venues on the northern side of the IJ in Amsterdam North.

For easily accessible **jazz and pop festivals outside Amsterdam**, see the relevant sections below.

Concert Halls and Multi-Media Centres

Amstelveen Cultureel Centrum, Plein 1960, Amstelveen; ☎645 84 44. Down in the southern suburbs of the city and a long way from the centre (bus #64, #66), it offers a varied, if middle-of-the-road, programme of pop, classical music and dance. Worth keeping an eye on for the occasional gem.

Beurs van Berlage, Beursplein 1; ☎627 04 66. The splendid interior of the former stock exchange (see p.57) has been put to use as a venue for theatre and concerts. It's becoming increasingly important as a city centre venue.

Carre Theatre, Amstel 115–125; ☎622 52 25. A splendid 100-year-old structure (originally built as a circus) that now hosts all kinds of top international acts: anything from the Peking Circus to rap and Russian folk dance, with Elvis Costello and Alison Moyet squeezed in between. Tickets range from *f*25 to *f*60 depending on who's performing.

Jaap Eden Hal, Radioweg 64; ☎694 98 94. Large concert hall in the east of the city which occasionally stages big-name gigs. Heavy metal bands a favourite. Prices *f*15–40; tram #9.

Meervaart, Osdorpplein 205; ☎610 73 93. A modern multi-media centre on the outskirts of town (tram #1, bus #19, #23) with a varied programme of international music, film, theatre and dance. Rock performances irregularly (there's a blues festival in March), classical music/opera Sunday at midday and the occasional Monday, as well as a good, varied selection of films, with lots of reruns. Film tickets *f*9, other events *f*10–*f*25.

Melkweg, Lijnbaansgracht 234a; ☎624 17 77. Probably Amsterdam's most famous entertainment venue, and these days one of the city's prime arts centres, with a young, hip clientele at odds with Melkweg's erstwhile hippy image. Its theatre space serves as an outlet for small, inventive international groups, virtually all of which perform in English, and the concert hall plays host to a broad range of bands, with the emphasis on

Nightlife

Nightlife

The following also host pop and rock concerts: the Amstelveen Cultureel Centrum, p.145; Carre Theatre, p.145; Jaap Eden Hal, p.145; Kleine Komedie, p.151; Meervaart, p.145; Melkweg, p.145.

For jazz and Latin concerts see also Concertgebouw, p.148, De Engelbewaarder, p.128; Morlang, p.131.

African music and lesser-knowns. Later, on Friday and Saturday nights, excellent, offbeat disco sessions go on well into the small hours – admission ƒ5 plus ƒ4 membership (valid one month). Those intending to visit more than once should buy a longer validity membership card – three months cost ƒ6, one year ƒ20. Other features include a fine monthly film programme, a tea room selling dope and space cake (hash brownies), and a bar and restaurant (Marnixstraat entrance) open 11am–midnight on weekdays, 2pm–midnight on weekends. Otherwise, concerts begin around 10.30pm and admission ranges from ƒ10 to ƒ25. The Melkweg is closed Mon.

Stadsschouwburg, Leidseplein 26; ☎624 23 11. These days somewhat overshadowed by the Muziektheatre, but still staging significant opera and dance (it's a favourite of the Netherlands Dance Theatre), as well as – in its small hall – performances by ESTA and ART (see below). Tickets ƒ15 and up.

Pop and Rock

Until recently, **Dutch rock** was almost uniformly dire, divided fairly evenly between the traditional songs, accompanied by a loud accordian, being belted out of cafés in the Jordaan – a brash and sentimental adaptation of French chansons – and, with a few notable exceptions, the anaemic copies of English and American groups by bands lacking identity, and singing (uncon-vincingly) in English. The best place to hear the former – if you must – is still the Jordaan, at cafés such as *Nol* and the *Twee Zwaantjes*, detailed in *Bars*. As for modern pop and rock, times have mercifully changed, and Dutch groups nowadays have both quality and originality. Look out for the much praised Urban Dance Squad or the recently reborn Claw Boys Claw and other manifestations of the dance music and House scene, or try to see new rock bands like Betty Serveert. Bear in mind, too, that Amsterdam is often on the circuit of up-and-coming British bands, and keep a sharp eye on the listings. As far as **prices** go, for big names you'll pay anything between ƒ30 and ƒ50 a ticket; ordinary gigs go for ƒ5 to ƒ15. If no price is listed, entrance is usually free.

Aside from summer Sundays in the Vondelpark, Amsterdam doesn't have any **outdoor festivals**. Of those outside the city, the most famous is the *Pink Pop Festival* in June, down in the south at the Draf en Renbaan in Landgraaf, near Maastricht. Others include the spring *Halfway Festival* in Spaarnwoude (Sparnwoude is halfway between Amsterdam and Haarlem), the May *Goffert Pop* in Nijmegen, and the June *Park Pop*, in The Hague. Dates change, so check with the VW before heading out.

Where to Go

Bamboo Bar, Lange Leidsedwarsstraat 66; ☎624 39 93. Unpretentious, friendly bar which hosts a variety of different sounds every night: everything from Country & Western to jazz; and a great refuge from the disco kids of nearby Leidseplein. Open 10pm–2am or 3am

Cruise Inn, Zeeburgerdijk 271; ☎692 71 88. Off the beaten track, but good music from the 1950s and 1960s. Saturdays is R&B night.

Iboya, Korte Leidsedwarsstraat 29; ☎639 13 83. In the slightly less tacky of two ropey tourist streets. Theatre, club and restaurant combined; piano bar, Saturday night cabaret and live Latin music late into the night.

De Kikker, Egelantiersstraat 130; ☎627 91 98. Easy-listening music accompanies pricey French cuisine in a chic Art Deco interior in the middle of the Jordaan. Smooth trios playing bossa nova and French chansons. Normally open Fri–Sun; ƒ10 if you don't eat. From 10.30pm.

Korsakoff, Lijnbaansgracht 161; ☎625 78 54. Performances by some of the better-known local bands in a lively setting with cheap drinks and a post-punk clientele. Free admission.

Miles, Lijnbaansgracht 163; ☎628 89 10. Small bar that hosts regular live bands of the jazzier variety. Older, unpretentious crowd.

Morlang, Keizersgracht 451; ☎625 26 81. Super-trendy café with live music every Tues. Soul, jazz and classical.

Paradiso, Weteringschans 6–8; ☎623 73 48. A converted church that features bands ranging from the up-and-coming to well-known names on the brink of stardom. Also hosts classical concerts, lectures and debates. Entrance ƒ12–30, plus ƒ3.50 membership. The bands usually get started at 9pm.

PH 31, Prins Hendriklaan 31; ☎673 68 50. A bare, whitewashed room smack in the middle of the posh Vondelpark neighbourhood, that hosts amply amplified hardcore punk and new wave bands from 11pm on Thurs nights and jazz and blues sessions from 8.30pm on Sun nights. Tram #2.

Sleep-In/Arena, 's-Gravesandestraat 51; ☎694 74 44. Recently reopened under the grandiose name of *International Centre for Youth Culture, Tourism and Information*, this is part of the big budget hostel listed on p.119. Live music is usually on Wed, Thurs & Fri (usually up-and-coming bands), with films on Tues and a disco on Sat. Check ahead first; ƒ5–10.

Jazz and Latin

For jazz fans, Amsterdam can be a treat. Ther's an excellent range of jazz outlets for such a small city, varying from tiny bars staging everything from traditional to avant-garde, to the *Bimhuis* – the city's major jazz venue – which plays host to both international names and homegrown talent. Saxophonists Hans Dulfer, William Breuker and Theo Loevendie, and percussionist Martin van Duyhhoven, are among the Dutch names you might come across – and they're well worth listening to if you do.

It's worth remembering, too, that The Netherlands has one of the best jazz **festivals** in the world, the *North Sea Jazz Festival*, held in the *Congresgebouw* in The Hague during July: three days and nights of continuous jazz on twelve stages, involving over 700 musicians and costing about ƒ75 a day – a bargain if you've got the time to travel there. October is also a special time for jazz, with extra concerts and small festivals all over the country. For information on this and (if your Dutch is up to it) jazz all over Holland at any time of year, phone *Jazzline* on ☎626 77 64.

Latin American music is less in evidence, but far from nonexistent. *De Kroeg*, Lijnbaansgracht 163 (☎420 02 32), is a wonderful place for salsa (and more besides), *Canecao Rio*, Lange Leidsedwarstraat 86 (☎626 15 00), for Brazilian music, while *Rum Runners* (see below) specializes in Latin American music in a neo-colonial Latin atmosphere.

Where to Go

Café Alto, Korte Leidsedwarsstraat 115; ☎626 32 49. Legendary little jazz bar just off Leidseplein. Quality modern jazz every night from 10pm until about 2.30am (though often much later). Big on atmosphere, though slightly cramped. Drinks prices are hiked up, so fill up before you go.

Casa Blanca, Zeedijk 26; ☎625 56 85. Live jazz every night.

Bimhuis, Oude Schans 73–77; ☎623 13 61. Recently rebuilt, with an excellent auditorium and ultra-modern bar. Concerts Thurs–Sat at 9pm (ƒ15–25), free jazz sessions Mon–Tues at 10pm. Live music in the bar, Sun afternoons at 4pm, also free.

De Engelbewaarder, Kloveniersburgwal 59; ☎625 37 72. Live jazz on Sun afternoons and evenings.

Du Lac, Haarlemmerstraat 118; ☎624 42 65. Rather trendified bar with jazz sessions on Sunday.

Joseph Lamm Jazz CLub, Van Diemenstraat 242; ☎622 80 86. Traditional jazz centre which encourages dancing. Live Dixieland jazz Sat 9pm–3am, ƒ5; jam sessions Sun 8pm–2am, free.

Latin Club, Oude Zijds Voorburgwal 254 ☎624 22 70. Salsa/cocktail bar with occasional live bands and a selection of tapes imported from South America. Mon–Fri 2pm–2am, weekends until 3am.

Le Maxim, Leidsekruisstraat 35; ☎624 19 20. Intimate piano bar with mainstream and undemanding live music nightly.

Rum Runners, Prinsengracht 277; ☎627 40 79. Trendy Caribbean restaurant and cocktail bar in the former hall of the Westerkerk, with live – mainly laid-back Latin American – bands Sun at 10pm.

Nightlife

Nightlife

For contemporary and classical music see also Amstelveen Cultureel Centrum, p.145; Paradiso, p.146; Morlang, p.131; Meervaart, p.145; Stadsschouwburg, p.146.

Folk and Ethnic

The Dutch **folk music** tradition is virtually extinct. But there is a small and thriving scene in Amsterdam, due mainly to a handful of American and British expatriates and a few sympathetic cafés – as well as a couple of good outlets for **ethnic** and **world music**. For more information, call the Amsterdam folk organization *Mokum Folk* (☎626 04 26).

Where to Go

Akhnaton, Nieuwe Zijds Kolk 25; ☎624 33 96. Calls itself a "Centre for World Culture", specializing in African, Latin American music, etc. Admission ƒ15 and up.

Blarney Stone, Nieuwendijk 29; ☎623 38 30. An Irish pub and hangout with Irish music at weekends.

Mulligans, Amstel 100; ☎622 13 30. Irish bar which often features Gaelic musicians.

Soeterijn, Linnaeusstraat 2; ☎568 85 00. Part of the Tropenmuseum, this theatre specializes in the drama, dance, film and music of developing countries. A great place for ethnic music and to pick up on acts that wouldn't normally come to Amsterdam. Admission ƒ10–20; political and ethnic films, ƒ10; ethnic dance and theatre, much of it in English, ƒ15. Tram #9, #10, #14.

The String, Nes 98; ☎625 90 15. Small centrally situated bar that has live folk acts every evening.

Contemporary and Classical music and Opera

Under its new conductor, Riccardo Chailly, the *Concertgebouworkest* is one of the most dynamic orchestras in the world. The *Rotterdam Philharmonic* and *Utrecht Symphony* orchestras also have worldwide reputations, while Ton Koopman's *Amsterdam Baroque Orchestra* and Frans Bruggen's *Orchestra of the 18th Century* are two internationally renowned period instruments orchestras. In addition, the **opera scene** has been drastically improved with the opening of the *Muziektheater*, now home of the *Netherlands Opera Company*, which has a reputation for incisive, modern

and sometimes controversial productions. The *Concertgebouw* is Amsterdam's principal outlet for **classical music**, while **contemporary** and **chamber music** have an excellent home in the *IJsbreker* – and many notable Dutch exponents of contemporary music in the *ASKO Ensemble*, *Circle Ensemble* and *Volharding Orchestra*. Note, also, that a number of Amsterdam's churches (and former churches) host regular performances of classical and chamber music.

Where to Go

Concertgebouw, Concertgebouwplein 2–6; ☎571 83 45. After a facelift and renewal of its crumbling foundations, the Concertgebouw is now looking – and sounding – better than ever. Two halls, the smaller one used for chamber concerts, have regular performances by the resident Concertgebouw Orchestra and Netherlands Philharmonic, as well as a star-studded international programme. They also do free lunchtime concerts Sept–May (doors open 12.15pm, arrive early), and swing/jazz nights from time to time. Tickets ƒ25 minimum.

Engelse Kerk, Begijnhof 48; ☎624 96 65. Of the churches, this has the biggest programme – three to four performances a week, lunchtime, afternoon and evening. ƒ13–17.

IJsbreker, Weesperzijde 23; ☎668 18 05. Large, varied programme of international modern, chamber and experimental music. Out of the town centre by the Amstel, but scheduled to move to the Westergasfabrik, Haalemmerweg 8–10. Phone ahead to find out the latest. Tram #3, #6, #7, #10.

Muziektheater, Amstel 3; ☎625 54 55. Via the Netherlands Opera, which is resident here, the fullest programme of opera in Amsterdam. Tickets (ƒ23–65, except for weekends) go very quickly. Check out the programme for free, Tuesday lunchtime concerts.

Villa Baranka, Prins Hendrikkade 140 ☎627 64 80. New arts forum which aims to create a "salon" in a six-storey building and which stages (mainly classical) theatre and music, poetry readings and art workshops. Performances on afternoons and evenings, but mainly confined to the weekends. *f*10–20.

Waalse Kerk, Oude Zijds Achterburgwal 157. Weekend afternoon and evening concerts *f*7.50–22.

Discos and Clubs

Nightclubbing in Amsterdam is not the exclusive, posing, style-conscious business it is in many other capitals. There is no one really extravagant night spot, and other than those in hotel chains such as the Hilton or Sonesta, or the tacky pick-up joints around Leidseplein, most Amsterdam clubs – even trendy ones – are not very expensive nor difficult to get into, and you go more to dance than to people-watch. This is good news if funds are low, bad if the city's reputation has led you to expect more. There's a growing hip-hop scene, and House and Acid have taken off in a big way, in the form of special nights at the Roxy, and far-out events in the city's dock areas. Also, in addition to the following listings, it's worth checking out some of the city's **gay night spots**, which are – the non-exclusive ones at least – often among the best clubs in the city.

Technically, **membership** is required to get in to some clubs (those that call themselves "societies"), though in practice this can either be waived or inexpensively arranged at the door. Most clubs open around 10pm and close up around 4am or slightly later, but there's no point in arriving before midnight. On the whole – and unless we state otherwise – music is basic Top 40 fodder, drink prices normally 50 percent or so more than you would pay in a bar.

Where to Go

Cash, Leidseplein 8; ☏ 627 81 28. Former theatre, and one of the flashiest of the loud and unappealing Leidseplein discos. Plush black decor, business-orientated clientele and dress leaning towards the formal. Top 40 music. On the whole best avoided. Fri & Sat 10pm–5am, admission *f*10, and expensive drinks.

Dansen bij Jansen, Handboogstraat 11; ☏ 620 17 79. Founded by – and for – students, and now a firmly functional disco for a predominantly young set. Sun–Thurs 11pm–4am, Fri & Sat 11am–5.30pm; admission *f*4, though officially you need student ID to get in.

Escape, Rembrandtsplein 11; ☏ 622 35 42. Though by no means its best, this is Amsterdam's largest disco, with a dance floor that can accommodate 2000 people, half a million watts of computerized light show, and a superb sound system. Otherwise unexciting. Thurs 10pm–4am, Fri–Sat 10pm–5am; admission *f*10.

Havana Club, Reguliersdwarsstraat 17–19; ☏ 620 67 88. Recently opened and already very popular with a mixed clientele (gay, yuppie, art crowd). Also perhaps the only place in town to cater for people who want to dance but still get up for work the next day. Sun–Thurs open until 1am, Fri & Sat until 2am; free admission.

Herenhuis, Herengracht 114; ☏ 622 76 85. One of the longest established disco locations in Amsterdam, a large and brimming place that plays a broad selection of music, and puts on Wed, Thurs and Sun jazz jam sessions. Open at 11pm, admission *f*5 weekends, weekdays free.

iT, Amstelstraat 24; ☏ 625 01 11. Large disco with a superb sound system. Often features well-known live acts. The largest venue in the city, especially popular for Thursday and Sunday House nights. Admission *f*10. Open 11pm–4am. Saturday night is exclusively gay, but it's popular with gays throughout the week.

Mazzo, Rozengracht 114; ☏ 626 75 00. One of the city's hippest discos. Originally set up as a club for media people, now more or less anyone can get in. Angular bar, video screen and a sharp, image-obsessed crowd. Open every night 11pm–4am, Fri & Sat until 5am; admission *f*7.50, weekends *f*10 (includes free drink).

Odeon, Singel 460; ☏ 624 97 11. Open again after renovation since it burned down, this converted seventeenth-century building has two dance floors (the upstairs one only open weekends) and a stylishly

Nightlife

Nightlife

elegant interior playing host to an invariably student gang. Open throughout the week, Sun–Thurs 10pm–4am, Fri & Sat 10pm–5am; admission ƒ7.50.

Pacha, Oude Zijds Voorburgwal 216 ☎627 19 77. Medium-sized club that usually plays variants of House. Admission ƒ10.

(Op de schaal van) Richter 36, Reguliersdwarsstraat 36; ☎626 15 73. Reopened after a shutdown due to drug violations, this is a small, split-level club supposed to resemble a building after an earthquake, with shattered mirrors, broken-down walls and cracked ceilings, mocked up to draw in one of the city's most conspicuously chic crowds. Fairly flexible door policy. Open throughout the week midnight–5am; admission ƒ7.50, Fri & Sat ƒ10.

The Roxy, Singel 465; ☎620 03 54. Housed in an old cinema with varied music, this has one of the city's best sound systems, and is one of its hippest clubs, a good place to get invited to parties. The Pussy Lounge in the upper bar is held every two months for women only, gay nights are Wednesday, and they have New Age nights once a month, with aromatherapy, soft lighting and bubble machines. Wed–Sun 11pm–5am. Admission ƒ7.50–12.50, although the door policy is highly selective, and it's sometimes near-impossible to get in if you're not a member.

Soul Kitchen, Amstelstraat 32a; ☎620 23 33. Relaxed club thats refreshingly oriented towards soul and funk rather than the usual House stuff. Consequently a slightly older clientele than usual, and no real door policy. Admission ƒ5.

House parties

As in other capital cities, House parties in weird and wonderful venues are the rage in Amsterdam. The two big organized venues are OCCII, Amstelveenseweg 134 (☎671 77 78), and **Marcanti Plaza**, Jan van Galenstraat. However, for the best, impromptu happenings you have to ask around in the clubs, look out for fly posters or try calling the house party **info line** on ☎06/350 32015; this costs 50c a minute.

Lesbian and Gay Clubs

Clit Club, in the *Web Club*, Oude Zijds Voorburgwal 15–17, every Friday evening (☎624 87 64). Outrageous and energetic boogying down that attracts women of all persuasions. Can get highly erotic as the night hots up and inhibitions (and clothes) are cast away. Women only.

COC Disco, Rozenstraat 14; ☎626 30 87. Women's night every Sat until 3am, popular with younger lesbians. Mixed on Friday night.

C'Ring (Cockring), Warmoesstraat 96; ☎623 96 04. Currently Amsterdam's most popular gay men's disco. Light show and bars on two levels. Get there early at the weekend to avoid queuing. 11pm–5am.

Exit, Reguliersdwarsstraat 42; ☎625 87 88. Along with *iT* (see below), the city's most popular gay club. Sister to the *April* café on the same street, with a similiar crowd. Nightly 11pm–5am; very popular at weekends. Admission ƒ5.

Homolulu, Kerkstraat 23; ☎624 63 87. Well-established gay/lesbian disco with restaurant. Door policy in force, but many straights on Sat. Nightly 10pm–4am, 5am on weekends. Sun night is women's night.

iT, Amstelstraat 24; ☎625 01 11. See "Where to Go" p.148.

De Trut, Bilderdijkstraat 165. Housed in a former factory building, *De Trut* has a large dance floor, cheap drinks, and plays non-commercial music. Sunday nights are exclusively gay. Very hot, since it's in a basement, and rather seedy. Open 11pm–3.30am; arrive early to be sure of getting in. For more details, call in (there's no phone).

Film

Most of Amsterdam's thirty or so commercial cinemas are huge, multiplex picture palaces showing a selection of general releases – and are interesting for just that. However, there is one – the extravagantly Art Deco *Tuschinski*, Reguliersbreestraat 26 (☎626 26 33) – which is worth visiting no matter what's showing; screen 1 tends to be especially interesting. If you're more into film than architecture, the multi-media centres and film houses (*filmhuizen*) show

revival and art films and often hold retro-spectives – as does, though less regularly, the Netherlands Film Museum (p.176).

The Dutch use subtitles for foreign films, (most of which are in English), which means that language isn't a problem. Films are very rarely dubbed into Dutch: if you want to be sure, look out for the words *Nederlands Gesproken* printed next to the title in the listings – this indicates it's been dubbed. Most major cinemas have four showings a day, two in the afternoon, two in the evening and, sometimes, a late-night showing, beginning just after midnight on Friday and Saturday. Tickets cost about ƒ13, though *Alfa, Bellevue, Cinerama* and *De Uitkijk* have considerably reduced prices Monday to Thursday. Prices for the *filmhuizen* are always substantially cheaper.

Programmes change on Friday: most bars and cafés have a weekly film schedule pinned up; or check the usual listings sources, principally the what's-on supplement of *Time Out* magazine, Thursday's *Het Parool*, Friday's *Volkskrant* or *Uitkrant's Filmagenda* section.

Filmhuizen and Revival Cinemas

De Boomspijker, Recht Boomsloot 52; ☎626 40 02. An inexpensive alternative film showcase within walking distance of Centraal Station. Admission ƒ7.50 evenings, matinees ƒ5.

Cinecenter, Lijnbaansgracht 236; ☎623 66 15. Opposite the Melkweg, this shows attractive independent and quality commercial films.

Desmet, Plantage Middenlaan 4a; ☎627 34 34. Often used by the Dutch company Film International to promote independent films. Gay movies every Sunday afternoon. Tram #9, #14.

Filmmuseum Cinematheek, Vondelpark 3; ☎589 14 00. Dutch films showing every Tuesday evening, international films (with English and Dutch subtitles) the rest of the week at 7pm and 9.30pm. Admission ƒ8.50 evenings, matinees ƒ6.

Kriterion, Roeterstraat 170; ☎623 17 08. Stylish duplex cinema around the corner from the *Desmet*. Shows arthouse and quality commercial films. Weesperplein metro.

The Movies, Haarlemmerdijk 161; ☎638 60 16. Another beautiful Art Deco cinema, and with it's own distribution company, this triplex is the place for intellectual, arty or independent films. Also, a café with live music every Fri & Sat from 9pm. Admission ƒ12.50. Tram #3, bus #18 or #22.

Rialto, Ceintuurbaan 338; ☎675 39 94. The main forum for retrospectives or film series with a theme. Admission ƒ12–17, ƒ9–13 with CJP. Tram #3, #12, #24, #25.

Theatre

Surprisingly, for a city that functions so much in English, there is only one English-language theatre group: the Stalhouderij company (see below). There are also regular English-language productions and performances by touring groups at the theatres listed below and at multi-media centres. For details of annual festivals, see p.36.

Theatres with English-language productions

Bellevue, Leidsekade 90; ☎624 72 48. Regular venue of ESTA.

Felix Meritis, Keizersgracht 324; ☎623 13 11. Avant-garde dance and drama – sometimes both combined – and base for the experimental group *Maatschappij Discordia*. Admission ƒ15–20.

Kleine Komedie, Amstel 56; ☎624 05 34. One of Amsterdam's oldest theatres, established in 1786, with occasional English-language shows, ƒ15–25, and performances by the odd pop mega-star, around ƒ20.

Stalhouderij, 1e Bloemdwarsstraat 4; ☎626 22 82. Amsterdam 's only non-subsidized English language theatre company, mounting new productions every six weeks or so in one of the city's smallest, most intimate theatre spaces. Contemporary and modern works, Shakespeare, readings, classes and workshops. Admission ƒ15.

Studio Theater, Lijnbaansgracht 238; ☎625 54 54. Behind the Stadtsschouwburg. Has occasional English language productions.

University Theatre, Nieuwe Doelenstraat 16; ☎623 01 27. Home to the *Caterwauling Company* among others, who perform regularly in English.

Nightlife

The following venues also show films: Meervaart, p.145; Melkweg, p.145; Soeterijn, p.148.

Nightlife

*For theatre see
also Meervaart,
P.145; Melkweg,
p.145; Soeterijn,
p.148;
Stadschouwburg,
p.146.*

*Dance sometimes
takes place at
Amstelveen
Cultural
Centrum, p.145;
Bellevue, p.151;
Meervaart, p.145;
Soeterijn, p.148;
Stadsschouwburg,
p.146.*

Other theatres

Otherwise, most of the city's larger companies concentrate either on foreign works in translation or Dutch-language theatre, neither of which, for the non-speaker, are likely to be terribly interesting. If, however, your Dutch is strong enough, **other theatres** include:

Balie, Kleine Gartmanplantsoen 10; ☎623 29 04.

Brakke Grond, Nes 45; ☎626 68 66. The Flemish cultural centre.

De Engelenbak, Nes 71; ☎624 03 94.

Frascati, Nes 63; ☎623 57 23.

Nieuwe De La Mar, Marnixstraat 404; ☎623 34 62.

Polanen Theatre, Polanenstraat 174; ☎682 13 11.

Theater Instituut Nederland, Herengracht 168; ☎ 623 51 04.

Dance

Of the three **major Dutch dance companies**, the most innovative is the *Netherlands Dance Theatre*, with a repertoire of ballet and modern dance and inspired choreography by director Jiri Kylian. In comparison, the Muziektheatre-based *Dutch National Ballet* under Hans van Manen, although very accomplished, can seem lacking in verve and imagination – as can the third company, the largely traditional *Scapino Ballet*. Two other notable Dutch choreographers, Toer van Schayk and Rudi van Dantzig, work regularly in Amsterdam; and for folk dance fans, there's the excellent *Folklore Dance Theateristisch* – also frequent visitors to the city.

On a smaller scale, Amsterdam is particularly receptive to the latest trends in **modern dance**, and has many experimental dance groups, often incorporating other media into their productions; small productions staged by dance students also abound. Modern Dutch companies include *Dansproduktie*, one of the most original; *IntroDans*, similar in style to the *Netherlands Dance Theatre*; and *Danskern*, who have humour, imagination and vitality.

The listings that follow are theatres for dance only; dance also takes place on occasions at a number of places city-wide, so check the usual sources, in particular for those places detailed in the margin.

Where to Go

Captain Fiddle, Kloveniersburgwal 86 ☎626 03 63. Small theatre specializing in modern dance performances. Tickets *f*10.

Danslab, Overamstelstraat 139; ☎694 94 66. Experimental, and occasionally very interesting, dance. Rather far from the city centre though: nearest metro Wibautstraat. Tickets *f*10–13.

Liefde, Da Costakade 102; ☎683 31 14. A dance school studio where students put on their own productions. Admission *f*7.50.

Muziektheater, Amstel 3; ☎625 54 55. Home of the National Ballet, but with a third of its dance schedule given over to international companies. Tickets *f*23–65.

Het Veerm, Van Diemenstraat 410–412; ☎626 01 12. Old warehouse converted into dance studios and a small theatre. Good modern dance. Tickets *f*7.50–12.50.

Chapter 11

Shops and Markets

Unless you come from a very small town or do all your **shopping** in designer stores, you'll be able to find much of what's available in Amsterdam's shops at home – and often more cheaply. Where Amsterdam scores, however, is in some excellent, unusual speciality shops (designer clocks, rubber stamps, Indonesian arts, condoms – to name just a few), a handful of good **markets**, and its shopping convenience: the city's centre concentrates most of what's interesting within its tight borders.

There are few specific **shopping areas**. But broadly, **Nieuwendijk** and **Kalverstraat** are where you'll find mass-market clothes and mainstream department stores; **Leidsestraat** and **Rokin** are more pricey; the **Jordaan**, west of the centre, is home to more specialized, more adventurous clothes shops; the northern edge of the Red Light district, along **Damstraat** and **Hoogstraat**, has some exciting new stores; while to the south, **P.C. Hoofstraat, Van Baerlestraat** and **Beethovenstraat** play host to designer clothiers, upmarket ceramics stores, confectioners and delicatessens. There's also the **Spiegelkwartier**, centre of Amsterdam's antique and art trade, which cuts through the main canals near the Rijksmuseum. Many of the most interesting and more specialized shops are scattered among the small streets which connect the main canals.

As for **opening hours**, most shops take Monday morning off, and open from 9am until 6 or 6.30pm Monday to Friday, 9am to 5pm Saturday, and close all day Sunday; late opening (until 9pm) is on Thursday.

Larger shops will accept **payment** with a major credit card (*American Express, Visa, Access/Mastercard*, etc), but never by travellers' cheque. Most shops will, however, take *Eurocheques*.

Art and Design

Amsterdam is full of private **commercial art galleries**. They're scattered all over the city centre rather than confined to any specific areas, though often, because of the space the older houses offer, you'll find them along the major canals. *What's On In Amsterdam* carries listings of major shows, as does (with more informed entries) *City Life*. For an overall picture of what each gallery is about, it's best to supplement our brief listings with a current edition of *Museumkrant* or a *Gallery Guide*, available from *Athenaeum* or any art bookshop. Since original art may be out of your price range, we've included listings of places to pick up **prints, posters and cards**, as well as a couple of shops selling **artists' materials**. Many of the card and gift shops that have opened of late have highly questionable tastes, from the tacky to the openly pornographic. The card shops below are a cut above the usual dross.

Galleries

Amazone, Singel 72; ☎627 90 00.
Women's art and related exhibitions.

Amsterdamse Beeldhouwers Kollektief, Zeilmakersstraat 15; ☎625 63 32.
Permanent exhibit of contemporary Dutch sculptors.

Shops and Markets

For more on cycling in the city, see "Getting Around" in Basics.

Animation Art Name That Toon, Berenstraat 19; ☎627 76 00. Comic art specialist.

E. H. Ariens Kappers, Nieuwe Spiegelstraat 32; ☎623 53 56. Old prints and engravings, often affordable, covering a wide range of subjects

Arti, Spui 1a; ☎623 33 67. Impressive nineteenth-century exhibition space showing art by the members of the Arti et Amicitae society. Another, more internationally slanted space at Rokin 112.

D'eendt, Spuistraat 272; ☎626 57 77. Well-known modern art gallery whose critics claim has declined in recent months. Still, it shouldn't be overlooked.

Elisabeth den Bierman de Haas, Nieuwe Spiegelstraat 44; ☎626 10 12. Twentieth-century paintings and graphics; focus on the Cobra group.

Espace, Keizergracht 548; ☎624 08 02. Paintings and drawings from the 1960s and 1970s.

Barbara Farber, Keizersgracht 265; ☎627 63 43. American avant-garde and graffiti art.

Galerie Amsterdam, Warmoesstraat 101; ☎624 74 08. Paintings and graphic art relating to Amsterdam and environs.

Galerie de Drie Gratien, Weteringstraat 39; ☎624 19 45. Erotic art by Dutch artists.

Jurka, Singel 28; ☎626 67 33. Up-to-the-minute paintings and photographs.

C. M. Kooring-Verwindt, Spiegelgracht 14–16; ☎623 65 38. Twentieth-century Dutch art. A wide selection.

The Living Room, Laurierstraat 70; ☎625 84 49. Current trends in Dutch art.

Modern African Art Gallery, Kerkstraat 123 (☎620 19 58); Prinsengracht 472 (☎620 66 92). Pretty much what it says.

Mokum, Oude Zijds Voorburgwal 334; ☎624 39 58. Interesting art from the "New Dutch Realism" School.

Montevideo, Singel 137; ☎623 71 01. Video arts.

Nieuw Perspectief, Rokin 109; ☎626 39 52. Contemporary art and photography.

René Shand, Prinsengracht 821; ☎620 62 50. Specializes in both modern and contemporary art.

Taller, Keizersgracht 607; ☎624 67 34. Group of Latin American artists who work and exhibit in this converted coach house.

Torch, Lauriergracht 94; ☎626 02 84. Exhibitions of new photography.

Fons Welters, Bloemstraat 140; ☎622 71 93. Recent sculpture and other 3–D work.

Posters, Prints and Art Supplies

Art Unlimited, Keizersgracht 510; ☎624 84 19. Enormous card and poster shop. Good for communiqués home that don't involve windmills.

Lourie Kopie, Rosengracht 63 (☎420 02 47) and other branches. Cheapest place for quality photocopying.

Van Beek, Stadhouderskade 63–65; ☎662 16 70. Long-established outlet for artists' materials.

Van Ginkel, Bilderdijkstraat 99; ☎618 98 27. Supplier of artists' materials, with the emphasis on print making.

Paper Moon, Singel 419; ☎626 16 69. Well-stocked card shop.

Vlieger, Amstel 34–52; ☎623 58 34. Artists' materials supplier, with the emphasis on paper.

Bikes

Bikes can be **rented** from Centraal Station (and other train stations), as well as a number of private outlets all over town – see *Basics*. And you may well be approached on the street or in a bar by someone offering you a bike to **buy**. For a legal purchase, try the shops listed below, or one of the stations, which sell, repair and store (*stalling*) bikes. If you find no-one in the shop speaks English, there's a **glossary** of basic bike terms on p.19.

De Fietsenmaker, Nieuwe Hoogstraat 23–25; ☎624 61 37. Every bike part you could need. Recently voted the best bike shop in Amsterdam in a newspaper poll.

Freewheel, Singel 268; ☎420 11 50. Bike repairs and sales in a shop run by women.

R. P. van Heel, Hofmeijerstraat 15; ☎665 68 68. Bike repairs.

P. Jonkerk, Lange Leidsedwarsstraat 145; ☎623 25 42. Good selection of used bikes.

Lautenbach, Bethaniendwarsstraat 9; ☎627 92 89. New and secondhand bikes.

Lohman, De Clercqstraat 70–76; ☎618 39 06. New and used bikes.

Ton Kroonenberg, Van Wonstraat 59–63; ☎671 64 66. Helpful and courteous repair and sales.

Tweewielercentrum, Haarlemmerstraat 30; (☎625 15 81); Linnaeusparkweg 142 (☎692 81 66). New and used bikes, sales and repairs. Little English spoken.

Books and Magazines

Though prices are upped, virtually all Amsterdam bookshops stock at least a small selection of **English-language books**, and, in the city centre, at least, it's possible to pick up most English **newspapers** the day they come out. English-language **magazines**, too, are available from newsstands and bookshops.

General Bookshops

Albert de Lange, Damrak 62; ☎624 67 44. Perhaps the best bookshop in the city, with a great stock of Penguins, a marvellous travel section, and an informed staff.

Athenaeum, Spui 14–16; ☎622 62 48. Excellent all-round bookshop, with a more adventurous stock than *WH Smith*. Also a good source of international newspapers and magazines.

De Bijenkorf, Dam 1; ☎621 80 80. Best of the department stores for English-language books.

Bruna. A nationwide chain, and a safe bet for popular paperbacks and mainstream newspapers and magazines. Branches all over town; for the nearest, look in the phone book under *Bruna*.

Scheltema Holkema Vermeulen, Koningsplein 20; ☎523 14 11. One of Amsterdam's biggest and best bookshops. Five floors of everything from fiction to philosophy. The top floor has remaindered and bargain books.

English-language bookshops

American Discount Book Centre, Kalverstraat 185; ☎625 55 37. As the name suggests, entirely English-language, and with especially good gay and pulp fiction sections.

The English Bookshop, Lauriegracht 71; ☎626 42 30. Exclusively English-language bookshop with a small but quirky collection of titles, many of which you won't find elsewhere.

W H Smith, Kalverstraat 152; ☎638 38 21. Dutch branch of the UK high street chain, with four floors of books and magazines. A predictable selection but strong on travel and language, and with a useful ordering service. Prices are sometimes cheaper here than in regular Dutch bookshops.

Discount and secondhand bookshops

N. C. Berg, Oude Schans 8–10; ☎624 08 48. Delightfully untidy old bookshop.

The Book Exchange, Kloveniersburgwal 58; ☎626 62 66. Good on fairly up-to-date English-language paperbacks.

Book Traffic, Leliegracht 50; ☎620 46 90. Run by an American, with an excellent and well-organized selection of mainly English-language secondhand books.

Van Gennep, Nieuwe Zijds Voorburgwal 330; ☎626 44 48. Excellent discount book-shop; many bargains if you look carefully. Also good for politics, art and sciences.

De Kloof, Kloveniersburgwal 44; ☎622 38 28. Enormous higgledy-piggledy used bookshop on four floors. Great for a rummage.

A. Kok, Oude Hoogstraat 14–18; ☎623 11 91. Large and well-stocked secondhand bookshop. Loads of bargains, with prices down to a guilder.

Lorelei, Prinsengracht 495; ☎623 43 08. Women's/feminist secondhand books. Open Wed–Sat from noon.

De Slegte, Kalverstraat 48–52; ☎622 59 33. The Amsterdam branch of a nationwide operation specializing in used and new books at a discount.

Vrouwenindruk, Westermarkt 5; ☎624 50 03. Secondhand feminist books.

Shops and Markets

Shops and Markets

Westmann's Winkel, Korte Lijnbaaansteeg 1; ☎624 94 87. Wonderfully cluttered and small secondhand bookshop with a fine selection of old paperbacks at reasonable prices. The best bet for re-stocking your holiday reading.

Art and architecture books

Architectura & Natura, Leliegracht 44; ☎623 61 86. Books on architecture and interior design.

Art Book, Prinsengracht 645; ☎625 93 37. The city's best source of high-gloss art books. Keep in mind, also, the shops of the main museums, particularly the Stedelijk.

Asian Art Bookshop, Nieuwe Spiegelstraat 18; ☎620 17 82. The name says it all.

Boekie Woekie, Berenstraat 16; ☎639 05 07. Books by and on Dutch artists.

Premsela, Van Baerlestraat 78; ☎662 42 66. Slightly snooty art book specialist.

Children's books

De Kinderboekwinkel, Rozengracht 34 (☎622 47 61); Nieuwe Zijds Voorburgwal 344 (☎622 77 41). Children's books, some in English. See also "Comics", below.

Comics

Lambiek, Kerkstraat 78; ☎626 75 43. The city's largest comic bookshop and gallery.

Strip Antiquariaat, Reestraat 24; ☎622 04 02. Secondhand comics and collectors' items.

Stripwinkel Kapitein Rob, 2e Egelantiersdwarsstraat 7; ☎622 38 69. Cartoon books, old and new.

Cookery books

Kookboekhandel, Runstraat 26; ☎622 47 68. Cookery books in a variety of languages, including English; also some out-of-print treasures. The owner is a cookery journalist well known in Holland, and can be grumpy if you don't display enough knowledge.

Gay and Lesbian books

Intermale, Spuistraat 251–253; ☎625 00 09. Gay men's bookshop.

Vrolijk, Paleisstraat 135; ☎623 51 42. Gay and lesbian bookshop.

Language books

Intertaal, Van Baerlestraat 76; ☎671 53 53. Teach-yourself books and dictionaries in every language you could think of.

Religion, Occult, Astrology, Mind And Body

Arcanum, Reguliersgracht 54; ☎625 08 13. Specialists in astrology and the occult.

Au Bout du Monde, Singel 313; ☎625 13 97. Astrology, psychology, mysteries, mysticism. With record shop downstairs.

International Evangelist Bookshop, Raadhuisstraat 14; ☎620 18 59. Bibles, Christian books and records, and God knows what else.

Het Martyrium, Van Baerlestraat 170; ☎673 2092. Enormous selection of books on religious and humanist subjects.

Politics and the Third World

Fort van Sjakoo, Jodenbreestraat 24; ☎625 89 79. Anarchist bookshop, stocking a wide selection of radical political publications.

Milieuboek, Plantage Middenlaan 2H; ☎624 49 89. Right next to the Hortus Botanicus, and specializing in books on green and environmental issues.

Tropenmuseum Bookstore, Linnaeusstraat 2 ☎568 82 00. Books on Third World politics and culture, many in English. See also *De Derde Winkel*, listed under "Miscellaneous Shops", p.163.

Tweede Wereld Centrum, Rosmarijnsteeg 10; ☎627 94 91. Books, records, posters, etc, from Eastern Europe.

Theatre books

Theatre Bookshop, Leidseplein 26a; ☎622 64 89. Theatre books, magazines, cards.

Travel books and guides

A la Carte, Utrechtsestraat 110–112; ☎625 06 79. Travel guides and maps.

Evenaar, Singel 348. Travel bookshop catering for travellers to far-flung destinations. Basically books on everywhere except Europe and North America.

Island International, Westerstraat 15 ☎638 92 52. General bookshop whose speciality is books concerning Greece.

Pied a Terre, Singel 393; ☎627 44 55. Hiking maps and guides, many in English.

Stadsboekwinkel, Waterlooplein 18; ☎622 45 37. The shop for all books on Amsterdam: architecture, transport, history, urban planning, geography, etc.

Jacob van Wijngaarden, Overtoom 97; ☎612 19 01. A travel bookshop with a huge selection, including many titles in English.

Women's books

Xantippe, Prinsengracht 290; ☎623 58 54. Women's and feminist books and literature.

Clothes

When it comes to **clothes**, Amsterdam is in many ways an ideal place to shop: prices aren't through the roof, you're not overwhelmed by the selection, and the city is small enough that a shopping trip doesn't have to destroy your feet.

But don't expect a huge selection. The city's **department stores** tend to be conservative, and the big international designers appear to have boycotted Amsterdam altogether. What you will find are good-value **mainstream styles** along Kalverstraat and – south of Dam Square – Nieuwendijk, and more upmarket stuff along the parallel Rokin and down in the south of the city on P. C. Hooftstraat, Van Baerlestraat and Beethovenstraat. More interestingly, there's a fair array of one-off, individually run places, youth-oriented clothes shops and or secondhand clothing shops in the Jordaan, on Nieuwe Hoogstraat (a handful), or along the narrow streets that connect the major canals west of the city centre. The Waterlooplein flea market (see p.162) can also be a good hunting ground for **secondhand clothes**. What follows is a brief rundown of some of the more exciting outlets:

New and Designer Clothes

Agnes B, Rokin 126; ☎627 14 65. Shop of the French designer.

Antonia, Gasthuismolensteeg 12; ☎627 24 33. A gathering of adventurous Dutch designers under one roof. Good on shoes and bags too.

Columbine, Nieuwe Hoogstraat 6; ☎623 15 99. Exciting designer outfits; well worth a look, especially during sale times.

Confetti, Prinsenstraat 11; ☎ 622 53 06. Bright, fun, easy to wear and affordable women's clothes.

Diabolo, Oude Zijds Voorburgwal 242; ☎625 45 06. Black gear for Goths and Hell's Angels.

Diversi, 1e Leliedwarsstraat 6; ☎625 07 73. Small but inspired collection of reasonably priced, mainly French clothes for women.

Exota, Nieuwe Leliestraat 32 (☎620 91 24); Hartenstraat 10 (☎623 18 88). Good, fairly priced selection of both new and used clothing.

Hobbit, Van Baerlestraat 34 and 42–44; ☎664 07 79. High prices but a good, varied selection of women's and men's clothes. Watch for sales.

Kamikaze, Kalverstraat 158; ☎626 11 94. Pretty standard Kalverstraat clothing outlet.

Local Service, Keizersgacht 400–402; ☎626 68 40. Men and women's fashions. Ultra-trendy and expensive.

Look Out, St. Luciensteeg 22 (☎627 76 49); Utrechtsestraat 91 (☎625 50 32). Colourful coats and knits – not cheap.

Mac and Maggie, Kalverstraat 6 (☎626 10 39); Kalverstraat 172 (☎624 10 00); Spuistraat 110 (☎638 22 52). A rare find on the downscale reaches of Kalverstraat. Unusual colours, nice cuts, decent prices. Men and women's clothes.

Mateloos, Bilderdijkstraat 62; ☎683 23 84. Clothes for women in larger sizes.

De Mof, Haarlemmerdijk 107–111; ☎623 17 98. Basically an industrial clothier, selling heavy-duty shirts, baggy overalls and the like for rock-bottom prices.

Margariet Nannings, Prinsengracht 8. Spacious wooden-floored studio with always interesting women's clothing. Also a men's shop on the same street at number 24.

Pauw, Leidsestraat 16 (☎626 56 98); and branches all over town. Mainstream

Shops and Markets

For children's clothes, see Kids' Amsterdam, *p.167.*

Shops and Markets

and often unexceptional seperates for women.

Raymond Linhard, Van Baerlestraat 50; ☎679 07 55. Cheerful, well-priced seperates.

Roybczinsky, Reestraat 12. Stylish women's clothes shop with a slightly exotic/Indian feel.

Sissy Boy, Van Baerlestraat 15 (☎671 51 74); Kalverstraat 210 (☎626 00 88); Leidsestraat 15 (☎623 89 49). Pricey but nice clothes.

Studio Chazo, Herenstraat 34; ☎624 53 58. Small, cosy women's clothing shop specializing in wedding and party clothes.

Edgar Vos, P. C. Hoofstraat 132–134; ☎662 63 36. Amsterdam shop of the Dutch designer.

Western Classic, Kalverstraat 154; ☎622 32 29. Jeans, jackets, leathers, hats, jewellery and accessories.

Wild!, Kerkstraat 104; ☎626 73 02. Basement shop selling ultra-trendy dance clothes for clubbing types. A good place, too, to pick up on what's happening on the nightlife scene.

ZX, Kerkstraat 113; ☎625 73 08. On the other side of the street from *Wild!*, this is aiming at a similiar crowd – secondhand fashion with an arty flavour.

Secondhand clothes

Daffodil, Jacob Obrechtstraat 41; ☎679 56 34. Designer labels only in this posh secondhand shop down by the Vondelpark.

Laura Dols, Wolvenstraat 7; ☎624 90 66. Vintage clothing and lots of hats.

The End, Nieuwe Hoogstraat 26; ☎625 31 62. Unspectacular but inexpensive.

Jojo, Prinsengracht 11 (☎624 40 02); Huidenstraat 23 (☎623 34 76). Good secondhand clothes from all eras. Particularly good for trench coats and Fifties jackets.

Lady Day, Hartenstraat 9; ☎623 58 20. Good-quality secondhand clothes at reasonable prices.

Puck, Nieuwe Hoogstraat 1; ☎625 42 01. Vintage secondhand clothes.

Rose Rood, Kinkerstraat 159; ☎618 23 34. Period women's clothing – Victorian undergarments and the like.

Second Best, 2e; Anjelierdwarsstraat 8 ☎623 23 00. More Jordaan cast-offs.

Zipper, Huidenstraat 7 (☎623 73 02); Nieuwe Hoogstraat 10 (☎627 03 53). Mainly used clothes selected for style and quality – or so it says on the door. Prices start high, but it's very popular, and everything is in good condition.

Accessories: Shoes, Hats, Jewellery

Big Shoe, Leliegracht 12; ☎622 66 45. Specially commissioned Italian shoes for larger-sized feet.

Body Sox, Leidsestraat 35; ☎627 65 53. Socks, tights and stockings in every conceivable colour and design.

Bonnier, Haarlemmerstraat 58; ☎622 16 41. Very reasonably priced bag and umbrella shop.

Dr Adam's, Oude Doelenstraat 5–9 (☎622 37 34); P C Hoofstraat 90 (☎662 38 35). One of the city's broadest selection of shoes.

The English Hatter, Heiligeweg 40; ☎623 47 81. Classic menswear shop; everything from ties, and other accessories to shirts, cricket sweaters, and, of course, hats.

Fleco, Westerstraat 189; ☎622 79 83. Hats, ties and socks for men.

De Grote Tas, Oude Hoogstraat 6; ☎623 01 10. Good selection of bags and suitcases.

Hoeden M/V, Herengracht 422; ☎626 30 38. Designer hats galore, from felt Borsalinos to straw Panamas. Gloves and umbrellas too. Intimidating prices, though.

Robin & Rik, Runstraat 30; ☎627 89 24. Leather belts and hats produced in the shop.

Roxanne, St Antoniebreestraat 126; ☎638 47 88. Modern rather arty shoe shop, with a limited choice.

Sambara, 2e Tuindwarsstraat 7; ☎623 06 60. Shoes; unusual styles.

Shoebaloo, Koningsplein 7–9 (☎626 79 93); P. C. Hooftstraat 80(☎671 22 10).

Unisex shoes, trendy styles. See also *Bagbaloo* around the corner.

Tie Rack, Heiligeweg 7 (☎627 29 78); Kalverstraat 138 (☎623 30 52). Amsterdam branches of the ubiquitous English chain.

Tulips, Nieuwe Leliestraat 25; ☎627 55 95. Tights and socks – a vast array.

Department Stores

Amsterdam's **department stores**, like many of the city's shops, err on the side of safety. Venture inside only if you have an unfulfilled shopping urge; otherwise save them for specifics.

De Bijenkorf, Dam 1; ☎621 80 80. Dominating the northern corner of Dam Square, this is the city's top shop, a huge bustling place (the name means "beehive") that has an indisputably wide range and little of the snobbishness of a place like *Harrods* or even *Metz* (see below).

HEMA, Nieuwendijk 174 (☎624 65 06); Reguliersbreestraat 10 (☎24 65 06). A kind of Dutch Woolworth's, but of a better quality: good for stocking up on toiletries and other essentials, and occasional designer delights – it's owned by *De Bijenkorf*, and you can sometimes find the same items at knock-down prices.

Magna Plaza, Nieuwe Zijds Voorburgwal 182. Not really a department store, but a cluster of shops and stores in the converted former post office.

Maison de Bonneterie, Rokin 140–142; ☎626 21 62. Apart from the building, which rises through balustraded balconies to a high central dome, nothing special: very conservative and, on the whole, extremely expensive.

Marks & Spencer, Kalverstraat 66; ☎620 00 06. The place to head for if you're feeling homesick.

Metz & Co., Keizersgracht 455; ☎624 88 10. By far the city's swishest shop, with the accent on Liberty prints (it used to be owned by Liberty of London), stylish ceramics and designer furniture of the kind that is exhibited in modern art museums: just the place to pick up a Rietveld chair. If your funds won't stretch quite that far, settle for

a cup of coffee in the top floor Rietveld restaurant, which affords great views over the canals.

Peek & Cloppenberg, Dam 20; ☎623 28 37. Less a department store than a multi-floored clothes shop with some painfully middle-of-the-road styles. Nonetheless, an Amsterdam institution.

Vromm & Dreesmann, Kalverstraat 201–221 & 212–224; ☎622 01 71. The main Amsterdam branch of the middle-ground nationwide chain. Again, useful for essentials.

Food and Drink

Below are listings of **speciality food shops**, together with a selection of **wine and spirits shops** noted for their centrality, speciality, or sheer value; and **night shops**, which sell provisions and (often) hot meals to take away and are open 4pm–1am.

Supermarkets

For home cooking and economical eating and drinking, the most central **supermarket** is the *Mignon* at Leidsestraat 76 ☎627 19 00. There are also branches of the larger *Albert Heijn* chain at P. C. Hooftstraat 129 (☎662 03 77); Westerstraat 79–87 (☎623 68 52); Haarlemmerdijk 1 (☎625 69 31); Nieuwmarkt 18 (☎623 24 61); and a very large one at Waterlooplein 129–131 (☎624 12 49). Otherwise, for supermarkets in your area, look in the Yellow Pages under *Supermarkten*.

Breads, pastries and sweets

Paul Annee, Runstraat 25 (☎623 53 22); Bellamystraat 2–4 (☎618 31 13). The best wholemeal bread in town; also try the *speculaas* and fruit and nut loaf.

J. G. Beune, Haarlemmerdijk 156–158; ☎624 83 56. Handmade cakes and chocolates in an old-style interior.

Arnold Comelis, Van Baerlestraat 93 (☎662 12 28); 1ᵉ Constantyn Huygenstraat 88 (☎618 36 88). The apple tart is a treat.

Errol Trumpie, Leidsestraat 46; ☎624 02 33. Elegant handmade pastries and chocolates.

Shops and
Markets

Shops and Markets

Kwekkeboom, Reguliersbreestraat 36 (☎623 68 47); Damstraat 20 (☎624 83 65); Linnaeusstraat 80–86 (☎665 04 43). One of the city's most famous pastry shops, showered with awards for its goods. Not cheap, but you're paying for the *chocolatier's* equivalent of Gucci.

Lanskroon, Singel 385; ☎623 77 43. Amsterdam's best pastry shop, with a small area for on-the-spot consumption.

Lensen, Kalverstraat 94; ☎623 67 68. Centrally situated bakers on Kalverstraat, good also for ready-made sandwiches, and with a few tables inside.

Mediterrané, Haarlemmerdijk 184; ☎620 35 50. Great croissants, North African pastries, French bread, etc

Pompadour, Húidenstraat 12; ☎623 95 53. Chocolates and lots of homemade pastries (usually smothered or filled with chocolate).

Cheese

Arxhoek, Damstraat 23; ☎622 91 18. Good, centrally situated general cheese shop.

Hoving's Comestibles, Herenstraat 32. Excellent selection of cheeses and other goodies.

De Kaaswaag, Nieuwemarkt 6; ☎622 86 10. Handily located for all your cheese needs.

Robert & Abraham Kef, Marnixstraat 192; ☎626 22 10. A wide range of French cheeses – and facilities for tasting.

Coffee and tea

Geels & Co., Warmoesstraat 67; ☎624 06 83. Oddly situated among Warmoesstraat's porno shops, this is one of the city's oldest and best-equipped specialist in coffee and tea.

Keyser, Prinsengracht 180; ☎624 08 23. Beautiful old-fashioned interior and friendly service.

Simon Levelt, Prins Hendrikkade 26; ☎622 84 28. Aromatic coffee specialist opposite Centraal Station that you can smell almost as soon as you arrive in the city.

't Zonnetje, Haarlemmerdijk 45; ☎623 00 58. Tea and coffee dealer, and herbalist.

Delis

Dikker & Thijs, Prinsengracht 444; ☎626 77 21. The city's best-known gourmet shop, with an unrivalled selection of fine wines, fish, cooked meats, cheeses and hors d'oeuvres. The prices are, to say the least, sobering.

Eichholtz, Leidsestraat 48; ☎622 03 05. Smaller and cheaper than *Dikker & Thijs*.

The Fresh Co., Koningsplein 6; ☎624 57 21. Posh, deli-style foodshop, very central, that does great salads and sandwiches for picnics, as well as all kinds of delicious items for more adventurous self-catering.

Fish and seafood

Dikker & Thijs (above) are good for fish, and for both lunchtime snacks and takeaway meals there are centrally located fish and seafood **stalls** on Nieuwmarkt, Westermarkt, Utrechtsestraat at Herengracht, Raadhuisstraat at Singel, and on Stadhouderskade near Leidseplein. Otherwise, among a number of good central **shops** are *De Kreeft*, on Muntplein at Vijzelstraat 3, *Hendrik's*, Oude Doelenstraat 18, and the *Volendammer Vishandel*, Nieuwe Spiegelstraat 54.

Health food

De Belly, Nieuwe Leliestraat 174; ☎624 52 81. Small and very friendly shop stocking all things organic.

Manna, Ferdinand Bolstraat 122; ☎671 65 14. Largest of the city's health food shops, with a small upstairs café.

Markus, Nieuwe Kerkstraat 8; ☎625 12 23. Long-established health food shop.

De Natuurwinkel, Weteringschans 133 (☎638 40 83); Van Woustraat 80 (☎671 47 19); 1e C Huygenstraat 49–55 (☎664 1 04). New supermarket chain devoted to health food and natural products.

De Weegchaal, Jodenbreestraat 20; ☎624 17 65. Friendly shop near the Waterlooplein flea market. Much the best place if you're not in a hurry.

De Zonnebloem, Haarkemmerdijk 174; ☎626 63 10. Small, adequately stocked health food shop. Now owned by *Manna*; (see above).

Butchers

De Groene Weg, Huidenstraat 11; ☎627 91 32. Organic meat. Also at 1e C. Huygenstraat 55 (☎683 48 59) as part of *De Natuurwinkel*.

Rodrigues, Vijzelgracht 20; ☎623 28 62. Traditional Amsterdam butcher – much the best place to go if you're a carnivore.

Beer, wine and spirits

De Bierkoning, Paleisstraat 125; ☎625 23 36. 750 different beers and glasses to drink them from.

Chateau P. C. Hooft, Honthorststraat 1 ☎664 93 71. Extensive but expensive off-licence on the corner of the chic P. C. Hoofstraat.

Drinkland, Spuistraat 116; ☎638 65 73. Largest and most central off-licence in the city.

Eerste Amsterdamse Waterwinkel, Roelof Hartstraat 10; ☎675 59 32. When you've had enough of alcohol this is the place to head for. Sells bottled waters from all over the world. Try the wonderful German *Statl Fasching*.

Hart's Wijnhandel, Reestraat 1 (☎623 28 58); Vijzelgracht 3 (☎623 83 50); Nieuwe Spiegelstraat 41 (☎623 40 21); Koninginneweg 143 (☎662 52 50). Beer, wine and spirits from the cheap to the pocket-stinging.

Het Karbeel, Warmoesstraat 58; ☎627 49 95. Wine and cheese shop with a small mezzanine café for lunch and exhibitions of contemporary art. Open Thurs until 9pm.

De Kievit, Haarlemmerstraat 7; ☎622 27 81. Central and well-stocked wine and spirits shop.

1001 Bieren, Huidenstraat 21; ☎623 77 11. International beer shop.

H. P. de Vreng, Nieuwendijk 75; ☎624 45 81. Nine thousand miniature bottles for sale in this celebrated wine and spirits shop.

Night shops

Night shops are open in the evenings, usually from 6pm to midnight or 1am. Expect to pay a little over the odds for being able to shop late.

Aubergine, Prinsenstraat 28; ☎625 99 48. Centrally located and reliable night shop.

Avondmarkt, De Wittenkade 94–96; ☎686 49 19. The biggest, best and cheapest of the night shops, just west of the city centre.

Baltus, Vijzelstraat 127; ☎626 90 69. Central but very expensive.

Big Bananas, Leidsestraat 73; ☎627 70 40. Reasonable and convenient, if not especially cheap, night shop.

Dolf's, Willemstraat 79; ☎625 95 03. One of the better night shops, and reasonably central, in the Jordaan.

Van Doomeveld, De Clercqstraat 3; ☎618 17 27. Pricey, but handy for satisfying late-night hankerings for champagne.

Holland Belgie, Roeterstraat 2; ☎622 97 97. Small friendly night shop whose owner has his own show on local cable television.

Sterk, Waterlooplein 241; ☎626 88 10. Centrally located night shop, close by the Amstel.

Shops and Markets

Markets

Amsterdam's markets are more diverting than its shops. There's a fine central **flea market** on Waterlooplein, vibrant **street markets** such as the Albert Cuyp, emphasizing food and cheap clothing, and smaller **weekly markets** devoted to anything from stamps to flowers.

General and Flea Markets

Albert Cuypstraat. Amsterdam's best-known – and best – general market. Mon–Sat 9am–4.30pm.

Boerenmarkt, Noordermarkt. Organic produce, handicrafts, chickens, pets and exotic birds. Sat 10am–1pm.

Dapperstraat. Daily general market. Mon–Sat 9am–4pm.

Lindengracht. Weekly general market, good for a taste of Jordaan atmosphere. Sat 9am–4pm.

Ten Katestraat. Daily general market. Mon–Sat 9am–4pm.

Waterlooplein. New and secondhand clothes, antiques, junk, books and bikes. Amsterdam's best and most enjoyable

Shops and Markets

browse. Daily 9am–5pm. On Sundays there's also an antiques market.

Westerstraat. General market. Mon 7.30am–1.30pm.

Antiques and art markets

De Looier, Elandsgracht 109. Indoor antiques stalls, selling a variety of goods. Sat–Wed 11am–7pm, Thurs 11am–9pm.

Noordermarkt. More junk than antiques. Mon 7.30am–1.30pm.

Rommelmarkt, Looiersgracht 38. Indoor junk market, with two floors of everything from old coins, stamps, books and records to secondhand clothes. Daily except Fri.

Spui. Irregular art market. Sun 10am–6pm.

Thorbeckeplein. Art market. Sun noon–6pm.

Waterlooplein. Good-quality antiques market. Sun 10am–5pm.

Book markets

Oudemanhuispoort. Mon–Sat 10am–4pm.
Spui. Fri 9am–6pm.

Flower markets

Amstelveld, Kerkstraat at Reguliersgracht. Mon 10am–3pm.

Bloemenmarkt, on the Singel between Muntplein and Koningsplein. Plants and flowers, pots and bulbs, sold from stalls on floating barges. Very reasonable prices. Mon–Sat 9am–4.30pm.

Stamp markets

Nieuwe Zijds Voorburgwal, between Dam Square and Spui. Wed & Sat 10am–4pm.

Records

Record prices in Amsterdam are fairly reasonable. However, the selection tends to be limited, and vinyl is even more a thing of the past than it is in Britain or North America – CDs, and to a lesser extent cassette tapes, are the order of the day. Still, the city does have one or two specialized dealers – particularly strong in secondhand and used jazz and reggae – who may be able to turn up something you couldn't find back home.

Backbeat Records, Egelantiersstraat 19; ☎627 16 57. Small specialist in soul, blues, jazz, funk, etc, with a helpful and enthusiastic owner.

Boudisque, Haringpakkersteeg 10–18; ☎623 26 03. New wave, reggae and other black music. Videos too.

Concerto, Utrechtsestraat 54–60; ☎623 52 28. New and used records – pop, jazz and classical. Perhaps the best all-round selection in the city.

Dance tracks, Nieuwe Nieuwestraat 69; ☎639 08 53. Import dance music, hip-hop, soul and house.

Falstaff, Muiderstraat 11; ☎626 09 88. Specializes in classical music and opera.

FAME, Kalverstraat 2–4; ☎638 25 25. Subtitled "Nederlands Grootste Platenzaak", this place carries a large general selection of CDs and tapes.

Forever Changes, Bilderdijkstraat 148; ☎612 63 78. New wave, collector's items, secondhand and new.

Free Record Shop, Kalverstraat 32 & 230 (☎626 58 08; ☎625 73 78); Ferdinand Bolstraat 79 (☎671 60 74). One of the better pop/rock chains.

Get Records, Utrechtsestraat 105; ☎622 34 41. Emphasis on new wave.

Golden Age Records, Nieuwe Nieuwestraat 26; ☎625 22 81. Specialist in jazz and blues.

Jazz Inn, Spui 5; ☎623 56 62. Just jazz.

Outland, Zeedijk 22; ☎638 75 76. Zeedijk record shop specializing in the latest House and Techno sounds.

Record Palace, Weteringschans 33; ☎622 39 04. Opposite Paradiso, a small shop specializing in records from the Fifties and Sixties.

The Sound of the Fifties, Prinsengracht 669; ☎623 97 45. 1950's and 1960's pop and jazz, secondhand and new.

Staalplaat, Jodenbreestraat 24; ☎625 41 76. Noise, avant-garde, obscure music. Good range of cassettes.

Virgin Megastore, Nieuwe Zijds Voorburgwal 182; ☎ 622 89 29. The familiar record chain, here filling the entire ground floor of the Magna Plaza shopping centre.

Miscellaneous and Ethnic

Perhaps more than any other place in Europe, Amsterdam is a great source of odd little shops devoted to one particular product or inetrest. What follows is a selection of favourites.

Akkerman, Kalverstraat 149; ☎ 623 16 49. Vast array of pens, inks and writing implements.

Backstage, Rosengracht 68; ☎ 622 12 67. Make-up and clothes for parties.

Baobab, Elendsgracht 128; ☎ 626 83 98. Textiles, jewellery and ceramics from Indonesia and the Far East.

Jan Best, Keizersgracht 357; ☎ 623 27 36. Famed antique lamp shop, with some wonderfully kitsch examples.

Body Shop, Kalverstraat 157–159 (☎ 623 97 89); Nieuwendijk 196 (☎ 626 61 35). The Amsterdam outlets of the wildly successful eco-friendly smellies and cosmetics chain. Part of the global movement to demystify travel.

Centro Cultural Jose-Marti, Herengracht 259; ☎ 626 95 90. Latin American culture, particularly books.

Compendium, Hartenstraat 14; ☎ 638 15 79. The place to go if you're into games. All kinds (including video and computer games, etc), mainly for adults.

Condomerie Het Gulden Vlies, Warmoesstraat 141; ☎ 627 41 74. Condoms of every shape, size and flavour imaginable. All in the best possible taste.

Demmenie Sports, Marnixstraat 2; ☎ 624 36 52. Sports shop selling everything you might need for hiking, camping, survival, etc.

De Derde Winkel, Huidenstraat 16; ☎ 625 22 45. Crafts from – and books about – developing countries.

De Droomdoos, Oude Leliestraat 1; ☎ 620 10 75. Flashy fabric-covered cardboard boxes for knick-knacks.

D. Eberhardt, Damstraat 16; ☎ 624 07 24. Chinese and southeast Asian crafts, ceramics, clothes and jewellery.

Electric Lady, 2e Leliedwarsstraat 5. Pungent 1970s collection of psychedelia of all kinds, most of it luminous.

Gerda's Bloemenwinkel, Runstraat 16; ☎ 624 29 12. Amsterdam is full of flower shops, but this is its most imaginative and sensual. An aesthetic experience.

Hanky Panky, Oude Zijds Voorburgwal 141; ☎ 627 48 48. Perhaps the best known of a number of places in the city centre where you can get a tattoo. Has a "Tattoo Museum" as well.

P. G. C. Hajenius, Rokin 92–96; ☎ 623 74 94. Old, established tobacconist selling its own (and other brands of) cigars, tobacco, smoking accessories and every make of cigarette you can think of.

The Head Shop, Kloveniersburgwal 39; ☎ 624 90 61. Every dope-smoking accessory you could possibly need, along with assorted marijuana memorabilia.

Heimwee & Nu, 1e Hugo de Grootstraat 28; ☎ 681 71 31. Antiques, but painted in colourful "punkish" style. Inexpensive.

Jacob Hooij, Kloveniersburgwal 10–12; ☎ 624 30 41. Homeopathic chemist with an ancient interior and a huge stock of *drop* – Dutch liquorice.

't Japanese Winkeltje, Nieuwe Zijds Voorburgwal 175; ☎ 627 95 23. Japanese arts and crafts.

Joe's Vliegerwinkel, Nieuwe Hoogstraat 19; ☎ 625 01 39. Kites, frisbees, etc. More down-to-earth than its Jordaan rival.

Donald E. Jongejans, Noorderkerkstraat 18; ☎ 624 68 88. Hundreds of spectacle frames, none of them new, some of them very ancient. Supplied the specs for Bertolucci's *The Last Emperor*.

't Klompenhuisje, Nieuwe Hoogstraat 9a; ☎ 622 81 00. Amsterdam's best and brightest array of clogs.

Knopenwinkel, Wolvenstraat 14; ☎ 624 04 79. Buttons in every conceivable shape and size.

Shops and Markets

For general toy shops, see Kids' Amsterdam p.167.

Shops and Markets

Kramer, Reestraat 20; ☎ 626 52 74. Candles, oils and incense specialist.

Eduard Kramer, Nieuwe Spiegelstraat 64; ☎ 623 08 32. Specialists in fifteenth-to-twentieth-century Dutch tiles. A marvellous selection. Great for souvenirs and gifts to take home.

Nieuws Innovations, Prinsengracht 297; ☎ 627 95 40. Specialists in modern designer items for the home – projector clocks, remote control lamps, Philippe Starck vases, etc.

Old Prints, Spiegelgracht 27 (☎ 628 88 52); Singel 496 (☎ 625 55 78). Old prints of Amsterdam and much else besides, at discount prices.

1001 Kralen, 1e Bloemdwarsstraat 38; ☎ 624 36 81. "Kralen" means "beads", and 1001 would seem a conservative estimate in this place, which sells nothing but.

Out of Africa, Herengracht 215; ☎ 623 46 77. African arts and crafts.

Partyhouse, Rozengracht 40–42 (☎ 624 78 51); Utrechtsestraat 90 (☎ 620 83 04). Every conceivable fun-making object – masks, rentable costumes and wigs, talking clocks, crazy feet, streamers and hats. You name it.

Posthumus, St. Luciensteeg 23–25; ☎ 625 58 12. Posh stationery, cards and, best of all, a choice of hundreds of rubber stamps.

Schaak-en Go-winkel Het Paard, Haarlemmerdijk 147; ☎ 624 11 71. Many different types of chess and Go games and books.

Taste of Ireland, Herengracht 228; ☎ 625 67 04. Irish sausages, draught Guinness and freshly baked soda bread, to name just the most obvious items for those sick for home.

't Winkeltje, Prinsengracht 228; ☎ 625 13 52. Jumble of cheap glassware and crockery, candlesticks, antique tin toys, kitsch souvenirs, old apothecaries jars and flasks. Perfect for browsing.

Witte Tanden Winkel, Runstraat 5; ☎ 623 34 43. Wacky toothbrushes and just about every dental hygeine accoutrement you could ever need.

Chapter 12

Kids' Amsterdam

Amsterdam's attractions are aimed mainly at adults, such that things to keep **kids** entertained on a wet afternoon are few and far between. However, there's plenty more to do than drag yourself around canals and press your nose up against shop windows, and attractions include tram rides, circuses and a great zoo. The attitude to children, too, is as understanding as you'd expect. If museums don't allow prams they do provide snugglies to carry small children in; most restaurants have high chairs and children's menus (though they're not always that wonderful); and bars don't seem to mind accompanied kids, as long as they're reasonably under control. In short, in very few places will having a small child in your care close doors to you. Teenagers, while less welcome in bars, should have enough to gawk at in the city streets to keep them amused.

Babysitting services and equipment hire

It's worth noting that not all hotels welcome young children (they'll make this clear when you book), but many of those that do, offer **babysitting services**. Otherwise there are a couple of agencies worth contacting, and even one place which hires out babycare equipment.

Baby-Rent, Hoptille 180; ☎696 30 47. Somebody had to think of it. You can hire anything you might possibly need for your baby here, from buggies to bottle warmers. A bit far out, in the southeast of the city, but handy if you're travelling light.

Babysit Centrale Kriterion, 2e Rozendwarsstraat 24; ☎624 58 48. Long-established agency with a high reputation, using students of at least 18 years old. Inexpensive 24-hour service: ƒ5–10 per hour, plus a ƒ4 administrative charge depending on the time of day. Book sitters between 5.30 and 7pm.

International Baby Nanny Sit Centrale, Asingabourg 36; ☎646 29 44. Reliable babysitting service.

Parks, playgrounds and trips

The city's most central green spot, the **Vondelpark**, has an excellent playground with sandpits, paddling pools, and ducks to feed. During the summer there's always some (free) entertainment for kids, either in the afternoon programme or in the park's open-air theatre. Most city parks have things to keep the kids entertained, but the best, the **Gaasperpark**, is outside of the centre (metro stop Gaasperplas; buses #60, #61, #157, #158, #174), with terrific play facilities and paddling pools. The **Amsterdamse Bos** (see Chapter Five) has playgrounds, lakes, and wild animals, and you can hire canoes to explore the waterways for ƒ7.50 per hour from 8am to sunset.

A good introduction for older children are the **canal trips** from Centraal Station or Damrak, or, less historical but much more fun, a ride on a **canal bike**. This can get tiring, but jetties where boats can be picked up and dropped off are numerous, and it's quite safe; addresses on p.19. For a great

Kids'
Amsterdam

view of the city, try a trek up the **towers** of the Oude Kerk and Westerkerk (open summer only; see p.59, and 79).

Museums, exhibitions and the zoo

Artis Zoo, Plantage Kerklaan 38–40; ☎523 34 00. Tram #7, #9, #14. Daily 9am–5pm, planetarium opens at 1pm on Mon; adults ƒ17.50, children under 9 ƒ10. Open year-round and, on top of the usual creatures and creepy-crawlies, has a farm where kids can torment sheep, calves, goats, etc. If it's raining it's best to visit the aquarium – one of the best-stocked in Europe – and the Zeiss Planetarium, which organizes special kid's events. Both covered by one ticket.

Aviodome Aeroplane Museum, Schiphol Airport; ☎604 15 21. Train from Centraal Station. May–Sept daily 10am–5pm; Oct–April Tues–Fri 10am–5pm, Sat & Sun noon–5pm, closed Mon; adults ƒ6, children under-12 ƒ4.50. If you find yourself with time to kill, and the kids have tired of watching the planes take off, this offers a few ancient aircraft plus a flight simulator. Buy an all-in ticket at Centraal Station, which includes the return rail fare, museum entrance, a cup of coffee and *appelgebak* at the Schipol station bar.

Madame Tussaud's, Dam 20; ☎622 99 49. Tram #4, #9, #14, #16, #24, #25 . Daily 10am–6pm; adults ƒ16, children under 15 ƒ11; family tickets (2 adults, 2 children) ƒ43. Newly reopened and greatly enlarged waxwork collection similar to the one in London. Among the few unique features, there's an attempt to recreate Hieronymous Bosch's *Garden of Earthly Delights* and a room devoted to Rembrandt. Hardly the high point of anyone's trip to the city, but there are parts which might excite the kids.

NINT Technological Museum, Tolstraat 129; ☎570 81 11. Tram #3, #4. Mon–Fri 10am–5pm, Sat & Sun noon–5pm; adults ƒ8, children (5–12) ƒ6. A fairly dull collection of mostly mechanical exhibits designed to fire Dutch youth's enthusiasm in industry. Hardly any information in English.

TM Junior Museum, Linnaeusstraat 2; ☎568 83 00. Tram #3, #6, #9, #10. Bus #22 . Open afternoons during the school

year, plus weekends; phone for complete hours. Admission ƒ7.50 for adults, ƒ4 for children, . Conceived especially for children between the ages of 6 and 12, its aim is to promote international understanding by holding exhibitions about other cultures. Not as dry as it might sound, with lively exhibits and lots of things to get your hands on, it's best on Sunday, when school groups aren't visiting. For those especially interested, the *Tropenmuseum*, of which the TM is an adjunct, is also worth exploring.

Museum Tramline, Haarlemmermeerstation, Amstelveenseweg 264; ☎673 75 38. Tram #6, #16 . April–Oct Sun and public holidays 10.30am–5.30pm; July & Aug also Tues, Wed, Thurs & Sat 1–3.30pm. Phone for exact dates; adults ƒ4, children under 11 ƒ2. Not so much a museum as a set of working antique trams that run along adapted railway tracks down to the Amsterdamse Bos and, beyond, into Amstelveen. Can be fun for kids, and it's good to get to the Bos.

Zoological Museum, Plantage Middenlaan 53 ☎523 34 00. Tram #7, #9, #14. Tues–Sun 9am–5pm; admission included in entry to the zoo (see above). Essentially a natural history museum, with a static collection of insects, birds, bats and whales, as well as skeletal remains. Only regularly changing exhibitions lighten an otherwise dull load.

Theatres, circuses and funfairs

A number of **theatres** have inexpensive (around ƒ5) entertainment for children in the afternoon, a fair proportion of which gets around the language problem by being mime- or puppet-based: check the children's section ("Jeugdagenda") of *Uitkrant*, and look for the words *mimegroep* (mime group) and *poppentheater* (puppet theatre). For general information on children's theatre in Amsterdam, call ☎622 29 99. Public holidays and the summer bring touring **circuses** and the occasional mobile **funfair** (*kermis*) to the city, the latter usually setting up on Dam Square and thus hard to miss. Check, too, the **festivals** listings on p.36: many, such as the Queen's birthday celebrations, can be enjoyed by kids.

Other theatres which regularly have good kids' programmes are *De Brakke Grond*, Nes 45 (☎ 626 68 66); *Cleynteater*, H. Cleyndertweg 63a (☎ 634 40 17); *De Meervaart*, Osdorpplein 205 (☎ 610 73 93); *Ostadetheater*, Van Ostadestraat 233 (☎ 679 50 96); *Polanentheater*, Polanenstraat 174 (☎ 682 13 11).

Carre Theatre, Amstel 115–125; ☎ 622 52 25. Occasionally books internationally famous circuses.

Deridas, Hobbemakade 68; ☎ 662 15 88. Puppet theatre very good for the very young, with activities on Sundays for the under-5s.

Elleboorg Kindertheater, Passeerdersgracht 32; ☎ 626 93 70. Circus performed by and for children. Sounds deadly, but we haven't seen it. Phone bookings required.

De Krakeling, Nieuwe Passeerdersstraat 1; ☎ 624 51 23. Full-time children's theatre, and a good place to begin. The emphasis is often on full-scale audience participation. Phone for a schedule.

Melkweg, Lijnbaansgracht 234a; ☎ 624 17 77. Sun afternoon activities for children from mid-Oct to early April.

Poppentheater Diridas, Hobbenmakade 68; ☎ 662 15 88. Kids' puppet theatre.

Shops

Azzurro Kids, P. C. Hoofstraat 122 ☎ 673 04 57. Perhaps the city's chic-est kids' clothes store.

Bell Tree, Spiegelgracht 10; ☎ 625 88 30. A beautiful shop full of old-fashioned toys, mobiles, models, simple toys and kids' books.

Berend Botje, Zocherstraat 87; ☎ 618 33 49. Secondhand kids' clothes store near the Vondelpark.

De Bijenkorf. Dam 1; ☎ 621 80 80. A department store, but with one of the best (and most reasonable) toy sections in town.

Intertoys, Heiligeweg 26–28 (☎ 622 11 22); and branches throughout the city. Amsterdam's largest toy shop.

Joe's Vlieger en Frisbeehandel, Nieuwe Hoogstraat 19; ☎ 625 01 39. Kites, frisbees, etc. More down-to-earth than its Jordaan rival.

Kids' World, Utrechtsestraat 73. Wonderful clothes and shoes for children.

De Kinderboekwinkel, Rozengracht 34 (☎ 622 47 61); Nieuwe Zijds Voorburgwal 344 (☎ 622 77 41). Children's books, some of which are in English.

De Kleine Bloem, Bloemstraat 44; ☎ 622 72 40. Children's clothes at reasonable prices. Nought to six-year-olds.

Portobello Giftshop, Rokin 107; ☎ 622 69 03. A good source of educational wooden toys that salve the conscience and please the eye.

Speelboom, Kalverstraat 30; ☎ 624 95 72. Toy shop, with models, train sets and chess boards – and not a video game in sight.

Speel-Goed, Bilderdijkstraat 61; ☎ 616 26 94. Specializes in toys for under-fives.

Kids' Amsterdam

See also
"Miscellaneous and Ethnic Shops", p.163.

Chapter 13

Sport and Outdoor Activities

Most visitors to laid-back Amsterdam tend to confine their exercise to walking around the major sights. But if you get the urge to stretch your muscles, there's a range of **participatory sports** available. In winter, skating is the most popular and enjoyable; other activities are based in private, health or sports clubs, to which you can usually get a day pass, though almost all are away from the immediate centre of town.

As a **spectator**, you're limited mainly to cheering on the talented local football team *Ajax* – though their Rotterdam rivals *Feyenoord* are just a train ride away. For up-to-the-minute details on all the sports listed here, or on where to find your own favourite sporting activity, phone the city council's sport information service on ☎ 552 24 90.

Beaches

The Netherlands has some great **beaches**, although the weather is unreliable and the water often murky and full of jellyfish. For swimming or sunbathing, the nearest resort is Zandvoort, a short train ride from Amsterdam – though beware of large crowds in season. Otherwise, there are resorts and long, sandy beaches all the way up to the dune-filled western coastline: Katwijk and Noordwijk can be reached by bus from Leiden, Castricum-aan-Zee and Bergen-aan-Zee, and Egmond-aan-Zee by bus from Alkmaar; or, with your own vehicle, it's possible to find any number of deserted spots in between.

Bowling, Snooker and Carambole

If it's raining or you're just an enthusiast, there are plenty of places to indulge yourself in less energetic sports, like **ten-pin bowling**, **snooker** and **pool**, or the more specifically Dutch **carambole** – a form of billiards, played on a table without pockets. You score by making cannons, and the skill of some of the locals, often spinning the ball through impossible angles, is unbelievable. It's considered unfashionable, but you'll find tables in many cafés, and get plenty of advice on how to play if you so much as look at a ball.

Bavaria Snooker Club, Van Ostadestraat 97; ☎676 40 59. Seven tables. ƒ9–13.50 per hour. Pool and carambole too.

Keizers' Snooker Club, Keizersgracht 256; ☎623 15 86. Eight high-quality tables in a seventeenth-century canal house. ƒ17 an hour.

Knijn Bowling Centre, Scheldeplein 3, opposite RAI complex; ☎664 22 11. The closest to the city centre, with 22 bowling lanes. Between ƒ26 and ƒ39 per hour per alley, maximum of six persons Mon–Sat 4pm–1am, Sun 2pm–11pm.

Snooker Centre, Rokin 28; ☎620 49 74. Twelve tables, ƒ13.50–15 an hour.

Snookercentrum de Munt, Reguliersbreestraat 16; ☎620 20 40. Twelve tables, ƒ11–14.50 per hour.

Chess and Draughts

Gambit, Bloemgracht 20, **Het Hok**, Lange Leidsedwarsstraat 134, and **Domino**, Leidsekruistraat 19, are cafes where both chess and draughts are played to the exclusion of (almost) everything else. There's a small charge for a board. See "Bars" for more details.

Football

Ajax Amsterdam, Middenweg 401; ☎694 65 15. A talented and entertaining young team still near the top of the Dutch league, although as far as crowd trouble goes Ajax's "F-side" mob are every bit as bad as anything Britain's fans can come up with. The Ajax stadium is at the eastern end of the tram #9 line, and the cheapest (standing) tickets start at ƒ12.50. For a full list of all league matches, consult the VVV.

Feyenoord Rotterdam, Feyenoord Stadium, Olympiaweg 50, Rotterdam; ☎010/419 04 57. One of the country's other top-league teams. A handy train stop near the grounds. Ticket prices similar to Ajax's.

Gambling

If you're itching to strike it rich with your last few guilders, Amsterdam is a disappointment. There's no horse racing to speak of and legal casinos are few and far between. You can, however, place bets on British horse races at Ladbroke's **Totalisator** offices: the two most central offices are at Lange Niezel 12 (☎622 91 98), and Leidestraat 101 (☎623 85 83). The most central place to play the tables is the new **Holland Casino**, Max Euweplein 62 (☎620 10 06). It's open daily from 1.30pm until 3am, and there's a cover charge of ƒ5. You need to wear a jacket if you're a man, and, since the minimum age for admission is 18 years, be prepared to show some sort of ID.

Hockey and Basketball

The RAI Centre, Europaplein 8; ☎549 12 12. Most major matches take place here, along with an unusual Dutch form of basketball called *Korfbal*, in which teams are mixed and the basket is much higher.

Horse Riding

Amsterdamse Manege, Nieuwe Kalfjeslaan 25; ☎643 13 42. The place for a ride – but only on dressage horses.

Hollandse Manege, Vondelstraat 140; ☎618 09 42. The most centrally located place to ride.

Jogging

The main circuits are the **Vondelpark** and **Amsterdamse Bos**, the latter having special routes of varying distances signposted throughout. The **Amsterdam Marathon**, should you be up for it (a little over 42km), takes place in May.

Pole Sitting

Every year in July/early August, there's the chance to witness the offbeat spectator sport of pole sitting.

In Noorderwijkerhout, just north of Scheveningen, there's a **pole sitting marathon** which lasts about five days. Although not exactly a dynamic sport, it generates a fair amount of excitement as some fifteen braves sit it out on poles perched in the North Sea. The last one left is the winner.

Saunas and Gyms

Deco, Herengracht 115; ☎623 82 15. In the running for Amsterdam's most stylish sauna and steam bath, with a magnificent Art Deco interior and a nice café. A great place to hang out for the day without a stitch on. Highly recommended. Day tickets up to 2pm ƒ16, after 2pm ƒ24. Mon–Sat 11am–11pm, Sun 1–6pm.

Garden Gym, Jodenbreestraat 158; ☎626 87 72. Weight-training and dance-workout studio with saunas, solarium, massage and self-defence classes. Mainly, but not exclusively, for women. Day pass ƒ14.50 with shower, ƒ21.50 including use of sauna. Mon, Wed & Fri 9am–11pm, Tues & Thurs noon–11pm, Sat 11am–6pm, Sun 10am–7pm.

Sauna Damrak, Damrak 54; ☎622 60 12. Centrally located sauna. ƒ23.50, ƒ27.50 with towels.

Sport and
Outdoor
Activities

Sport and Outdoor Activities

Splash, Looiersgracht 26–30; ☎624 84 04. Very popular hi-tech fitness centre with sauna, tanning salon and Turkish bath. Daily aerobic classes, gender-seperated training rooms. Day pass ƒ25. Mon–Fri 10am–10pm, Sat & Sun 11am–6pm.

De Stokerij, 1e Rozendwarsstraat 8; ☎625 94 17. Council fitness centre with facilities for football, tennis, volleyball, etc, and a gym. Price ƒ3 an hour during instruction periods, otherwise ƒ40 a month. Tram #13, #14, #17.

Skating

When it's **really cold**, skaters can get spoiled in Amsterdam: almost every drop of available water is utilized, and the canals provide an exhilarating way to whizz round the city – much more fun than going round a rink. But before you venture out, a few **safety points**:

• Wait till you see others on the ice – locals have a better idea of its thickness.

• If in doubt, start off on the smaller ponds in the Vondelpark.

• Be careful under bridges, where the ice takes longest to freeze.

• If the ice gives way and you find yourself in the water, head for the darkest spot you can see in the ice above – that's the hole.

It's also possible to skate out of Amsterdam and into surrounding towns – through the Waterland or to Muiderslot and Naarden, for example. One of the great events in Holland's sporting calendar is the annual *Elfstedentocht*, a race across eleven towns and 200km of frozen waterways in Friesland. Though the race couldn't be held for twenty years, a recent spate of cold winters has meant two competitions in a row and an increasing number of partici-pants – over 16,000 when it was last held in 1986. If you're around in January and the ice is good, you'll hear talk of little else.

Most Amsterdammers have their own skates, and there are surprisingly few places where you can **hire** a pair. If Dutch friends can't help, you can hire some at one of the rinks (only Jaap Eden Baan offi-cially allows them to be taken from the rink). **Buying** a pair from a department store or sports shop will cost upwards of ƒ70; the best place to look for a secondhand pair is from one of the noticeboards in bars and suchlike.

Jaap Eden Baan, Radioweg 64; ☎694 98 94. Tram #9, or bus #8 from Amstel Station as far as the last stop on Kruislaan. Large indoor rink with all facilities, open Oct – March.

Leidseplein rink, Leidseplein. Small, free, outdoor rink, good for a trial run before hitting the canals. Open Nov–Feb.

Swimming

Flevoparkbad, Zeeburgerdijk 630; ☎692 50 30. Tram #3, #10. The best outdoor pool in the city; gets very busy on sunny days. Adults ƒ4, kids ƒ3.50. Mid-May to late Sept, daily 10am–5pm; on warm days, till 9pm.

Jan van Galenbad, Jan van Galenstraat 315; ☎612 80 01. Outdoor pool in the west of the city, open May–Sept only.

Marnixbad, Marnixplein 9; ☎625 48 43. Central swimming pool complete with slides, whirlpools, etc. Admission ƒ4.

De Mirandabad, De Mirandalaan 9; ☎642 80 80. Superbly equipped swimming centre (outdoor and indoor pools), with wave machine, whirlpools and slides. Adults ƒ5.75, kids ƒ4.50. Outdoor pool mid-May to mid-Sept 10am–9pm. Indoor pool roughly Mon–Fri 7am–10pm, weekends 10am–5pm; women only Wed 9am–11am, small children Sun 10–11am.

Zuiderbad, Hobbemastraat 26; ☎679 22 17. Lovely old pool that's been around for close on 100 years and is thus refreshingly free of the gimmicks that clutter up the others. Admission ƒ4.

Tennis, Squash and Table Tennis

Most outdoor tennis courts are for members only, and those that aren't need to be booked well in advance. Your best bets for getting a game at short notice are at the following places :

Frans Otten Stadion, Stadionstraat 10; ☎662 87 67. Five indoor tennis courts and 20 squash courts. Tennis around ƒ25–30 per hour, squash ƒ15 per half-hour, ƒ18.75

in the evening. Racket hire ƒ5. Open Mon–Fri 9am–11pm, Sat & Sun 9am–8pm.

Gold Star Tennis, K. Lotsylaan 20 near Vrije Universiteit, Buitenveldert; ☎644 54 83. Sneltram #51. Ten indoor tennis courts, rates for around ƒ25–35 per hour for non-members. Racket hire ƒ5. Summer hours 7am–11pm.

Squash City, Ketelmakerstraat 6; ☎626 78 83. ƒ27 per court for 45 minutes between 9am and 5pm, ƒ37 after 5pm; all prices include sauna. Racket hire ƒ5. Open daily 9am–midnight. Phone ahead to book courts.

Table Tennis Institute Amsterdam, Keizersgracht 209; ☎624 57 80. Very central table tennis hall – an increasingly popular sport in Amsterdam. Open daily 1pm–1am, ƒ10 per table per hour. Phone to book.

Tafelcentrum Leoos, 1 Marnixplantsoen 1; ☎624 22 87. Table tennis centre that's slightly cheaper than the above, at ƒ9 per hour. Mon–Fri 5pm–1am.

Sport and Outdoor Activities

Chapter 14

Museums

Slogging around museums isn't everyone's idea of fun, and you may find more than enough visual stimulation in Amsterdam's mansions and canals. But the city has a superb concentration of art galleries, of which three – the **Rijksmuseum**, the **Van Gogh** and the **Stedelijk** – rank among the best in the world. Add to this over thirty small museums – including the **Anne Frank House**, an excellent **Jewish Historical Museum**, and the beautiful hidden church of the **Amstelkring** – and you get some idea of just how impressive that concentration is. The listings below, combined with the map on the following pages and the accounts in the guide itself, should help you choose.

If you intend to visit more than a couple of museums it's advisable to buy a **museumcard**, either from the VVV or direct from a museum. It costs ƒ15 if you're under 18, ƒ40 for adults and ƒ25 for senior citizens. It's valid for a year and grants free entry to all state and municipally run Museums throughout the country. You need to take a passport photo along to get one, but considering it costs ƒ6.50 to visit the Rijksmuseum alone, it's a bargain if you intend to visit more than a couple of museums; where museumcards *aren't* accepted we've indicated. An alternative is the **Cultureel Jongeren Passport** or **CJP**, which for ƒ20 gets you reductions in museums, and on theatre, concert and *filmhuis* tickets – though these can vary, and are often not that substantial. Valid throughout the country and in Belgium, it's available only to those under 26 and can be

bought from the *Uitburo* in the Stadsschouwburg on Leidseplein. Incidentally, **entry-prices for kids** are usually half that of the adult admission.

Opening times, particularly of state-run museums, tend to follow a pattern: closed on Monday, open from 10am to 5pm Tuesday to Saturday and from 1 to 5pm on Sunday and public holidays. Almost all the museums offer at least basic **information** in English or a written English guide. Most have temporary special exhibitions or *tentoonstelling*; the best way to find out what's showing is to pick up a free copy of the English *Museum Magazine*, available from any museum. "Museum Agenda" in *Uitkrant* and *What's On In Amsterdam* are also useful for up-to-the-minute listings.

Finally, if you like to take your museums the easy way, between April and October the VVV runs a **museum boat** from the Centraal Station: it stops at the Anne Frank House, Amsterdam Historical Museum, Rijksmuseum, Van Gogh and Stedelijk Museums, Rembrandt House, Jewish Historical Museum and the Maritime Museum. Tickets cost around ƒ19 (ƒ13 with Museumcard) and are valid all day, allowing gentle canal hops; the first of five boats leaves at 9.30am, Tuesday to Saturday only. There's also the **Canal Bus** service, which takes in the central museums all year round.

Allard Pierson Museum
Oude Turfmarkt 127. Tram #4, #9, #14, #16, #24, #25. Tues–Fri 10am–5pm; Sat–Sun and holidays 1–5pm; ƒ5, kids ƒ2.

The city's premier archeological museum; see p.65.

Amstelkring Museum

Oude Zijds Voorburgwal 40. Walking distance from Centraal Station. Mon–Sat 10am–5pm, Sun 1–5pm; f4.50, kids f3.
Known as "Our Dear Lord in the Attic", this is a well-preserved seventeenth-century clandestine Catholic church and house; see p.60.

Amsterdam Historical Museum

Kalverstraat 92. Tram #1, #2, #4, #5, #9, #14, #16, #24, #25. Mon–Fri 10am–5pm, Sat & Sun 11am–5pm; f6.50, kids f3.50; guided tours on Wed at 2pm and 3pm.
Modern and engaging collection of artefacts relating to the history of the city; see p.65.

Anne Frank House

Prinsengracht 263. Tram #13, #14, #17. Mon–Sat 9am–5pm, Sun 10am–5pm; f7, children 10–17 f3.50, under 10s free; no museumcard.
The secret annexe where Anne Frank and her family hid during the occupation, now a museum; see p.82.

Bijbels Museum

Herengracht 366. Tram #1, #2, #5. Tues–Sat 10am–5pm, Sun 1–5pm; f3.
Ecumenical museum of the world's religions; see p.72.

Bosmuseum ·

Koenenkade, Amsterdamse Bos. At the end of the Tram Museum's line, or bus #170, #171 or #172 from Centraal Station. Daily 10am–5pm; free.
Museum and information centre of the Amsterdam Bos, in the south of the city; see p.110.

Geels & Co. Museum

Warmoesstraat 67. Fri & Sat noon–5pm.
Museum of coffee- and tea-related displays above a shop selling the same; see p.59.

Geological Museum

Nieuwe Prinsengracht 130. Tram #6, #7, #9, #10, #14. Mon–Fri 9am–5pm; free.
The geological collection of Amsterdam University; see p.78.

Hash Info Museum

Oude Zijds Achterburgwal 148. Tram #4, #9, #16, #24, #25. Daily, 11am–10pm f6.
Collection of artefacts relating to the imbibing of cannabis, not popular with the Amsterdam authorities; see p.60.

Hollandse Schouwburg

Plantage Middenlaan 24. Tram #7, #9, #14. Summer daily 11am–4pm; free. Monument daily 11am–4pm.
Exhibition on the horrors of World War II, with special reference to Jewish families who were deported via the Schouwburg building; see p.91.

Hortus Botanicus

Plantage Middenlaan 2. Tram #7, #9, #14. April–Oct Mon–Fri 9am–5pm, Sat–Sun 11am–5pm; Nov–March Mon–Fri 9am–4pm, Sat–Sun 11am–4pm; f56.
Botanical gardens of Amsterdam University; see p.91.

Jewish Historical Museum

J. D. Meijerplein. Metro to Waterlooplein, or tram #9, #14. Daily, except Yom Kippur, 11am–5pm; f7, children f3.50.
Innovative museum of the Jewish faith, with reference to the history of the Jews in Amsterdam; see p.90.

Kattenkabinet

Herengracht 468. Tram #16, #24, #25. Tues–Sat 11am–5pm, Sun noon–5pm f7.50.
Hundreds of paintings and art objects related to cats, on display in an old canal house; see p.70.

Kromhout Shipyard Museum

Hoogte Kadijk 147. Bus #22, #28. Mon–Fri 10am–4pm; f3.50, kids f1.50; no museumcards.
Old shipyard that is part museum, part restorer of old vessels; see p.94.

Maritime Museum

Kattenburgerplein 1. Bus #22, #28. Tues–Sat 10am–5pm, Sun 1–5pm; f10, kids f7.50.
Impressive collection of maritime objects, large and small; see p.93.

Museums

The museums and galleries listed here are covered in more detail in the relevant city chapters.

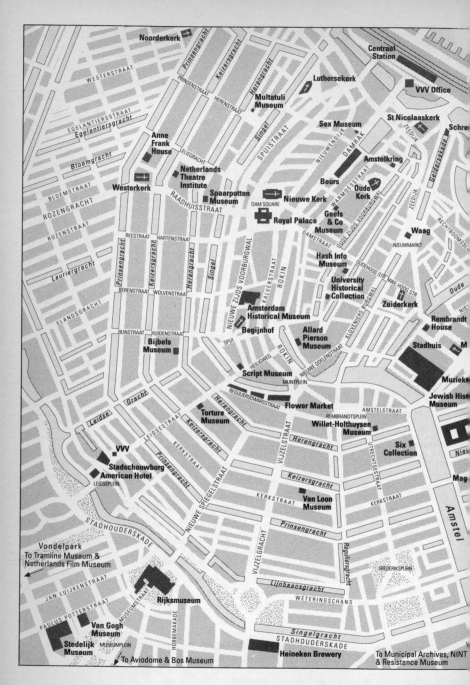

Het Ij

Dijksgracht

arthuis

Oosterdok

Montelbaanstoren

PRINS HENDRIKKADE

KATTENBURGERSTRAAT

Maritime Museum

KATTENBURGERGRACHT

Nieuwe

WITTENBURGERGRACHT

Vaart

OOSTENBURGERGRACHT

To the
Netherlands
Press Museum

n Kerk

Herengracht

ENTREPOTDOK

HOOGTEKADIJK

Trade
Union Museum

Kromhout
Shipyard
Museum

MUIDERSTRAAT

Hortus Botanicus

PLANTAGE DOKLAAN

Hollandse
Schouwburg

Artis Zoo

PLANTAGE MIDDENLAAN

Keizersgracht

Zoological
Museum

Singelgracht

Suriname Historical
Museum

PLANTAGE MUIDERGRACHT

NIEUWE KERK STRAAT

Geological
Museum

Muiderpoort

Achtgracht

Nieuwe

WEESPERPLEIN

SARPHATISTRAAT

Tropenmuseum

MAURITSKADE

Oosterpark

WIBAUTSTRAAT

0   500 m

Museums

Max Euwe Centre
Max Euweplein 30. Tram #1, #2, #5, #6, #7, #10. Tues–Fri 10.30am–4pm; free.
Eponymous museum of the only Dutch chess champion, full of chess-related bits and pieces; see p.74.

Municipal Archives
Amsteldijk 67. Tram #3, #4. Mon–Fri 8.45am–4.45pm, Sat 9am–12.15pm; free.
A mass of historical material on the city, displayed by way of regular exhibitions, although research is the archives' chief concern; see p.107.

Mutatuli Museum
Korsjespoortsteeg 20. Tram #1, #2, #5, #13, #17. Tues 10am–5pm, other times phone ☎ 638 19 38 for an appointment; free.
Museum in the former home of the eighteenth-century Dutch writer; see p.66.

Netherlands Film Museum
Vondelpark 3, near the southern end of Roemer Visscherstraat. Tram #1, #2, #3, #6, #12. Mon–Fri 3–9.30pm, Sat & Sun 4–9.30pm; library and documentation centre Tues–Sat 11am–5pm; film shows daily 4–9.30pm; free; film shows f8.50.
Basically a showcase for obscure films on a variety of subjects – not always Dutch and usually organized by theme; see p.106.

Netherlands Press Museum
International Institute for Social History, Cruquiusweg. Mon–Fri 9am–5pm, by appointment only, (☎ 668 58 66).
The history of the Dutch press since 1903, as revealed in newspapers, leaflets, posters and political cartoons; see p.112.

Netherlands Theatre Museum
Herengracht 168. Tram #13, #14, #17. Tues–Sun 11am–5pm; f5, kids f3.
Recreations of contemporary stage sets alongside models that trace the earlier days of the theatre in The Netherlands; see p.72.

Open Harbour Museum
KNSM-Laan 311 (aka Surinamekade 3). Bus #28. Wed–Fri 1–5pm; f3.50, f2.50 with museumcard.
History of the harbour of Amsterdam, presented from a social viewpoint. Interesting and broadly "alternative" historical analysis.

Rembrandt House
Jodenbreestraat 4–6. Metro to Waterlooplein, tram #9, #14. Mon–Sat 10am–5pm, Sun 1–5pm; f5, kids f2.50.
The home of Rembrandt at the height of his fame and popularity, home to a display of his engravings; see p.88.

Resistance Museum
Lekstraat 63. Tram #4, #12, #25. Tues–Fri 10am–5pm; Sat–Sun 1–5pm; f3.50.
Excellent display on the rise of the resistance from the German invasion of The Netherlands in May 1940 to the country's liberation in 1945; see p.109.

The Rijksmuseum
Stadhouderskade 42. Tram #5, #6, #7, #10, #16, #24, #25. Tues–Sat 10am–5pm, Sun 1–5pm; f10. The Dutch paintings section is always open; if, however, you specifically want to see another department, phone ☎ 673 21 21 to check opening hours. Free half-hourly films give the background to the major paintings; for more on Dutch art and artists, see Contexts.
The country's national museum, with marvellous collections of Dutch art and history, as well as furniture, oriental ceramics, etc; see p.97.

Rijksmuseum Vincent Van Gogh
Paulus Potterstraat 7. Tram #2, #3, #5, #12, #16. Mon–Sat 10am–5pm, Sun 1–5pm; f10, children under 17 f5.
Informative cassettes are on hire to guide you around the highlights of the permanent collection. During summer there are sometimes also half-hour playlets on different aspects of the artist's life, roughly every hour in the downstairs auditorium, price f3.50. For information on courses, held in spring and autumn, and on the walk-in studio sessions (summer and winter), ask at the workshop.
Perhaps the world's finest collection of work, on paper and canvas, by Vincent Van Gogh; see p.104.

Script Museum
University library, Singel 425. Tram #1, #2, #4, #5, #9, #16, #24, #25. Mon–Fri 11am–4pm; free.
Collection of different writing materials and alphabets from around the world; p.68.

Sex Museum
Damrak 18. Daily 10am–11pm; f3.95.
Rather tawdry exhibition of sex-related art
and artefacts; see p.57.

Six Collection
*Amstel 218. Tram #4. Apply first, with
passport, at the Rijksmuseum for a ticket.
Guided tours on Mon, Wed, Fri at 10am
and 11am; closed public holidays; free.*
A private home that displays a handful of
the finest paintings of the Dutch golden age
in a period setting. Be warned, though,
that you must follow the procedure
outlined above; the house is still lived in
and is extremely protective of its privacy;
see p.77.

Stedelijk Museum
*Paulus Potterstraat 13. Tram #2, #3, #5,
#12, #16. Daily 11am–5pm; f7.50. For
details of the museum's Sunday
performances of classical music, see
"Nightlife".*
The city's prime venue for modern art.
Displays from its excellent permanent
collection, as well as regular temporary
exhibitions; see p.105.

Tropenmuseum
*Linnaeusstraat 2. Tram #3, #6, #9, #10,
#14. Mon–Fri 10am–5pm, Sat–Sun noon–
5pm; f7.50, children f4.*
Applied arts from all over the world, imaginatively displayed through a variety of
media; see p.111.

Torture Museum
Leidsestraat 27. Daily 10am–7pm; f7.50.
A macabre but well-displayed and informative collection of medieval punishment
equipment; see p.73.

Trade Union Museum
*Henri Polaklan 9. Tram #7, #*9, #14. Tues–
Fri 11am–5pm, Sun 1–5pm; f5.*
A small collection of documents, cuttings
and photos relating to the Dutch labour
movement; see p.92.

University of Amsterdam Historical Collection
*Oude Zijds Voorburgwal 231. Tram #4, #9,
#16, #24, #25. Mon–Fri 9am–5pm, but
phone first for an appointment (☎ 525 33
39 or ☎ 525 33 41), free.*
Collections of books, prints, letters and
suchlike, related to the city university's
history; see p.62.

Van Loon Museum
*Keizersgracht 672. Tram #16, #24, #25.
Mon 10am–5pm, Sun 1–5pm; f5.*
Period canal house with a pleasantly
down-at-heel interior of peeling stucco and
shabby paintwork; p.72.

Willet-Holthuysen Museum
*Herengracht 605. Tram #4, #9, #14. Mon–
Fri 10am–5pm, Sat & Sun 11am–5pm; f5,
kids f2.50.*
Rococo-style, period canal house, some-
what more pristinely restored than the Van
Loon; see p.76.

Museums

*For details of
museums that
specifically appeal
to children, see
Kids' Amsterdam.*

Out of the City

Chapter 15

Introduction and Practicalities

A lthough Amsterdammers may try to persuade you that there's nothing remotely worth seeing outside their own city, The Netherlands is a compact country, its rail services fast and frequent, and day trips can be made easily to a number of extremely worthwhile destinations from the capital.

The options really split into two groups: the cities of the **Randstad** conurbation which stretches south of Amsterdam, and the comparatively rural area to the **north**, where your journeys are more likely to focus on the old ports of the IJsselmeer. The quickest and most convenient method of getting anywhere is by *Nederlandse Spoorwegen* or *NS*, the Dutch **rail network**. It offers return (*retour*) tickets that give substantial savings on the normal return fare. Also, if you're heading for one specific attraction or taking kids along, it might be worth using one of their day excursion fares (*dagtochten*), which combine travel and admission on a reduced ticket. Those intending to take a longer tour of the country should consider Rail Rover tickets (currently *f*152 for a seven day *weekkaart*), which allow travel throughout the Dutch rail network. There's copious literature published by Dutch Railways outlining these offers, available from most Dutch train stations, and, in Great Britain, from the *NS* office at 25-28 Buckingham Gate, London SW1E 6LD (☎071/630 1735).

Road connections are fast, the Dutch road network is comprehensive and efficient. **Car rental** costs are fairly standard for Europe: prices for the smallest vehicle (inclusive of collision damage waiver and insurance) start at f45 a day. The international rental companies all have offices in Amsterdam although you may be able to make some small savings by going to local operators.

If you're not pressed for time, **cycling** is an ideal way of seeing the countryside: the landscape is gentle and there's an extensive system of bike paths, often diverted from the main roads. Bikes can be hired from almost all train stations (see *Basics* for details of Amsterdam bike hire). Companies like *Awks Bike Tours* (☎692 35 84) also offer leisurely

See Basics, *p.22, for details of car rental companies in Amsterdam, and the main rules of the road in The Netherlands.*

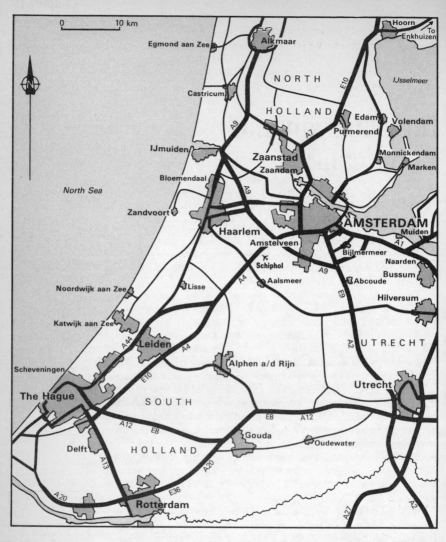

tours in the city environs. Cycling maps (scale 1:100,000) are available from the VVV (around ƒ8 each) or from the ANWB (ƒ9.95 each).

The VVV offices in Amsterdam (see p.24) can advise on travel in any part of the country .

A good starting point wherever you go is the local VVV office, which can help with detailed maps, restaurant listings and accommodation – usually at around ƒ35 per person per night in a lower-grade hotel, a little less in private rooms. Opening times listed are for summer (April – Sept); expect hours to be slightly reduced at other times of the year.

OUT OF THE CITY: CHAPTER 15

Chapter 16

The Randstad Cities

Amsterdam forms the northeasternmost point of the dense urban conglomeration known as the **Randstad**, made up primarily of the cities that were the principal power bases of the Dutch trading empire during the seventeenth century. Despite their close proximity to each other, most of these retain surprisingly distinct characters, and they're also well connected by a major train line, making it possible to visit more than one on a day out from the capital.

Haarlem is the closest to Amsterdam, just fifteen minutes by train but with a character all of its own, and with enticing attractions like the Frans Hals Museum. Further down the line, **Leiden** has a highly respected university and a number of excellent museums; **The Hague** is the rather pompous political capital of the country, although it has plenty to see, most notably a fine collection of pictures in its Mauritshuis gallery; while to the east, **Utrecht** exudes a pleasant provincialism that offers a refreshing change from the capital. Bear in mind, too, that in between most of the Randstad cities lie the best of the Dutch **bulbfields**, a blaze of colour if you're here between March and June; and all along the nearby coast are some of the country's finest **beaches** – long sandy strands fringed by endless expanses of dunes.

Haarlem

Just over ten minutes from Amsterdam by train, **HAARLEM** has quite a different pace and feel from the capital, an easily absorbed city of around 150,000 people that sees itself as a step above its neighbours. The Frans Hals Museum, in the almshouse where the artist spent his last – and for some, his most brilliant – years, is worth an afternoon in itself; there are numerous beaches within easy reach, as well as some of the best of the bulbfields; and the city's young and vigorous nightlife may well keep you up until the last train back – which is, conveniently, after midnight.

Arrival, information and accommodation

The **train station** is located on the north side of the city, about ten minutes' walk from the centre; **buses** stop right outside. The **VVV**, attached to the station (April–Sept Mon–Sat 9am–5.30pm, Oct–March Mon–Fri 9am–5.30pm; ☎31 90 59), has maps (50c) and can book **private rooms** for around ƒ30 a head, though you'll find more choice in Zandvoort, about twenty minutes away by hourly bus #80 (every fifteen minutes from Tempelierstraat) or #81 (every half hour from the railway station). The same goes for **hotels**, though Haarlem has a few reasonably priced alternatives. The *Carillon*, centrally placed at Grote Markt 27 (☎31 05 91), has doubles from about ƒ85, as does the *Waldor*, close to the station at Jansweg 40 (☎31 26 22). There's also a **youth hostel** at Jan Gijzenpad 3 (open March–Oct; ☎37 37 93); bus #2 or #6 runs frequently from the station – a ten-minute journey. **Campers** should either try the campsites among the dunes along Zeeweg out at Bloemendaal-aan-zee (bus #81), though these tend to be open during spring and summer only, or Haarlem's own site at Liewegie 17, which is open all year – to get there take bus #80 from Tempelierstraat.

The Harlem area telephone code is ☎023.

The Town

For a long time the residence of the counts of Holland, Haarlem was sacked by the Spanish under Frederick of Toledo in 1572. There are reminders of this all over the town, since, after a seven-month siege, the revenge exacted by the inconvenienced Frederick was terrible: nearly the whole population was massacred, including the entire Protestant clergy. Recaptured in 1577 by William the Silent, Haarlem went on to enjoy its greatest prosperity in the seventeenth century, becoming a centre for the arts and home to a flourishing school of painters.

Nowadays, the place retains an air of quiet affluence, with all the picturesque qualities of Amsterdam but little of the sleaze. The core of the city is **Grote Markt**, an open space flanked by a concentration of Gothic and Renaissance architecture, most notably the gabled and balconied **Stadhuis**, at one end. This dates from the fourteenth century, though it has been much rebuilt over the years, the last time in 1630 – a date recorded on the facade. Inside, the main hall is normally left open for visitors during office hours; it's decorated with a few fifteenth-century paintings. At the other end of Grote Markt there's a statue of one **Laurens Coster**, who, Haarlemmers insist, is the true inventor of printing. Legend tells of him cutting a letter "A" from the bark of a tree and dropping it into the sand by accident. Plausible enough, but most authorities seem to agree that Gutenburg was the more likely source of the printed word.

Coster stands in the shadow of the **Grote Kerk of St Bavo** (Mon–Sat 10am–4pm; Oct–Jan closes at 3.30pm; ƒ2.50), where he is believed to be buried. If you've been to the Rijksmuseum in

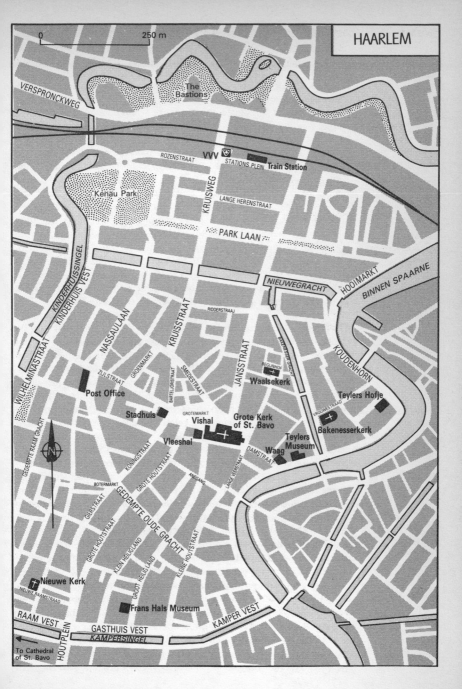

Haarlem

Amsterdam, the church may seem familiar, at least from the outside, since it was the principal focus of the seventeenth-century painter Berckheyde's many views of this square – only the black-coated burghers are missing. Finished in the early sixteenth century, it dwarfs the surrounding clutter of streets and houses, and serves as a landmark from almost anywhere in the city. Inside, it is breathtakingly high, its beauty enhanced by the bare, white-painted power of the Gothic vaulting. The mighty Christian Muller organ of 1738 is said to have been played by Handel and Mozart and is one of the biggest in the world, with 5000 pipes and razzmatazz Baroque embellishment. You can hear it played on Tuesday evenings between mid-May and mid-September. Beneath the organ, Xaverij's lovely group of draped marble figures represents Poetry and Music, offering thanks to the town, represented as patroness of the arts, for her generosity, while in the choir there's a late fifteenth-century painting that the church traditionally (though dubiously) attributes to Geertgen tot Sint Jans, along with memorials to painters Pieter Saenredam and Frans Hals – both of whom are buried here. Outside, at the church's western end, the **Vishal** and, opposite that, Lieven de Key's profusely decorated **Vleeshal** (the former fish and meat markets), hold regular art exhibitions (Mon–Sat 11am–5pm, Sun 1–5pm). There is usually no admission fee.

The Frans Hals Museum

Haarlem's chief attraction, the **Frans Hals Museum** at Groot Heiligland 62 (Mon–Sat 10am–5pm, Sun 1–5pm; *f*6), is just a five-minute stroll from Grote Markt, housed in the Oudemannenhuis almshouse where the aged Hals is supposed to have lived out his last destitute years on public funds. Little is known about Frans Hals. Born in Antwerp, the son of Flemish refugees who settled in Haarlem in the late 1580s, his extant oeuvre is relatively small: some two hundred paintings and nothing like the number of sketches and studies left behind by Rembrandt – partly because Hals wasn't fashionable until the nineteenth century, and a lot of his work was lost before it became collectable. His outstanding gift was as a portraitist, showing a sympathy with his subjects and an ability to capture fleeting expression that some say even Rembrandt lacked. Seemingly quick and careless flashes of colour form a coherent whole, leaving us a set of seventeenth-century figures that are curiously alive.

The museum begins with the work of other artists: first a small group of **sixteenth-century works**, the most prominent a triptych by Gerard David, and an early anti-imperialist painting – *West Indian Scene* by Jan Mostaert, in which the naked natives try fruitlessly to defend themselves against the cannon and sword of their invaders. Van Scorel's *Baptism of Christ* and *Knights of Jerusalem* follow, along with works by van Goyen, Brouwer, and van Ostade, and a good group of paintings by the **Haarlem mannerists**, including works by Carel van Mander, leading light of the Haarlem School and mentor of many of the other painters represented here. Cornelis Cornelisz van Haarlem

186

OUT OF THE CITY: CHAPTER 16

best follows van Mander's guidelines: *The Marriage of Peleus and Thetis* was a popular subject, probably because it was interpreted as a warning against discord, appropriate during the long war with Spain – though Cornelisz gives as much attention to the arrangement of elegant nudes as to his subject. The same is true of his *Massacre of the Innocents*, which could refer to the siege of Haarlem just twenty years earlier.

Frans Hals was a pupil of van Mander, too, though he seems to have learned little more than the barest rudiments from him. His paintings in the west wing – a set of "Civic Guard" portraits of the companies initially formed to defend the country from the Spanish, later on just local social clubs – established his reputation as a portraitist, and earned him a regular income. There was a special skill involved in painting these: for the first time Hals made the group portrait a unified whole instead of a static collection of individual portraits; his figures are carefully arranged, but so cleverly as not to appear contrived. For a time, Hals himself was a member of the Company of Saint George, and in the *Officers of the Militia Company of Saint George* he appears in the top left-hand corner – one of his few self-portraits.

After this, there are numberless scenes of Haarlem by Berckheyde and Saenredam, among others; landscapes by the Ruisdaels and Berchem; and some group portraits by Veerspronck and the elderly Frans Hals. Hals' later paintings are darker, more contemplative works, closer to Rembrandt in their lighting. The *Governors of the Saint Elizabeth Gasthuis*, painted in 1641, is a good example, as are the portraits of the *Regents* and *Regentesses of the Oudemannhuis* itself – perhaps the museum's finest treasures. These were commissioned when Hals was in his eighties, a poor man despite a successful painting career, hounded for money by the town's tradesmen and by the mothers of his illegitimate children, and dependent on the charity of the people depicted here. Their cold, hard faces stare out of the gloom, the women reproachful, the men only slightly more affable – except for the character just right of centre who has been labelled (and indeed looks) completely drunk. There are those who claim Hals had lost his touch by the time he painted these, yet the sinister, almost ghostly power of these paintings, facing each other across the room, suggests quite the opposite. Van Gogh's remark that "Frans Hals had no fewer than twenty-seven blacks" suddenly makes perfect sense.

Other galleries hold lesser works by lesser artists. There's a new wing, which houses temporary exhibitions, usually of modern and contemporary artists, and permanent paintings by Israëls, Appel, and Jan Sluyters – though lamentably few of the latter. More interesting is the Oudemannhuis itself, a fairly typical *hofje* whose style of low buildings and peaceful courtyards you'll see repeated with slight variations all over town – and indeed the country. Classical concerts are held here regularly throughout the year except June to August, usually in the afternoon on the third Sunday of each month; however, they didn't run in 1993. To find out if they're starting up again, phone ☎ 31 91 80.

The Hofjes . . . and Haarlem's other sights

As for the rest of town, Haarlem has a greater number of hofjes than most Dutch cities – over twenty in fact – proof of the town's prosperity in the seventeenth century. The VVV has information on where to find them in their "Hofjestocht" brochure, and they run guided tours every Saturday at 10am, and, in July and August, on Wednesdays at 10am. Most are still inhabited, so you're confined to looking around the courtyard, but the women who sit outside seem used to the occasional visitor and won't throw you out.

Second in the pecking order of Haarlem sights, the **Teylers Museum**, at Spaarne 16 (Tues–Sat 10am–5pm; Sun 1–5pm; *f*6.50), is Holland's oldest museum, founded in 1778 by wealthy local philanthropist Pieter Teyler van der Hulst. This should appeal to scientific and artistic tastes alike, containing everything from fossils, bones and crystals, to weird, H.G. Wells-type technology (including an enormous eighteenth-century electrostatic generator), and sketches and line drawings by Michelangelo, Raphael, Rembrandt, and Claude, among others. The drawings are covered for protection from the light, but don't be afraid to pull back the curtains and peek. Look in, too, on the rooms beyond, filled with work by eighteenth- and nineteenth-century Dutch painters, principally Breitner, Israëls, Weissenbruch, and, not least, Wijbrand Hendriks, who was the keeper of the art collection here.

Teyler also lent his charity to the **Teyler's Hofje**, a little way east around the bend of the Spaarne at Koudenhorn 64, a solid late eighteenth-century building that is more monumental in style than the town's other *hofjes*. Nearby, the elegant tower of the **Bakenesser Kerk** forms the other main protrusion on the Haarlem skyline, a late fifteenth-century church which is usually kept closed. Two other sights which may help structure your wanderings are on the opposite side of town. Van Campen's **Nieuwe Kerk** was built – rather unsuccessfully – on to Lieven de Key's bulbed, typically Dutch tower in 1649, though the interior is symmetrical with a soberness that is quite chilling after the soaring heights of the Grote Kerk. Just beyond, and much less self-effacing, the Roman Catholic **Cathedral of St Bavo** (April–Oct Mon–Sat 10am–noon & 2–4.30pm) is one of the largest ecclesiastical structures in Holland, designed by Joseph Cuijpers and built between 1895 and 1906. It's broad and spacious inside, cupolas and turrets crowding around an apse reminiscent of Byzantine churches or mosques, the whole surmounted by a distinctive copper dome.

Eating and Drinking

For **lunches and snacks**, try *Mephisto*, Grote Markt 29, which is open all day Wednesday to Sunday and serves very reasonable Dutch food and snacks. *Café 1900*, Barteljorisstraat 10, is also good for lunch, a trendy locals' hangout serving drinks and light meals in an impressive turn-of-the-century interior (it also has live music on Sundays); *H.*

Ferd. Kuipers is an excellent patisserie and tea room at Barteljorisstraat 22. In the evening, there's *Alfonso's* Tex-Mex restaurant just behind the Grote Kerk at Oude Groenmarkt 8; the *Piccolo* restaurant, Riviervischmarkt 1, serves pasta and decent pizzas; or try the Indonesian food at *De Lachende Javaen*, on Frankestraat, which serves *rijstaffels*.

Once you've eaten, *Ze Crack*, at the junction of Lange Veerstraat and Kleine Houtstraat, is a dim, smoky **bar** with good music and – unsurprisingly perhaps – lots of English people and beer by the pint. On the same street, closer to Grote Markt at Lange Veerstraat 9, *'t Ouwe Proef* is more typically Dutch, a *proeflokaal* that also sells beer – it's lively early evening.

Around Haarlem: Bloemendaal and Zandvoort

West of Haarlem, the monied outskirts of the town give way to the thick woodland and rugged dune landscape of the **Kennemerduinen National Park**, which stretches down to the sea. Bus #81 from the train station runs to the coast at **BLOEMENDAAL-AAN-ZEE**, which is the rather grandiose name for a group of beachside shacks that house a thriving ice-cream trade, while a little further south, and reachable direct on bus #80, **ZANDVOORT**, an agglomeration of modern and faceless apartment complexes that rise out of the dunes, is a major Dutch seaside resort. As resorts go it's pretty standard – packed and oppressive in summer, depressingly dead in winter. The best reason to visit is the championship motor racing circuit, which provides background noise to everyone's sunbathing. If you come for the beach, and manage to fight your way through the crush to the water, watch out – the sea here is murky and ominously close to the smoky chimneys of IJMUIDEN to the north.

You can also visit the Keukenhof Gardens from Haarlem; special express buses run twice an hour during the season every day except Sunday.

Leiden

The home of Holland's most prestigious university, **LEIDEN** has an academic air. Like Haarlem to the north, you get the feeling it regards itself as separate from and independent of Amsterdam – which is fair enough. There's enough here to justify at least a day trip, and the town's energy, derived largely from its students, strongly counters the myth that there's nothing worth experiencing outside the capital. Leiden museums, too, are varied and comprehensive enough to merit a visit in themselves – though be selective. The town's real charm lies in the peace and prettiness of its gabled streets and canals.

The university was a present from William the Silent, a reward for Leiden enduring (like Haarlem and Alkmaar) a year-long siege by the Spanish. The town emerged victorious on October 3, 1574, when William cut through the dykes around the city and sailed in with his fleet for a dramatic eleventh-hour rescue. This event is still commemorated with an annual fair on 2 and 3 October, fireworks, and the

Leiden

consumption of two traditional dishes: herring and white bread, which the fleet was supposed to have brought with them, and *hutspot*, or stew and mashed potato – a cauldron of which was apparently found simmering in the abandoned Spanish camp.

Arrival, information and accommodation

The Leiden area telephone code is ☎071.

Leiden's **train and bus stations** are situated on the northwest edge of town, about ten minutes' walk from the centre. The VVV is opposite at Stationsplein 210 (Mon–Fri 9am–5.30pm, Sat 9am–4pm; ☎14 68 46); they have maps and various leaflets and can advise on **accommodation** or make **room bookings** in private homes for ƒ35 a person. Other than that, Leiden is fairly short on **hotel** space for a town of its size, and there are no special bargains. *De Ceder*, out beyond the station at Rijnsburgerweg 80 (☎17 59 03), has rooms starting at ƒ100 for a double, not including breakfast; turn left outside the station and left again under the train tracks; *De Doelen*, better placed at Rapenburg 2 (☎12 05 27), has doubles for ƒ125, including breakfast. On the whole, though, accommodation is cheaper in the seaside resorts of Katwijk and Noordwijk (p.195). Of the two, Katwijk is the more pleasant place to stay, with several hotels and pensions along its seafront Boulevard; try *Het Anker*, at Boulevard 129 (☎01718/13890), or the *Seahorse*, Boulevard 14 (☎01718/15921), both of which have rooms starting at about ƒ40 per person. The nearest **youth hostel** is in Noordwijk, at Langevelderlaan 45 (☎02523/72920) – take bus #60 from opposite the station. If you're **camping**, the closest large site is the *Koningshof* in Rijnsburg, north of Leiden; take bus #40; otherwise, Noordwijk has several campsites, Katwijk one. All are open from March to October.

The Town

Leiden's most appealing quarter is that bordered by Witte Singel and Breestraat, focusing on Rapenburg, a peaceful area of narrow pedestrian streets and canals. Here, at Rapenburg 28, is perhaps the city's best-known attraction, the **Rijksmuseum Van Oudheden** (Tues–Sat 10am–5pm, Sun noon–5pm; ƒ3.50, children ƒ2), Holland's principal archeological museum, with a huge collection. You can see one of its major exhibits, the *Temple of Taffeh*, for free. Situated in a courtyard in front of the museum entrance, this was a gift from the Egyptian government in gratitude for the Dutch part in the 1960s UNESCO excavations in Abyssinia (Ethiopia), which succeeded in uncovering submerged Nubian monuments. Dating back to the first century AD, the temple was adapted in the fourth century to the worship of Isis, eventually being sanctified as a Christian church four hundred years later. The Egyptians placed very firm conditions on their legacy: no one should have to pay to see it, and the temperature and humidity must be carefully regulated, with the lights overhead simulating the passage – and shadow – of the sun.

Inside the museum proper, the first exhibit is the remains of a temple to Nehellania – a goddess of sailors – which was uncovered in Zeeland. Next come classical Greek and Roman sculpture, leading chronologically through Hellenistic works to busts, statues, and friezes of Imperial Rome. The best collection, though, is the Egyptian, beginning with wall reliefs, statues, and sarcophagi from tombs and temples, and continuing in the rooms immediately above with a set of mummies and sarcophagi as complete as you're likely to see outside Egypt. The *Three Figures of Maya*, to name just one exhibit, are exceptionally well preserved. The third floor is specifically Dutch: an archeological history of the country, from prehistoric, Roman and medieval times, that is, perhaps inevitably, less interesting than the rest of the museum.

Further along Rapenburg, at no. 73, the original home of the **university** still stands, part of which is open as a **museum** (Wed–Fri 1–5pm; free) that details its history. Through the courtyard, the **Hortus Botanicus** gardens (Mon–Sat 9am–5pm, Sun 10am–5pm; f3.50) make a lovely spot, lushly planted and subtly landscaped across to the Witte Singel canal. Planted in 1587, they are supposedly among the oldest botanical gardens in Europe, a mixture of carefully tended beds of shrubs and hothouses full of tropical foliage. Leave by the exit off to the left, across the canal, where a red door hides a reconstruction of the original garden, the **Clusiustuin** (April–Oct only Mon–Fri 9am–5pm), named after the botanist who first brought tulips to Holland.

Cross Rapenburg from the university museum, and you're in the network of narrow streets that constituted the medieval town, converging on a central square and the **Pieterskerk** (daily 1.30–4pm; free), the town's principal church. This is deconsecrated now, used occasionally for a Saturday antique market, and it has an empty warehouse-like feel. But among the fixtures that remain are a simple and beautiful Renaissance rood screen in the choir, and a host of memorials to the sundry notables buried here – among them **John Robinson**, leader of the Pilgrim Fathers.

Robinson lived in a house on the site of what is now the **Jan Pesijn Hofje** on Kloksteeg. A curate in England at the turn of the seventeenth century, he was suspended from preaching in 1604, later fleeing with his congregation to pursue his Puritan form of worship in the more amenable atmosphere of Calvinist Holland. Settling in Leiden, Robinson acted as pastor to growing numbers, but still found himself at odds with the establishment. In 1620, a hundred of his followers ("The Pilgrim Fathers") sailed via Plymouth for the freedom and abundance of America, though Robinson died before he could join them; he's buried in the church.

If you want to find out more, stroll down to the **Leiden Pilgrim Collection** at Vliet 45 (Mon–Fri 9.30am–4.30pm; free), part of the city archives and a mine of information on Robinson's group during their stay in Leiden. Otherwise, continue east onto **Breestraat**, which marks the edge of Leiden's commercial centre, flanked by the long, ornate Renaissance front of the late sixteenth-century **Stadhuis**, the only part of the building to survive a fire in 1929. Behind, the rivers which cut Leiden into islands converge at the busiest point in town, the site of a vigourous Wednesday and Saturday general **market** which sprawls right over the sequence of bridges into the blandly pedestrian **Haarlemmerstraat** – the town's major shopping street.

The junction of the Oude and Nieuwe Rijn is marked by the mid-seventeenth-century **Waag**, a replacement for a previous Gothic structure, built to a design by Pieter Post and fronted with a naturalistic frieze by Rombout Verhulst. Across the water from here, on an island formed by the fork in the two sections of river, the **Burcht** (daily 10am–11pm; free) is the rather ordinary, graffiti-daubed shell of a fort perched on a mound, the battlements of which you can clamber up for a view of Leiden's roofs and towers. The **Hooglandsekerk** (April–Oct only Mon 1–3.30pm, Tues–Sat 11am–4pm, Sun 11am–4pm; free), nearby, is a light, lofty church with a central pillar that features an epitaph to the burgomaster at the time of the 1574 siege, Pieter van der Werff, who became a hero during its final days. When the situation became so desperate that most people were all for giving up, the burgomaster, no doubt remembering the massacre of Haarlem, offered his own body to them as food. His invitation was rejected, but – the story goes – it succeeded in instilling new determination in the flagging citizens.

Across the Oude Rijn from here, is the **Museum Boerhaave** at Lange St Agnietenstraat 10 (Tues–Sat 10am–5pm, Sun noon–5pm; ƒ3.50), named after the seventeenth-century Leiden surgeon, and a brief but absorbing guide to scientific and medical developments over the last three centuries, with particular reference to Dutch achievements, including some gruesome surgical implements, pickled brains, and suchlike. Five minutes' walk away, Leiden's municipal museum, housed in the old Lakenhal ("cloth-hall") at Oude Singel 28–32 (Tues–Fri 10am–5pm, Sat & Sun 1–5pm; ƒ5), is similarly engaging, with a picture gallery devoted to natives of the town as well as mixed rooms of furniture, tiles, glass, and ceramics. It's also the only museum in Leiden to regularly exhibit modern Dutch art. Upstairs, the rooms are grouped around the Grote Pers ("Grand Press"), and look much as they would have when Leiden's cloth trade was at its height – though most have since been decorated with paintings or now house temporary exhibitions. Downstairs are sixteenth-century paintings centring on Lucas van Leyden's *Last Judgment* triptych, plus canvases by Jacob van Swanenburgh, the first teacher of the young Rembrandt; by Rembrandt himself; and associated Leiden painters – among them Jan Lievens (with whom he shared a studio), Gerrit Dou (who initiated the Leiden tradition of small, minutely detailed pictures), and the van Mieris brothers. There's also a painting depicting the sixteenth-century siege that shows the heroic van der Werff in full flow.

Around the corner on Molenwerf, the **Molenmuseum de Valk**, Tweede Binnenvestgracht 1 (Tues–Sat 10am–5pm, Sun 1–5pm; ƒ3), is a restored grain mill, one of twenty that used to surround Leiden. The downstairs rooms are furnished in simple, period style; upstairs a slide show recounts the history of windmills in Holland, while displays detail their development and showcase their tools and grinding apparatus, all immaculately preserved. An absorbing way to spend an hour, it's only five minutes' stroll from the station.

There's one other museum between here and the station, the **Rijksmuseum Voor Volkenkunde** at Steenstraat 1 (Tues–Fri 10am–5pm, Sat & Sun 1–5pm; ƒ5), the national ethnological museum, which has complete sections on Indonesia and the Dutch colonies, along with reasonable ones on the South Pacific and Far East. However, it gives most other parts of the world a less than thorough showing and is not an essential stop by any means.

The university makes Leiden a good place to buy **books**. *Kooyker*, Breestraat 93, has a superb selection of books in English; there's also a decent branch of *De Slegte* at Breestraat 73. Consider also taking a **canal trip** around the city centre. These run from Beestenmarkt during summer and cost ƒ8 per person for a forty-minute tour.

Eating and Drinking

It's easy to **eat and drink** cheaply in Leiden. The streets around the Pieterskerkhof and the Hoogslandskerk both hold concentrations of bars and restaurants. For lunch, *Noroc*, just off Breestraat on Pieterskerk Choorsteeg, is a pleasant café with a light menu; *Barrera*, opposite the old university building on Rapenburg, is a cosy bar that serves sandwiches. For dinner, *Annie's Verjaardag*, pleasantly located on the waterside at Hoogstraat 1a, serves reasonably priced main courses, and *Het Huis de Bijlen*, just off Noordeinde, has even cheaper daily specials. *De Brasserie*, Lange Mare 38, has Dutch food; *Eethuis de Trommelaar* is a pleasant and reasonably priced vegetarian restaurant at Apothekersdijk 22; *Eethuis de Stoep*, Oude Rijn 1a, has à la carte dishes and well-priced three-course menus ranging in price from ƒ22.50 to ƒ45 for a very varied selection of food. With more money, you might try *Bistro Malle Jan*, just off Pieterskerkhof at Nieuwesteeg 11, and includes a vegetarian dish on its menu. If you want something non-Dutch, *Radja Mas*, on Maarsmansteeg, next door to *Vroom & Dreesman* off Breestraat, is a reasonably priced Indonesian restaurant, though it closes at 8pm; *Cojico*, at Breestraat 33, is an amiable Mexican restaurant.

Around Leiden: the Bulbfields and the Coast

Along with Haarlem to the north, Leiden is the best base for seeing something of the Dutch **bulbfields** which have flourished here since the late sixteenth century when one Carolus Clusius, a Dutch botanist, brought the first tulip bulb over from Asia Minor and watched it prosper on Holland's sandy soil. Although bulbs are grown in North Holland, too, the centre of the Dutch bulb-growing industry is the area around Leiden and up toward Haarlem. The flowers are inevitably a major tourist pull, and one of Holland's most lucrative businesses, supporting some ten thousand growers in what is these days a billion-guilder industry. Obviously spring is the best time to see something of the blooms, when the view from the train – which cuts directly through the main growing areas – can be sufficient in itself, the fields divided into stark geometric blocks of pure colour. With your own transport you can take in the full beauty of the bulbfields by way of special routes marked by hexagonal signposts – local VVVs sell pamphlets listing the best vantage points.

You can also visit the Keukenhof Gardens from Haarlem, see p.183.

Lisse and the Keukenhof Gardens

Should you want to get closer to the flowers, **LISSE**, halfway between Leiden and Haarlem, is the place to look at the best of the Dutch flower industry, home to the **Keukenhof Gardens** (late March–end of May daily 8am–7.30pm; ƒ14.50), the largest flower gardens in the world. The Keukenhof was set up in 1949, designed by a group of prominent bulb growers to convert people to the joys of growing flowers from bulbs in their own gardens. Literally the "kitchen garden", its site is the former estate of a fifteenth-century countess, who used to grow herbs and vegetables for her dining table here – hence the name. Some seven million flowers are on show for their full flowering period, complemented, in case of especially harsh winters, by five thousand square metres of greenhouses holding indoor displays. You could easily spend a whole day here, swooning among the sheer abundance of it all. There are three restaurants in the seventy acres of grounds, and well-marked paths take you through the gardens, which hold daffodils, narcissi, and hyacinths in April, and tulips from mid-April until the end of May. A special Express bus – #54 – run to the Keukenhof from both Leiden (and Haarlem) bus stations twice an hour, every day including Sunday.

If you can't visit in the spring, the **Bulbdistrict Museum**, also in Lisse at Heereweg 219 (Tues–Sun 1–5pm; f2.50), offers the history of the bulb business, dating from the time the first tulip was brought over from Turkey – but it's a poor substitute for the real thing.

Aalsmeer and More Bulbs

You can see the industry in action in **AALSMEER**, 23km north of Leiden towards Amsterdam, whose flower auction, again the largest in the world, is held daily in a building approximately the size of 75 football fields (Mon–Fri 7.30–11am; f4). The dealing is fast and furious, and the turnover staggering. In an average year around f1.5 billion (about £500 million) worth of plants and flowers are traded here, many of which arrive in florist's shops throughout Europe on the same day. In case it all seems a mystery, there are headphones placed strategically around with recorded information in English. Be sure, incidentally, to arrive well before 10am; otherwise you won't see a single flower.

There are other places, too, with bulbs and flowers, though none as spectacular as the Keukenhof, nor as vibrant as the Aalsmeer auction. The **Frans Roozen nurseries** at Vogelenzangseweg 49 in **VOGELENZANG**, a little way south of Haarlem (April–May Mon–Sun 8am–6pm, July–Sept Mon–Fri 9am–5pm; free), have a show greenhouse displaying blooms. **RIJNSBURG**, just north of Leiden, has a flower parade in early August, from Rijnsburg to Leiden and Noordwijk. There's a similar parade from Haarlem to Noordwijk (see below) at the end of April, culminating in a display of the floats in the town.

The Coast: Katwijk and Noordwijk

Like all of the towns in this part of·Holland, Leiden has easy access to some fine beaches, though the coastal resorts themselves aren't much to write home about, and unless you're keen to swim the only reason for visiting is for their larger – and cheaper – supply of accommodation and campsites. **KATWIJK-AAN-ZEE**, accessible by bus #31, #41, or Express bus #35 from the stop opposite the bus station (every 20min; the journey takes 25min), is the stock Dutch

Leiden

seaside town, less crowded than Zandvoort and without the pretensions of Scheveningen, but pretty dreary nonetheless – although it does preserve some of the features of an old coastal village in the lines of terraced houses that spread out around the seventeenth-century lighthouse. The undeveloped sand dunes, though, which stretch along the shore south toward The Hague, make an ideal area for secluded sunbathing. Otherwise its main attraction is the **Katwijk Sluices**, just north of the resort area, beside the main bus route. Completed in 1807, these are a series of gates that regulate the flow of the Oude Rijn as it approaches the sea: around high tide, the gates are closed; when they are opened, the pressure of the accumulated water brushes aside the sand deposited at the mouth of the river by the sea – a simple system that finally determined the course of the Oude Rijn, which for centuries had been continually diverted by the sand deposits, turning the surrounding fields into a giant swamp.

NOORDWIJK-AAN-ZEE, some 3km up the coast and accessible by bus #40, #42 or Express bus #25 from the same stop is of even less appeal, not much more than a string of grandiose hotel developments built across the undulating sand dunes behind the coast. The beach is excellent, but the one time it's worth coming to see the town itself is the last weekend in April when the **flower parade** arrives from Haarlem and makes an illuminated tour of night-time Noordwijk.

The Hague and Scheveningen

With its urbane atmosphere, **THE HAGUE** differs from any other Dutch city. Since the sixteenth century it's been Holland's political capital and the focus of national institutions, in a country built on civic independence and munificence. Frequently disregarded until the development of central government in the nineteenth century, The Hague's older buildings are a rather subdued and modest collection with little of Amsterdam's flamboyance. Most of it's canal houses are demurely classical with an overpowering sense of sedate prosperity. In 1859 English poet Matthew Arnold wrote: "I never saw a city where the well-to-do classes seemed to have given the whole place so much of their own air of wealth, finished cleanliness, and comfort; but I never saw one, either, in which my heart would so have sunk at the thought of living". Things haven't changed much: the "well-to-do classes" – mostly diplomats in dark Mercedes and multinational executives – ensure that many of the hotels and restaurants are firmly in the expense account category, and the nightlife is similarly packaged. But, away from the mediocrity of wealth, The Hague does have cheaper and livelier bars and restaurants – and even its share of restless adolescents hanging around the pizza joints.

The Hague area telephone code, including Scheveningen (p.206), is ☎070.

The town may be rather drab, but it does have some excellent museums, principally the famed collection of old Dutch masters at the

Mauritshuis, and more modern works of art at the **Gemeente Museum**. And when you're tired of the art, the satellite town of **Scheveningen** is the country's largest resort, with wide sandy beaches to laze on.

Arrival, information and accommodation

The Hague has two **train stations** – *Den Haag H.S.* (*Hollands Spoor*) and *Den Haag C.S.* (*Centraal Station*). Of the two, Den Haag C.S. is the more convenient, situated five minutes' walk east of the town centre next door to the complex housing the VVV (April–Sept Mon–Sat 9am–9pm, Sun 10am–5pm; Oct–March Mon–Sat 9am–6pm, Sun 10am–5pm; ☎34 03 50 51, 50c per minute). This is immediately outside the main entrance, on the right in the same complex as the Babylon shopping centre; the bus and tram stations are also right outside. Den Haag H.S. is 1km to the south, and frequent rail services connect the two. The Hague may be the country's third largest city, but almost everything worth seeing is within easy walking distance of Den Haag C.S.; if you intend to use the city's buses and trams, the VVV and counters at the railway station sell the standard *strippenkaart* and a *dagkaart* – the best bet if you're only here for the day.

Accommodation in The Hague proper is hard to find and/or expensive – you might be better off basing yourself in Scheveningen, twenty minutes' ride away by tram (see below), where rooms are more plentiful and slightly cheaper. If you do want to stay in town, the best bet is to pay the extra guilders and let the VVV arrange somewhere for you to stay – especially as the cheaper pensions are spread out all over the city. Otherwise, there's a cluster of seedy but reasonably priced **hotels** just outside Den Haag H.S. station: the *Aristo*, Stationsweg 164–166 (☎389 08 47), which has doubles from ƒ75; the *Astoria*, Stationsweg 139 (☎384 04 01), which charges ƒ85; the *Limburg*, Stationsplein 49 (☎384 01 02), with double rooms for ƒ95; and the *Du Commerce*, Stationsplein 64 (☎380 85 11), from ƒ90 for a double. There are also two relatively central **pensions** with doubles at about ƒ90 per night: the *Huize Bellevue*, northwest of the centre along Laan Van Meerdervoort – right at Groot Hertoginne, then first left along the northern part of Beeklaan at no. 417 (☎360 55 52); and the *Minnema*, a short journey north of the centre just east of Koningskade/Raamweg at Dedelstraat 25.

The **youth hostel** *Ockenburgh* (☎397 00 11) is at Monsterseweg 4, some 10km to the west of the town centre just behind the beach at Kijkduin (bus #122, #123 or #124 from Centraal Station), charging ƒ65 per double. It's attached to a small budget hotel, with double rooms for ƒ100, and adjoins the best and largest **campsite** in the area, *Camping Ockenburgh*, Wijndaelerweg 25 (open March–Oct; ☎325 23 64) – bus #4 from the station. Both the youth hostel and the camp-site are about ten minutes' walk from the nearest bus stop – ask the driver to let you off.

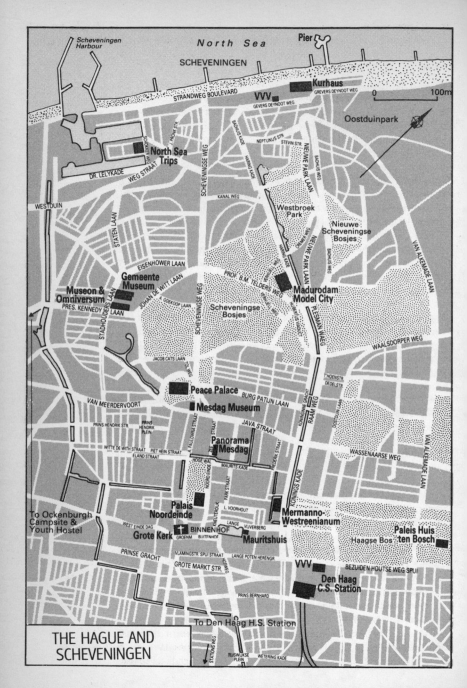

North Sea

Scheveningen
Harbour

SCHEVENINGEN

Pier

STRANDWEG BOULEVARD

Kurhaus

GREVERS DEYNOOT WEG

VVV

GEVERS DEYNOOT WEG

Oostduinpark

0   100m

North Sea
Trips

SCHOKKER WEG

DR. LELYKADE

WEG STRAAT

FR. TROMP STR.

SCHEVENINGSE WEG

BADHUIS KADE

HARING KADE

NEPTUNUS STR.

STEVIN STR.

NIEUWE PARK LAAN

BADHUIS WEG

WESTDUIN

STATEN LAAN

EISENHOWER LAAN

KANAL WEG

Westbroek
Park

Nieuwe
Scheveningse
Bosjes

VAN ALKEMADE LAAN

Museon &
Omniversum

Gemeente
Museum

PRES. KENNEDY LAAN

STADHOUDERSLAAN

JOHAN DE WITT LAAN

PROF. B.M. TELDERS WEG

KERSSEL WEG

NIEUWE PARK LAAN

HARING KADE

Madurodam
Model City

PLESMAN WEG

GOEKOOP LAAN

SCHEVENINGSE WEG

Scheveningse
Bosjes

KONINGIN EMMA GRACHT

WAALSDORPER WEG

JACOB CATS LAAN

TEL WEG

Peace Palace

BURG PATIJN LAAN

T.HOENSTR.
DEDELSTR.

OOSTDUIN LAAN

VAN MEERDERVOORT

Mesdag Museum

JAVA STRAAT

WASSENAARSE WEG

PRINS HENDRIK STR.

PRINS
HENDRIK
PLEIN

A. PAULOWNA STRAAT

ZEE STRAAT

Panorama
Mesdag

FREDER STRAAT

RAAM WEG

WITTE DE WITH STRAAT

PIET HEIN STRAAT

ELAND STRAAT

HOGE WAL

MAURITS KADE

NOORD EINDE

PARK STRAAT

KONINGS KADE

To Ockenburgh
Campsite &
Youth Hostel

Palais
Noordeinde

L. VOORHOUT

Mermanno-
Westreenianum

Paleis Huis
ten Bosch

Haagse Bos

WEST EINDE DAG

Grote Kerk

BINNENHOF

GROENM. BUITENHOF

LANGE
VIJVERBERG

Mauritshuis

PRINSE GRACHT

VLAMINGSTR. SPUI STRAAT

LANGE POTEN HERENGR.

BEZUIDEN HOUTSE WEG SPUI

GROTE MARKT STR.

VVV

Den Haag
C.S. Station

PRINS BERNHARD

To Den Haag H.S. Station

STATIONS WEG

RIJSWIJKSE
PLEIN

WETERING KADE

THE HAGUE AND
SCHEVENINGEN

The City Centre

Right in the centre, and the oldest part of the city, the **Binnenhof**
("inner court") is the home of Holland's bicameral parliament. Count
William II built a castle here in the thirteenth century, and the settlement that grew up around it became known as the "Count's Domain" –
'*s Gravenhage*, literally "Count's Hedge" – which is still the city's official name. As the embodiment of central rather than municipal power,
the Binnenhof had a checkered history – empty or occupied, feted or
ignored – until the nineteenth century when The Hague shared political capital status with Brussels during the uneasy times of the United
Kingdom of the Netherlands. Thereafter it became the seat of government, home to an effective legislature. The present rectangular
complex is a rather mundane affair, a confusing mixture of shape and
style that irritated nineteenth-century Dutch parliamentarians with its
obvious lack of prestige.

The best view is from the front, where a small lake – the **Hof
Vijver** ("Court Pond") – mirrors the attractive symmetry of the facade.
Behind the lake, the Binnenhof is a major tourist attraction, but there's
precious little to see except the **Ridderzaal** ("Hall of the Knights"), a
slender-turreted structure used for state occasions. It's been a
courtroom, market, and stable, and so repeatedly replaced and
renovated that little of the thirteenth-century original remains. An
undramatic guided tour of the Ridderzaal and the chambers of
parliament (often closed on Mon & Tues) starts regularly from the
information office at Binnenhof 8a (Mon–Sat 10am–4pm; July & Aug
also Sun noon–4pm; ƒ5).

The Mauritshuis Collection

To the immediate east of the Binnenhof, the **Royal Picture Gallery
Mauritshuis**, Korte Vijverberg 8 (Tues–Sat 10am–5pm, Sun 11am–
5pm; ƒ7.50 paid as you leave the gallery) is located in a magnificent
seventeenth-century mansion. Generally regarded as one of the best
galleries in Europe, it's famous for its extensive range of Flemish and
Dutch paintings from the fifteenth to the eighteenth centuries, based
on the collection accumulated by Prince William V of Orange (1748–
1806). All the major Dutch artists are represented, and it's well laid
out, with multilingual cards in each room providing background notes
on all the major canvases. At present the rooms are not numbered, and
the policy of the museum is (rather awkwardly) to spread the works of
many of the key artists through several rooms, rather than place them
together. For further detailed information, the museum shop sells an
excellent guidebook for ƒ25, or you can join one of the irregular and
expensive conducted tours – prices depend on length; ask at reception
for times.

The entrance and museum shop are in the **basement** on the east
side of the building, together with **Andy Warhol**'s *Queen Beatrix*, a
twentieth-century aperitif to the collection above. Heading up the

stairs to the **first floor**, walk back toward the old front doors and enter the room on the left, where **Hans Memling**'s *Portrait of a Man* is a typically observant work, right down to the scar on the nose. Close by, **Rogier van der Weyden**'s *The Lamentation of Christ* is a harrowing picture of death and sorrow, with Christ's head hanging down toward the earth, surrounded by the faces of the mourners, each with a particular expression of anguish and pain. **Quinten Metsys** was the first major artist to work in Antwerp, where he was made a Master of the Guild in 1519. An influential figure, he attempted to imbue his religious pictures with spiritual sensitivity, and his *Descent from the Cross* is a fine example – Christ's suffering face under the weight of the Cross contrasted with the grinning, taunting onlookers behind.

Proceeding in a counterclockwise direction, through a series of rooms on either side of the Italianate dining room, exhibits include two giant allegorical canvases by Jan Sanders van Hemessen; Lucas Cranach the Younger's spirited *Man with a Red Beard*; and two works by **Hans Holbein the Younger**, a striking *Portrait of Robert Cheeseman*, where all the materials – the fur collar, the falcon's feathers and the cape – seem to take on the appropriate texture, and his *Portrait of Jane Seymour*, one of several pictures commissioned by Henry VIII, who sent him abroad to paint matrimonial candidates. Holbein's vibrant technique was later to land him in hot water: an over-flattering portrait of Anne of Cleves swayed Henry into an unhappy marriage with his "Flanders' Mare" that was to last only six months.

Of a number of paintings by **Adriaen Brouwer**, *Quarrel at a Card Table* and *Inn with Drunken Peasants* are two of the better known, with thick, rough brush strokes recording contemporary Flemish lowlife. Brouwer could approach this subject with some authority, as he spent most of his brief life in either taverns or prison. **Peter Paul Rubens**, the acclaimed painter and diplomat, was a contemporary of Brouwer, though the two could hardly be more dissimilar: Rubens' *Portrait of Isabella Brant*, his first wife, is a typically grand, rather statuesque work, not perhaps as intriguing as *Adam and Eve in Paradise*, a collaboration between Rubens, who painted the figures, and **Jan Brueghel the Elder**, who filled in the dreamlike animals and landscape behind. In the same room are two examples of the work of Rubens' chief assistant, **Anthony van Dyck**, a portrait specialist who found fame at the court of King Charles I. His *Pieter Stevens of Antwerp* and *Quinton Simons of Antwerp* are good, early examples of his tendency to flatter and ennoble his subjects that no doubt helped him into the job. Nearby, and again showing the influence of Rubens, is the robust *Adoration of the Shepherds* by Jacob Jordaens.

On the **second-floor** landing, the broad brush strokes of **Frans Hals**' *Laughing Boy* are far removed from the restrained style he was forced to adopt in his more familiar paintings of the burghers of Haarlem. **Carel Fabritius**, pupil of Rembrandt and (possibly) the

teacher of Vermeer, was killed in a gunpowder explosion at Delft when
he was only 22. Few of his canvases have survived, but an exquisite
exception is *The Goldfinch*, a curious, almost impressionistic work,
with the bird reduced to a blur of colour. One of his Delft contemporaries was Gerard Houckgeest, who specialized in church interiors,
like *The Tomb of William of Orange*, a minutely observed study of
exact architectural lines lightened by expanses of white marble.

Off the second-floor landing, on the left at the front of the
museum, is the Mauritshuis' most famous painting, **Jan Vermeer**'s
View of Delft, a superb townscape of 1658, with the fine lines of the
city drawn beneath a cloudy sky, a patchwork of varying light and
shade – though the dispassionate, photographic quality the painting
has in reproduction is oddly lacking in the large canvas. In the same
room, Gerard Ter Borch's *Lice Hunt* is in striking contrast to
Vermeer's detachment, a vignette of seventeenth-century domestic life.

Heading in a counterclockwise direction, other highlights include
the busy stick-like figures of the *Winter Scene* by Hendrik Avercamp,
the deaf and dumb artist from Kampen, and Paulus Potter's lifelike
Young Bull, a massive canvas complete with dung and rather frightening testicles. Best known of the **Rembrandts** is the *Anatomy Lesson of
Dr Tulp*, from 1632, the artist's first commission in Amsterdam. The
peering pose of the "students" who lean over the corpse solved the
problem of emphasis falling on the body rather than on the subjects of
the portrait, who were in fact members of the surgeons' guild.
Hopefully Tulp's skills as an anatomist were better than his medical
advice, which included the recommendation that his patients drink
fifty cups of tea a day.

Dotted throughout the museum are no fewer than thirteen paintings by **Jan Steen**, including a wonderfully riotous picture carrying the
legend *"The way you hear it, is the way you sing it"* – a parable on
the young learning bad habits from the old – and a typically salacious
Girl Eating Oysters.

The rest of the city centre

A few metres to the west of the Binnenhof, the **Gevangenpoort** or
"Prisoner's Gate Museum", at Buitenhof 33 (Mon–Fri 10am–4pm;
April–Sept also Sun 1–5pm; hourly tours only; last tour 4pm; ƒ5), was
originally part of the city fortifications. Used as a prison until the nineteenth century, it now contains an array of instruments of torture and
punishment centred around its Chamber of Horrors. As well as the
guillotine blades, racks, and gallows, the old cells are in a good state
of repair – including the *ridderkamer* for the more privileged captive.
Here Cornelius de Witt, Burgomaster of Dordrecht, was imprisoned
before he and his brother Johan, another staunch Republican and
leader of the States of Holland, were dragged out and murdered by an
Orangist mob in 1672. The brothers were shot, beheaded, and cut into
pieces which were then auctioned to the crowd; Johan's tongue is
preserved for macabre posterity in the storerooms of the Gemeente

Museum. The Gevangenpoort is understandably popular; join the line about fifteen minutes before each hourly tour to guarantee a place.

Down the street at Buitenhof 35, the **Prince William V Gallery** (Tues–Sun 11am–4pm; ƒ2.50 or free with Mauritshuis ticket) has paintings by Rembrandt, Jordaens, and Paulus Potter among others, but it's more interesting as a reconstruction of a typical eighteenth-century gallery – or "cabinet" as they were known. The fashion then was to sandwich paintings together in a cramped patchwork from floor to ceiling: though it's faithful to the period, this makes viewing difficult for eyes trained by spacious modern museums.

A five-minute walk away to the west, and easily the best of The Hague's old churches, St Jacobskerk or the **Grote Kerk** (July & Aug Mon 11am–4pm; free. Otherwise closed to the public except when there are exhibitions, usually Mon–Fri 11am–4pm, Sun 1–5pm) is a hall church with an exhilarating sense of breadth and warmly decorated vaulting. The one thing you can't miss, as it's placed where the high altar should be, is the memorial to the unmemorable Admiral Opdam, who was blown up with his ship during the little-remembered naval battle of Lowestoft in 1665. Keep an eye open for the Renaissance pulpit: similar to the one in Delft's Oude Kerk, it has carved panels framing the apostles in false perspective. For the energetic, the **church tower** (open Wed noon for groups of eight to ten people; ☎365 86 65) provides blustery views over the town.

Back in the centre, **Lange Voorhout** is fringed by an impressive spread of diplomatic mansions and the *Hotel des Indes*, where the ballerina Anna Pavlova died in 1931 and where today you stand the best chance of being flattened by a chauffeur-driven limousine. Just to the east, the **Meermanno-Westreenianum Museum**, Prinsessegracht 30 (Mon–Sat 1–5pm; free), has a small collection of remarkably well-preserved medieval illuminated manuscripts and Bibles; and nearby, the **Hague Historical Museum**, Korte Vijverberg 7 (Tues–Fri 11am–5pm, Sat & Sun noon–5pm; ƒ4), mixes local history with temporary exhibitions on topical issues.

To the immediate west of Lange Voorhout, the sixteenth-century **Paleis Noordeinde** (admission free) is one of several royal buildings that lure tourists to this part of town. In 1980, Queen Juliana abdicated in favour of her daughter Beatrix, who proceeded to return the royal residence from the province of Utrecht to The Hague. Despite the queen's attempts to demystify the monarchy, there's no deterring the enthusiasts who fill the expensive "Royal Tours" around the peripheries of the palace and Beatrix's other residence just outside town, the seventeenth-century **Huis ten Bosch** ("House in the woods"; no entrance).

Much of the rest of the centre is drab and dreary, an apparently unformulated mixture of the stately old and the brashly new (the giant "Babylon" shopping complex by the Centraal Station wins the ugliness award). During the war the occupying German forces built a V2 launching site just outside the city: as a result it was almost as badly bombed by the Allies as its neighbour Rotterdam had been by the Luftwaffe.

North of the city centre

Ten minutes' walk north of the centre along Noordeinde, the **Panorama Mesdag**, Zeestraat 65b (Mon–Sat 10am–5pm, Sun noon–5pm; f4), was designed in the late nineteenth century by Hendrik Mesdag, banker turned painter and local citizen become Hague School luminary. His unremarkable seascapes are tinged with an unlikable bourgeois sentimentality, but there's no denying the achievement of his panorama, a depiction of Scheveningen as it would have appeared in 1881. Completed in four months with help from his wife and the young G.H. Breitner, the painting is so naturalistic that it takes a few moments for the skills of lighting and perspective to become apparent. Five minutes' walk from the Panorama at Laan van Meerdervoort 7f is the house Mesdag bought as a home and gallery. At the time it overlooked one of his favourite subjects, the dunes, the inspiration for much of his work, and today contains the **Mesdag Museum** (Tues–Sat 10am–5pm, Sun 1–5pm; f3.50). Although currently closed for restoration, his collection includes a number of Hague School paintings which, like his own work, take the seascapes of the nearby coast as their subject. There are also paintings by Corot, Rousseau, Delacroix, and Millet, though none of them represents the artists' best achievements. Perhaps the most interesting exhibits are the florid and distinctive paintings of Antonio Mancini, whose oddly disquieting subjects are reminiscent of Klimt.

The Peace Palace

Round the corner from the Mesdag Museum, framing the Carnegieplein, the **Peace Palace** (Mon–Fri hourly guided tours at 10am, 11am, 2pm, 3pm; May–Oct also at 4pm; f5. Check with the VVV for times of tours in English) is home to the Court of International Justice and, for all the wrong reasons, a monument to the futility of war. Toward the end of the nineteenth century, Tsar Nicholas II called an international conference for the peaceful reconciliation of national problems. The result was the First Hague Peace Conference of 1899 whose purpose was to "help find a lasting peace and, above all, a way of limiting the progressive development of existing arms". This in turn led to the formation of a Permanent Court of Arbitration housed obscurely in The Hague until Andrew Carnegie donated \$1.5 million for a new building – the Peace Palace. These honorable aims came to nothing with the mass slaughter of World War I: just as the donations of tapestries, urns, marble, and stained glass were arriving from all over the world, so Europe's military commanders were preparing their offensives. Backed by a massive law library, fifteen judges are still in action today, conducting trade matters in English and diplomatic affairs in French. Widely respected and generally considered neutral, their judgments are nevertheless not binding.

The Gemeentemuseum, Museon, and Omniversum

North of the Peace Palace, the **Gemeentemuseum**, Stadhouderslaan 41
(Tues–Sun 11am–5pm; ƒ7; bus #4 from Centraal Station), is arguably
the best and certainly the most diverse of The Hague's many museums.
Designed by H.P. Berlage in the 1930s, it's generally considered to be
his masterpiece, although its layout can be confusing, and the labelling
is erratic. However, the musical instruments are outstanding – especially the harpsichords and early pianos – and the selection of Islamic
ceramics is extraordinary. The collection of modern art is frustrating,
but it does attempt to outline the development of Dutch painting
through the Romantic, Hague, and Expressionist schools to the De Stijl
movement. **Mondrian**, the De Stijl group's most famous member, dominates this part of the gallery: the museum has the world's largest collection of his paintings, though much of it consists of (deservedly)
unfamiliar early works painted before he evolved the abstraction of
form into geometry and pure colour for which he's best known.

Adjoining the Gemeentemuseum is a modern building that houses
the **Museon** (Tues–Fri 10am–5pm, Sat–Sun noon–5pm; ƒ5), a
sequence of nonspecialist exhibitions of human activities related to the
history of the earth. Self-consciously internationalist, it's aimed at
school parties, as is the adjoining **Omniversum** or "Space Theatre"
(shows on the hour, Tues–Thurs 11am–4pm, Fri–Sun 11am–9pm;
ƒ16). A planetarium in all but name, it possesses all the technical
gadgetry you'd expect.

Madurodam Miniature Town

Halfway between The Hague and Scheveningen, the **Madurodam
Miniature Town** (daily March–May 9am–10.30pm, June–Aug 9am–
11pm, Sept 9am–9.30pm, Oct–Dec 9am–6pm; closed Jan–March;
ƒ12.50), accessible by tram #1 or #9, is heavily plugged by the tourist
authorities, though its origins are more interesting than the trite and
expensive present, a copy of a Dutch town on a 1:25 scale. The original
money was put up by J.M.L. Maduro, who wished to establish a memorial to his son who had distinguished himself during the German invasion of 1940, and died in Dachau concentration camp five years later.
There's a memorial to him just by the entrance, and profits from the
Miniature Town are used for general Dutch social and cultural
activities.

Eating and Drinking

For cheap **food**, there's a cluster of places along Herenstraat, off Plein
near the Binnenhof, the best of which is *De Apendans* at no. 13a, a
no-frills, popular restaurant serving a simple Dutch menu for ƒ17 and
up. Other reasonably priced, centrally sited alternatives include good
fishy snacks at *Noordzee*, Spuistraat 44; pizzas at *Pinelli*, on the way
to the Grote Kerk at Dag. Groenmarkt 31; good quality light lunches
and decent pizzas at *Brasserie Renoir*, at the bottom of Noordeinde,

> The **North Sea Jazz Festival**, held every year in mid-July at the Nederlands
> Congresgebouw, Churchillplein 10, is The Hague's most prestigious event,
> attracting international media coverage and many of the world's most
> famous musicians. Details of performances are available from the VVV,
> which will also reserve accommodation, virtually impossible to find after the
> festival has begun. Various kinds of tickets can be purchased; a *dagkaart*,
> for example, valid for an entire day, costs ƒ75.

no. 2a; vegetarian meals at *De Dageraad*, just east of Lange Voorhout
at Hooikade 4, for around ƒ25; and snacks at the *Bodega De
Posthoorn*, Lange Voorhout 39a. Failing that, there's a good choice at
Eetcafé Hardans, Nobelstraat 11b, behind the post office, while
Grand Café Popacatepetl, Buitenhof 4–5, is a great venue for
Mexican meals or just drinks and tapas. On an expense account you
could do worse than sample the seafood delights of the *Oesterbar
Saur*, at Lange Voorhout 47–53, or Italian specialities at *La Liguria*,
Noordeinde 97, though you'll spend at least ƒ40–50 at either place.

For **bars**, head for the streets to the immediate east of Lange
Voorhout, including the quiet canals around Smidswater and Hooikade,
where *De Landman* and the *Pompernickel* are at Denneweg 48 and
27. In the other direction, along Papestraat, *Café de Paap*, at no. 32,
has live music on Tuesday nights and Sunday afternoons.

Listings

Bikes Can be rented from either of The Hague's train stations for ƒ7.50 a day,
plus a ƒ200 deposit.

Bookshop *Boekhandel Plantijn*, Noordeinde 62. Good for art books.

Car Rental *Avis*, Theresiastraat 210 (☎385 06 98); *Budget*, Juliana van
Stolberglaan 214 (☎382 43 86); *Europcar* (at the *Hotel Sofitel*), Koningin
Julianaplein 35 (☎385 17 08).

Dentist Daily 7am – midnight ☎365 46 46, Sat & Sun ☎397 44 91.

Embassies *Australia*, Carnegielaan 12 (☎310 82 00); *Canada*, Sophialaan 7
(☎361 41 11); *Great Britain*, Lange Voorhout 10 (☎364 58 00); *Eire*, Dr
Kuyperstraat 9 (☎363 09 93); *USA*, Lange Voorhout 102 (☎362 49 11).

Gay Scene There are several gay bars: try *Boko*, Nieuwe Schoolstraat 2, or
Stairs, Nieuwe Schoolstraat 11.

Hospital Ambulances ☎06 11; general medical care at night ☎345 53 00.

Information A free monthly magazine with details of concerts, theatre performances, special events, and entertainments in The Hague and environs is available from the VVV.

Jazz Records *Jazz Inn*, Groenmarkt 32. A superb jazz record shop.

Markets General: Herman Costerstraat (Mon & Sat 8am–5pm). Food: Markthof,
Gedempte Gracht/Spui (Mon 11am–6pm, Tues–Fri 9am–6pm). Antiques, books,
and curios: Lange Voorhout (mid-May to Sept Thurs & Sun 11am–9pm); Plein
(Oct to mid-May Thurs 11am–9pm).

Chemists Night services listed in newspapers and at the VVV.

Post Office Nobelstraat; Prinsenstraat; Kerkplein (Mon–Fri 8.30am–6.30pm,
Thurs also 6.30–8.30pm, Sat 9am–4pm).

Scheveningen

Situated on the coast about 4km from the centre of The Hague, the old
fishing port of **SCHEVENINGEN** has none of its neighbour's business-
like air, enjoying instead its status as Holland's top coastal resort,
attracting more than nine million visitors a year to its beach, pier, and
casino. It's not a particularly attractive place, but it can make a good
alternative base if you're keen to see something of The Hague, since
hotels are cheaper and more plentiful. At certain times of year, too, it's
worth a special visit – in mid-June for example, when the town hosts a
massive international **kite festival** that takes over the beach and much
of the town, or during its international **fireworks festival** in August.

Scheveningen was a fashionable resort in the nineteenth century,
but faded after the 1920s; it's currently being redeveloped as an all-
year resort. The centre of town is called **Scheveningen Bad**, grouped
around the massive **Kurhaus** hotel that's the most potent symbol of
the town's bygone era. Sadly, it's the only reminder, the rest of the
town centre being a rather tacky mix of shopping precinct, guest-
houses, and amusement arcades, both around the hotel and along the
busy seafront. Inside, the *Kurhaus* has recently been refurbished and
is worth a peek into for its main central hall, which looks much as it
would have done in the town's heyday, richly frescoed, with mermaids
and semi-clad maidens cavorting high above the gathered diners. You
can enjoy the atmosphere for the price of a cup of coffee, or attend
one of the classical concerts occasionally held here.

The town **museum** at Neptunusstraat 92 (Tues–Sat 10am–5pm; ƒ3)
recaptures some of the atmosphere of old Scheveningen, with a collection of figures in nineteenth-century costume, dioramas showing the
cramped conditions on board the primitive fishing boats, and items
such as nets and compasses from the boats themselves. But most
people come here for the **beach** – a marvellous stretch, though very
crowded in summer, and it's hard to be sure about the condition of the
water. The pier isn't especially impressive either, its appendages
packed with the rods of fishermen and various amusements, and you'd
do better to either indulge yourself in the beachfront **Wave Pool** recreation centre, complete with a sub-tropical climate, whirlpools, and water-
slides, or stroll a little way north to emptier stretches of beach and
dunes in the **Oostduinpark**. Otherwise, a kilometre or so in the opposite direction, Scheveningen's harbour and fishing port still flourish in
the more workaday environs of **Scheveningen Haven**: the site of a large
container depot and an early morning **fish auction**, by the more north-
erly of the two docks, at Visafslagweg 1 (Mon–Sat 7–10am), though this
is very much a technical, computerized affair. **Boat trips** on the North
Sea (June–Sept daily at 4pm) start from Dr. Lelykade, beside the southern dock.

Practicalities

Trams #1, #7, and #9 run from The Hague C.S. to Scheveningen,
stopping by the *Kurhaus*; from The Hague H.S., take tram #8. Tram

One of the difficulties involved in getting to Scheveningen is pronouncing the name. During World War II, resistance groups tested suspected Nazi infiltrators by getting them to say "Scheveningen" – an impossible feat for a German-speaker apparently, and not much easier if you happen to speak English.

#1 also connects with Delft. If you decide to stay in Scheveningen, the VVV at Gevers Deyjnootweg 126 (April–Sept Mon–Sat 9am–9pm, Sun 10am–5pm; Oct–March Mon–Sat 9am–6pm, Sun 10am–5pm; ☎06/3403 5051, 50c per minute) can book **rooms** in private homes for about ƒ35 a head (for room reservations call ☎350 05 00) Failing that there are plenty of **hotels**. The *Martin*, Gevers Deynootweg 23 (☎352 41 45), has double rooms starting at ƒ95; the *Albion* across the road (☎355 79 87) has doubles for ƒ110; or there's a grouping of hotels on the other side of the *Kurhaus* on the seafront Zeekant, including the comfortable *Aquarius*, where charges start at ƒ115 for a double. There's another, smaller **youth hostel**, the *Marion*, at Havenkade 3a (☎354 3501), with rooms for ƒ25 a head. Other cheap options include the *Meyer* (ƒ70), near the town museum at Stevinstraat 64 (☎355 8138); the *Hage*(ƒ90), closer to the sea at Seinpostduin 23 (☎351 4696); and *El Cid* (ƒ75), Badhuisweg 51 (☎354 6667).

As for **eating**, the *Big Bell*, on the seafront next to the *Kurhaus*, is about the cheapest place to eat in the town centre, serving huge portions of Dutch food for under ƒ20; the *Olympiade*, underneath the *Martin* hotel, is a cosy Greek eatery, similarly priced. In Scheveningen Haven there are a couple of decent waterside fish restaurants, both by the outer harbour: the *Havenrestaurant* is simple and inexpensive, the *Mero*, further down toward the sea, is more upscale and pricier. For evening **drinking**, try the *Kings Arms*, a friendly mock-pub outside the *Kurhaus* on Gevers Deyjnootplein.

Delft

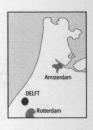

DELFT has considerable charm: gabled red-roofed houses stand beside tree-lined canals, and the pastel colours of the sidewalks, brickwork, and bridges give the town a faded, placid tranquillity – a tranquillity that from spring onward is systematically destroyed by tourists. They arrive in their air-conditioned busloads and descend to congest the narrow streets, buy an overpriced piece of gift pottery, and photograph the spire of the Nieuwe Kerk. And beneath all the tourists, the gift shops, and the tea rooms, old Delft itself gets increasingly difficult to find.

The Town

Why is Delft so popular? Apart from its prettiness, the obvious answer is **Delftware**, the clunky and monotonous blue-and-white ceramics to which the town gave its name in the seventeenth century. If you've

Delft

See p.97 for
details of the
Rijksmuseum.

already slogged through the vast collection in Amsterdam's Rijksmuseum it needs no introduction; and though production of the "real" Delftware is down to a trickle, cheap mass-produced copies have found a profitable niche in today's shops. For those sufficiently interested, *De Porceleyne Fles* at Rotterdamsweg 119, a factory producing Delftware, is open for visits (April–Oct Mon–Sat 9am–5pm, Sun 10am–4pm; Nov–March Mon–Fri 9am–5pm, Sat 10am–5pm; free), and the **Huis Lambert van Meerten Museum** at Oude Delft 199 (Tues–Sat 10am–5pm, Sun 1–5pm; *f*3:50) has a large collection of Delft (and other) tiles.

Another reason for Delft's popularity is the **Vermeer** connection. The artist was born in the town and died here, too – leaving a wife, eleven children, and a huge debt to the local banker. He had given the man two pictures as security, and his wife bankrupted herself trying to retrieve them. Only traces remain of the town as depicted in Vermeer's famous *View of Delft*, now in the Mauritshuis in The Hague. You'll find them most easily on foot – it's not a difficult place to explore. The **Markt** is the best place to start, a central point of reference with the Renaissance Stadhuis at one end and the Nieuwe Kerk at the other. Lined with cafés, restaurants, and teenagers blaring disco music on ghetto blasters, it really gets going with the Thursday general market – not, therefore, the ideal day to visit.

The **Nieuwe Kerk** (April–Oct Mon–Sat 9am–5pm, Nov–March Mon–Sat 11am–4pm; *f*2.50) is new only in comparison with the Oude Kerk, as there's been a church on this site since 1381. Most of the original structure, however, was destroyed in the great fire that swept over Delft in 1536, and the remainder in a powder magazine explosion a century later – a disaster, incidentally, which claimed the life of the artist Carel Fabritius, Rembrandt's greatest pupil and (debatably) the teacher of Vermeer. The most striking part of the restoration is in fact the most recent – the 100-metre spire (May–mid-June Tues–Sat 10am–4.30pm, mid-June–Aug Mon–Sat 10am–4.30pm; *f*3.25), replaced in 1872 and from whose summit there's a great view of the town. Unless you're a Dutch monarchist, the church's interior is uninspiring: it contains the burial vaults of the Dutch royal family, the most recent addition being Queen Wilhelmina in 1962. Only the Mausoleum of William the Silent grabs your attention, an odd hodgepodge of styles concocted by Hendrik de Keyser, architect also of the Stadhuis opposite.

South of the Stadhuis, signs direct you to the **Koornmarkt**, one of the town's most characteristic seventeenth-century streets. At number 67 is the **Museum Tétar van Elven** (May–mid-Oct Tues–Sat 1–5pm; *f*3), slightly drab in appearance but an authentic restoration of the eighteenth-century patrician house that was the studio and home of Paul Tétar van Elven, a provincial and somewhat forgettable artist/collector. **Wynhaven**, another old canal, leads to Hippolytusbuurt and the Gothic **Oude Kerk** (April–Oct Mon–Sat 10am–5pm; *f*2.50), arguably the town's finest building. Simple and unbuttressed, with an unhealthily leaning tower, it's the result of a succession of churches

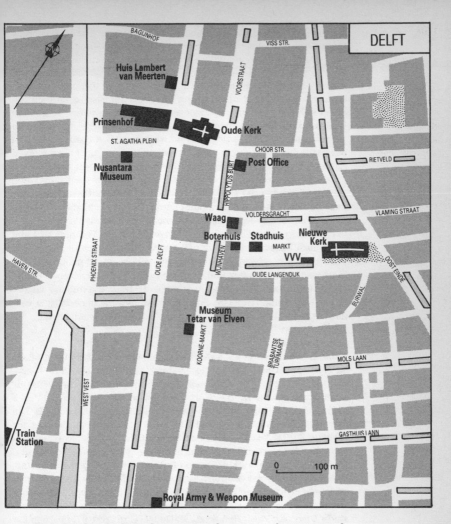

here from the thirteenth to the seventeenth century; the strong and unornamented vaulting proves interiors don't have to be elaborate to avoid being sombre. The pride of the church is its pulpit of 1548, intricately carved with figures emphasized in false perspective, but also notable is the modern stained glass, depicting and symbolizing the history of The Netherlands – particularly the 1945 liberation – in the north transept. If you're curious about the tombs – including that of Admiral Maarten van Tromp, famed for hoisting a broom at his masthead to "sweep the seas clear of the English" as he sailed up the Medway – take a look at the *Striking Points* pamphlet available at the entrance.

Opposite the Oude Kerk is the former Convent of Saint Agatha or **Prinsenhof** as it came to be known (Tues–Sat 10am–5pm, Sun 1–5pm; June–Aug also Mon 1–5pm; ƒ3.50). Housing Delft's municipal art collection (a good group of works including paintings by Aertsen and Honthorst), it has been restored in the style of the late sixteenth century – an era when the building served as the base of **William the Silent** in his Protestant revolt against the Spanish invaders. From here William planned sorties against the Imperial Catholic troops of Phillip II, achieving considerable success with his *Watergeuzen* or sea beggars, a kind of commando-guerrilla unit that initially operated from England. He met his death here at the hands of a French assassin: the bullets that passed through him, made by three pellets welded into one, left their mark on the Prinsenhof walls and can still be seen. Tickets for the Prinsenhof also include admission to the unremarkable **Nusantra** ethnographical museum and the Huis van Meerten tile collection.

Finally, if you have the time, the **Royal Army and Weapon Museum** (Tues–Sat 10am–5pm, Sun 1–5pm; ƒ3:50), near the station, is worth a visit. It has a good display of weaponry, uniforms, and military accoutrements – which may sound supremely dull, but isn't, even if you're not an enthusiast. The museum attempts to trace the military history of The Netherlands from the Spanish wars up to the imperialist adventures of the 1950s – which are shown in surprisingly candid detail.

Practicalities

From the train station it's a short walk into town and the VVV at Markt 85 (Mon–Fri 9am–6pm, Sat 11am–3pm; April–Sept also Sun 11am–3pm; ☎015/12 61 00). Cheapest **accommodation** is in the pensions around the station or the Markt: expect to pay around ƒ70 for a double; details from the VVV. Otherwise the cheapest hotel is *Les Compagnons*, Markt 61 (☎015/14 01 02), which has doubles for around ƒ85; *De Kok*, Houttuinen 15 (☎015/12 21 25), has doubles at about the same price. The **campground**, *De Delftse Hout*, Kortftlaan 5 (bus #60 from the station) is open from April to October. For **eating**, the *Hotel Monopole*, centrally located on the Markt, is pretty tourist-oriented but has reasonably priced pancakes, *uitsmijters*, light meals and three-course menus; *De Koornbeurs*, close by, is an even cheaper student mensa. *Locus Publicus*, Brabantse Turfmarkt 67, is a popular local hangout, serving a staggering array of beers as well as sandwiches. Try also *Café de Wynhaven* on Wynhaven, or *Stadskoffiehuis*, Oude Delft 135, a lunchroom that serves pancakes.

Gouda

A pretty little place some 25km northeast of Rotterdam, **GOUDA** is almost everything you'd expect of a Dutch country town: a ring of quiet canals that encircle ancient buildings and old docks. More surprisingly, its **Markt**, a ten-minute walk from the train station, is the

largest in Holland – a reminder of the town's prominence as a centre
of the medieval cloth trade, and later of its success in the manufacture
of cheeses and clay pipes.

Gouda's main claim to fame is its **cheese market**, held in the Markt
every Thursday morning from June to August. Traditionally, some
thousand local farmers brought their home-produced cheeses here to
be weighed, tested, and graded for moisture, smell, and taste. These
details were marked on the cheeses and formed the basis for negotia-
tion between buyer and seller, the exact price set by an elaborate
hand-clapping system, which itself was based on trust and memory, for
deals were never written down. Today, the cheese market is a shadow
of its former self, a couple of locals in traditional dress standing
outside the Waag, surrounded by modern open-air stands. The promised mixture of food and tradition is mercilessly milked by tour operators, who herd their victims into this rather dreary scene every week –
but don't let this put you off a visit, since Gouda's charms are found
elsewhere.

If you happen to be in the area in mid-December, it's worth phoning
the Gouda VVV to find out exactly when the town will be holding its
splendid candlelit pre-Christmas festival. All electric lights are extin-
guished on the main square, and it's lit by thousands of candles, giving
a magical, picture-book atmosphere.

The Town

Slap-bang in the middle of the Markt, the **Stadhuis** is an elegant
Gothic building dating from 1450, whose facade is fringed by statues
of counts and countesses of Burgundy above a tinkling carillon that
plays every half hour. Nearby, on the north side of the square, the
Waag is a tidy seventeenth-century building, decorated with a detailed
relief of cheese weighing, with the remains of the old wooden scales
inside. To the south, just off the Markt, **St Janskerk** (March–Oct Mon–
Sat 9am–5pm, Nov–Feb Mon–Sat 10am–4pm; ƒ2:50) was built in the
sixteenth century and is famous for its magnificent **stained glass
windows**. As well as their intrinsic beauty, the windows show the way
religious art changed as Holland moved from a society dominated by
the Catholic Church to one dominated by a Calvinist Church. The biblical themes executed by Dirk and Wouter Crabeth between 1555 and
1571, when Holland was still Catholic, have an amazing clarity of
detail and richness of colour. Their last work, *Judith Slaying
Holofernes* (window no. 6) is perhaps the finest, the story unfolding in
intricate perspective. By comparison, the post-Reformation windows,
which date from 1572 to 1603, adopt an allegorical and heraldic style
typical of a more secular art. *The Relief of Leiden* (window no. 25)
shows William the Silent retaking the town from the Spanish, though
Delft and its burgomasters take prominence – no doubt because they
paid the bill for its construction. All the windows are numbered and a
detailed guide is available at the entrance for ƒ3.

*Holland's other
major cheese
market is held in
Alkmaar, detailed
in the following
chapter.*

Gouda

By the side of the church, the flamboyant **Lazarus Gate** of 1609 was once part of the town's leper hospital, until it was moved to form the back entrance to the **Catharina Gasthuis**, a hospice till 1910. A likable conglomeration of sixteenth-century rooms and halls, including an old isolation cell for the insane, the interior of the Gasthuis has been turned into the municipal **Stedelijk Museum** (Mon–Sat 10am–5pm, Sun noon–5pm; ƒ3.50). The collection incorporates a fine sample of early religious art, notably a large triptych, *Life of Mary*, by Dirk Barendsz and a characteristically austere *Annunciation* by the Bruges artist Pieter Pourbus. Other highlights include a spacious hall, *Het Ruim*, that was once a sort of medieval hostel, but is now dominated by paintings of the civic guard, principally two group portraits by Ferdinand Bol; the intricate silver-gilt *Chalice and Eucharist Dish* was presented to the guard in the early fifteenth century. Two later rooms have a modest selection of Hague and Barbizon School canvases, notably work by Anton Mauve and Charles Daubigny.

Gouda's other museum, **De Moriaan** (Mon–Sat 10am–5pm, Sun noon–5pm; use Stedelijk Museum ticket), is in a cosy old merchant's house at Westhaven 29, with a mixed bag of exhibits from clay pipes to ceramics and tiles. Westhaven itself is a charming jumble of old buildings that head off toward the old toll house and a dilapidated mill beside the Hollandse IJssel river, on the southern edge of the town centre. There's a restored, fully operational **grain mill** (Mon–Sat 9am–5pm; ƒ1.50) to the immediate west of the Markt, at Vest 65.

Practicalities

Gouda's **train** and **bus stations** are to the immediate north of the town centre, ten minutes from the VVV, Markt 27 (Mon–Fri 9am–5pm, Sat 10am–4pm; ☎01820/13666), which has a limited supply of private **rooms** from ƒ60 for a double per night; they will ring ahead to make a booking, and there's a cover charge of ƒ3.50. Otherwise, the cheapest place in town is an unofficial **youth hostel**, conveniently sited at Westhaven 46 (☎01820/12879), with dorm beds for ƒ25. The most reasonably priced **hotel** is the *Het Blauwe Kruis*, Westhaven 4 (☎01820/12677), where grim and grimy doubles start at ƒ65. There are two other, more agreeable hotels in the centre, the *De Keizerskroon*, to the west of Westhaven at Keizerstraat 11 (☎01820/28096), with doubles from ƒ90, and the *De Utrechtse Dom*, a couple of minutes' walk to the east of St Janskerk at Geuzenstraat 6 (☎01820/27984), with doubles from ƒ60.

For **food**, Gouda has literally dozens of cafés and snack bars catering to the hundreds of tourists who day-trip here throughout the season. *Borsalino*, Naalerstraat 4, serves a variety of dishes, including vegetarian options starting at ƒ12.75; look out as well for Balkan specialities at the imaginatively named *Balkan*, Markt 10; pancakes at *'t Goudse Winkeltje*, Achter de Kerk 9a; and cheap pizzas at the *Rimini*, Markt 28.

Utrecht

"I groaned with the idea of living all winter in so shocking a place", wrote Boswell in 1763, and **UTRECHT** still promises little as you approach: surrounded by shopping centres and industrial developments, the town only begins to reveal itself in the old area around the Dom Kerk, roughly enclosed by the Oude and Nieuwe Grachts. These distinctive sunken canals date from the fourteenth century, and their brick cellars, used as warehouses when Utrecht was a river port, have been converted to chic cafés and restaurants. Although the liveliest places in town, they don't disguise Utrecht's provincialism: just half an hour from Amsterdam, all the brashness and vitality of the capital is absent, and it's for museums and churches rather than nightlife that the town is enjoyable.

Founded by the Romans in the first century AD, the city of Utrecht became the site of a wealthy and powerful medieval bishopric, which controlled the surrounding region under the auspices of the German emperors. In 1527 the bishop sold off his secular rights and shortly afterward the town council enthusiastically joined the revolt against Spain. Indeed, the **Union of Utrecht**, the agreement that formalized the opposition to the Habsburgs, was signed here in 1579. Some two hundred years later the **Treaty of Utrecht** brought to an end some of Louis IV of France's grand imperial ambitions.

The area telephone code for Utrecht is ☎ 030.

The Town

The focal point of the centre is the **Dom Tower**, at over 110m the highest church tower in the country. It's one of the most beautiful, too, its soaring, unbuttressed lines rising to a delicate octagonal lantern added in 1380. A guided tour (April–Oct Mon–Fri 10am–5pm, Sat 11am–5pm, Sun noon–5pm; Nov–March Sat 11am–5pm & Sun noon–5pm; last entry one hour before closing; ƒ3.50) takes you unnervingly near to the top, from where you can see Rotterdam and Amsterdam on a clear day. Only the eastern part of the great cathedral remains, the nave having collapsed (with what must have been an apocalyptic crash) during a storm in 1674. It's worth peering inside (May–Sept daily 10am–5pm; Oct–April Mon–Sat 11am–4pm, Sun 2–4pm; free) to get a sense of the hangar-like space the building once had, and to wander through the **Kloostergang**, the fourteenth-century cloisters that link the cathedral to the chapterhouse. The Kloostertuin, or cloister gardens, are reckoned to be the best place in town to listen to the carillon concerts from the Dom Tower, which you can do from a pleasant tea house. If bells are not your thing, you might be lucky enough to catch music on more conventional instruments – classical concerts are regularly held here.

Except for the Dom, Utrecht's churches aren't all that interesting: the oldest is the **St Pieterskerk** (Tues–Fri 11am–4.30pm, Sat 11am–3pm), a shabbily maintained building that's a mixture of Romanesque and Gothic styles with twelfth-century paintings and reliefs. You'll

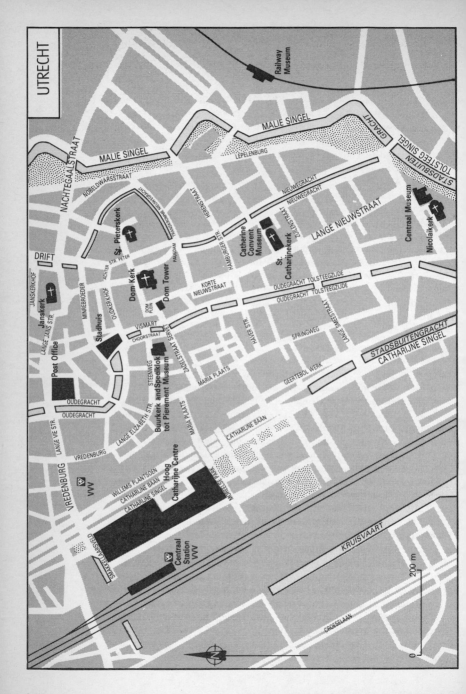

UTRECHT

Railway
Museum

MALIE SINGEL

MALIE SINGEL

NACHTEGAALSTRAAT

NOBELDWARSSTRAAT

LEPELENBURG

STADSBUITEN TOLSTEEG SINGEL

GRACHT

NIEUWEGRACHT

NIEUWEGRACHT

LANGE NIEUWSTRAAT

TRANSSTRAAT

HERENSTRAAT

St. Pieterskerk

ZUILENSTRAAT

HAMBURGER STR.

Catherine
Convent
Museum

Centraal Museum

Nicolaikerk

ACHTER STR. PETER

PAUSDAM

St.
Catharijnekerk

DRIFT

JANSKERKHOF

Dom Kerk

Dom Tower

KORTE
NIEUWSTRAAT

OUDEGRACHT TOLSTEEGZIJDE

OUDEGRACHT TOLSTEEGZIJDE

Janskerk

MINREBROEDER

DOM
PLEIN

LANGE JANS STR.

OUDKERK HOF

Stadhuis

VISMART

HAVER STR.

SPRINGWEG

LANGE SMEESTRAAT

Post Office

CHOORSTRAAT

ZADELSTRAAT SERVET

STEENWEG

Buurkerk and
tot Pierement Museum

SpeelKlok

MARIA PLAATS

GEERTEBOL WERK

STADSBUITENGRACHT

CATHARIJNE SINGEL

OUDEGRACHT

OUDEGRACHT

LANGE ELIZABETH STR.

LANGE VIE STR.

VREDENBURG

CATHARIJNE BAAN

VREDENBURG

VVV

WILLEMS PLANTSOEN

CATHARIJNE BAAN

CATHARIJNE SINGEL

Hoog
Catharijne Centre

MARIA PLAATS

MOREELSE PARK

KRUISVAART

SMAKKELAARSVELD

Centraal
Station
VVV

GROESELAAN

200 m

0

come across more striking fare if you head northwest to the bend in the Oude Gracht, between the grandiose nineteenth century **Stadhuis**, and the huge brick Amsterdam School **post office**. Across the canal from here is the oldest house in Utrecht, the fourteenth century **Huis Oudaen**. It's recently been renovated and now has a café on the ground floor, the *Proeflokaal*, where you can sample beer brewed in the steam brewery in its basement.

Not far from the Stadhuis are a couple of unusual little museums. **Den Dubbelden Arend** (Tues & Thurs 10.30 am; guided tours only) at Schoutenstraat 13, is the oldest bakery in the city; the **Museum voor het Kruideniersbedrijf** at Hoogt 8 (Tues–Sat 12.30–4.30pm) is possibly the world's only museum devoted to groceries. Also in the vicinity, further down Oude Gracht, is the **Buurkerk**, home of one sister Bertken, who was so ashamed of being the illegitimate daughter of a cathedral priest that she hid away in a small cell here – for 57 years, until her death in 1514. Now the church is a peculiar home to the **Speelklok tot Pierement Museum** (Tues–Sat 10am–5pm, Sun 1–5pm; ƒ6, children ƒ3), a collection of burping fairground organs and ingenious musical boxes that's worth an hour of anyone's time.

The city's other museums are a little way from the centre. The national collection of ecclesiastical art, the **Catharijne Convent Museum** (Tues–Fri 10am–5pm, Sat & Sun 11am–5pm; ƒ5), at Nieuwe Gracht 63, has a mass of paintings, manuscripts, and church ornaments from the ninth century on, brilliantly exhibited in a complex built around the old convent. This excellent collection of paintings includes work by Geertgen tot Sint Jans, Rembrandt, Hals, and, best of all, a luminously beautiful *Virgin and Child* by van Cleve. Part of the convent is the late Gothic St Catherine's church, its radiant white interior enhanced by floral decoration.

Keep walking down along Nieuwe Gracht and you reach Utrecht's other important museum, the **Centraal**, at Agnietenstraat 1 (Tues–Sat 10am–5pm, Sun noon–5pm; ƒ5). Its claim to hold "25,000 curiosities" seems a bit exaggerated, but it does have a good collection of paintings by Utrecht artists of the sixteenth and seventeenth centuries. Van Scorel lived in Utrecht before and after he visited Rome, and he brought the influence of Italian humanism north. His paintings, like the vividly individual portraits of the *Jerusalem Brotherhood*, combine High Renaissance style with native Dutch observation. The central figure in white is van Scorel himself: he made a trip to Jerusalem around 1520, which accounts for his unusually accurate drawing of the city in *Christ's Entry into Jerusalem*. A group of painters influenced by another Italian, Caravaggio, became known as the Utrecht School. Such paintings as Honthorst's *The Procuress* adapt his chiaroscuro technique to genre subjects, and develop an erotic content that would itself influence later genre painters like Jan Steen and Gerrit Dou. Even more skilled and realistic is Terbrugghen's *The Calling of St Matthew*, a beautiful balance of gestures dramatizing the tax collector's summoning by Christ to become one of the apostles.

Utrecht

The Museumboot

Perhaps the easiest and most pleasant way of seeing Utrecht's museums is by the **Museumboots**. There are two of these: one leaves every hour from Oude Gracht (opposite no. 85; Mon–Sat noon–4pm, Sun 11am–4pm; ƒ7) and plies along to the Centraal Museum and the National Railway Museum/Catharijne Convent; the other leaves from the Viebrug (daily 10am, 11.30am, 1pm, 2.30pm & 4pm; ƒ11, which gives a 50 percent discount at the museums), which spans Oude Gracht near the main post office, and chugs along to Gaardbrug (for the Speelklok tot Pierement Museum and Dom tower), to the Centraal Museum/Railway Museum and the Catharijne Convent Museum.

Gerrit Rietveld, the de Stijl designer, was most famous for both his brightly coloured zig-zag and geometrical chairs, displayed in the applied art section. Part of the de Stijl philosophy (see *Contexts*) was that the approach could be used in any area of design, though Rietveld's angular furniture is probably better to look at than to sit on. There are more pieces of his furniture out of town, in the **Schröderhuis** (Prins Hendriklaan 50, bus #4 from the railway station) which he designed and built in 1924 for Truus Schröder and her three children. It's hailed as one of the most influential pieces of modern architecture in Europe, demonstrating the organic union of lines and rectangles characteristic of the movement. To join a conducted tour (Wed–Sat 11am–5pm, Sun noon–5pm; ƒ9), call first (☎030/ 362310) as the maximum number of people allowed is twelve. The design of the ground floor had to meet the rigours of the building license, and Rietveld got around the planning restrictions by letting his imagination rip only on the top floor, the actual living space. Only the outer walls here are solid; the entire floor can be subdivided in different ways by means of sliding walls.

Back in Utrecht itself, there's one final museum that might detain you: the **Spoorweg (Railway) Museum** (Tues–Sat 10am–5pm, Sun 1–5pm; ƒ8.50, children ƒ4) at Maliebaanstation – bus #3 from the station – with trains, buses, and trams sitting in Utrecht's out-of-use train station: not much information, but enthusiastic attendants.

Practicalities

Train and bus stations both lead into the Hoog Catharijne shopping centre: the **main VVV office** is at Vredenburg 90 (Mon–Fri 9am–5.30pm, Sat 9am–1.30pm; ☎340 34085, 50c per minute), a seven-minute walk away. They offer the usual help with accommodation – the cheapest places, such as *Van Ooyen*, Dantelaan 117 (☎93 81 90), or *Hotel Ouwi*, FC Donderstraat 12 (☎71 63 03) cost around ƒ70 a double. The *Domstad*, Parkstraat 5 (☎31 01 31) is slightly more expensive. The **youth hostel** at Rhijnauwenselaan 14, Bunnik, linked to the train station by bus #40 or #43, is a little far out but beautifully sited in an old country manor house; the well-equipped **campground** at Arienslaan 5 can be reached by a #57 bus from the Central Station.

Though the city is compact enough to explore on foot, touring the **Utrecht**
canals, either by boat, or by cycling along towpaths, adds another
dimension to a visit. To rent a **bike**, head for *Canal Bikes* on Oude
Gracht opposite the former City Hall (Mon–Wed & Sun 10am–7pm,
Thurs–Sat 10am–9pm) whose hire prices include a map of the canal
network. Canal trips **by boat** depart hourly from Oude Gracht at the
corner of Lange Viestraat and Potterstraat near the Vieburg (Oct–May
daily from 11am-5pm; June-Sept also Tues and Thurs from 6-9pm;
ƒ10; ☎030-720111).

Restaurants mostly lie along the Oude Gracht, Lange Janstraat and
Nobelstraat. Best of those on Oude Gracht are the *Tussen Hemel en
Aarde*, and the medieval *Huis Oudaen* at number 99, with mid-priced
meals served on the first floor; further along at number 123, *De
Werfkring* is mostly vegetarian. The cheapest option here is a *dags-
chotel* at *Eetcafé De Baas* on Lijnmarkt 6. Along Lange Janstraat and
Nobelstraat, try *Café Zeezicht* on Nobelstraat 2, which serves reasonably priced breakfasts, lunches and dinners, to an accompaniment of
live music on Tuesday nights. Also check out nearby *Grand Café
Polman's Huis*, on the corner of Jansdam and Keistraat, if only for its
turn-of-the-century interior. *Stadscafé Broers*, on Janskerkhof 9 opposite the St Jans church, in the same building as *Hotel Pays-Bas*, has a
beautiful stained glass dome inside, and serves good, though not
cheap, *dagschotels*.

The town's best **bars** cluster around the junction of Oude Gracht
and Wed: check out the lively *De Witte Ballons* at Lijnmarkt 10-12,
and, around the corner at Oude Gracht 196, the very pleasant Café
Belgie. As for Utrecht's **gay scene**, try *De Wolkenkrabber* bar at Oude
Gracht 47, and the gay & lesbian disco, *De Roze Wolk*, right underneath. For further dancing go to *Fellini* on Tues, Fri and Sat from
10.30pm, in the former prison below the former City Hall.

Every spring Utrecht hosts the **Springdance Festival**, a festival of
international modern dance. In June, this is followed by an open-air art
festival throughout the city centre, known as **Festival a/d Werf**.

Chapter 17

North and East of Amsterdam

N orth of Amsterdam, there are more beaches and bulbfields, and a more rural atmosphere in general prevails. Among the towns, **Alkmaar** is perhaps the most renowned, primarily for its cheese market, although its consequent popularity with visitors can be offputting during the busy summer months, when it can be besieged with visitors. The same goes for the villages on the edge of the IJsselmeer, a short way northeast of the city, where places like **Marken**, **Volendam** and **Edam** sport a self-consciously packaged prettiness that is the epitome of the rather bogus image of Holland manufactured for the tourist. A couple of places southeast of the capital, **Muiden** and **Naarden**, are a fair antidote, each with highly individual – and enjoyable – historical centres, easily combined for a day out. Consider, too, travelling a little further afield, to either **Hoorn** or **Enkhuizen**. Two old Zuider Zee trading ports, both can be reached on a day trip from Amsterdam (they're 40min and 1hr respectively away by train, on the same line); they preserve lovely old centres and quiet, mast-spiked harbours, and Enkhuizen is the home of the impressive **Zuider Zee Museum**, which attempts (fairly successfully) to recreate life as it was before it was closed off by the barrier dam and the IJsselmeer was created.

Zaandam and Zaanse Schans

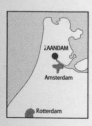

Most of the trains heading north from Amsterdam pass through the build-up of settlements that spreads north from the banks of the IJ and is known as ZAANSTAD. Looking out of the train window, it's arguable that there's no real reason to get off, and you really wouldn't be missing all that much if you didn't. The central core of Zaanstad is ZAANDAM, a small, largely modern town that was a popular tourist hangout in the nineteenth century, when it was known as "La Chine d'Hollande" for the faintly oriental appearance of its windmills, canals, masts, and row upon row of brightly painted houses. Claude Monet spent some time here in the 1870s, and, despite being suspected of spying and under constant police surveillance, immortalized the place in a series of paintings.

Follow the main street of Gedempte Gracht from the train station for five minutes, turn right down Damstraat, right again and left down Krimp, and you can see something of this former look, the harbour spiked with masts beyond a little grouping of wooden houses. On Krimp itself is Zaandam's main claim to fame, the **Czaar Petershuisje** (Jan–Nov Tues–Fri 10am–5pm, Sat & Sun 1–5pm; Dec Sat & Sun only 1–5pm; ƒ1.50), a house in which the Russian Tsar Peter the Great stayed when he came to study shipbuilding here. In those days Zaandam was an important centre for shipbuilding, and the Tsar made four visits to the town, the first in 1697 when he arrived incognito and stayed in the simple home of one Gerrit Kist, who had formerly served with him. A tottering wooden structure enclosed within a brick shelter, the house is no more than two rooms really, decorated with a handful of portraits of the benign-looking emperor and the graffiti of tourists that goes back to the mid-nineteenth century. Among the few things to see is the cupboard bed in which Peter is supposed to have slept, together with the calling cards and pennants of various visiting Russian delegations; around the outside of the house is a display on the shipbuilding industry in Zaandam. As Napoleon is supposed to have remarked on visiting the house, "Nothing is too small for great men."

Most visitors to Zaanstad are, however, here to visit **ZAANSE SCHANS** (April–Oct daily 9am–5pm; rest of the year the site is open but the individual museums and exhibitions are not; admission free, but entrance to exhibitions and museums between 25c and ƒ3.50 apiece), a recreated Dutch village made up of houses, windmills, and workshops assembled from all over the country. An energetic, but ultimately rather fake attempt to reproduce a Dutch village as it would have looked at the end of the seventeenth century, it's a pretty enough place, but it gets crammed in summer, and is not frankly worth the bother for its clog-making displays and pseudo-artisans' premises. However, it does represent the closest chance to Amsterdam to see windmills if that's what you're after, some of them working mills grinding mustard and producing oil. Among other specific attractions are a clock museum and period room, and you can also take boat trips on the river (April–Sept 10am–5pm). To get to Zaanse Schans from Zaandam, take bus #97; the same bus runs direct from Amsterdam (Marnixstraat) – an hour's trip in all.

Marken, Volendam and Edam

The majority of visitors heading out of Amsterdam make for the settlements on the banks of the IJsselmeer. **MARKEN** is the first of these, accessible direct from Amsterdam by way of bus #111 from opposite the St Nicolaaskerk – a thirty-minute journey. It's a popular place, a

former island in the Zuider Zee that was, until its road connection to the mainland in 1957, largely a closed community, supported by a small fishing industry. At one time its biggest problem was the genetic defects caused by close and constant intermarrying; now it's how to contain the tourists, whose numbers increase yearly. Marken's distinctness has in many ways been its downfall; its character – or what remains of it – has been artificially preserved: the harbour is still brightly painted in the local colours, and local costumes and clogs are worn. Recently a series of eel-smoking houses have been converted into the **Marken Museum**, Kerkbuurg 44 (open April–Oct Mon–Sat 10am–4.30pm) devoted to the history of the former island and its fishing industry. Although visitors now supply the income lost when the Zuider Zee was closed off, it turns out to have been a desperate remedy.

Volendam

Beyond the Marken causeway turn-off the road follows the dike as far as **VOLENDAM** – accessible direct from Amsterdam on bus #110 or by ferry from Marken, which takes twenty munutes and costs ƒ2 each way (March–Oct daily every 30–45min). Volendam is a larger village than Marken and retains some semblance of its fishing industry in conjunction with the more lucrative business of tourism – into which it, too, has thrown itself wholeheartedly. This is everyone's picturebook view of Holland: fishermen in baggy trousers sit strategically along the harbour wall, women scurry about picturesquely to piped music, clad in the winged lace caps that form the most significant part of the well-publicized village costume. Stop off if it's lunchtime, when you can snack your way along the waterfront fish stands; otherwise give the place a wide berth.

Edam

Further on down the #110 bus route, almost connected to Volendam, you might expect **EDAM** to be just as bad, especially considering its reputation for the red balls of cheese that the Dutch produce for export. In fact, it's a relief after the mob rule of Volendam, a pretty little town that is these days more a suburb of the capital than a major cheese-producer. It has only a fraction of the souvenir shops of its neighbours, and a charm that they have long since lost. The main draw is the **Grote Kerk** (April–Sept daily 2–4.30pm), an enormous building almost totally rebuilt after a fire in 1602, with some remarkable stained glass dating from that time. Damplein, Edam's nominal centre, is home to the eighteenth-century **Raadhuis**, which, although rather plain from the outside, has a superabundance of luxuriant stucco work within. On the other side of Damplein, Edam's oldest brick house, dating from 1530, houses **The Captain's House Museum** (Easter–Sept only Mon–Sat 10am–4.30pm, Sun 1.30–4.30pm; ƒ2), famous for its floating cellar, allegedly built by a retired captain who could not bear the thought of sleeping on dry land. Around the corner in the sixteenth century cheese-weighing house (open daily 10am–5pm) on Kaamarkt, a **cheese market** is held every Wednesday morning between mid-July and mid-August. The VVV is housed in the Raadhuis (April–Sept Mon–Sat 10am–5pm, Oct–March Mon–Sat 10am–12.30pm; ☎02993/71727), and has free maps of Edam, though not much else.

Hoorn

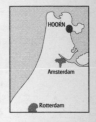

A little way north of Edam, **HOORN**, the ancient capital of an area known as West Friesland, "rises from the sea like an enchanted city of the east, with its spires and its harbour tower beautifully unreal". So wrote the English travel writer E.V. Lucas in 1905, and the town is still very much a place you should either arrive at or leave by sea – though you probably won't get the chance to do either. During the seventeenth century this was one of the richest of the Dutch ports, referred to by the poet Vondel as the trumpet and capital of the Zuider Zee, handling the important Baltic trade and that of the Dutch colonies. The Dutch East India Company was run from here, Tasman went off to "discover" Tasmania and New Zealand, and in 1616 William Schouten sailed out to navigate a passage around South America, calling its tip "Cape Hoorn" after his native town. The harbour silted up in the eighteenth century, however, stemming trade and gradually turning Hoorn into one of the so-called "dead cities" of the Zuider Zee – a process completed with the creation of the IJsselmeer.

The Town

Not surprisingly, Hoorn's former glories are hard to detect in what is today a quiet provincial backwater: the harbour is a yacht marina, and the elegant streets and houses, almost entirely surrounded by water, give only the faintest of echoes of the town's balmy seventeenth-century prosperity. The centre is **Rode Steen**, literally "red stone," an unassuming square that used to hold the town scaffold and now focuses on the swashbuckling statue of **J.P. Coen**, founder of the Dutch East Indies Empire and one of the bright lights of the seventeenth century. Coen was a headstrong and determined leader of the Dutch imperial effort, under whom the Far East colonies were consolidated, and rivals, like the English, were fought off. His settling of places like Moluccas and Batavia was something of a personal crusade, and his austere, almost puritanical way of life was in sharp contrast to the wild and unprincipled behaviour of many of his compatriots on the islands.

On one side of Rode Steen stands the early seventeenth-century **Waag**, designed by Hendrik de Keyser and now a smart restaurant. On the other side, and dominating the square, the **Westfries Museum** (Mon–Fri 11am–5pm, Sat & Sun 2–5pm; ƒ3.50) is Hoorn's most prominent sight, housed in the elaborately gabled former West Friesland government building, and decorated with the coats of arms of the house of Orange-Nassau, West Friesland, and the seven major towns of the region. Inside, the museum recreates – convincingly – the interiors of the time when Hoorn's power was at its height. Along with portraits, furniture, and ceramics, the walls of the council chamber (room 7) are covered with militia portraits by Jan Rotius, who portrays himself in the painting by the window – he's the figure by the flag on the left – and employs some crafty effects in the other canvases. Walk past the figure in the far right of the central painting and watch his foot change position from left to right as you pass. On the second floor, in room 16, there's a painting of 1632 by Jan van Goyen (*Landscape with a Peasant Cart*) and a wooden fireplace carved with tiny scenes showing a whaling expedition – Hoorn was once a whaling port of some importance. Other items of interest include a view of Hoorn painted in 1622, a room containing portraits of various East India Company dignitaries, including one of the severe Coen, while on the top floor are mock-ups of trades and shops of the time, even a prison cell.

There's not all that much of special interest in the rest of Hoorn, but it's a good place to drift around aimlessly, and the old **harbour** and the canals which lead down to it (follow G. Havensteeg from Rode Steen), are very pretty, the waterfront lined with gabled houses looking out to the stolid **Hoofdtoren**, a defensive gateway from 1532. On the other side of Rode Steen, on Kerkstraat, the **Boterhal**, formerly the St Jans Gasthuis, permanently exhibits works by Hoorn artists. It's a delightful building with a trap gable, tapering to a single window and built at an angle to the main body; it too holds a small permanent exhibition of work by local artists.

Practicalities

Hoorn's **train station** is on the northern edge of town, about ten minutes' walk from the centre and the VVV, which occupies the leaning former town hall at Nieuwstraat 23 (Sept–June Mon 1–5pm, Tues–Fri 9.30am–5pm, Sat 10am–4pm; July & Aug Mon 1–6pm, Tues–Sat 9.30am–6pm (and Thurs nights till 9pm); ☎02290/18342). There's a youth hostel about 2km out from the centre at Schellinkhouterdijk 1a (☎02290/14256) – take bus #132, #137, or #147 from the station and get off at the home for stray animals; otherwise the cheapest **hotels** are *De Magneet*, close to the harbour at Kleine Oost 5–7 (☎02290/15021), with doubles for around ƒ100, and *De Posthoorn*, Breed 25–27 (☎02290/14057), which charges about ƒ90. As for **eating**, *Sweet Dreams*, at Kerkstraat 1, is a good cheap place for lunch, and couldn't be more central, with omelettes and Mexican dishes – though it closes at 9pm. *Het Witte Paard*, by the Grote Kerk at Lange Kerkstraat 27, has Dutch food and vegetarian dishes though it, too, closes at 9pm. Later on there's *Isola Bella*, Grote Oost 65, five minutes from Rode Steen, which has pizza and pasta, and a number of bars and restaurants grouped around the harbour.

Between May and October, Hoorn is the starting point of **steam train services** to Medemblik, which run once a day in May, June, September and October (at 11am), and twice a day in July and August (at 10.45am and 2.15pm). They can be a pleasant way of getting to the town if you have kids – journey time is one hour, and tickets cost ƒ11. Outside summer, if you want to get from Hoorn to Medemblik, catch express bus #139, which takes about 25 minutes.

Enkhuizen

Another "dead city", though much smaller than Hoorn, **ENKHUIZEN**, twenty minutes further east by train, was also an important port during the seventeenth century, with the largest herring fleet in the country. However, it too declined at the end of the seventeenth century, and the town now offers much the same sort of attractions as Hoorn, retaining its broad mast-spattered harbours and peaceful canals. It also has a genuinely major attraction in the **Zuider Zee Museum**, which brings busloads of tourists up here during the summer to experience what is a very deliberate attempt to capture the lifestyle that existed here when the town was still a flourishing port – and which was destroyed once and for all with the building of the Afsluitdijk. Enkhuizen is also a good place to visit for its summer ferry connections to Stavoren and Urk across the IJsselmeer.

The Town and the Zuider Zee Museum

A few hundred metres from the two main harbours, **Westerstraat** is Enkhuizen's main spine, a busy pedestrianized street that is home to most of the town's shops and restaurants. At one end, the **Westerkerk** is an early fifteenth-century Gothic church with an odd wooden belfry, added in 1519. A right turn from here leads into a residential part of town, very pretty, with its canals crossed by white-painted footbridges. The other end of Westerstraat is marginally more monumental, zeroing in on the mid-sixteenth-century **Waag** on Kaasmarkt, which houses the **Stedelijk Waagmuseum** of local odds and ends (mid-April–mid-Oct Tues–Fri 11am–5pm, Sat & Sun 2–5pm; ƒ1.50). Nearby is the solid classically styled mid-seventeenth-century **Stadhuis** – behind which the dangerously leaning **Gevangenis** was once the town prison. This is closed to the public, but a peek through its barred windows gives some idea of the bleakness of conditions for the average prisoner in those days, most of the main furnishings still being in place.

Close by here, along the waterfront at Wierdijk 18, the indoor section of the Zuider Zee Museum, the **Binnenmuseum** (daily 10am–5pm; ƒ5, but see Buitenmuseum below), has a collection of fishing vessels and equipment, and Zuider Zee arts and crafts, recently spruced up and displayed in bright new surroundings. Exhibits include regional costumes and painted furniture from Hindeloopen (see *West of the Dam*); an ice-cutting boat from Urk, once charged with the responsibility of keeping the shipping lanes open between the island and the port of Kampen; displays of sail- and rope-making implements; and much else besides

Most people, however, give the Binnenmuseum a miss and instead make straight for the **Buitenmuseum** on the far side of the harbour (early April–end Oct daily 10am–5pm; ƒ12.50, children ƒ8), where buildings have actually been transported from 39 different locations to form a period portrayal of the vanished way of life around the Zuider Zee in a recreation of various towns and villages. The only way to get there is by boat, either from the train station or, if you're driving, from the museum parking area by the end of the Lelystad road. The ticket entitles you to either a free boat trip or free parking. Once there, you can either tour the museum by way of the free hourly guided tours, or – rather nicer – simply wander around taking it all in at your own pace.

Close by the ferry wharf there's a series of lime kilns, conspicuous by their tall chimneys, from which a path takes you through the best of the museum's many intriguing corners, beginning with a row of cottages from Monnickendam, nearby which there's an information centre. A number of streets lined with cottages lead off from here, a mock-up of a typical Zuider Zee fishing village basically, with examples of buildings from Urk among other places, their modest, precisely furnished interiors open to visitors and sometimes peopled by characters in traditional dress hamming it up for the tourists. Further on, a number of buildings sit along and around a central canal. There's a post office from Den Oever; a grocery from Harderwijk; an old laundry, thick with the smell of washing; a pharmacy and a bakery from Hoorn, the latter selling pastries and chocolate; while a cottage from Hindeloopen doubles up as a restaurant. It all sounds rather kitsch, and in a way it is: there are regular demonstrations of the old ways and crafts, goats and sheep roam the stretches of meadow, and the exhibition is mounted in such an earnest way as to almost beg criticism. But the attention to detail is very impressive, and the whole thing is never overdone, with the result that many parts of the museum are genuinely picturesque. If you see nothing else in Enkhuizen (and many people don't), you really shouldn't miss it.

Practicalities

Trains to Enkhuizen – the end of the line – stop right on the corner of the harbour, close by the main **bus stops** and **ferry wharves**. There's a VVV office in the train station (Tues–Sat 10am–5pm; April–Oct also open Sun 10am–5pm; ☎02280/13164) which has free maps but can't help with much else. From here it's a five- to ten-minute walk to Westerstraat and the centre of the small town. If you're staying, the least expensive option is the wonderful circular dormitory in the Dromendaris Tower (☎02280/12076) on Paktuinen in the outer harbour, possibly the cheapest place in Holland. If you prefer to sleep in privacy, the cheapest hotel is *Het Wapen*, conveniently located close to the Zuider Zee museums and the harbours at Breedstraat 59 (☎02280/13434), which has double rooms for around ƒ100. Apart from camping that's about it on the budget accommodation front. For camping, there are two sites handily located on the northern side of town: closest is the *Enkhuizer Zand* on the far side of the Zuider Zee Museum at Kooizandweg 4; there's also *De Vest* – follow Vijzelstraat north off Westerstraat, continue down Noorderweg, and turn left by the old town ramparts. Both sites are open April to September only.

Restaurants in Enkhuizen tend to be expensive. *Het Shoutwje*, Westerstraat 98, is less pricey than most, but the food is only average; *Holle Bolle Gijs*, on the waterfront of the outer harbour, has decent main meals and especially good-value lunch dishes; while the *Café Dromedaris*, in the Dromedaris tower, serves well-priced food for lunch and dinner.

During summer you can travel on from Enkhuizen **by ferry** to Stavoren, Urk, or Medemblik. These leave from behind the train station. Ferries to Stavoren run roughly three times daily; and to Urk and Medemblik twice daily. To Stavoren and Urk, reckon on paying ƒ10 to ƒ12 plus ƒ5 or so for a bike.

Alkmaar

An hour from Amsterdam by train, **ALKMAAR** is typical of small-town Holland, its pretty, partially canalized centre surrounded by water and offering a low-key, undemanding provincialism which makes a pleasant change after the rigours of the big city. It's also a good base for exploring the nearby dunes and beaches, or even the towns of West Friesland. Alkmaar is probably best known for its **cheese market**, an ancient affair which these days ranks as one of the most extravagant tourist spectacles in Holland. Cheese has been sold on the main square here since the 1300s, and although no serious buying goes on here now, it's an institution that continues to draw crowds – though nowadays they're primarily tourists. If you do want to see it (it's held every Friday morning, mid-April to mid-Sept), be sure to get there early, as by the 10am opening the crowds are already thick. The ceremony starts with the buyers sniffing, crumbling, and finally tasting each cheese, followed by heated bartering. Once a deal has been concluded, the cheeses – golden discs of Gouda mainly, laid out in rows and piles on the square – are borne away on ornamental carriers by four groups of porters for weighing. Payment, tradition has it, takes place in the cafés around the square.

The Town

Even if you've only come for the cheese market, it's a good idea to see something of the rest of the town before you leave. On the main square, the **Waag** was originally a chapel dedicated to the Holy Spirit, but was converted, and given its magnificent east gable, shortly after the town's famous victory against the Spanish in 1573, when its citizens withstood a long siege by Frederick of Toledo – a victory which marked the beginning of the end for the Spaniards. Nowadays the Waag houses the VVV (see below) and the **Kaasmuseum** (April–Oct Mon–Sat 10am–4pm except Fri 9am–4pm; *f*2), which has displays on the history of cheese and cheese-making equipment and suchlike. Across the other side of the square, the **Biermuseum de Boom**, Houttil 1 (April–Sept Tues–Sat 10am–4pm, Sun 1–4pm; Oct–March Thurs–Sun 1–4pm; *f*3), is housed in the building of the old De Boom brewery, and has displays tracing the brewing process from the malting to bottling stage, aided by authentic props from this and other breweries the world over. There's lots of technical equipment, enlivened by mannikins and empty bottles from once innumerable Dutch brewers – though few, curiously, from De Boom itself. It's an engaging little museum, lovingly put together by enthusiasts; it also has a top floor shop in which you can buy a huge range of beers and associated merchandise, as well as a downstairs bar serving some eighty varieties of Dutch beer.

The **Stedelijk Museum** (Tues–Sat 10am–5pm, Sun 1–5pm; *f*2), on the other side of the town centre in Doelenstraat, displays pictures and plans of the siege of 1573, along with a *Holy Family* by Honthorst and portraits by Maerten van Heemskerk and Caesar van Everdingen, the latter a local and very minor seventeenth-century figure who worked in the Mannerist style of the Haarlem painters. Close by, at the far end of **Langestraat**, the town's main shopping street, the **St Laurenskerk**, a Gothic church of the later fifteenth century, is worth looking into for its huge organ, commissioned at the suggestion of Constantijn Huygens by Maria Tesselschade, local resident and friend of the Golden Age elite. The case was designed by Jacob van Campen and painted by Caesar van Everdingen. In the apse is the tomb of Count Floris V, penultimate in the line of medieval counts of North Holland, who did much to establish the independence of the towns hereabouts but who was murdered by nobles in 1296 (see p.227). On Langestraat itself the only notable building is the **Stadhuis**, a florid affair, half of which (the eastern side and tower) dates from the early sixteenth century.

Practicalities

Alkmaar's **train station** is about ten minutes' walk west of the centre of town on Stationsstraat; to get to the centre from the station, turn right outside, then left, and follow the road for five minutes to the St Laurenskerk. The VVV is five minutes away from here, housed in the Waag on Waagplein (Mon–Wed 9am–5.30pm, Thurs–Sat 9am–6pm; ☎072/11 42 84). They have **private rooms** for *f*25 per person, including breakfast; failing that, *De Nachtegaal* is the cheapest and most central **hotel**, opposite the town hall at Langestraat 100 (☎072/11 28 94), with reasonable double rooms, without bath, from about *f*85. Failing that, *Pension Ida Margaretha*, Kanaaldijk 186 (☎072/61 39

89), has doubles for *f*90. If you're **camping**, there's a site (open April–Sept) ten minutes' bus ride northwest of the town centre; take bus #168 or #169 from the train station.

There are quite a few decent places to **eat**. *Jelle's Eethuisje*, between Laat and Oude Gracht on Ridderstraat 24, is good for light lunches and cheap evening meals; *Ikan Mas*, one of several restaurants in the old part of town at Fnidsen 101–103, is an OK Indonesian that does a reasonable *rijstaffel*, while *Rose's Cantina*, two doors down, serves Tex-Mex dishes. For splurges, try *Bistro Wladimir* at Waagplein 36, which offers French and Dutch food in an intimate atmosphere. **Drinking**, too, is well catered for. There are two main groupings of bars: one on Waagplein itself, the other on the nearby canal of Verdronken Noord, by the old Vismarkt. Of the former, *De Kaasbeurs*, at Houttil 30, is a lively place during the day but closes in the early evening; *Café Corridor*, virtually next door, is a lively hangout that plays loud music late into the night and has a small dancefloor at the back. On Verdronken Noord, *De Pilaren* is also noisy, though catering to a slightly older crowd; *Café Stapper*, next door, is a good refuge if the music gets too much.

If you just want to have a quick look around Alkmaar after the cheese market, in summer you can take a **boat trip** around the town, from near the Waag. They run from April to October, last 45 minutes and cost *f*6.

Around Alkmaar – and Points North

The seashore close to Alkmaar is the area's best feature and, if the weather is warm, it's a good place to cool off after the crush of the cheese market. Bus #168 runs out to **BERGEN**, a cheerful village that has been something of a retreat for artists since the Expressionist Bergen School of the early twentieth century worked here. There are a number of galleries around the village, including the **KCB** gallery next door to the VVV at Plein 7 (Tues–Sat 11am–5pm, Sun 2–5pm; *f*1), which holds regular exhibitions of work by contemporary Bergen artists, and there's a small collection of older work in the **Sterkenhuis Museum** on Oude Prinsweg (May–Sept Tues–Sat 10am–noon & 3–5pm; July & Aug also 7–9pm; *f*1.50), which also contains documentation on the defeat of the Duke of York here in 1799, along with period rooms and old costumes.

There's a permanent exhibition of Bergen School paintings on display at the **Smithuizen Museum**, Stationsweg 83 (Fri–Sun 2–6pm; Nov & Dec Fri & Sat only 2–6pm; free), in **HEILOO**, just south of Alkmaar. Heiloo is also important for bulbs, and has a summer exhibition of flowers and plants in its **Hortus Bulborum** – fair compensation if you missed the Keukenhof. If you're interested in bulbs, there's a museum devoted to bulb cultivation south of the town in **LIMMEN** at Dusseldorpweg 64, with exhibits on two centuries of bulb-growing in Holland (mid-April to mid-Sept Mon & Tues 9am–noon & 2–5pm, Fri 9am–noon; free).

Bus #168 runs on from Bergen to **BERGEN-AAN-ZEE**, a bleak place in itself but with access to some strikingly untouched dunes and beach. It also has an **aquarium** (daily 10am–6pm), crammed full of marine life, if the weather turns or you have kids in tow. About 3km south, **EGMOND-AAN-ZEE** (also directly accessible from Alkmaar) is a little larger but not much more attractive, though it also has huge expanses of sand. A short way inland across the dunes, in **EGMOND-AAN-DE-HOEF**, you can see the remains of the castle of the counts of North Holland, destroyed in 1574. Egmond is also an entry point of the **Noordhollands Duinreservaat**, an area of woods and dunes that stretches south beyond Castricum and holds a couple of campsites and any number of cycle paths, not to mention the superb beach.

The coast north of Bergen, from CAMPERDUIN to PETTEN, has no dunes, and the sea is kept at bay by means of a four-and-a-half kilometre-long **dike** – something you can learn more about at the **"de dijk te kijk"** ("the dike on show") exhibition on Zuiderhazedwarsdijk, outside Petten, on the dike, which has old maps, photos, and drawings illustrating the building of the defence (May, June & Sept Sat & Sun 2–5pm; July & Aug Mon–Fri 10am–5pm, Sat & Sun 2–5pm; free).

Muiden and Naarden

MUIDEN, just thirteen kilometres east of Amsterdam, is squashed around the Vecht, a river usually crammed with pleasure boats and dinghies sailing out to the IJmeer and beyond to the IJselmeer. It's the most famous sailing harbour in the Gooi area, not least because the royal yacht *De Groene Draek* is often moored here. As well as the harbour there are two beaches on the IJmeer, Muiderberg and Muiderzand. Although most of the sightseeing is done by weekend admirals eyeing up each other's boats, the **Muiderslot** (April–Sept Mon–Fri 10am–5pm, Sun 1–5pm; Oct–March Mon–Fri 10am–4pm, Sun 1–4pm; ƒ5) provides an extra spark of interest. In the thirteenth century this was the home of Count Floris V, a sort of aristocratic Robin Hood who favoured the common people at the nobles' expense. They replied by kidnapping the Count, imprisoning him in his own castle and stabbing him to death. Destroyed and rebuilt in the fourteenth century, Muiderslot's interior is these days a recreation of the period of a more recent occupant, the poet Pieter Hooft. He was chatelain here from 1609 to 1647, a sinecure that allowed him to entertain a group of artistic and literary friends who became known as the Muiden Circle, and included Grotius, Vondel, Huygens, and other Amsterdam intellectuals. The obligatory guided tours (April–Sept every 15 min, Oct–March hourly) centre on this clique, in a restoration that is both believable and likable – two things period rooms generally aren't.

From the jetty outside the Muiderslot, boats depart regularly for the imposing fortress-island of **Pampus**, a couple of kilometres out to sea. It was built at the end of the nineteenth century as part of Amsterdam's defence system, but has now fallen into ruin. The VVV, Kazernestraat 10 (April–Sept Mon–Fri 10am–5pm, Sat 10am–1pm; ☎02942/61389) has details on renting watersports equipment. If you fancy pottering around in **boats**, the *Muiden Jachtverhuur Station* (MYCS), Naarderstraat 10 (02942/61413) rents out sailboats, *Van Deursen* at Herengracht 119 (02942/61385) rowboats. If you want to bypass Muiden you can get to Muiderberg from Amsterdam on bus #136.

Naarden

Take a look at a postcard of **NAARDEN**, about 10km east, and it seems as if the town was formed by a giant pastry cutter: the double rings of ramparts and moats, unique in northern Europe, were engineered between 1675 and 1685 to defend Naarden and the eastern approach to Amsterdam. They were still in use as recently as the 1920s, and one of the fortified spurs is now the wonderfully explorable **Fortification Museum** at Westwalstraat 6 (April–Oct Mon–Fri 10am–4.30pm, Sat & Sun noon–5pm; *f*3.50), whose claustrophobic underground passages show how the garrison defended the town for 250 years.

The rest of Naarden's tiny centre is peaceful rather than dull. The small, low houses mostly date from after 1572 when the Spanish sacked the town and massacred the inhabitants, an act designed to warn other settlements in the area against insurrection. Fortunately they spared the late Gothic **Grote Kerk** (June–mid Sept daily 2–4pm) and its superb vault paintings. Based on drawings by Dürer, these twenty wooden panels were painted between 1510 and 1518 and show an Old Testament story on the south side, paralleled by one from the New Testament on the north. To study the paintings without breaking your neck, borrow a mirror at the church's entrance. A haul up the Grote Kerk's **tower** (May–Aug hourly tours daily 1–4pm; *f*3) gives the best view of the fortress island and, less attractively, Hilversum's TV tower.

If you've never heard of Jan Amos Komenski, or Comenius, a seventeenth-century polymath and educational theorist, it's unlikely that the **Comenius Museum** at Turfpoortstraat 27 (guided tours only Nov–March Tues–Sun 2–5pm; April–Oct Tues–Sat 10am–5pm, Sun noon–5pm; *f*2.50) will fire your enthusiasm for the man. A religious exile from Moravia (now in the Czech Republic), Comenius lived in Amsterdam and is buried in Naarden. He's a national hero to the Czechs, and they donated most of the exhibits in the museum and also constructed his **Mausoleum** in the **Waalse Kapel** on Kloosterstraat – a building permanently on loan to the Czech people.

Practicalities

CN bus #136 leaves Amsterdam every half hour from Weesperplein, stopping first at Muiden (travel time 40min) then Naarden (55min). The Naarden VVV is at Adriaan Dortmansplein 1b (May–Sept Mon–Fri 9am–5pm, Sat 10am–4pm, Sun noon–4pm; Oct–April Mon–Fri 9am–5pm, Sat 10am–2pm; closed Sun; ☎02159/42836).

The Contexts

History of Amsterdam

To a great extent, a history of Amsterdam is a history of the whole of The Netherlands. The city has been at the centre of events in the country since its sixteenth-century ascendancy: it was the most glorious cultural and trading centre throughout the Golden Age, and, despite a brief downturn in the eighteenth century, has grown in stature in the last few decades, gaining notoriety for its progressive policies and population during the Sixties and Seventies, and increasing credibility again as a centre for commerce and business.

The Earliest Years

Amsterdam's earliest history is as murky as the marshes from which it arose. A settlement appeared in the eleventh century, founded with a number of other small towns on the barely populated coast. Previously, this stretch of peat bogs and marshes had been uninhabitable, and it was only when the level of the sea fell and floods became less frequent that colonies sprang up, settling on the higher ground of river banks and dams for protection against the floods.

As the name suggests, Amsterdam was founded on a dam on the River Amstel, and the first mention of the settlement comes in a toll privilege charter granted by Count Floris V in 1275 (a document that can be seen in the city archives). By this time Haarlem, Delft and Leiden were already established; Amsterdam itself began to flourish in 1323, when the Count of Holland designated the small town as a toll port

for beer imported from Hamburg. Amsterdam soon became an important transit port for grain and a trading force within the Baltic.

As the city grew, its **market** diversified. English wool was imported, made into cloth in Leiden and Haarlem and exported via Amsterdam; the cloth trade drew workers into the town to work along Warmoesstraat and the Amstel, and ships were able to sail right up to Dam Square to pick up the finished work and drop off imported wood, fish, salt and spices.

Though the city's **population** rose steadily throughout the sixteenth century to around 12,000, Amsterdam was relatively small compared to Antwerp or London: building on the waterlogged soil was difficult and slow, requiring timber piles to be driven into the firmer sand below. And with the extensive use of timber and thatch, fires were a frequent occurrence. A particularly disastrous blaze in 1452 resulted in such destruction that the city council made building with slate and stone obligatory – one of the few wooden houses that survived the fire stands at the entrance to the Begijnhof. In the mid-sixteenth century the city underwent its first expansion as burgeoning trade with the Hanseatic towns of the Baltic made the city second only to Antwerp as a marketplace and warehouse to northern and western Europe. The trade in cloth, grain, gems and wine brought craftspeople to the city, and the city's merchant fleet grew: by the 1550s three-quarters of all grain cargo going out of the Baltic was carried in Amsterdam vessels. The foundations were being laid for the supreme wealth of the Golden Age.

The Rise of Protestantism

At the beginning of the sixteenth century the superstition and elaborate ritual in the established **Church** was being attacked throughout northern Europe. Erasmus of Rotterdam advanced the concept of an idealized human, seeing man as the crowning of creation rather than the sinful creature of The Fall. In 1517 Martin Luther produced his 95 theses against the church practice of indulgences; his writings and Bible translations were printed in The

Netherlands. But it was Calvin (who differed from Luther in his views on the role of church and state) who gained the most popularity in Amsterdam. In 1535 the Anabaptists, an early **Protestant movement**, rioted, occupying Amsterdam Town Hall and calling on passers-by to repent. Previously the town had accepted the Anabaptists, but it acted swiftly when civic rule was challenged: the town hall was besieged and the surviving Anabaptists executed on Dam Square. Following this, an atmosphere of anti-Protestant repression temporarily prevailed.

Around this time, the fanatically Catholic **Philip II** succeeded to the Spanish throne. Through a series of marriages the Spanish monarchy had come to rule over the Low Countries, and Philip was determined to rid the country of the heresy of Protestantism. He came face to face with a rapidly spreading Calvinist movement, and in 1564 Amsterdam Calvinists voiced complaints about nepotism in the city administration to Margaret of Palma, Philip's sister and regent of the Low Countries. Their protests were acknowledged, thus once again reinforcing the power of the Protestant movement, which was by now gaining favour among Amsterdam nobles, too. In 1565 a winter crop failure caused a famine among mainly Calvinist workers and roused discontent against Catholic Spain and Philip's anti-Protestant edicts. Later that year, a wave of **iconoclasm** swept the country: in Amsterdam, Calvinist mobs ran riot in the churches, stripping them of their wealth and their rich decoration; only by being promised the Franciscan church for worship were they mollified. Many churches, particularly in North Holland, were never restored, leaving most with the plain whitewashed interiors seen today. The ferocity of the outbreak shocked the nobility into renewed support for Spain; most radical Protestant leaders saw what was coming and quietly slipped away abroad.

War with Spain

Philip's answer to the iconoclasm was to send in an army of 10,000 men led by the **Duke of Alva** to suppress the heresy absolutely; his first act was to condemn to death 12,000 of those who had taken part in the rebellion the previous year. **William the Silent**, an apostate Prince of the House of Orange-Nassau and the country's largest landowner, organized the Protestant revolt against Spanish rule, taking the cities of Delft,

Haarlem and Leiden from Alva's troops. Amsterdam, however, prudently remained on the side of the stronger force until it became clear that William was winning – and his forces had surrounded the town. After the fall of Amsterdam the Catholic clergy was expelled and Catholic churches and monasteries were handed over for Protestant use.

In 1579 the seven Dutch provinces signed the Union of Utrecht and brought about the formation of the **United Provinces**, an alliance against Spain that was the first consolidation of the northern Low Countries into an identifiable country. The Utrecht agreement stipulated **freedom of religious belief**, ensuring that anti-Spanish sentiment wasn't translated into divisive anti-Catholicism. Though this tolerant measure didn't extend to freedom of worship, a blind eye was turned to the celebration of mass if it was done privately and inconspicuously – a move that gave rise to "clandestine" Catholic churches like that of the **Amstelkring** on Oude Zijds Voorburgwal.

With the revolt against Spain concluded, Amsterdam was free to carry on with what it did best – trading and making money.

The Golden Age

The brilliance of Amsterdam's explosion on to the European scene is as difficult to underestimate as it is to detail. The size of its **merchant fleet** had long been considerable, carrying Baltic grain into Europe. Even the determined Spaniards had been unable to undermine Dutch **maritime superiority**, and, following the effective removal of Antwerp as a competitor, Amsterdam became the emporium for the products of northern and southern Europe and the new colonies in the West Indies. The city didn't only prosper from its market; its own ships carried the produce, a cargo trade that greatly increased its wealth.

Dutch **banking and investment** brought further prosperity, and by the mid-seventeenth century Amsterdam's wealth was spectacular. The Calvinist bourgeoisie indulged themselves in fine and whimsically decorated canal houses, and commissioned images of themselves in group portraits. Civic pride knew no bounds as great monuments to self-aggrandisement such as the new **Town Hall** were hastily erected, and if some went hungry, few starved, as the poor were cared for in municipal almshouses.

The arts flourished and **religious tolerance** extended even to traditional scapegoats, the

Jews (especially the Sephardis), who had been hounded from Spain by the Inquisition but who were guaranteed freedom from religious persecution under the terms of the Union of Utrecht. They brought with them their skills in the gem trade, and by the end of the eighteenth century accounted for ten percent of the city's population. Guilds and craft associations thrived and in the first half of the century the city's population increased fourfold. Agricultural workers were drawn to the better wages offered in Dutch industry, arriving along with Huguenot refugees from France and Protestants escaping persecution in the still-Catholic south.

To accommodate its growing populace, Amsterdam **expanded** several times during the seventeenth century. The grandest and most elaborate plan to enlarge the city was begun in 1613, with the building of the western stretches of the **Herengracht, Keizersgracht** and **Prinsengracht,** the three great canals that epitomize the wealth and self-confidence of the Golden Age. In 1663 the sweeping crescent was extended east and north beyond the IJ, but by this time the population had begun to stabilize, and the stretch that would have completed the ring of canals around the city was left only partially developed – an area that would in time become the *Jodenhoek* or Jewish quarter.

One organization that kept the city's coffers brimming throughout the Golden Age was the **East India Company.** Formed by the newly powerful Dutch Republic in 1602, the Amsterdam-controlled enterprise sent ships to Asia, Indonesia, and as far as China to bring back spices, wood and other assorted plunder. Given a trading monopoly in all lands east of the Cape of Good Hope, it had unlimited military powers over the lands it controlled, and was effectively the occupying government in Malaya, Ceylon and Malacca. Twenty years later the **West Indies Company** was inaugurated to protect new Dutch interests in the Americas and Africa. Expending most of its energies in waging war on Spanish and Portugese colonies from a base in Surinam, it never achieved the success of the East India company, and was dismantled in 1674, ten years after its small colony called New Amsterdam had been captured by the British – and renamed New York. Elsewhere, Amsterdam held on to its colonies for as long as possible – **Java** and **Sumatra** were still under Dutch control after World War II.

Gentle Decline – 1650 To 1800

Part of the reason Amsterdam achieved such economic pre-eminence in the first part of the seventeenth century was that its rivals were expending their energies elsewhere: England was in the turmoil of the Civil War, France was struggling with economic problems brought on by skirmishes with the Spanish, and Germany was ravaged by the Thirty Years' War. By the second half of the century all three countries were back on their feet and fighting: England's navy was attacking the Dutch fleet, Louis XIV of France attempted an invasion of the Low Countries which all but reached Amsterdam, and the troops of the Bishop of Münster occupied the east of the country. While none of these threats became a reality, they signalled the passing of Amsterdam's – and the country's – headiest days.

Though the French had been defeated, Louis retained designs on the United Provinces. When his grandson succeeded to the Spanish throne and control of the Spanish Netherlands (Brabant, Flanders and Antwerp), Louis forced him to hand the latter over into French hands. The United Provinces, England and Austria, formed an alliance against the French and so began the **Wars of the Spanish Succession,** a haphazard conflict that dragged on until 1713. The fighting tarnished Amsterdam's dazzling riches, draining the nation's wealth. A slow decline in the city's fortunes began, furthered by a mood of conservatism growing out of a reaction against the lucrative speculation of the previous century. Towards the end of the eighteenth century, Amsterdam, and the United Provinces, saw a rising tension between Dutch loyalists and pro-French ruling families (who styled themselves "Patriots"). By the 1780s there was near-civil war, and in 1795 the French, aided by the Patriots, invaded, setting up the **Batavian Republic** and administering it from Amsterdam. Effectively under French control, the Dutch were enthusiastically at **war with England,** and in 1806 Napoleon installed his brother **Louis** as King of The Netherlands in Amsterdam's town hall (giving it, incidentally, its name, **Royal Palace**) in an attempt to create a commercial gulf between the country and England. Amsterdam merchants, with an ever-canny eye to profit, had continued trading with England while the naval battles raged. From his headquarters Louis, however, wasn't willing to allow the country to become a simple satellite of France: he ignored Napoleon's directives and after just four years of rule was forced to abdicate. Following Napoleon's disastrous retreat from Moscow, French rule weakened, and eventually the country was returned to **Dutch control** under William I.

The Nineteenth Century

With the **unification of The Netherlands** in 1813, a process that incorporated parts of the former Spanish Netherlands and brought about the formation of Belgium, the **status of Amsterdam** changed. Previously the self-governing city, made bold by its economic independence, could (and frequently did) act in its own self-interest at the expense of the national interest; now it was integrated within the country with no more rights than any other city – it was the capital in name, but the seat of government and all decision-making was The Hague.

Though the **industrial revolution** arrived late, in the first years of the nineteenth century Amsterdam regained parts of its **colonies** in the West and East Indies. Colonial trade improved, but like other trade, it was hampered by the Zuider Zee, whose shallows and sandbanks prevented new, larger ships from entering. The North Holland Canal, completed in 1824 to bypass the Zuider Zee, made little difference, and it was Rotterdam, strategically placed on the Rhine inlets between the industries of the Ruhr and Britain, that prospered at Amsterdam's expense. Even the opening of the **North Sea Canal** in 1876 failed to push Amsterdam's trade ahead of Rotterdam's, though the capital did house the country's **shipbuilding industry**, remnants of which can still be seen at the Kromhout yard in the Eastern Islands.

Between 1850 and the turn of the century the population of Amsterdam, which had remained static since the 1650s, doubled. Most of the newcomers to the city were poor and the **housing** built for them reflected this; the small homes around De Pijp in the Old South remain good examples of the low-cost housing that the more affluent working classes could afford. The Jordaan, for the early parts of the century one of the city's most impoverished quarters, was cleared. Its polluted canals were filled in and small, inexpensive homes were built. The Jordaan project was one of many put together by philanthropic social organizations, and the council, too,

had what were, for the time, forward-looking policies to **alleviate poverty** and increase education for the poor. The political climate was outstandingly liberal, influenced by cabinet leader J. R. **Thorbecke** and an increasingly socialist contingent on the Amsterdam City Council.

Before the hard years of the depression the city continued to grow. The rise in the standard of living among working people meant that they could afford better homes, usually under the auspices of housing associations or the city's own building programmes. The most interesting of these were the estates built in what came to be called the **New South**: designed by a group known as the **Amsterdam School** of architects, they combined modernism with the best of home-grown styles – and were extremely successful.

War

At the outbreak of **World War I** The Netherlands had remained neutral, though it suffered privations as a result of the Allied blockade of ports through which the Germans might be supplied. Similar attempts to remain neutral in **World War II** soon failed: German troops invaded on May 10, 1940, and the Dutch were quickly overwhelmed; Queen Wilhelmina fled to London, and Arthur Seyss-Inquart was installed as Berlin's puppet leader. Members of the **NSB**, the Dutch fascist party which had welcomed the invaders, found themselves rapidly promoted to positions of authority, but, in the early years of the occupation at least, life for the ordinary Amsterdammer went on much as usual. Even when the first roundups of the Jews began in 1941, most people pretended they weren't happening, the single popular demonstration against the Nazi action being the quickly suppressed **February strike**.

The **Dutch Resistance** was instrumental in destroying German supplies and munitions and carrying out harassing attacks in the city, and as the resistance grew, underground newspapers flourished – today's *Trouw* (Loyalty) and *Het Parool* (The Password) began life as illegal newsletters. Around 13,000 Resistance fighters and sympathizers lost their lives during the war, and the city's old **Jewish quarter**, swollen by those who had fled Germany during the persecutions of the 1930s, was obliterated, leaving only the deserted Jodenhoek and the diary of a young girl as testaments to the horrors.

After the War

The years immediately after the war were spent patching up the damage of occupation and liberation. It was a period of intense **poverty** in the capital, as food, fuel and building materials were practically nonexistent; a common sight on the streets were handcart burials of those who had died of hunger or hypothermia, black cardboard coffins being trundled to mass graves. As the liberating Canadians had moved nearer to Amsterdam, the Germans had blown up all the dikes and the sluices at IJmuiden, and repairing these further slowed the process of rebuilding. The sea itself claimed victims in 1953, when an unusually high tide swept over Zeeland's coastal defences, flooding 40,000 acres of land and drowning more than 1800 people. The resultant **Delta Project**, which secured the area, also ensured the safety of cities to the south of Amsterdam, although the city had already been more affected by the 1932 completion of the **Asfluitdijk**, which closed off the traditional way of reaching the city by ship through the Zuider Zee – which became the freshwater IJseelmeer. The later opening of the **Amsterdam-Rhine canal** did much to boost the fortunes of the city, with massive cargo-handling facilities being built to accommodate the imports of grain and the supply of ore for the Ruhr furnaces. Steadily the rebuilding continued: in Amsterdam all the land projected for use by the year 2000 was used up by the "garden cities". Giant suburbs such as **Bijlmermeer** to the southeast were the last word in 1960s large-scale residential plans, with low-cost modern housing, play areas and traffic-free foot and bicycle paths. Today, however, Bijlmermeer is a ghetto few willingly visit.

The Sixties and Seventies

The 1960s were above all a period of change and some notoriety for Amsterdam. The city witnessed the growth of a number of radical causes and protest movements. In 1965, for example, a group of young people made it a weekly ritual to gather round a statue in the centre of Amsterdam to watch a remarkable performer, one-time window cleaner and magician extraordinaire, Jasper Grootveld. Grootveld had won notoriety a couple of years earlier by painting K for kanker ("cancer") on cigarette billboards throughout the city. Later he set up an "anti-smoking temple" and proclaimed the statue

of the Lieverdje ("Lovable Rascal") on the Spui the symbol of "tomorrow's addicted consumer", since it had been donated to the city by a cigarette manufacturer.

Grootveld wasn't the only interesting character around town: Roel van Duyn, a philosophy student at Amsterdam University and initiator of a New Left movement, and the **Provos** (short for *provocatie* – "provocation") started joining in Grootveld's magic happenings, sparking a chain of rebellion that would influence events in The Netherlands for the next twenty years.

The number of real Provos never exceeded about 25, but their actions and street "Happenings" appealed to a large number of young people. The group had no coherent structure: they emerged into public consciousness through one common aim – to bring points of political or social conflict to public attention by spectacular means. More than anything they were masters of publicity, and pursued their "games" with a spirit of fun rather than grim political fanaticism. They reflected the swinging sixties attitude of young people all over the western world.

In July 1965 the police intervened at the Saturday night "Happening" for the first time, and set a pattern for future confrontations; they had already confiscated the first two issues of the Provos' magazine in which their initiator, van Duyn, published the group's manifesto and in which their policies later appeared under the title "The White Plans". These included the famous but unsuccessful **white bicycle plan**, which proposed that the Council ban all cars in the city centre and supply 20,000 bicycles (painted white) for general public use – the idea being that you picked up a bike, rode it to your destination, and then left it for someone else to use.

There were regular incidents throughout 1965 and 1966 involving a variety of Provo protests, but it was the action taken on March 10, 1966, the wedding day of Princess Beatrix and Claus von Amsberg, that provoked the most serious unrest: smoke bombs were thrown at the wedding procession and fights with the police broke out across the city. The following month Provo Hans Tuynman was arrested for handing a policeman a leaflet protesting police actions. Street demonstrations followed, along with further arrests, and when Tuynman was sentenced to three months' imprisonment on May 11, anger spread. Through all this conflict, however, the Provos were also winning increased public support: in the municipal elections of 1966 they received over 13,000 votes – two and a half percent of the total, and enough for a seat on the Council. But this achievement didn't mean the end of the Provos' street actions. Indeed, the next event in which they were involved was one of the most violent of the 1960s. It started with a demonstration by city construction workers on June 13, during which one worker suddenly died. Such was the anti-police feeling that it was assumed he had been killed by police patrolling the protest, and the following day the workers staged a strike and marched through the city with thousands of supporters, including the Provos who by now were regarded as the champions of the public versus the police. The worker actually died of a heart attack, but the mood had been set and there were clashes between police and rioters for four days. A month later The Hague government ordered the dismissal of Amsterdam's Police Chief and, a year later, that of the mayor.

But by May 1967 the Provos' inspiration was waning, and at a final gathering in the Vondelpark they announced that they would disband, even though they still had a member on the City Council.

The next phase in the Provo phenomenon was the creation of the "Oranje Free State", a so-called alternative society set up by van Duyn in 1970 in the form of a mock government with its own "ministers" and "policies". The new movement, whose members were named **Kabouters** after a helpful gnome in Dutch folklore, was successful if short-lived. It adopted some of the more reasonable "white policies" of the Provos and went so far as to win seats in six municipalities, including five in Amsterdam on a vaguely socialist ticket. "No longer the socialism of the clenched fist, but of the intertwined fingers, the erect penis, the escaping butterfly . . . ", their manifesto proclaimed. But before long the Kabouter movement, too, faded amid disputes over methodology.

As the Provo and Kabouter movements disappeared, many of their members joined **neighbourhood committees**, set up to oppose certain plans of the City Council. By far the most violently attacked scheme was that of building a **metro line** through the Nieuwmarkt to the new suburb of Bijlmermeer. The initial idea was conceived in 1968 and consisted of a plan to build a four-line network for an estimated f250 million. By 1973, the cost had risen to f1500 million – for just one line.

It was the Council's policy of coping with the ever-growing problem of housing by **moving residents** to these suburbs that infuriated Amsterdammers, who felt that their town was being sold off to big businesses and their homes converted to banks and offices, thereby creating a city centre that ordinary people couldn't afford to live in. The opponents of the metro plan objected to the number of houses that would have to be demolished, contending that it was merely an elitist development, of no real use to the public.

Official **clearance of the Nieuwmarkt** area was scheduled for February 1975 but confrontation between police and protesters began the previous December. Many residents of the condemned houses refused to move, and further violent clashes were inevitable. The worst came on March 24, 1975, a day that became known as **Blue Monday**: the police began a clearing action early in the morning and their tactics were heavy-handed. Tear-gas grenades were fired through windows smashed by water cannons, armoured cars ripped through front doors, and the police charged in to arrest occupants (residents and supporters), who threw paint cans and powder bombs in retaliation. The fighting went on late into the night with thousands of demonstrators joining in. At the end of the day, thirty people – including nineteen policemen – had been wounded, and 47 arrested; 450 complaints were filed against the police. A couple of weeks later came another big clash, but this time the demonstrators used different tactics, forming human barricades in front of the houses to be cleared. The police charged, armed with truncheons; it was an easy eviction. But the protestors had made their point, and afterwards showed their spirit of rebellion by holding parties on the rubble-strewn sites. Despite continuing opposition, the metro eventually opened in 1980.

The Squatting Movement

Meanwhile the ever-increasing problem of housing was bringing about the emergence of a new movement – the **squatters**. At first the squatters' movement was peripheral, consisting mainly of independently operating neighbourhood committees. There was little sense of unity until joint actions to defend a handful of symbolic

Amsterdam squats took place. These shaped the development of the squatters' movement, today a strong political force with clearly defined rights and the ear of the City Council.

Four events help explain how this transformation of the squatters' movement occurred: the actions at the key squats of Vondelstraat, Lucky Luyk and Wyers – and the national day of squatting on April 30, 1980.

The end of the **Vondelstraat** squat in Amsterdam's most prestigious neighbourhood near the Rijksmuseum was perhaps the most famous squatting event in The Netherlands. Three days after the empty office premises were occupied in March 1980, police tanks were ordered to remove the squatters. About 500 police took part and the resulting riots spread through the streets and reached the tourist area of Leidseplein. Battles raged the whole day and fifty people were wounded. The squatters were evicted, but it wasn't long before they reoccupied the building. The significance of the Vondelstraat squat was that the attempted eviction and ensuing riots cost the Council a considerable amount of money – a fact the squatters used tactically, making future evictions too expensive for the authorities to undertake.

The next major event involved not a specific squat but protest actions on April 30, 1980 – the **coronation day** of Queen Beatrix. Squatters in Amsterdam and throughout The Netherlands staged protests against the huge amounts of money being spent on the festivities, in addition to the reputed f84 million spent on the rebuilding of her residence in The Hague. Two hundred buildings in 27 cities were squatted; half of these squats were cleared the same day, and it was one of these clearances that sparked off the first battle in Amsterdam. Then, in the afternoon, a protest demonstration set off to march through the city to Dam Square where the crowning ceremony was taking place. Confrontation with the police began almost immediately on Waterlooplein, and from then on the city centre turned into complete chaos. The squatters' ranks were swelled by other protesters angered by the coronation expenditure at a time when the Amsterdam City Council claimed it could not afford to build homes. Public festivities came to an abrupt halt as fighting broke out in the streets and continued until the early hours. Tear gas enveloped the city while Special Squad Police made repeated charges, and many revellers

were caught up with the rebels as the police cordoned off the most militant areas.

By 1982 the squatting movement was reaching its peak. After the success of the Vondelstraat squat in 1980, an estimated 10,000 squatters took over buildings across Amsterdam. The eviction of those who had occupied **Lucky Luyk**, a villa on the Jan Luykenstraat, was the most violent and the most expensive (damage ran into millions of guilders) the city had known to date.

Lucky Luyk was originally squatted in 1981 after standing empty for a few years. In October 1980 squatters were forcibly evicted by the *knokploegen* – groups of heavies rented by property owners to protect their investments. Two months later the owners of the villa won a court order for the evacuation of the building. At this stage, the Amsterdam City Council stepped in to pre-empt the violence that was certain to accompany such an action: they bought the villa for f350,000 – giving the owners an easy f73,000 profit. The squatters weren't happy, but agreed to leave the building if it were used for young people's housing. On October 11, 1982, two days before a meeting between the Council and the squatters, twelve policemen from the Special Squad broke into Lucky Luyk through the roof and arrested the five occupants – a surprise attack that enraged squatters across the country and resulted in sympathy actions in many other cities.

In Amsterdam, riots soon started and lasted for three days. Supporters of the Lucky Luyk, who included many non-squatters, built barricades, wrecked cars, destroyed property and set fire to a tram, while police retaliated with tear gas and water cannons. The mayor declared unprecedented emergency measures, permitting police to arrest anyone suspected of disrupting public order.

The squatters had learned a lesson: the authorities had had enough and were learning new and easier methods of eviction – and were prepared to evict at any cost. Squatters needed to develop a new defence tactic. They hit on politics, and found a new case to fight – **Wyers**. This building, a former distribution centre for a textile firm, had been occupied in October 1981 by about a hundred squatters from all over the city. They were soon informed that *Hollandse Beton Maatschappij*, one of the country's largest building companies, had just obtained permission to build luxury apartments and shops on the site. Trouble was postponed, however, when *HBM* decided the time was not right for their financial investment and scrapped their plans. But in the spring of 1982 they reapplied for building rights, this time to put up a hotel on behalf of Holiday Inn. The initial application was turned down, but an amended plan was approved by the Council in June 1983. An eviction order was presented to the Wyers inhabitants, but the squatters found legal loopholes within the eviction order and the clearance was delayed.

The squatters were also busy preparing an alternative plan to present to the Council, which involved using the building as a combined cultural-residential complex with space for small businesses and studios. This constructive alternative won the support of many people, and even the Council considered it a viable idea. Dialogue between the Council and the squatters continued, but Wyers was cleared in February 1984, with the usual pictures of water cannons and tear gas spread across the front pages of Europe's newspapers. The eviction itself was relatively peaceful: the squatters had decided not to resist and instead linked arms around the site and waited for the police onslaught. Today the Holiday Inn stands on Nieuwe Zijds Voorburgwal as a testament to the fact that the squatters failed here: but as banners proclaimed after the eviction, "You can demolish Wyers but will never destroy the ideas behind Wyers".

Amsterdam Today

The social consciousness and radicalism of the 1960s reached Amsterdam early, and word of the psychedelic revolution was quick to catch on. Dam Square and the Vondelpark became open-air urban campsites, and the pilgrims of alternative culture descended on the easy-going, dope-happy capital. Just as quickly the revolution faded, replaced by the cynicism of the 1970s and, more recently, the resurgence of the right. The city's **housing problems** became a counter-culture focus in the 1960s and early 1970s (see above), and US deployment of **cruise missiles** in The Netherlands temporarily galvanized opposition in the early 1980s. In spite of large-scale protest (over 4 million people signed an anti-cruise petition, the *volkspetitonnment*, and there were many demonstrations in the city), the missiles were scheduled to be deployed in 1985; the nearest missile base to Amsterdam, **Woensdrecht**, was seventy miles away and the focus of popular opposition. However, arms

negotiations between the US and USSR meant that the missiles never arrived – and that the buildings created to house them were all a waste of time and money.

Today, even under the socialist mayor Ed van Thijn, new housing is firmly aimed at Amsterdam's luxury hotel market rather than at its residential needs, and the city's former radicalism seems – for the moment at least – suspended. One of the controversial issues of recent years has been the building of the **Muziektheater/Stadhuis** on Waterlooplein. Historically the site chosen for the new opera building was sensitive, as it was part of the old Jodenhoek and had been a public space for centuries; politically, the building of a highbrow cultural centre was attacked as elitist; and architecturally, the plans were a clumsy hybrid, different designers being responsible for each section.

The Muziektheater was bound to come in for flak, and got it from the **Stopera** campaign, named after the early label for the building and a convenient contraction of "Stop the Opera". No doubt the fact that Amsterdam was angling for the 1992 Olympics was reason for the Council to railroad the plans through, yet, compared to the previous fracas, protest was surprisingly slight. Though the building is today an ugly intruder on the Amstel, it seems to have won over many of its erstwhile opponents – perhaps because Amsterdammers can accommodate any public building more easily than a private one. On the other hand, it's a sign of the times (and the city's gentrification) that there's been little protest over the new casino that's about to open just off the Leidseplein, or the private residential and shopping development – of massive and unappealing proportions – that is being built alongside it.

Yet some of the ideas (and idealism) of a few years back seem to be bearing fruit on a national level. In the elections of 1989 **Groen Links**, the Green-Left coalition of mainly small left and ecology parties, had a strong showing, and a year previously, The Netherlands had become the first European country to officially adopt a **National Environment Plan**, a radical agenda of Green policies: as yet, however, the Plan has still to be implemented. Also, the city council has recently adopted a plan for a **traffic-free centre** after a narrow majority voted for the policy in an admittedly low turnout referendum. On the other hand, the far-right **Centrum Democratische** party, led by Hans Janmaat, also won enough votes to enable him to gain an unprecedented seat in the Lower House of the country's parliament, an event which occasioned multiple demonstrations. There's something naggingly illiberal, too, in the City Council's decision to set up an employment-scheme-cum-"Guardian Angels"-type force, the *Stadswacht*, to patrol Leidseplein, Rembrandtsplein and other hot spots on the lookout for drug dealers and sundry petty criminals; although this has largely sunk without trace, the days of "Happenings", helpful gnomes and white bicycles now seems a world away. As the most powerful group in the Social Democratic Party put it, the *Nieuw Links* ("New Left") has largely given way to the era of the *Nieuw Flinks* ("New Firm").

The success of the traffic-free centre scheme focused attention on other transport-related developments: with new contruction methods that allow lengthy tunnelling without razing everything above ground, the **metro** seems to be returning to favour, though to remove associations of the earlier protests it's now referred to as the *snelltram*. Similarly the **IJ-Boulevard** scheme is intended to link the western harbours to the east (where a new housing project is planned), with modern office developments and high income housing running along the route.

Schiphol airport is increasingly a problem. Essential to the national economy (it's Europe's most important airport, after Heathrow), it will need to grow in the next few years, which means the area aound it will suffer further. Already there are doubts abouts the airport's safety: in October 1992 an El Al Boeing 747 freighter plane **crashed** into the Bijlmermeer housing estate, narrowly missing a block scheduled for demolition and destroying the showpiece of the redesigned estate. Around fifty people were killed, though the exact total will never be known: the estate was densly filled with people from Surinam and the Antillian communities, some of whom were probably in the country illegally. The plane's cargo of kerosene and secret unspecified "military chemicals" destroyed a vast swathe of the estate, and it's fortunate that casualties were relatively low.

One aftermath of the disaster was that the government ordered an amnesty on Surinam and Antillian immigrants who had entered the country illegally, in order that a full death toll could be worked out. The resulting racist backlash this caused added to the attacks on foreign immigrants in western Europe at the time, though this was not nearly as bad as those in Germany.

Dutch Art

This is the very briefest of introductions to the subject, designed to serve only as a quick reference on your way round the major galleries. For more in-depth and academic studies, see the recommendations in the Books listings, below. And for where to find the paintings themselves, turn to the hit list at the end.

Beginnings

Until the sixteenth century the area now known as the Low Countries was in effect one country, the most artistically productive part of which was Flanders in modern Belgium, and it was there that the solid realist base of later Dutch painting developed. Today the works of these **early Flemish painters** are pretty sparse in Holland, and even in Belgium few collections are as complete as they might be; indeed, many ended up as the property of the ruling Habsburgs and were removed to Spain. Most Dutch galleries do, however, have a few examples.

Jan van Eyck (1385–1441) is generally regarded as the originator of Low Countries painting, and has even been credited with the invention of oil painting itself – though it seems more likely that he simply perfected a new technique by thinning his paint with the recently discovered turpentine, thus making it more flexible. His most famous work still in the Low Countries, the Ghent *altarpiece* (debatably

painted with the help of his lesser-known brother, Hubert), was revolutionary in its realism, for the first time using elements of native landscape in depicting biblical themes.

Firmly in the van Eyck tradition were the **Master of Flemalle** (1387–1444) and **Rogier van der Weyden** (1400–64). The Flemalle master is a shadowy figure: some believe he was the teacher of van der Weyden, others that the two artists were in fact the same person. There are differences between the two, however: the Flemalle master's paintings are close to van Eyck's, whereas van der Weyden shows a more emotional and religious intensity. Van der Weyden influenced such painters as **Dieric Bouts** (1415–75), who was born in Haarlem but was active in Louvain, and is recognizable by his stiff, rather elongated figures. **Hugo van der Goes** (d. 1482) was the next Ghent master after van Eyck, most famous for the *Portinari altarpiece* in Florence's *Uffizi*; after a short painting career, he died insane. Few doubt that **Hans Memling** (1440–94) was a pupil of van der Weyden: active in Bruges throughout his life, he is best remembered for the pastoral charm of his landscapes and the quality of his portraiture, much of which survives on the rescued side panels of triptychs. More renowned are **Hieronymus Bosch** (1450–1516), whose frequently reprinted and discussed religious allegories are filled with macabre visions of tortured people and grotesque beasts, and **Pieter Bruegel the Elder** (1525–69), whose gruesome allegories and innovative interpretations of religious subjects are firmly placed in Low Countries settings.

Meanwhile, there were movements based to the north of Flanders. **Geertgen tot Sint Jans** ("Little Gerard of the Brotherhood of St. John") (d. 1490), a student of **Albert van Ouwater**, had been working in **Haarlem**, initiating – in a strangely naive style – an artistic tradition in the city that would prevail throughout the seventeenth century. **Jan Mostaert** (1475–1555) took over after Geertgen's death, and continued to develop a style that diverged more and more from that of the southern provinces. **Lucas van Leyden** (1489–1533) was the first painter to effect real changes in northern painting. Born in Leiden, his bright colours and narrative technique were refreshingly new at the time, and he introduced a novel dynamism into what had become a rigidly formal treatment of devotional subjects. There was rivalry, of course. Eager to publicize Haarlem as the artistic capital of the northern Netherlands, Carel van Mander (see below) claimed Haarlem native **Jan van Scorel** (1495–1562) as the better painter, complaining, too, of van Leyden's dandyish ways.

Certainly van Scorel's influence should not be underestimated. At this time every painter was expected to travel to Italy to view the works of Renaissance artists. When the Bishop of Utrecht became Pope Hadrian VI, he took van Scorel with him as court painter, giving him the opportunity to introduce Italian styles into what had been a completely independent tradition. Hadrian died soon after, and van Scorel returned north, combining the ideas he had picked up in Italy with Haarlem realism and passing them on to **Maerten van Heemskerck** (1498–1574), who went off to Italy himself in 1532, staying there five years before returning to Haarlem.

The Golden Age

The seventeenth century begins with **Carel van Mander**, Haarlem painter, art impressario and one of the few chroniclers of the art of the Low Countries. His *Schilderboek* of 1604 put Flemish and Dutch traditions into context for the first time, and in addition, specified the rules of fine painting. Examples of his own work are rare, but his followers were many, among them **Cornelius Cornelisz van Haarlem** (1562–1638), who produced elegant renditions of biblical and mythical themes; and **Hendrik Goltzius** (1558–1616), who was a skilled engraver and an integral member of van Mander's Haarlem academy. These painters' enthusiasm for Italian art, combined with the influence of a late revival of Gothicism, resulted in works that combined Mannerist and Classical elements. An interest in realism was also felt, and for them, the subject became less important than the way in which it was depicted: biblical stories became merely a vehicle whereby artists could apply their skills in painting the human body, landscapes, or copious displays of food – all of which served to break religion's stranglehold on art, and make legitimate a whole range of everyday subjects for the painter.

In Holland (and this was where the north and the south finally diverged) this break with tradition was compounded by the **Reformation**: the austere Calvinism that had replaced the Catholic faith in the northern provinces had no use for images or symbols of devotion in its churches. Instead, painters catered to the public, and no longer visited Italy to learn their craft; the real giants of the seventeenth century – Hals, Rembrandt, Vermeer – stayed in The Netherlands all their lives. Another innovation was that painting split into more distinct categories – genre, portrait, landscape, etc. – and artists tended (with notable exceptions) to confine themselves to one field throughout their careers. So began the greatest age of Dutch art.

Historical and Religious Painting

If Italy continued to hold sway in The Netherlands it was not through the Renaissance painters but rather via the fashionable new realism of Caravaggio. Many artists – Rembrandt for one – continued to portray classical subjects, but in a way that was totally at odds with the Mannerists' stylish flights of imagination. The Utrecht artist, **Abraham Bloemaert** (1564–1651), though a solid Mannerist throughout his career, encouraged these new ideas, and his students – **Gerard van Honthorst** (1590–1656), **Hendrik Terbrugghen** (1588–1629), and **Dirck van Baburen** (1590–1624) – formed the nucleus of the influential **Utrecht School**, which followed Caravaggio almost to the point of slavishness. Honthorst was perhaps the leading figure, learning his craft from Bloemaert and travelling to Rome, where he was nicknamed "Gerardo delle Notti" for his ingenious handling of light and shade. This was, however, to become in his later paintings more routine technique than inspired invention, and though a supremely competent artist, Honthorst remains somewhat discredited among critics today. Terbrugghen's reputation seems to have aged rather better: he soon forgot Caravaggio and developed a more personal style, his later, lighter work having a great influence on the young Vermeer. After the obligatory jaunt to Rome, Baburen shared a studio with Terbrugghen and produced some fairly original work – work which also had some influence on Vermeer – but today he is the least studied member of the group and few of his paintings survive.

But it's **Rembrandt** who was considered the most original historical artist of the seventeenth century, painting religious scenes throughout his life. In the 1630s, the poet and statesman Constantijn Huygens procured for him his greatest commission – a series of five paintings of the Passion, beautifully composed and uncompromisingly realistic. Later, however, Rembrandt received fewer and fewer commissions, since his treatment of biblical and historical subjects was far less dramatic than that of his contemporaries. It's significant that while the more conventional Jordaens, Honthorst, and van Everdingen were busy decorating the Huis ten Bosch near The Hague for patron Stadholder Frederick Henry, Rembrandt was having his monumental *Conspiracy of Claudius Civilis* (painted for the new Amsterdam Town Hall) rejected – probably because it was thought too pagan an interpretation of what was an important symbolic event in Dutch history. **Aert van Gelder** (1645–1727), Rembrandt's last pupil and probably the only one to concentrate on historical painting, followed the style of his master closely, producing shimmering biblical scenes well into the eighteenth century.

Genre Painting

Genre refers to scenes from everyday life, a subject that, with the decline of the church as patron, became popular in Holland by the mid-seventeenth century. Many painters devoted themselves solely to such work. Some genre paintings were simply non-idealized portrayals of common scenes, while others, by means of symbols or carefully disguised details, made moral entreaties to the viewer.

Among early-seventeenth-century painters, **Hendrik Terbrugghen** and **Gerard Honthorst** spent much of their time on religious subjects, but also adapted the realism and strong chiaroscuro learned from Caravaggio to a number of tableaux of everyday life. **Frans Hals**, too, is better known as a portraitist, but his early genre paintings no doubt influenced his pupil, **Adriaen Brouwer** (1605–38), whose riotous tavern scenes were well received in their day and collected by, among others, Rubens and Rembrandt. Brouwer spent only a couple of years in Haarlem under Hals before returning to his native Flanders where he influenced the younger **David Teniers**. **Adriaen van Ostade** (1610–85), on the other hand, stayed there most of his life, skilfully painting groups of peasants and tavern brawls – though his later acceptance by the establishment

led him to water down the realism he had learnt from Brouwer. He was teacher to his brother **Isaak** (1621–49), who produced a large number of open-air peasant scenes, subtle combinations of genre and landscape work.

The English critic E. V. Lucas dubbed Teniers, Brouwer and Ostade "coarse and boorish" compared with **Jan Steen** (1625–79), who, along with Vermeer, is probably the most admired Dutch genre painter. You can see what he had in mind: Steen's paintings offer the same Rabelaisian peasantry in full fling, but they go their debauched ways in broad daylight, and nowhere do you see the filthy rogues in shadowy hovels favoured by Brouwer and Ostade. Steen offers more humour, too, as well as more moralizing, identifying with the hedonistic mob and reproaching them at the same time. Indeed, many of his pictures are illustrations of well-known proverbs of the time – popular epithets on the evils of drink or the transience of human existence that were supposed to teach as well as entertain.

Gerrit Dou (1613–75) was Rembrandt's Leiden contemporary and one of his first pupils. It's difficult to detect any trace of the master's influence in his work, however; Dou initiated a style of his own: tiny, minutely realized, and beautifully finished views of a kind of ordinary life that was decidedly more genteel than Brouwer's – or even Steen's for that matter. He was admired, above all, for his painstaking attention to detail: and he would, they say, sit in his studio for hours waiting for the dust to settle before starting work. Among his students, **Frans van Mieris** (1635–81) continued the highly finished portrayals of the Dutch bourgeoisie, as did **Gabriel Metsu** (1629–67) – perhaps Dou's greatest pupil – whose pictures often convey an overtly moral message. Another pupil of Rembrandt's, though a much later one, was **Nicholaes Maes** (1629–93), whose early paintings were almost entirely genre paintings, sensitively executed and again with a moralizing message. His later work shows the influence of a more refined style of portrait, which he had picked up in France.

As a native of Zwolle, **Gerard ter Borch** (1619–81) found himself far from all these Leiden/Rembrandt connections; despite trips abroad to most of the artistic capitals of Europe, he remained very much a provincial painter all his life, depicting Holland's merchant class at play and becoming renowned for his curious doll-like figures and his enormous ability to capture the textures of different cloths. His domestic scenes were not unlike those of **Pieter de Hooch** (1629– after 1684), whose simple depictions of everyday life are deliberately unsentimental, and, for the first time, have little or no moral commentary. De Hooch's favourite trick was to paint darkened rooms with an open door leading through to a sunlit courtyard, a practice that, along with his trademark rusty red colour, makes his work easy to identify and, at its best, exquisite. That said, his later pictures reflect the encroaching decadence of the Dutch republic: the rooms are more richly decorated, the arrangements more contrived and the subjects far less homely.

It was, however, **Jan Vermeer** (1632–75) who brought the most sophisticated methods to painting interiors, depicting the play of natural light on indoor surfaces with superlative skill. And it's for this and the curious peace and intimacy of his pictures that he's best known. Another recorder of the better-heeled Dutch households, and, like de Hooch, without the moral tone, he is regarded (with Hals and Rembrandt) as one of the big three Dutch painters – though he, was, it seems, a slow worker, and only about forty small paintings can be attributed to him with any certainty. Living all his life in Delft, Vermeer is perhaps the epitome of the seventeenth-century Dutch painter – rejecting the pomp and ostentation of the High Renaissance to quietly record his contemporaries at home, painting for a public that demanded no more than that.

Portraits

Naturally, the ruling bourgeoisie of Holland's flourishing mercantile society wanted to put their success on record, and it's little wonder that portraiture was the best way for a young painter to make a living. **Michiel Jansz Miereveld** (1567–1641), court painter to Frederick Henry in The Hague, was the first real portraitist of the Dutch Republic, but it wasn't long before his stiff and rather conservative figures were superseded by the more spontaneous renderings of **Frans Hals** (1585–1666). Hals is perhaps best known for his "corporation pictures" – portraits of the members of the Dutch civil guard regiments that had been formed in most larger towns while the threat of invasion by the Spanish was still imminent. These large group pieces demanded superlative technique, since the painter had to create

a collection of individual portraits while retaining a sense of the group, and accord prominence based on the importance of the sitter and the size of the payment each had made. Hals was particularly good at this, using innovative lighting effects, arranging his sitters subtly, and putting all the elements together in a fluid and dynamic composition. He also painted many individual portraits, making the ability to capture fleeting and telling expressions his trademark; his pictures of children are particularly sensitive. Later in life, his work became darker and more akin to Rembrandt's.

Jan Cornelisz Verspronck (1597–1662) and **Bartholomeus van der Helst** (1613–70) were the other great Haarlem portraitists after Frans Hals – Verspronck recognizable by the smooth, shiny glow he always gave to his sitters' faces, van der Helst by a competent but unadventurous style. Of the two, van der Helst was the more popular, influencing a number of later painters and leaving Haarlem while still young to begin a solidly successful career as portrait painter to Amsterdam's burghers.

The reputation of **Rembrandt van Rijn** (1606– 69) is still relatively recent – nineteenth-century connoisseurs preferred Gerard Dou – but he is now justly regarded as one of the greatest and most versatile painters of all time. Born in Leiden, the son of a miller, he was apprenticed at an early age to **Jacob van Swanenburgh**, a then quite important, though uninventive, local artist. He shared a studio with **Jan Lievens**, a promising painter and something of a rival for a while (now all but forgotten), before going up to Amsterdam to study under the fashionable **Pieter Lastman**. Soon he was painting commissions for the city elite and he also became an accepted member of their circle. The poet and statesman Constantin Huygens acted as his agent, pulling strings to obtain all of Rembrandt's more lucrative jobs, and in 1634 Rembrandt married Saskia van Ulenborch, daughter of the burgomaster of Leeuwarden and quite a catch for the still relatively humble artist. His self-portraits at the time show the confident face of security – on top of things and quite sure of where he's going.

Rembrandt would not always be the darling of the Amsterdam smart set, but his fall from grace was still some way off when he painted the *Night Watch* – a group portrait often associated with the artist's decline in popularity. But, although Rembrandt's fluent arrangement of his subjects was totally original, there's no evidence that the military company who commissioned the painting was anything but pleased with the result. More likely culprits are the artist's later pieces, whose obscure lighting and psychological insight took the conservative Amsterdam burghers by surprise. His patrons were certainly not sufficiently enthusiastic about his work to support his taste for art collecting and his expensive house on Jodenbreestraat, and in 1656 possibly the most brilliant artist the city would ever know was declared bankrupt; he died thirteen years later – as his last self-portraits show, a broken and embittered old man. Throughout his career Rembrandt maintained a large studio, and his influence pervaded the next generation of Dutch painters. Some – Dou and Maes – more famous for their genre work, have already been mentioned. Others turned to portraiture.

Govert Flinck (1615–60) was perhaps Rembrandt's most faithful follower, and he was, ironically, given the job of decorating Amsterdam's new town hall after his teacher had been passed over. He died at a tragically young age before he could execute his designs, and Rembrandt was one of several artists commissioned to paint them – though his contribution was removed shortly afterwards. The work of **Ferdinand Bol** (1616–80) was so heavily influenced by Rembrandt that for a long time art historians couldn't tell the two apart. Most of the pitifully slim extant work of **Carel Fabritius** (1622–54) was portraiture, but he too died young, before he could properly realize his promise as perhaps the most gifted of all Rembrandt's students. Generally regarded as the teacher of Vermeer, he forms a link between the two masters, combining Rembrandt's technique with his own practice of painting figures against a dark background, prefiguring the lighting and colouring of the Delft painter.

Landscapes

Aside from Bruegel, whose depictions of his native surroundings make him the first true Low Countries' landscape painter, **Gillis van Coninxloo** (1544–1607) stands out as the earliest Dutch landscapist. He imbued the native scenery with elements of fantasy, painting the richly wooded views he had seen on his travels around Europe as backdrops to biblical scenes. In the early seventeenth century, **Hercules Seghers** (1590–1638), apprenticed to Coninxloo,

carried on his mentor's style of depicting forested and mountainous landscapes, some real, others not: his work is scarce but is believed to have had considerable influence on the landscape work of Rembrandt. **Esaias van der Velde**'s (1591–1632) quaint and unpretentious scenes show the first real affinity with the Dutch countryside but – though his influence, too, was great – he was soon overtaken in stature by his pupil **Jan van Goyen** (1596–1656), a remarkable painter who belongs to the so-called "tonal phase" of Dutch landscape painting. Van Goyen's early pictures were highly coloured and close to those of his teacher, but it didn't take him long to develop a markedly personal touch, using tones of greens, browns and greys to lend everything a characteristic translucent haze. His paintings are, above all, of nature, and if he included figures it was just for the sake of scale. Neglected until a little over a century ago, his fluid and rapid brushwork became more accepted as the Impressionists rose in stature.

Another "tonal" painter and a native of Haarlem, **Salomon van Ruisdael** (1600–70) was also directly affected by van der Velde, and his simple but atmospheric, though not terribly adventurous, landscapes were for a long time consistently confused with those of van Goyen. More esteemed is his nephew, **Jacob van Ruisdael** (1628–82), generally considered the greatest of all Dutch landscapists, whose fastidiously observed views of quiet flatlands dominated by stormy skies were to influence European painters' impressions of nature right up to the nineteenth century. Constable, certainly, acknowledged a debt to him. Ruisdael's foremost pupil was **Meindert Hobbema** (1638–1709), who followed the master faithfully, sometimes even painting the same views (his *Avenue at Middelharnis* may be familiar).

Nicholas Berchem (1620–83) and **Jan Both** (1618–52) were the "Italianizers" of Dutch landscapes. They studied in Rome and were influenced by Claude, taking back to Holland rich, golden views of the world, full of steep gorges and hills, picturesque ruins and wandering shepherds. **Allart van Everdingen** (1621–75) had a similar approach, but his subject matter stemmed from travels in Scandinavia, which, after his return to Holland, he reproduced in all its mountainous glory.

Aelbert Cuyp (1620–91), on the other hand, stayed in Dordrecht all his life, painting what was probably the favourite city skyline of Dutch land-scapists. He inherited the warm tones of the Italianizers, and his pictures are always suffused with a deep, golden glow.

Of a number of **specialist seventeenth-century painters** who can be included here, **Paulus Potter** (1625–54) is rated as the best painter of **domestic animals**. He produced a fair amount of work in a short life, the most reputed being his lovingly executed pictures of cows and horses. The accurate rendering of **architectural features** also became a specialized field, in which **Pieter Saenredam** (1597–1665), with his finely realized paintings of Dutch church interiors, is the most widely known exponent. **Emanuel de Witte** (1616–92) continued in the same vein, though his churches lack the spartan crispness of Saenredam's. **Gerrit Berckheyde** (1638–98) worked in Haarlem soon after but he limited his views to the outside of buildings, producing vari-ations on the same scenes around town.

In the seventeenth century another thriving category of painting was the **still life**, in which objects were gathered together to remind the viewer of the transience of human life and the meaninglessness of all worldly pursuits: often a skull would be joined by a book, a pipe or a goblet, and some half-eaten food. Again, two Haarlem painters dominated this field: **Pieter Claesz** (1598–1660) and **Willem Heda** (1594–1680), who confined themselves almost entirely to these carefully arranged groups of objects.

The 18th and 19th Centuries

With the demise of Holland's economic boom, the quality – and originality – of Dutch painting began to decline. The delicacy of some of the classical seventeenth-century painters was replaced by finicky still lifes and minute studies of flowers, or finely finished portraiture and religious scenes, as in the work of **Adrian van der Werff** (1659–1722). Of the era's big names, **Gerard de Lairesse** (1640–1711) spent most of his time decorating the splendid civic halls and palaces that were going up all over the place, and, like the buildings he worked on, his style and influ-ences were French. **Jacob de Wit** (1695–1754) continued where Lairesse left off, receiving more commissions in churches as Catholicism was allowed out of the closet. The period's only painter of any true renown was **Cornelis Troost** (1697–1750) who, although he didn't produce anything really new, painted competent portraits

and some neat, faintly satirical pieces that have since earned him the title of "The Dutch Hogarth". Cosy interiors also continued to prove popular and the Haarlem painter, **Wybrand Hendriks** (1744–1831), satisfied demand with numerous proficient examples.

Johann Barthold Jongkind (1819–91) was the first great artist to emerge in the nineteenth century, painting landscapes and seascapes that were to influence Monet and the early Impressionists: he spent most of his life in France and his work was exhibited in Paris with the Barbizon painters, though he owed less to them than to the landscapes of van Goyen and the seventeenth-century "tonal" artists.

Jongkind's work was a logical precursor to the art of the **Hague School**, a group of painters based in and around that city between 1870 and 1900 who tried to re-establish a characteris-tically Dutch national school of painting. They produced atmospheric studies of the dunes and polderlands around The Hague, nature pictures that are characterized by grey, rain-filled skies, windswept seas, and silvery, flat beaches – pictures that, for some, verge on the sentimental. **J. H. Weissenbruch** (1824–1903) was a founding member, a specialist in low, flat beach scenes dotted with stranded boats. The banker-turned-artist **H. W. Mesdag** (1831–1915) did the same but with more skill than imagination, while **Jacob Maris** (1837–99), one of three artist brothers, was perhaps the most typically Hague School painter, with his rural and sea scenes heavily covered by grey chasing skies. His brother **Matthijs** (1839–1917) was less predictable, ulti-mately tiring of his colleagues' interest in straight observation and going to London to design windows, while **Willem** (1844–1910), the young-est, is best known for his small, unpretentious studies of nature.

Anton Mauve (1838–88) is more famous, an exponent of soft, pastel landscapes and an early teacher of van Gogh. Profoundly influenced by the French Barbizon painters – Corot, Millet et al. – he went to Hilversum in 1885 to set up his own group, which became known as the "Dutch Barbizon". **Jozef Israëls** (1826–1911) has often been likened to Millet, though it's generally agreed that he had more in common with the Impressionists, and his best pictures are his melancholy portraits and interiors. Lastly, **Johan Bosboom**'s (1817–91) church interiors may be said to sum up the nostalgia of the Hague

School: shadowy and populated by figures in seventeenth-century dress, they seem to yearn for Holland's Golden Age.

Vincent van Gogh (1853–90), on the other hand, was one of the least "Dutch" of Dutch artists, and he lived out most of his relatively short painting career in France. After countless studies of peasant life in his native North Brabant – studies which culminated in the sombre *Potato Eaters* – he went to live in Paris with his art-dealer brother Theo. There, under the influence of the Impressionists, he lightened his palette, following the pointillist work of Seurat and "trying to render intense colour and not a grey harmony". Two years later he went south to Arles, the "land of blue tones and gay colours", and, struck by the harsh Mediterranean light, his characteristic style began to develop. A disastrous attempt to live with Gauguin, and the much-publicized episode when he cut off part of his ear and presented it to a woman in a nearby brothel, led eventually to committal to an asylum at St-Remy, where he produced some of his most famous, and most expressionistic, canvases – strongly coloured and with the paint thickly, almost frantically, applied.

Like van Gogh, **Jan Toorop** (1858–1928) went through multiple artistic changes, though he didn't need to travel the world to do so; he radically adapted his technique from a fairly conventional pointillism through a tired Expressionism to Symbolism with an Art-Nouveau feel. Roughly contemporary, **G. H. Breitner** (1857–1923) was a better painter, and one who refined his style rather than changed it. His snapshot-like impressions of his beloved Amsterdam figure among his best work and offered a promising start to the new century.

The 20th Century

Most of the trends in the visual arts of the early twentieth century found their way to The Netherlands at one time or another: of many minor names, **Jan Sluyters** (1881–1957) was the Dutch pioneer of Cubism. But only one movement was specifically Dutch – **de Stijl** (literally "the Style").

Piet Mondrian (1872–1944) was de Stijl's leading figure, developing the realism he had learned from the Hague School painters – via Cubism, which he criticized for being too cowardly to depart totally from representation – into a complete abstraction of form which he called **neo-plasticism**. He was something of a mystic, and this was to some extent responsible for the direction that de Stijl – and his paintings – took: canvases painted with grids of lines and blocks made up of the three primary colours and white, black and grey. Mondrian believed this freed the work of art from the vagaries of personal perception, making it possible to obtain what he called "a true vision of reality".

De Stijl took other forms too: there was a magazine of the same name, and the movement introduced new concepts into every aspect of design, from painting to interior design to architecture. But in all these media, lines were kept simple, colours bold and clear. **Theo van Doesburg** (1883–1931) was a de Stijl cofounder and major theorist: his work is similar to Mondrian's except for the noticeable absence of thick, black borders and the diagonals that he introduced into his work, calling his paintings "contra-compositions" – which, he said, were both more dynamic and more in touch with twentieth-century life. **Bart van der Leck** (1876–1958) was the third member of the circle, identifiable by white canvases covered by seemingly randomly placed interlocking coloured triangles.

Mondrian split with de Stijl in 1925, going on to attain new artistic extremes of clarity and soberness before moving to New York in the 1940s and producing atypically exuberant works such as *Victory Boogie Woogie* – so named because of the artist's love of jazz.

During and after de Stijl, a number of other movements flourished, though their impact was not so great and their influence largely confined to The Netherlands. The Expressionist **Bergen School** was probably the most localized, its best-known exponent **Charley Toorop** (1891–1955), daughter of Jan, who developed a distinctively glaring but strangely sensitive realism. **De Ploeg** ("The Plough"), centred in Groningen, was headed by **Jan Wiegers** (1893–1959) and influenced by Kirchner and the German Expressionists; the group's artists set out to capture the uninviting landscapes around their native town, and produced violently coloured canvases that hark back to van Gogh. Another group, known as the **Magic Realists**, surfaced in the 1930s, painting quasi-surrealistic scenes that, according to their leading light, **Carel Willinck** (b. 1900), reveal "a world stranger and more dreadful in its haughty impenetrability than the most terrifying nightmare".

Postwar Dutch art began with **CoBrA**: a loose grouping of like-minded painters from Denmark, Belgium and Holland, whose name derives from the initial letters of their respective capital cities. Their first exhibition at Amsterdam's Stedelijk Museum in 1949 provoked a huge uproar, at the centre of which was **Karel Appel** (b. 1921), whose brutal Abstract Expressionist pieces, plastered with paint inches thick, were, he maintained, necessary for the era – indeed, inevitable reflections of it. "I paint like a barbarian in a barbarous age", he claimed. In the graphic arts the most famous twentieth-century figure is **M. C. Escher** (1898–1970).

As for today, there's as vibrant an art scene as there ever was, best exemplified in Amsterdam by the rotating exhibitions of the Stedelijk or the nearby Overholland Museum. Of contemporary Dutch artists, look out for the abstract work of **Edgar Fernhout** and **Ad Dekkers**, the reliefs of **Jan Schoonhoven**, the multimedia productions of **Jan Dibbets**, the glowering realism of **Marlene Dumas**, the imprecisely coloured geometric designs of **Rob van Koningsbruggen**, the smeary expressionism of **Toon Verhoef**, and the exuberant figures of **Rene Daniels** – to name only the most important figures.

Dutch Galleries: a Hit List

In **Amsterdam**, the *Rijksmuseum* gives a complete overview of Dutch art up to the end of the nineteenth century, in particular the work of Rembrandt, Hals, and the major artists of the Golden Age; the *Van Gogh Museum* is best for the Impressionists and, of course, van Gogh; and for twentieth-century and contemporary Dutch art, there's the *Stedelijk*. Within easy reach of the city, the *Frans Hals Museum* in **Haarlem** holds some of the best work of Hals and the Haarlem School; also in Haarlem, the *Teyler's Museum* is strong on eighteenth- and nineteenth-century Dutch works. In **Leiden**, the *Lakenhal* has works by, among others, local artists Dou and Rembrandt, and the *Centraal* in **Utrecht** has paintings by van Scorel and the Utrecht School. Also in Utrecht, the *Catherine Convent Museum* boasts an excellent collection of works by Flemish artists and by Hals and Rembrandt.

Further afield, **The Hague's** *Gemeente Museum* owns the country's largest set of Mondrians, and its *Mauritshuis* collection contains works by Rembrandt, Vermeer and others of the era. The *Boymans van Beuningen Museum* in **Rotterdam** has a weighty stock of works by Flemish primitives and surrealists, as well as works by Rembrandt and other seventeenth-century artists, and nearby **Dordrecht's** *Municipal Museum* offers an assortment of seventeenth-century paintings that includes work by Albert Cuyp, and later canvases by the Hague School and Breitner.

The *Kroller-Muller Museum*, just outside **Arnhem**, is probably the country's finest modern art collection, and has a superb collection of van Goghs; a little further east, **Enschede's** *Rijksmuseum Twenthe* has quality works from the Golden Age to the twentieth century.

The City in Fiction

Amsterdam lives more frantically in fiction than in reality. It's the capital of Dutch literature not only in the sense that most Dutch writers have lived here at some time or are living here now, but it also forms the backdrop to most contemporary Dutch novels. A fair amount of Dutch literature has been translated into English recently, notably the work of Cees Noteboom, Marga Minco, Harry Mulisch and Simon Carmiggelt. There's also, of course, English-language fiction set in Amsterdam or The Netherlands, of which the detective writer Nicolas Freeling is perhaps the best-known exponent.

Simon Carmiggelt

A constant theme in Dutch literature is humour, and Simon Carmiggelt was one of the country's best-loved humorous writers – and a true poet of Amsterdam in his own way. He moved to the capital during the war, working as a production manager and journalist for the then illegal newspaper, Het Parool. In 1946, he started writing a daily column in the paper, entitled *Kronkel*, meaning "twist" or "kink". It was an almost immediate success, and he continued to write his *Kronkels* for several decades, in the end turning out almost 10,000. They're a unique genre – short, usually humorous anecdotes of everyday life, with a strong undercurrent of melancholy and a basic seriousness. They concern ordinary people, poignantly observed with razor-sharp – but never cruel – wit and intelligence. Some of the strongest have been bundled together in anthologies, two of which – *A Dutchman's Slight Adventures* (1966) and *I'm Just Kidding* (1972) – were translated into English. Simon Carmiggelt died in 1989.

Corner

In a café in the Albert Cuypstraat, where the open-air market pulses with sounds and colour, I ran into my friend Ben.

"Did you know Joop Groenteman?" he asked.

"You mean the one who sold fruit?" I replied.

"Yes. You heard about his death?"

I nodded. A fishmonger had told me. "It's a shame", said Ben. "A real loss for the market. He had a nice stall – always polished his fruit. And he had that typical Amsterdam sense of humour that seems to be disappearing. He'd say "Hi" to big people and "Lo" to little ones. If somebody wanted to buy two apples, he'd ask where the party was. No one was allowed to pick and choose his fruit. Joop handed it out from behind the plank. Somebody asked him once if he had a plastic bag, and he said, 'I got false teeth. Ain't that bad enough?' He never lost his touch, not even in the hospital".

"Did you go see him there?" I enquired. "Yes, several times", Ben said. "Once his bed was empty. On the pillow lay a note: 'Back in two hours. Put whatever you brought on the bed.' He had to go on a diet because he was too fat. They weighed him every day. One morning he tied a portable radio around his waist with a rope, put his bathrobe over it, and got on the scale. To the nurse's alarm he'd suddenly gained eight pounds. That was his idea of fun in the hospital. During one visit I asked him when he'd get out. He said, 'Oh, someday soon, either through the front door or the back.'"

Ben smiled sadly.

"He died rather unexpectedly", he resumed. "There was an enormous crowd at his funeral. I was touched by the sight of all his friends from the market standing round the grave with their hats on and each one of them shovelling three spadesful of earth on to his coffin. Oh well, he at least attained the goal of his life".

"What goal?" I asked.

"The same one every open-air merchant has", Ben answered, "a place on a corner. If you're on a corner, you sell more. But it's awfully hard to get a corner place".

"Joop managed it, though?"

"Yes – but not in the Albert Cuyp", said Ben. "That corner place was a sort of obsession to him. He knew his chance was practically nil. So then he decided that if he couldn't get one while he was alive, he'd make sure of it when he died. Every time the collector for the burial insurance came along, he'd say "Remember, I want a corner grave." But when he did die, there wasn't a single corner to be had. Well, that's not quite right. It just happened that there was one corner with a stone to the memory of someone who had died in the furnaces of a concentration camp. Nobody was really buried there. And the cemetery people gave permission to have the stone placed somewhere else and to let Joop have that plot. So he finally got what he wanted. A place on the corner".

Herring-man

It was morning, and I paused to buy a herring at one of those curious legged vending carts that stand along Amsterdam's canals

'Onions?' asked the white-jacketed herring-man. He was big and broad-shouldered, and his hair was turning grey – a football believer, by the looks of him, who never misses Sunday in the stadium.

'No onions,' I answered.

Two other men were standing there eating. They wore overalls and were obviously fellow-workers.

'There's them that take onions, and them that don't,' one of the men said tolerantly. The herring-man nodded.

'Take me, now, I never eat pickles with 'em,' said the other in the coquettish tone of a girl revealing some little charm that she just happens to possess.

'Give me another, please,' I said.

The herring-man cut the fish in three pieces and reached with his glistening hand into the dish of onions.

'No, no onions,' I said.

He smiled his apology. 'Excuse me. My mind was wandering' he said.

The men in overalls also ordered another round and then began to wrangle about some futility or other on which they disagreed. They were still at it after I had paid and proceeded to a café just across from the herring-cart, where I sat down at a table by the window. For Dutchmen they talked rather strenuously with their hands. A farmer once told me that when the first cock begins to crow early in the morning, all the other roosters in the neighbourhood immediately raise their voices, hoping to drown him out. Most males are cut from the same cloth.

'What'll it be?' asked the elderly waitress in the café.

'Coffee.' As she was getting it a fat, slovenly creature came in. Months ago she had had her hair dyed straw yellow, but later had become so nostalgic for her own natural brown that her skull was now dappled with two colours.

'Have you heard?' she asked.

'What?'

'The herring-man's son ran into a streetcar on his motorbike yesterday,' she said, 'and now he's good and dead. The docs at the hospital couldn't save him. They came to tell his pa about a half an hour ago.'

The elderly waitress served my coffee.

'How awful,' she said.

I looked across the street. The overalled quarrellers were gone, and the broad, strong herring-man stood cleaning his fish with automatic expertness.

'The kid was just seventeen,' said the fat woman. 'He was learning to be a pastry cook. Won third prize at the food show with his chocolate castle.'

'Those *motorbikes* are rotten things,' the waitress said.

The herring-man's face showed no expression at all. No pain, no dismay, no despair, no grief. Nothing. He was now busy wrapping up an order for a girl to take with her.

'And the kids always want to show off on 'em,' said the fat woman. 'But you can't impress a streetcar.'

Across the way the herring-man gave the girl her change. Then he went back to his fish-cleaning. You couldn't tell that anything at all had happened to him.

'People are mysterious,' a friend of mine once wrote, and as I thought of those words I suddenly remembered the onions the herring-man nearly gave me with my second fish, his smiling apology: 'My mind was wandering.'

Genius

The little café lay on a broad, busy thoroughfare in one of the new sections of Amsterdam. The barkeeper-host had only one guest: an ancient man who sat amiably behind his empty genever glass. I placed my order and added, 'Give grandfather something, too.'

'You've got one coming,' called the barkeeper. The old man smiled and tipped me a left-handed military salute, his fingers at his fragile temple. Then he got up, walked over to me, and asked, 'Would you be interested in a chance on a first-class smoked sausage, guaranteed weight two pounds?

'I certainly would be,' I replied.

'It just costs a quarter, and the drawing will take place next Saturday,' he said.

I fished out twenty-five cents and put it on the bar, and in return he gave me a piece of cardboard on which the number 79 was written in ink.

'A number with a tail,' he said. 'Lucky for you.'

He picked up the quarter, put on his homburg hat, and left the café with a friendly 'Good afternoon, gentlemen.' Through the window I saw him unlocking an old bicycle. Then, wheeling his means of transport, he disappeared from view.

'How old is he?' I asked.

'Eighty-six.'

'And he still rides a bicycle?'

The barkeeper shook his head.

'No,' he replied, 'but he has to cross over, and it's a busy street. He's got a theory that traffic can see someone with a bicycle in his hand better than someone without a bicycle. So that's the why and the wherefore. When he gets across, he parks the bike and locks it up, and then the next day he's got it all ready to walk across again.'

I thought it over.

'Not a bad idea,' I said.

'Oh, he's all there, that one,' said the barkeeper. 'Take that lottery, now. He made it up himself. I guess he sells about a hundred chances here every week. That's twenty-five guilders. And he only has to fork over one sausage on Saturday evening. Figure it out for yourself.'

I did so, cursorily. He really got his money's worth out of that sausage, no doubt of it.

'And he runs the drawing all by himself,' the barkeeper went on. 'Clever as all get out. Because if a customer says, "I've bought a lot of chances from you, but I never win," you can bet your boots he *will* win the very next Saturday. The old man takes care that he does. Gets the customer off his neck for a good long time. Pretty smart, huh?'

I nodded and said, 'He must have been a businessman?'

'Well no. He was in the navy. They've paid him a pension for ages and ages. He's costing them a pretty penny.'

All of a sudden I saw the old man on the other side of the street. He locked his bicycle against a wall and wandered away.

'He can get home from there without crossing any more streets,' said the barkeeper.

I let him fill my glass again.

'I gave him a drink, but I didn't see him take it,' I remarked.

The barkeeper nodded.

'He's sharp as tacks about that, too,' he said. 'Here's what he does. He's old and spry, and nearly everybody buys him something. But he never drinks more than two a day. So I write all the free ones down for him.' He glanced at a notepad that lay beside the cash register. 'Let's see. Counting the one from you, he's a hundred and sixty-seven to the good.'

Cees Noteboom

Cees Noteboom is one of Holland's best-known writers. He published his first novel in 1955, but only came to the attention of a wider public after the publication of his third novel, *Rituals*, in 1980. The central theme of all his work is the phenomenon of time: *Rituals* in particular is about the passing of time and the different ways of controlling the process. Inni Wintrop, the main character, is an outsider, a "dilettante" as he describes himself. The book is almost entirely set in Amsterdam, and although it describes the inner life of Inni himself, it also paints a vivid picture of the decaying city. Each section details a decade of Inni's life; the one reprinted below describes an encounter from his forties.

Rituals

There were days, thought Inni Wintrop, when it seemed as if a recurrent, fairly absurd phenomenon were trying to prove that the world is an absurdity that can best be approached with nonchalance, because life would otherwise become unbearable.

There were days, for instance, when you kept meeting cripples, days with too many blind people, days when you saw three times in succession a left shoe lying by the roadside. It seemed as if all these things were trying to mean something but could not. They left only a vague sense of unease, as if somewhere there existed a dark plan for the world that allowed itself to be hinted at only in this clumsy way.

The day on which he was destined to meet Philip Taads, of whose existence he had hitherto been unaware, was the day of the three doves.

The dead one, the live one, and the dazed one, which could not possibly have been one and the same, because he had seen the dead one first. These three, he thought later, had made an attempt at annunciation that had succeeded insofar as it had made the encounter with Taads the Younger more mysterious.

It was now 1973, and Inni had turned forty in a decade he did not approve of. One ought not, he felt, to live in the second half of any century, and this particular century was altogether bad. There was something sad and at the same time ridiculous about all these fading years piling on top of one another until at last the millennium arrived. And they contained a contradiction, too: in order to reach the hundred, and in this case the thousand, that had to be completed, one had to add them up; but the feeling that went with the process seemed to have more to do with subtraction. It was as if no one, especially not Time, could wait for those ever dustier, ever higher figures finally to be declared void by a revolution of a row of glittering, perfectly shaped noughts, whereupon they would be relegated to the scrap heap of history. The only people apparently still sure of anything in these days of superstitious expectation were the Pope, the sixth of his name already, a white-robed Italian with an unusually tormented face that faintly resembled Eichmann's, and a number of terrorists of different persuasions, who tried in vain to anticipate the great witches' cauldron. The fact that he was now forty no longer in itself bothered Inni very much.

"Forty," he said, "is the age at which you have to do everything for the third time, or else you'll have to start training to be a cross-tempered old man," and he had decided to do the latter.

After Zita, he had had a long-lasting affair with an actress who had finally, in self-preservation, turned him out of the house like an old chair.

"What I miss most about her," he said to his friend the writer, "is her absence. These people are never at home. You get addicted to that."

He now lived alone and intended to keep it that way. The years passed, but even this was noticeable only in photographs. He bought and sold things, was not addicted to drugs, smoked less than one packet of Egyptian cigarettes a day, and drank neither more nor less than most of his friends.

This was the situation on the radiant June morning when, on the bridge between the Herenstraat and the Prinsenstraat, a dove flew straight at him as if to bore itself into his heart. Instead, it smashed against a car approaching from the Prinsengracht. The car drove on and the dove was left lying in the street, a gray and dusty, suddenly silly-looking little thing. A blonde-haired girl got off her bicycle and went up to the dove at the same time as Inni.

"Is it dead, do you think?" she asked.

He crouched down and turned the bird onto its back. The head did not turn with the rest of the body and continued to stare at the road surface.

"Finito," said Inni.

The girl put her bike away.

"I daren't pick it up," she said, "Will you?"

She used the familiar form of you. As long as they still do that, I am not yet old, thought Inni, picking up the dove. He did not like doves. They were not a bit like the image he used to have of the Holy Ghost, and the fact that all those promises of peace had never come to anything was probably their fault as well. Two white, softly cooing doves in the garden of a Tuscan villa, that was all right, but the gray hordes marching across the Dam Square with spurs on their boots (their heads making those idiotic mechanical pecking movements) could surely have nothing to do with a Spirit which had allegedly chosen that particular shape in which to descend upon Mary.

"What are you going to do with it?" asked the girl.

Inni looked around and saw on the bridge a wooden skip belonging to the Council. He went up to it. It was full of sand. Gently he laid the dove in it. The girl had followed him. An erotic moment. Man with dead dove, girl with bike and blue eyes. She was beautiful.

"Don't put it in there," she said. "The workmen will chuck it straight into the canal."

What does it matter whether it rots away in sand or in water, thought Inni, who often claimed he would prefer to be blown up after his death. But this was not the moment to hold a discourse on transience.

"Are you in a hurry?" he asked.

"No."

"Give me that bag then." From her handlebar hung a plastic bag, one from the Athenaeum Book Store.

"What's in there?"

"A book by Jan Wolkers."

"It can go in there then," said Inni. "There's no blood."

He put the dove in the bag.

"Jump on the back."

He took her bike without looking at her and rode off.

"Hey," she said. He heard her rapid footsteps and felt her jumping on the back of the bike. In the shop windows he caught brief glimpses of something that looked like happiness. Middle-aged gentleman on girl's bicycle, girl in jeans and white sneakers on the back.

He rode down the Prinsengracht to the Haarlemmerdijk and from a distance saw the barriers of the bridge going down. They got off, and as the bridge slowly rose, they saw the second dove. It was sitting inside one of the open metal supports under the bridge, totally unconcerned as it allowed itself to be lifted up like a child on the Ferris wheel.

For a moment Inni felt an impulse to take the dead dove out of the plastic bag and lift it up like a peace offering to its slowly ascending living colleague, but he did not think the girl would like it. And besides, what would be the meaning of such a gesture? He shuddered, as usual not knowing why. The dove came down again and vanished invulnerably under the asphalt. They cycled on, to the Westerpark. With her small, brown hands, the girl dug a grave in the damp, black earth, somewhere in a corner.

"Deep enough?"

"For a dove, yes."

He laid the bird, which was now wearing its head like a hood on its back, into the hole. Together they smoothed the loose earth on top of it.

"Shall we go and have a drink?" he asked.

"All right."

Something in this minimal death, either the death itself or the summary ritual surrounding it, had made them allies. Something now had to happen, and if this something had anything to do with death, it would not be obvious. He cycled along the Nassaukade. She was not heavy. This was what pleased him most about his strange life – that when he had gotten up that morning, he had not known that he would now be cycling here with a girl at his back, but that such a possibility was always there. It gave him, he thought, something invincible. He looked at the faces of

the men in the oncoming cars, and he knew that his life, in its absurdity, was right. Emptiness, loneliness, anxiety – these were the drawbacks – but there were also compensations, and this was one of them. She was humming softly and then fell silent. She said suddenly, as if she had taken a decision, "This is where I live."

Translated by Adrienne Dixon; ©Louisiana State University Press, 1983.

Rudi Van Dantzig

Rudi van Dantzig is one of Holland's most famous choreographers, and was, until 1991, artistic director of the Dutch National Ballet. *For a Lost Soldier*, published in 1986, is his debut novel, an almost entirely autobiographical account of his experiences as a child during the war years. It's an extremely well-written novel, convincingly portraying the confusion and loneliness of the approximately 50,000 Dutch children evacuated to foster families during the hunger winter. The leading character of the novel, Jeroen, is an eleven-year-old boy from Amsterdam who is sent away to live with a family in Friesland. During the Liberation celebrations, he meets an American soldier, Walt, with whom he has a brief sexual encounter, and who disappears a few days later. The extract below details Jeroen's desparate search for Walt shortly after his return to Amsterdam.

For a Lost Soldier

I set out on a series of reconnoitering expeditions through Amsterdam, tours of exploration that will take me to every corner. On a small map I look up the most important streets to see how I can best fan out to criss-cross the town, then make plans on pieces of paper showing exactly how the streets on each of my expeditions join up and what they are called. To make doubly sure I also use abbreviations: H.W. for Hoofdweg, H.S. for Haarlemmerstraat. The pieces of paper are carefully stored away inside the dust-jacket of a book, but I am satisfied that even if somebody found the notes, they wouldn't be able to make head or tail of them. It is a well-hidden secret.

For my first expedition I get up in good time. I yawn a great deal and act as cheerfully as I can to disguise the paralysing uncertainty that is governing my every move.

'We're going straight to the field, Mum, we're going to build a hut,' but she is very busy and scarcely listens.

'Take care and don't be back too late.'

The street smells fresh as if the air has been scrubbed with soap. I feel dizzy with excitement and as soon as I have rounded the corner I start to run towards the bridge. Now it's beginning, and everything is sure to be all right, all my waiting and searching is about to come to an end; the solution lies hidden over there, somewhere in the clear light filling the streets.

The bright air I inhale makes me feel that I am about to burst. I want to sing, shout, cheer myself hoarse.

I have marked my piece of paper, among a tangle of crossing and twisting lines, with H.W., O.T., W.S.: Hoofdweg, Overtoom, Weteringschans.

The Hoofdweg is close by, just over the bridge. It is the broad street we have to cross when we go to the swimming baths. I know the gloomy houses and the narrow, flowerless gardens from the many times I've walked by in other summers, towel and swimming trunks rolled under my arm. But beyond that, and past Mercatorplein, Amsterdam is unknown territory to me, ominous virgin land.

The unfamiliar streets make me hesitate, my excitement seeps away and suddenly I feel unsure and tired. The town bewilders me: shops with queues outside, people on bicycles carrying bags, beflagged streets in the early morning sun, squares where wooden platforms have been put up for neighbourhood celebrations, whole districts with music pouring out of loudspeakers all day. An unsolvable jigsaw puzzle. Now and then I stop in sheer desperation, study my hopelessly inadequate piece of paper, and wonder if it would not be much better to give up the attempt altogether.

But whenever I see an army vehicle, or catch a glimpse of a uniform, I revive and walk a little faster, sometimes trotting after a moving car in the hope that it will come to a stop and he will jump out.

Time after time I lose my way and have to walk back quite far, and sometimes, if I can summon up enough courage, I ask for directions.

'Please, Mevrouw, could you tell me how to get to the Overtoom?'

'Dear me, child, you're going the wrong way. Over there, right at the end, turn left, that'll take you straight there.'

The Overtoom, when I finally reach it, seems to be a street without beginning or end. I walk, stop, cross the road, search: not a trace of W.S. Does my plan bear any resemblance to the real thing?

I take off my shoes and look at the dark impression of my sweaty foot on the pavement. Do I have to go on, search any more? What time is it, how long have I been walking the streets?

Off we sail to Overtoom,
We drink milk and cream at home,
Milk and cream with apple pie,
Little children must not lie.

Over and over again, automatically, the jingle runs through my mind, driving me mad.

As I walk back home, slowly, keeping to the shady side of the street as much as I can, I think of the other expeditions hidden away in the dust-jacket of my book. The routes I picked out and wrote down with so much eagerness and trust seem pointless and unworkable now. I scold myself: I must not give up, only a coward would do that. Walt is waiting for me, he has no one, and he'll be so happy to see me again.

At home I sit down in a chair by the window, too tired to talk, and when I do give an answer to my mother my voice sounds thin and weak, as if it were finding it difficult to escape from my chest. She sits down next to me on the arm of the chair, lifts my chin up and asks where we have been playing such tiring games, she hasn't seen me down in the street all morning, though the other boys were there.

'Were you really out in the field?'

'Ask them if you don't believe me!' I run onto the balcony, tear my first route map up into pieces and watch the shreds fluttering down into the garden like snowflakes.

When my father gets back home he says, 'So, my boy, you and I had best go into town straightway, you still haven't seen the illuminations.'

With me on the back, he cycles as far as the Concertgebouw, where he leans the bike against a wall and walks with me past a large green space with badly worn grass. Here, too, there are soldiers, tents, trucks. Why don't I look this time, why do I go and walk on the other side of my father and cling – 'Don't hang on so tight!' – to his arm?

'Now you'll see something,' he says, 'something you've never even dreamed of, just you wait and see.'

Walt moving his quivering leg to and fro, his warm, yielding skin, the smell of the thick hair in his armpits . . .

I trudge along beside my father, my soles burning, too tired to look at anything.

We walk through the gateway of a large building, a sluice that echoes to the sound of voices, and through which the people have to squeeze before fanning out again on the other side . There are hundreds of them now, all moving in the same direction towards a buzzing hive of activity, a surging mass of bodies.

There is a sweet smell of food coming from a small tent in the middle of the street in front of which people are crowding so thickly that I can't see what is being sold.

I stop in my tracks, suddenly dying for food, dying just to stay where I am and to yield myself up to that wonderful sweet smell. But my father has already walked on and I have to wriggle through the crowds to catch up with him.

Beside a bridge he pushes me forward between the packed bodies so that I can see the canal, a long stretch of softly shimmering water bordered by overhanging trees. At one end brilliantly twinkling arches of light have been suspended that blaze in the darkness and are reflected in the still water. Speechless and enchanted I stare at the crystal-clear world full of dotted lines, a vision of luminous radiation that traces a winking and sparkling route leading from bridge to bridge, from arch to arch, from me to my lost soldier.

I grip my father's hand. 'Come on,' I say, 'let's have a look. Come on!'

Festoons of light bulbs are hanging wherever we go, like stars stretched across the water, and the people walk past them in silent, admiring rows. The banks of the canal feel as cosy as candle-lit sitting-rooms.

'Well?' my father breaks the spell. 'It's quite something, isn't it? In Friesland, you'd never have dreamed that anything like that existed, would you now?'

We take a short cut through dark narrow streets. I can hear dull cracks, sounds that come as a surprise in the dark, as if a sniper were firing at us.

My father starts to run.

'Hurry, or we'll be too late.'

An explosion of light spurts up against the black horizon and whirls apart, pink and pale green fountains of confetti that shower down over a brilliant sign standing etched in the sky.

And another shower of stars rains down to the sound of muffled explosions and cheers from the crowd, the sky trembling with the shattering of triumphal arches.

I look at the luminous sign in the sky as if it is a mirage.

'Daddy, that letter, what's it for? Why is it there?' Why did I have to ask, why didn't I just add my own letters, fulfil my own wishful thinking?

'That W? You know what that's for. The W, the W's for Queen Wilhelmina...' I can hear a scornful note in his voice as if he is mocking me.

'Willy here, Willy there,' he says, 'but the whole crew took off to England and left us properly in the lurch.'

I'm not listening, I don't want to hear what he has to say.

W isn't Wilhelmina: it stands for Walt! It's a sign specially for me . . .

Reprinted by permission of The Bodley Head

Marga Minco

Marga Minco's *Empty House*, first published in 1966, is another wartime novel. During the German occupation, her entire family – they were Jewish – was deported and killed in concentration camps. Minco herself managed to escape this fate and spent much of the war in hiding in Amsterdam. In 1944 she moved to Kloveniersburgwal 49, which served as a safe house for various Dutch artists during the ensuing hunger winter; it's this house – or, rather, the house next door – that is the model for the various empty houses in the novel. In the following extract, the main character, Sepha, meets Yona, another Jewish survivor and later to become a great friend, when travelling back from Friesland to the safe house.

An Empty House

As soon as we were in the centre Yona put on her rucksack and tapped on the window of the cab. We'd been delayed a lot because the lorry which had picked us up at our spot beyond Zwolle had to go to all kinds of small villages and made one detour after another. We sat in the back on crates. Yona had grazed her knee heaving herself up over the tail-gate. I'd not seen it because I'd been making a place for us to sit.

'What have you done?' I asked.

'Damn it,' she cried, 'I'm not as agile as you. I told you. I spent all my time holed up in a kind of loft.' She tied a hanky round her knee. 'One step from the door to the bed. Do you think I did keep-fit exercises or something?'

I thought of the fire-escape which I'd gone up and down practically every day. In the end I could do it one-handed.

'Have you somewhere to go to in Amsterdam?'

I expected her to say it was none of my business, but she seemed not to hear me. The lorry thundered along a road where they'd just cleared away barricades.

'Do you know,' she said, 'at first I didn't know where I was?' Suddenly her voice was much less sharp. 'All I knew was that it was a low house with an attic window above the back door. "You don't live here," said the woman of the house. She always wore a blue striped apron. "But I am here though," I said. "No," she said, "you must remember that you're not here, you're nowhere." She didn't say it unpleasantly, she wished me no harm. But I couldn't get it out of my mind - you're nowhere. It's as if, by degrees, you start believing it yourself, as if you begin to doubt yourself. I sometimes sat staring at my hands for ages. There was no mirror and they'd white-washed the attic window. It was only by looking at my hand that I recognized myself, proved to myself that I was there.'

'Didn't anybody ever come to see you?'

'Yes. In the beginning. But I didn't feel like talking. They soon got the message. They let me come downstairs in the evenings occasionally, the windows were blacked out and the front and back doors bolted. It didn't impress me as being anything special. Later on, I even began to dislike it. I saw that they were scared stiff when I was sitting in the room. They listened to every noise from outside. I told them that I'd rather stay upstairs, that I didn't want to run any risks. You can even get used to a loft. At least it was mine, my loft.'

While talking, she had turned round; she sat with her back half turned towards me. I had to bend forward to catch her last words. Her scarf had slipped off. Her hair kept brushing my face. Once we were near Amsterdam, she started talking about her father who went with her to the Concertgebouw every week, accompanied her

on long walks and ate cakes with her in small tea-rooms. She talked about him as if he were a friend. And again I had to hear details of the house. She walked me through rooms and corridors, showed me the courtyard, the cellar with wine-racks, the attic with the old-fashioned pulley. I knew it as if I had lived there myself. Where would she sleep tonight?

'If you want to, you can come home with me,' I said. 'I shan't have any time. I've so much to do. There's a case of mine somewhere as well. I can't remember what I put in it.'

We drove across Berlage Bridge. It was still light. She'd fallen silent during the last few kilometres and sat with her chin in her hands. 'The south district,' I heard her say. 'Nothing has changed here, of course.'

I wrote my address on a little piece of paper and gave it to her. She put it in the pocket of her khaki shirt without looking at it.

'You must come,' I shouted after her when she had got out at Ceintuurbaan. She walked away without a backward glance, hands on the straps of her rucksack, hunched forward as if there were stones in it. I lost sight of her because I was looking at a tram coming from Ferdinand Bolstraat. The trams were running again. There were tiny flags on the front. Flags were hanging everywhere. And portraits of the Queen. And orange hangings. Everyone seemed to be in the streets. It was the last evening of the Liberation celebrations. The driver dropped me off at Rokin. I'd not far to go. If I walked quickly, I could be there in five minutes. The door was usually open, the lock was broken – less than half a minute for the three flights of stairs. I could leave my case downstairs.

People were walking in rows right across the full width of the street. The majority had orange buttonholes or red, white and blue ribbons. There were a lot of children with paper hats, flags and tooters. Two mouth-organ players and a saxophonist in a traditional *Volendammer* costume drifted with the mass, though far apart. I tried to get through as quickly as possible. I bumped into a child who dropped his flag, which was about to be trodden underfoot. I made room with my case, grabbed the flag from the ground and thrust it into his hand. Jazz music resounded from a bar in Damstraat. The door was open. Men and women were sitting at the bar with their arms around each other. Their bodies shook. All that was left in the baker's window were breadcrumbs. Here it was even busier. Groups of Canadians stood at the corners, besieged by whores, black-market traders and dog-end collectors.

I'd not seen much of the Liberation in the Frisian village. The woman I'd stayed with baked her own bread; she had done so throughout the war and she just went on doing it. When I was alone in the kitchen with her she asked with avid interest about my experiences in the hunger winter. She wanted to know everything about the church with corpses, the men with rattles, the people suffering from beriberi on the steps of the Palace, the emaciated children who went to the soup-kitchen with their pans. I spared her no details. About the recycled fat which gave us diarrhoea, the rotten fen potatoes, the wet, clay-like bread, about the ulcers and legs full of sores. I saw it as a way of giving something back.

At last I was at the bridge. I looked at the house with the large expanses of window and the grimy door. At the house next door, the raised pavement and the neck gable. The windows were bricked up. The debris was piled high behind. All that was left were bare walls. I put down my case to change hands. It was as if, only then, that I felt how hungry I was, how stiff my knees were from sitting for hours on the crate. There was something strange about the houses, as if I'd been away for years. But it could have been that I'd never stopped on the bridge before, never looked at them from that angle. The barge was still there. An oil-lamp was burning behind the portholes.

Our front door was closed. The lock had been mended in the meantime. I ought to have had a key somewhere. I didn't want to ring. I'd never realized that the staircase was so dark when the front door was shut. Without thinking, I groped for the banister and banged my hand against the rough wall. 'It's nice, soft wood,' Mark had said as he sawed the banister into logs. 'You can cut it nicely into pieces with a sharp knife.' The steps on the upper flight grated as if there were sand on them. I pushed the door open with my case.

There was a black lady's handbag on the bed. A leather bag with a brass clasp. Who had a bag like that? The leather was supple and smooth, except for some creases on the underside. I walked to the table which was full of bottles and glasses. I saw a long dog-end lying in one of the ashtrays. The cigarette must have

been carefully put out. Afterwards the burnt tobacco had been nipped off. I found the empty packet on the floor, Sweet Caporal. The divan was strewn with newspapers. Eisenhower standing in a car. Montgomery standing in a car. A new Bailey bridge built in record time.

I had to look among the piled-up crockery in the kitchen for a cup. I rinsed it a long time before I drank from it. I felt the water sink into my stomach; it gurgled as if it was falling into a smooth, cold hollow. The tower clock sounded the half-hour. The house became even quieter. There appeared to be nobody home on the other floors either. Half nine? It got dark quickly now. It was already dark under the few trees left along the canal. I opened one of the windows and leant outside. A man and a woman tottered along the pavement on the other side. They held each other firmly under the arm. They would suddenly lurch forward a few metres, slowly right themselves and start up again. The nine o'clock man always walked there too. I'd not heard him since the Liberation.

Reprinted by permission of Peter Owen Publishers, London.

Nicolas Freeling

Creator of the Dutch detective Van der Valk, Nicolas Freeling was born in England but has lived all his life in Europe, where most of his novels are set. He actually left Amsterdam over twenty years ago and nowadays rarely returns to the city. But in the Van der Valk novels he evokes Amsterdam (and Amsterdammers) as well as any writer ever has, subtly and unsentimentally using the city and its people as a vivid backdrop to his fast-moving action. The following extract is from A *Long Silence*, first published in 1972.

A Long Silence

Arlette came out into the open air and saw that spring had come to Amsterdam. The pale, acid sun of late afternoon lay on the inner harbour beyond the Prins Hendrik Kade: the wind off the water was sharp. It gave her a shock. A succession of quick rhythmic taps, as at the start of a violin concerto of Beethoven. That she noticed this means, I think, that from that moment she was sane again. But it is possible that I am mistaken. Even if insane one can have, surely, the same perceptions as other people, and this "click" is a familiar thing. Exactly the same happens when one takes a night train down from Paris to the Coast, and one wakes somewhere between Saint Raphael and Cannes and looks out, and there is the Mediterranean. Or was.

The pungent salt smell, the northern, maritime keynotes of seagull and herring, the pointed brick buildings, tall and narrow like herons, with their mosaic of parti-coloured shutters, eaves, sills, that gives the landscapes their stiff, heraldic look (one is back beyond Brueghel, beyond Van Eyck, to the primitives whose artists we do not know, so that they have names like the Master of the Saint Ursula Legend). The lavish use of paint in flat bright primary colours which typifies these Baltic, Hanseatic quay-sides is startling to the visitor from central Europe. Even the Dutch flags waving everywhere (there are no more determined flag-wavers) upset and worried Arlette: she had not realised how in a short time her eye had accustomed itself to the subtle and faded colourings of France, so that it was as though she had never left home. The sharp flat brightness of Holland! The painters' light which hurts the unaccustomed eye. . . Arlette never wore sunglasses in France, except on the sea, or on the snow, yet here, she remembered suddenly, she had practically gone to bed in them. It was all so familiar. She had lived here, she had to keep reminding herself, for twenty years.

She had no notion of where she wanted to go, but she knew that now she was here, a small pause would bring the spinning, whirling patterns of the kaleidoscope to rest. She crossed the road and down the steps to the little wooden terrace – a drink, and get her breath back! Everything was new – the pale heavy squatness of the Dutch café's cup-and-saucer, left on her table by the last occupant; the delightful rhythmic skyline across the harbour of the Saint Nicolaas church and the corner of the Zeedijk! Tourists were flocking into waterbuses, and now she was a tourist too. An old waiter was wiping the table while holding a tray full of empty bottles, which wavered in front of her eye.

"Mevrouw?"

"Give me a chocomilk, if at least you've got one that's good and cold".

Another click! She was talking Dutch, and as fluently as ever she had! He was back before she had got over it.

"Nou, mevrouwtje – cold as Finnegan's feet". His voice had the real Amsterdam caw to it. "You aren't Dutch though, are you now?"

"Only a tourist", smiling.

"Well now, by-your-leave: proper-sounding Dutch you talk there", chattily, bumping the glass down and pouring in the clawky chocomilk.

"Thank you very much".

Tot Uw dienst. Ja ja ja, kom er aan to a fussy man, waving and banging his saucer with a coin.

Neem mij niet kwa-a-lijk; een be-hoor-lijk Nederlands spreekt U daar. Like a flock of rooks. *Yah, yah ya-ah, kom er a-an.* And she was blinded by tears again, hearing her husband's exact intonation – when with her he spoke a Dutch whose accent sometimes unconsciously – ludicrously – copied hers, but when with the real thing, the *rasecht* like himself his accent would begin to caw too as though in self-parody.

Next door to her were sitting two American girls, earnest, quiet, dusty-haired, looking quite clean though their jeans were as darkly greasy as the mud the dredger over there was turning up off the harbour bottom. Scraps of conversation floated across.

She's a lovely person, ever so quiet but really mature, you know what I mean, yes, from Toledo". Arlette knew that Van der Valk would have guffawed and her eyes cleared.

I see her there, at the start of her absurd and terrifying mission. She has the characteristic feminine memory for detail, the naively earnest certainty that she has to get everything right. Had I asked what those two girls were drinking she would have known for sure, and been delighted at my asking.

I have not seen Amsterdam for four or five years, and it might be as long again before I shall. This is just as well. I do not want my imagination to get in the way of Arlette's senses. Piet, whose imagination worked like mine, saw things in an entirely different way to her. We were sitting once together on that same terrace.

"Look at that dam building", pointing at the Central Station, a construction I am fond of, built with loving attention to every useless detail by an architect of the last century whose name I have forgotten (a Dutch equivalent of Sir Giles Gilbert Scott). "Isn't it lovely?" Lovely is not the word I would have chosen but it is oddly right.

"The Railway Age", he went on. "Make a wonderful museum – old wooden carriages, tuff-tuff locos with long funnels, Madame Tussaud figures of station-masters with beards, police-men wearing helmets, huge great soup-strainer moustaches, women with bustle and reti-cules . . ." Yes, indeed, and children in sailor suits. Arlette's mind does not behave like this.

I am changed, thought Arlette, and unchanged. I am the same housewife, familiar with these streets, these people. I am not pricked or tickled by anything here, like a tourist. I see all this with the coolness and objectivity of experience. I am not going to rush into anything stupid or imprudent. This is a town I know, and I am going to find myself perfectly able to cope with the problem. I am not alone or helpless; I have here many friends, and there are many more who were Piet's friends and who will help me for his sake. But I am no longer the thought-less and innocent little wife of a little man in a little job, standing on the corner with shopping bag wondering whether to have a cabbage or a cauli. I am a liberated woman, and that is going to make a difference.

A tout was circling around the cluster of tables, sizing up likely suckers. A year or so ago he would have been handing out cards for a restaurant or hotel, looking for a quickie trip around the sights, with waterbus, Anne Frank and the Rembrandthuis all thrown in for only ten guilders. Now – he had closed in on the two American girls and she could hear his pidgin-German patois that is the international language of the European tout – selling live sex-shows. The two girls glanced up for a second with polite indifference, and went back to their earnest, careful, intense conversation, paying no further attention to him at all. He broke off the patter, circled backwards like a boxer and gave Arlette a careful glance: Frenchwomen, generally fascinated by the immoralities and debaucheries of these English and these Scandinavians – a likely buyer, as long as they have first done their duty with a really good orgy at Marks and Spencer's. Arlette met his eye with such a chill and knowing look that he shuffled back into the ropes and made off sideways: cow has been to the sex-show and has no money left. Amsterdam too has changed and not changed, she thought.

"Raffishness" was always the first cliché tour-ists used, the Amsterdammers were always intensely, idiotically proud of their red-light district and since time immemorial a stroll to look at "the ladies behind the windows" was proposed to every eager tourist the very first night.

They have taken now with such relish to the new role of exhibitionist shop-window that it is hard not to laugh – the visitor's first reaction generally is roars of laughter. The Dutch have a belief that sex has made them less provincial somehow – for few attitudes are more provincial than the anxious striving to be modern-and-progressive. Paris doesn't exist any more, and London is slipping, they will tell one with a boastful pathos, and Holland-is-where-it's-at. A bit immature, really, as the two nineteen-year olds from Dubuque were probably at that moment saying. Arlette was a humble woman. She saw herself as snobbish, narrow, rigid, French provincial bourgeois. Piet, born and bred in Amsterdam, used to describe himself as a peasant. This humility gave them both an unusual breadth, stability, balance. I remember his telling me once how to his mind his career if not his life had been an abject failure.

"But there", drinking brandy reflectively, being indeed a real soak and loving it, "what else could I have done?"

Arlette, walking through the lazy, dirty sunshine of late afternoon in Amsterdam, was thinking too, "What else could I have done?" She had come to lay a ghost. Not that she – hard-headed woman – believed in ghosts, but she had lived long enough to know they were there. Piet was a believer in ghosts. "I have known malign influences outside the bathroom door," he used to say. He was delighted when I gave him to read the finely-made old thriller of Mr A.E.W. Mason which is called The Prisoner in the Opal: he saw the point at once, and when he brought it back he said that he too, with the most sordid, materialistic, bourgeois of enquiries, always made the effort "to pierce the opal crust". Poor old Piet.

Once we were having dinner together in a Japanese restaurant. We had had three pernods, big ones, the ones Piet with his horrible Dutch ideas of wit which he took for esprit described as "Des Grand Pers". We were watching the cook slicing raw fish into fine transparent slices.

"There is poetry", said Piet suddenly, "in those fingers". I turned around suspiciously, because this is a paraphrase from a good writer, whom Piet had certainly not read. I used the phrase as an epigraph to a book I once wrote about cooks – which Piet had not read either. "Poetry in the fat fingers of cooks" – I looked at Piet suspiciously.

"So", with tactful calm, "is that a quotation?"

"No", innocent, "Just a phrase. Thought it would please you, haw". That crude guffaw; completely Piet. The stinker; to this day I don't know whether he was kidding me. A skilful user of flattery, but damn it, a friend.

The Damrak, the Dam, the Rokin. Squalid remnants of food, flung upon the pavements. The young were unable or unwilling to spend much on food, she thought, and what they got for their money probably deserved to be flung: one could not blame them too much, just because one felt revolted. But one did blame them: beastly children.

The Utrechtsestraat. The Fredericksplein. And once out of the tourist stamping-ground, Arlette knew suddenly where she was going. She was heading unerringly and as though she had never been away straight towards the flat where she had lived for twenty years. It was a longish way to walk, all the way from the Central Station and carrying a suitcase too. Why had she done it? She would have said, "What else could I have done?" crossly, for when she got there she was very tired and slightly footsore, dishevelled, her hair full of dust, smelling of sweat and ready to cry.

"Arlette! My dear girl! What are you doing? – but come in! I'm so happy to see you – and at the same time, my poor child, I'm so sad! Not that we know anything – what one reads in the paper nowadays – Pah! And again Pah! come in, my dear girl, come in – you don't mean to say you walked. . . from the station? You didn't! You couldn't! Sit down child, do. The lavy? But of course you know where it is, that's not something you'll have forgotten. I'll make some coffee. My dear girl, marvellous to see you, and the dear boys? – no no, I must be patient, go and have a pee child, and a wash, do you good". The old biddy who had always had a ground floor flat, and still did. . . She taught the piano. It had been the most familiar background noise to Arlette's life throughout the boys' childhood; her voice carried tremendously.

"One, Two, not so hasty. Pedal there, you're not giving those notes their value, that's a sharp, can't you hear it?" And coming back from shopping an hour later another one was being put through its hoops. "Watch your tempo, not so much espressivo, you're sentimentalising, this is the Ruysdaelskade, not the Wiener Wald or something".

"Lumpenpack", she would mutter, coming out on the landing for a breather and finding Arlette emptying the dustbin.

Old Mother Counterpoint, Piet always called her, and sometimes in deference to Jane Austen "Bates" ("Mother hears perfectly well; you only have to shout a little and say it two or at the most three times"). A wonderful person really. A mine of information on the quarter, possessor of efficient intelligence networks in every shop, an endless gabble on the telephone, forever fixing things for someone else. She could find anything for you; a furnished room, a second-hand pram scarcely used, a boy's bike, a shop where they were having a sale of materials ever so cheap – even if she didn't have her finger on it she knew a man who would let you have it wholesale. Warm-hearted old girl. Gushing, but wonderfully kind, and gentle, and sometimes even tactful.

"You take yours black, dear, oh yes, I hadn't forgotten – you think I'd forget a thing like that? Not gaga yet, thank God. Good heavens, it must be seven years. But you haven't aged dear, a few lines yes – badges of honour my pet, that's what I call them. Tell me – can you bear to talk about it? Where are you staying? By the look of you you could do with a square meal".

"I don't know, I was wondering . . ."

"But my poor pet of course, how can you ask, you know I'd be more than pleased and I've plenty of room, it's just can you bear all the little fussinesses of a frightened old maid – oh nonsense child, now don't be tiresome. Now I'll tell you what, no don't interrupt, I'm going to the butcher, yes still the same awful fellow, all those terrible people, how they'll be thrilled, just wait till he hears, I'll frighten him, he gave me an escalope last week and tough . . . my poor girl, since you left he thinks everything is permitted him. I'll get a couple of nice veal cutlets and we'll have dinner, just you wait and I'll get something to drink too, I love the excuse and what's more I'll make pancakes. I never bother by myself, you take your shoes off and put your feet up and read the paper, nonsense you'll do no such thing, I want to and anyway I'll enjoy it; would you perhaps love a bath, my pet?" The voice floated off into the hallway.

"Where's my goloshes, oh dear, oh here they are now how did they get that way, oh wait till I tell the wretch the cutlets are for you, he'll jump out of his skin . . ." The front door slammed. Arlette was home.

It was a nice evening. Bates brought Beaujolais – Beaujolais! "I remember you used to buy it, child, I hope you still like it. Cutlets".

"He practically went on his knees when he heard, with the tears in his eyes he swore on his mother's grave you'd be able to cut them with a fork and I just looked and said 'She'd better,' that's all".

"Bananas – I've got some rum somewhere, hasn't been touched in five years I'd say, pah, all dusty, do you think it'll still be all right dear, not gone poisonous or anything, one never knows now, they put chemicals in to make things smell better, awful man in the supermarket and I swear he squirts the oranges with an aerosol thing to make them smell like oranges, forlorn hope is all I can say".

The rum was tasted, and pronounced fit for pancakes.

"And how's Amsterdam?" asked Arlette, laughing.

It wasn't what it was; it wasn't what it had been. Arlette had been prepared to be bored with old-maidish gush about how we don't sleep safe in our beds of nights, not like when we had a policeman in the house, which did give someone a sense of security somehow. She ought to have known better really, because old mother Counterpoint had the tough dryness, the voluble energy, the inconsequent loquacity she expected – and indeed remembered, but the warm-hearted kindness was illuminated by a shrewd observation she had never given the old biddy credit for.

"Well, my dear, it would ill become me to complain. I'll have this flat for as long as I live and they can't put my rent up, I have to spread my butter thinner but I'm getting old and I need less of it. I have the sunshine still and the plants and my birds and they'll all last my time. I think it comes much harder on a girl your age, who can remember what things used to be, and who still has to move with the changes and accept them, whereas people expect me to be eccentric and silly. And I'm sorrier still for the young ones. They don't have any patterns to move by: it must give a terrible sense of insecurity and I think that's what makes them so unhappy. Everyone kowtows to them and it must be horrid really. Look at the word young, I mean it used to mean what it said and no more, young cheese or a young woman and that was that – and now they talk about a young chair or a young frock and it's

supposed to mean good, and when you keep ascribing virtue to people, and implying all the time that they should be admired and imitated, well dear, it makes their life very difficult and wearisome; I used to know a holy nun and she said sometimes that everybody being convinced one was good made a heavy cross to carry. When the young do wicked things I can't help feeling that it's because they're dreadfully unhappy. Of course there's progress, lots and lots of progress, and it makes me very happy. I don't have many pupils now, but I'm always struck when they come, so tall and healthy and active, so unlike the pale little tots when I was a young woman, and I remember very hard times, my dear, all the men drunk always because their lives were so hard, but they don't seem to me any happier or more contented and they complain more because they expect much more. I can't really see what they mean talking about progress because that seems to me that people are good and get better and the fact is, my pet, as you and I know, people are born bad and tend to get worse and putting good before evil is always a dreadful struggle dear, whatever they say. One is so vain and so selfish".

And Arlette, who had had a good rest, a delicious bath, and a good supper, found herself pouring out her whole tale and most of her heart.

"Well", said Bates at the end with great commonsense, "that has done you a great deal of good my dear, and that's a fact, just like taking off one's stays, girls don't wear stays any more and they don't know what they miss".

Arlette felt inclined to argue that it was a good thing to be no longer obliged to wear stays.

"Of course dear, don't think I don't agree with you, healthy girls with good stomach muscles playing tennis, and no more of that fainting and vapouring. But I maintain that it was a good thing for a girl to know constraint. Sex education and women's lib, all dreadful cant. Girls who married without knowing the meaning of the word sex were sometimes very happy and sometimes very unhappy, and I don't believe they are any happier now. I married a sailor, dear, and learned how to go without".

"It doesn't make me any happier now", said Arlette dryly.

"No dear, and that's just what I felt in 1940 when my ship got torpedoed. So now let's be very sensible. You've come here very confused and embittered, and you don't want anything to do with the police, and you're probably quite right because really poor dears they've simply no notion, but at the present you've no notion either. You'd never of thought about asking my advice because I'm a silly old bag but I'll give it you, and it is that you probably can find out who killed your husband, because it's surprising what you can do when you try, but it's as well to have friends you can count on, and you can count on me for a start, and with that my dear we'll go to bed, your eyes are dropping out".

"Did you join the resistance, in 1940 I mean?" asked Arlette.

"Yes I did, and what's more once I threw a bomb at a bad man in the Euterpestraat, and that was a dreadful place, the Gestapo head-quarters here in Amsterdam and it was very hard because I was horribly frightened of the bomb, and even more frightened of the bad man who had soldiers with him and most of all because I knew they would take hostages and execute them, but it had to be done, you see".

"I do see", said Arlette seriously, "it wasn't the moment to take off one's stays and feel comfortable".

"Right, my pet, right", said old mother Counterpoint.

Books

History

Dedalo Carasso *A Short History of Amsterdam*. Brief, socialist-slanted account, well illustrated with artefacts from the Historical Museum.

Geoffrey Cotterell *Amsterdam*. Popularized, offbeat history giving a highly readable account of the city up to the late 1960s.

Pieter Geyl *The Revolt of The Netherlands 1555–1609; The Netherlands in the Seventeenth Century 1609–1648*. Geyl's history of the Dutch-speaking peoples is the definitive account of Holland's history during its formative years, chronicling the uprising against the Spanish and the formation of the United Provinces. Quite the best thing you can read on the period.

Mark Girouard *Cities and People: A Social and Architectural History*. Has an informed and well-illustrated chapter on the city's social history.

Christopher Hibbert *Cities and Civilisation*. Includes a chapter on Amsterdam in the age of Rembrandt. Some interesting facts about seventeenth-century daily life.

J. H. Huizinga *Dutch Civilisation in the 17th Century*. Analysis of life and culture in the Dutch Republic by the country's most widely respected historian.

J. L. Price *Culture and Society in the Dutch Republic in the 17th Century*. An accurate, intelligent account of the Golden Age.

Simon Schama *The Embarrassment of Riches: An Interpretation of Dutch Culture in the Golden Age*. The most recent – and one of the most accessible – works on the Golden Age, drawing on a wide variety of archive sources.

Jan Stoutenbeek et al. *A Guide to Jewish Amsterdam*. Fascinating, if perhaps overdetailed, guide to just about every Jewish monument in the city. You can purchase a copy before you leave from the *Netherlands Board of Tourism*, or in better Amsterdam bookshops.

Sir William Temple *Observations upon the United Provinces of The Netherlands*. Written by a seventeenth-century English diplomat, and a good, evocative account of the country at the time.

Art and Architecture

Pierre Cabanne *Van Gogh*. Standard mix of art criticism and biography, drawing heavily on the artist's letters themselves.

Kenneth Clark *Civilisation*. This includes a warm and scholarly rundown on the Golden Age, with illuminating insights on the way in which the art reflected the period.

Eugene Fromentin *The Masters of Past Time: Dutch and Flemish Painting from Van Eyck to Rembrandt*. Entertaining essays on the major Dutch and Flemish painters.

R. H. Fuchs *Dutch Painting*. As complete an introduction to the subject – from Flemish origins to the present day – as you could wish for in just a couple of hundred pages.

Guus Kemme (ed.) *Amsterdam Architecture: A Guide*. Illustrated guide to the architecture of Amsterdam, with potted accounts of the major buildings.

Paul Overy *De Stijl*. Recently published reassessment of all aspects of the De Stijl movement. Clearly written and comprehensive.

Christian Rheinwald *Amsterdam Art Guide*. Comprehensive guide to the city's galleries, shops and contact points for both artists and those wanting to tour the art scene.

Jacob Rosenberg et al. *Dutch Art and Architecture 1600–1800*. Full and erudite anthology of essays on the art and buildings of the Golden Age and after. For dedicated Dutch-art fans only.

Irving Stone *Lust for Life*. Everything you ever wanted to know about van Gogh in a pop genius-is-pain biography.

Christopher White *Rembrandt.* The most widely available – and wide-ranging – study of the painter and his work.

Literature

Simon Carmiggelt *Kronkels.* Second collection of Carmiggelt's 'slight adventures', three of which are reprinted above.

Rudi van Dantzig *For a Lost Soldier.* Honest and convincing tale, largely autobiographical, that tells of a young boy's sexual awakening against a background of war and liberation. See the extract on p.254.

Anne Frank *The Diary of a Young Girl.* Lucid and moving, the most revealing thing you can read on the plight of Amsterdam's Jews during the war years.

Nicolas Freeling *A City Solitary; Love in Amsterdam; Cold Iron; Strike Out Where Not Applicable; A Long Silence.* Freeling writes detective novels, and his most famous creation is the rebel cop, Van der Valk, around whom a successful British TV series was made. Light, carefully crafted tales, with just the right amount of twists to make them classic cops 'n' robbers reading – and with good Amsterdam (and Dutch) locations. See the extract from *A Long Silence* on p.258.

Etty Hillesum *Etty: An Interrupted Life.* Diary of an Amsterdam Jewish young woman uprooted from her life in the city and taken to Auschwitz, where she died. As with Anne Frank's more famous journal, penetratingly written – though on the whole much less readable.

Margo Minco, *The Fall; An Empty House; The Glass Bridge* (Peter Owen). Prolific author wartime and survivor Minco is one of Holland's leading contemporary authors. Her work (especially *The Fall*) focuses on the city's Jewish community, particularly in the war years. See also the extract from *An Empty House* on p.256.

Harry Mulisch *The Assault.* Set part in Haarlem, part in Amsterdam, this traces the story of a young boy who loses his family in a reprisal-raid by the Nazis. A powerful tale, made into an excellent and effective film.

Multatuli *Max Havelaar: or the Coffee Auctions of the Dutch Trading Company.* Classic nineteenth-century Dutch satire of colonial life in the East Indies. Eloquent and, at times, amusing.

Cees Noteboom *Rituals.* An existentialist novel of the 1980s, mapping the empty existence of a rich Amsterdammer who dabbles in antiques. Bleak but absorbing. See the extract on p.252.

Jona Oberski *Childhood.* First published in 1978, this is a Jewish child's eye-witness account of the war years, the camps and executions. Written with feeling and precision.

Janwillem van de Wetering *Hard Rain.* An offbeat detective tale set in Amsterdam and provincial Holland. Like van de Wetering's other stories, sadly only available in the US, it's a humane, quirky and humourous story, worth reading for characters and locations as much as for inventive narrative.

Jan Wolkers *Turkish Delight.* Wolkers is one of The Netherlands' best-known artists and writers, and this is one of his early novels, examining closely a relationship between a bitter, working-class sculptor and his young, middle-class wife. A compelling, though at times misogynistic, even offensive, work, by a writer who above all seeks reaction.

Language

It's unlikely that you'll need to speak anything other than English while you're in Amsterdam: the Dutch have a seemingly natural talent for languages, and your attempts at speaking theirs may be met with some amusement. Outside Amsterdam people aren't quite as cosmopolitan, but even so the following words and phrases of Dutch should be the most you'll need to get by; supplement these with our detailed Food Glossary in Basics.

Pronunciation

Dutch is pronounced much the same as English, but with a few differences:

v is like the English f in **f**ar

w like the v in **v**at

j like the initial sound of **y**ellow

ch and **g** are like the Scottish lo**ch**

ng is as in bri**ng**

nj as in o**ni**on

Otherwise double consonants keep their separate sounds – kn, for example, is never like the English "knight".

Doubling the letter lengthens the vowel sound:

a is like the English cat

aa like cart

e like let

ee like late

o as in pop

oo in pope

u is like wood

uu the French tu

au and **ou** like how

ei and **ij** as in fine

oe as in soon

eu is like the dipthong in the French l**eur**

Dutch words and phrases

Basics and Greetings

yes	*ja*
no	*nee*
please	*alstublieft*
(no) thank you	*(nee) dank u* or *bedankt*
hello	*hallo* or *dag*
good morning	*goedemorgen*
good afternoon	*goedemiddag*
good evening	*goedenavond*
goodbye	*tot ziens*
see you later	*tot straks*
do you speak English?	*spreekt u Engels?*
I don't understand	*Ik begrijp het niet*
women/men	*vrouwen/mannen*
children	*kinderen*
when?	*wanneer?*
I want	*ik wil*
I don't want	*ik wil niet. . .(+verb)* *ik wil geen. . .(+noun)*
how much is. . .?	*wat kost. . .?*

Finding the way

how do I get to. . .?	*hoe kom ik in. . .?*
where is. . .?	*waar is. . .?*
how far is it to. . .?	*hoe ver is het naar. . .?*
far/near	*ver/dichtbij*
left/right	*links/rechts*
straight ahead	*rechtuit gaan*
platform	*spoor* or *perron*

Money

post office	*postkantoor*
stamp(s)	*postzegel(s)*
money exchange	*wisselkantoor*
cash desk	*kassa*
ticket office	*loket*

Useful Words

good/bad	*goed/slecht*
big/small	*groot/klein*
open/closed	*open/gesloten*
push/pull	*duwen/trekken*
new/old	*nieuw/oud*
cheap/expensive	*goedkoop/duur*
hot/cold	*heet* or *warm/koud*
with/without	*met/zonder*
here/there	*hier/daar*
men's/women's toilets	*heren/dames*

Days and Times

Sunday	*Zondag*
Monday	*Maandag*
Tuesday	*Dinsdag*
Wednesday	*Woensdag*
Thursday	*Donderdag*
Friday	*Vrijdag*
Saturday	*Zaterdag*
yesterday	*gisteren*
today	*vandaag*
tomorrow	*morgen*
tomorrow morning	*morgenochtend*
minute	*minuut*
hour	*uur*
day	*dag*
week	*week*
month	*maand*
year	*jaar*

Numbers

When saying a number, the Dutch generally transpose the last two digits: e.g., *drie guilden vijf en twintig* is *f*3.25.

0	*nul*
1	*een*
2	*twee*
3	*drie*
4	*vier*
5	*vijf*
6	*zes*
7	*zeven*
8	*acht*
9	*negen*
10	*tien*
11	*elf*
12	*twaalf*
13	*dertien*
14	*veertien*
15	*vijftien*
16	*zestien*
17	*zeventien*
18	*achttien*
19	*negentien*
20	*twintig*
21	*een en twintig*
30	*dertig*
40	*veertig*
50	*vijftig*
60	*zestig*
70	*zeventig*
80	*tachtig*
90	*negentig*
100	*honderd*
101	*honderd een*
200	*twee honderd*
201	*twee honderd een*
500	*vijf honderd*
1000	*duizend*

A Glossary of Dutch and Architectural Terms

AMBULATORY Covered passage around the outer edge of a choir of a church.

AMSTERDAMMERTJE Phallic-shaped objects placed alongside Amsterdam streets to keep drivers off the pavements and out of the canals.

APSE Semicircular protrusion at (usually) the east end of a church.

BAROQUE High-Renaissance period of art and architecture, distinguished by extreme ornateness.

BEGIJNHOF Similar to a *hofje* but occupied by Catholic women (*Begijns*) who led semi-religious lives without taking full vows.

BURGHER Member of the upper or mercantile classes of a town, usually with certain civic powers.

CABINET-PIECE Small, finely detailed painting of a domestic scene.

CARILLON A set of tuned church bells, either operated by an automatic mechanism or played by a keyboard.

FIETSPAD Bicycle path.

GASTHUIS Hospice for the sick or infirm.

GEMEENTE Municipal; e.g. *Gemeentehuis* – town hall.

GESLOTEN Closed.

GEVEL Gable. The only decoration practical on the narrow-fronted canal house was on its gables. Initially fairly simple, they developed into an ostentatious riot of individualism in the late seventeenth century before turning to a more restrained classicism in the eighteenth and nineteenth centuries.

GRACHT Canal.

HIJSTBALK Pulley beam, often decorated, affixed to the top of a gable to lift goods, furniture etc. Essential in canal houses whose staircases were narrow and steep, *hijstbalken* are still very much in use today.

HOF Courtyard.

HOFJE Almshouse, usually for elderly women who could look after themselves but needed small charities such as food and fuel; usually a number of buildings centred around a small, peaceful courtyard.

HUIS House.

KERK Church.

KONINKLIJK Royal.

MARKT Central town square and the heart of most Dutch communities, normally still the site of weekly markets.

MISERICORD Ledge on choir stall on which occupant can be supported while standing; often carved.

MOKUM A Yiddish word meaning "city", originally used by the Jewish community to indicate Amsterdam. Now in general usage.

NEOCLASSICAL Architectural style derived from Greek and Roman elements – pillars, domes, colonnades, etc. – popular in The Netherlands during French rule in the early nineteenth century.

POLDER An area of land reclaimed from the sea.

POSTBUS Post office box.

PLEIN A square or open space.

RAADHUIS Town hall.

RIJKS State.

SPIONNETJE Small mirror on canal house enabling occupant to see who is at the door without descending stairs.

STADHUIS Most commonly used word for a town hall.

STICHTING Can apply to either an institute or foundation.

STEDELIJK Civic, municipal.

WAAG Old public weighing-house, a common feature of most towns – usually found on the *Markt*.

Index

You are
A STUDENT

You travel
THE WORLD

You want
TO SAVE MONEY

Here's how

The International Student Identity Card

Available at Student Travel Offices Worldwide.

Entitles you to discounts and special services worldwide.

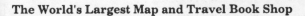